Threshold of
TERROR

The Last Hours of
the Monarchy in the
French Revolution

RODNEY ALLEN

SUTTON PUBLISHING

First published in the United Kingdom in 1999 by
Sutton Publishing Limited · Phoenix Mill
Thrupp · Stroud · Gloucestershire · GL5 2BU

This paperback edition first published in 2001

British Library Cataloguing in Publication Data
A catalogue record for this book is available from the British Library

ISBN 0 7509 2710 0

This book is dedicated to my wife Anne
without whose help it would not have been written

Typeset in 11/12pt Ehrhardt.
Typesetting and origination by
Sutton Publishing Limited.
Printed and bound in Great Britain by
J.H. Haynes & Co. Ltd, Sparkford.

Contents

Acknowledgements and Picture Credits

The author wishes to acknowledge his great appreciation to the Fondation pour l'Histoire des Suisses à l'Étranger at the Château de Penthes near Geneva for the provision of numerous texts and articles and the suggestion of sources, to Alain-Jacques Crouz-Tornare for providing a copy of his extensive thesis on Swiss troops in France at the time of the Revolution, to my sister Mrs. R.E. Bailey for encouragement and research, and to Professor Richard K. Redfern of Bradenton, Florida, for looking at my English and punctuation. Responsibility for failure in this respect lies with the author.

The illustrations in this book, unless stated otherwise, were kindly provided by the Mairie de Paris, and are © Photothèque des Musées de la Ville de Paris. The pictures on pp. 96, 102, 111, 150, 159 and 237 were loaned by courtesy of the Château de Penthes, and those on pp. 33, 56, 171 and 188 by the Bibliothèque Nationale, Paris. Grateful acknowledgement is made to Messrs Elwes & Hanham of 14 Old Bond Street, London W1, for permitting publication of their fine portrait of Louis XVI on p. 5, which shows the king very much as he would have looked towards the end of his reign. The unfinished portrait by Alexandre Kucharski of Marie Antoinette on p. 19 is from the Château de Versailles, courtesy of Giraudon/Bridgeman Art Library, London. The painting of the duc de Liancourt, which appears on p. 22, has been taken from a 1964 issue of *La Revue des Amis de Versailles, etc*, and the map on p. 9 from M.J. Sydenham's *The French Revolution*, published by Greenwood Press, London, in 1985.

Preface

The Revolution of 10 August 1792 saw the overthrow of France's 900-year-old Monarchy. This event is less well known in Britain than its antecedent of 14 July 1789 when the Bastille fell. Yet it had the same relationship as that of the Russian October Revolution to the February Revolution in 1917 (the old Russian calendar). In both instances, the first event cleared the ground, while the second planted the crop. Moreover, in each case, the first episode was largely spontaneous, whereas the second came about after deliberate preparation. Of course, over a century had passed and ideologies had changed. The end of social privilege in France became manifest from 10 August 1792, while 25 October 1917 signified the destruction of bourgeois capitalism in Russia. Both these revolutions aimed at establishing a new social and political era.

The many parallels between these two revolutions are well noted. Both engendered totalitarian politics, resulting in terror and civil war. Both embarked on external conflict to spread their ideology and as a means to weld together a fractured society. In the French case, this meant continuous aggressive war. After brief experimentation, Russia had to abandon such a policy owing to inadequate resources, substituting instead xenophobia at home and subversion abroad, although expanding territorially when opportunity allowed.

The Revolution of 1789 had started with high hopes. These were betrayed by the events of 10 August 1792. If liberal representative government under a constitutional monarchy had been successfully established in France shortly after 1789, much of Europe might have followed suit within a generation, and in Great Britain electoral reform could have come well before 1832. The fall and later execution of Louis XVI dashed these fair prospects, causing a conservative reaction outside France, while within France, political continuity was brutally ruptured and the door opened for totalitarian dictatorship. This proved to be a costly experience.

The traumatic nature of the events surrounding the end of the Monarchy caused many people to write about them. Much of this was tendentious, confused, and reported at second or third hand. However, a surprising number of direct eyewitness accounts make it possible to produce a detailed tapestry of the final hours of this political collapse and transformation, despite the untimely death of many leading participants in the two following years. This book's close focus in time and space allows the action to unroll as a drama possessing the classical unities. It also permits direct quotations and paraphrases from primary sources to be extensively interwoven in the text. I hope this will enhance the immediacy and authenticity of the narrative, especially as witnesses often reveal themselves with an openness one would not expect nowadays.

Texts, however, are not presented to the reader uncritically. Analytical commentary is added wherever necessary. Some witnesses who appear over several chapters become familiar characters, adding intimate personal drama to the historical events in which they participated. In the case of four of these witnesses, the overall narrative is extended in time to include the gripping stories of their escapes from France after the fall of the king. While these accounts are fascinating in themselves, their many incidental details help to establish the atmosphere of revolutionary France at that moment and to add depth to the main narrative.

The witnesses utilised can be divided into major and minor players. Two of the most important participants in the events leading up to the fall of the king were Pétion, the Mayor of the Commune or Municipality of Paris, and Roederer, Procureur Général Syndic of the Department of Paris and the Seine (Paris, for short). Both their accounts tend to be exculpatory. Pétion's was produced immediately after 10 August, and was influenced by the fear of being accused of having aided the defence of the Tuileries, the royal palace. In contrast, Roederer only published his detailed and most informative memoir forty years after the event, although taken from extensive notes made at the time. He can be accused of trying to conceal that he could have played a more forceful if dangerous role. Relations by rather less important actors are those produced by Dejoly, Minister of Justice, Sainte-Croix, Minister for Foreign Affairs, Leroux, a Municipal Officer, and Choudieu, a die-hard Jacobin Deputy. Dejoly, belonging to the radical Girondin faction, comes over as a decent man and honest reporter. Sainte-Croix's memoirs are less coherent, and the main impression is his fervent loyalty to the king. Leroux is a much better observer, as one might expect of a medical man, and provides a revealing picture of a moderate bourgeois official trying to cope with his duty in the face of inexorable revolutionary sentiment. Choudieu wrote a commentary on other people's memoirs after the overthrow of Charles X in 1830 allowed the fall of Louis XVI to be freely discussed. He provides some snippets of information from a Jacobin viewpoint.

Generally, the minor players had no need to defend their actions, and what they say, although prejudiced, is usually free from hidden bias. The most important of these are Liancourt, Madame Campan, Cléry, Madame Tourzel, Weber, Desbouillons, Langlade, Viard, Lucile Desmoulins, and Dr John Moore. The first five of these were royalists. The intense personal narrative produced by the aristocratic Liancourt is the best written and most useful. Weber also attempted a continuous narrative, but he was not so well placed to eavesdrop on the conversations of important people. The memoirs of the spirited Madame Campan, together with those of Madame de Tourzel and Cléry, all members of the royal household, are more episodic, but provide useful information and striking vignettes. Desbouillons from Brest commanded one of the detachments which attacked the Tuileries. He wrote a lengthy letter immediately after the event. This, and other correspondence, show him to be a conscientious reporter. Langlade was a gunner captain supposed to be defending the palace. He is the most genuinely committed radical among the leading witnesses. His account is extremely stimulating, generally reliable, and a useful balance against the predominance of royalist views. It is a pity his report ends just as the fighting begins. Captain Viard provides interesting details within the Tuileries during the night, and in the withdrawal of the royal family to the National Assembly. Lucile Desmoulins, wife of a leading anti-monarchist journalist, gives a domestic perspective to the insurrection. Dr John Moore, father of the famous general, gives a foreigner's view of 10 August.

Among other contemporary memoirs, I would specifically refer to those of Bertrand de Molleville, a former minister and confidant of Louis XVI, the journal of Gouverneur Morris, the United States Diplomatic Representative, the Marquis de Ferrières, a former deputy of the Constituent Assembly who was living in Paris at the time, and Ruault, a bookseller. None of these authors, except briefly the latter, witnessed directly the main events of 10 August, but the first two produce informed data on the background in the royalist camp leading up to that day, while the latter two provide second-hand details of the event itself. Also requiring mention are the memoirs of François Huë, a footman of the king's bedchamber and later a royalist agent, and certain observations by the young Napoleon Bonaparte.

Seven Swiss officers and one grenadier produced reports on their participation in the fighting, and in three cases described how they escaped from France. The best known account is the one produced by Captain Durler from Lucerne, written after he was able to leave France in February 1793. He submitted his manuscript to other officers who had shared his experiences, and the final draft was jointly signed by them. Despite this, it retains the naïve vanity of his personality and should be regarded more as a personal statement than an official report. Four other officers produced separate accounts from largely the same vantage-point. The earliest of these statements by Lieutenant Deluze was drafted only three days after the event. Two other officers related activities from entirely separate viewpoints. One, by Constant-Rebecque, who was later Chief of Staff of the Netherlands' forces at Waterloo, gives only a relatively few first-hand details of the action. The other, unpublished until 1928, is the extensive account by the nineteen-year-old Ensign Deville. It gives substantial coverage of important incidents not witnessed by any of his surviving colleagues. Grenadier Fonjallaz produced the only non-officer account among the Swiss who fought at the Tuileries. He makes few comments on the action itself, but relates a fascinating story on how he escaped being massacred in the palace and his return to Switzerland.

To these accounts must be added documents produced by official scribes, professional journalists, and some correspondence. The official minutes and newspaper reports on the sittings of the National Assembly are mines of useful material. They include not only speeches by deputies, but also details on individuals and deputations who continuously came to the symbolic barrier or bar of the Chamber to make statements. Minutes of the Paris Commune (Municipality) and some of its sections (wards) are also available. All these help to build up a comprehensive picture of what was going on throughout Paris during the hours concerned. Documents covering the interrogations of a number of Swiss officers and soldiers, as well as loyalist National Guards, have also survived. Their helpfulness is limited by the natural tendency of officers to conceal anything that might inculpate them, and of other ranks sometimes trying to please their captors.

Jean Gabriel Peltier, a royalist journalist who escaped to London, was the first person to attempt a comprehensive narrative of the events of 10 August. Written in the autumn of 1792, it was first entitled *Le Dernier Tableau de Paris*, and was subsequently republished as *Histoire de la Révolution du 10 Août 1792*. Although in Paris on the 10th, Peltier did not have a privileged vantage-point. However, he seems to have had access to a wide range of informants, not only French but Swiss as well. He claimed to have used some eighty sources, although unfortunately he hardly ever identifies them. Generally speaking, considering it was written when political feelings were high, Peltier's account of the preliminaries for the defence and the actual battle commands respect. Subject to critical appraisal, his work is a valuable source of information. The next significant attempt at a comprehensive account of the battle was first published long afterwards in 1819 by a former member of the Swiss Guards who had been on leave in Switzerland on 10 August 1792. Karl Pfyffer von Altishofen was raising money for the sculpting of the famous Lion of Lucerne, commemorating the heroism of the Swiss Guards who fell in the action. His account is uncritical, and leans heavily upon Peltier, and the reports produced by Durler and three fellow officers, namely Deluze, Glutz, and Gibelin. Nevertheless, he added some interesting details obtained from enquiries with survivors and their families.

I have generally relied on French secondary sources to cover the political situation leading up to the fall of the king. These also provide some essential information on 10 August itself, principally by providing original texts. First might be mentioned Buchez and Roux's massive *Histoires Parlementaires de la Révolution Française*, which is a leading source of documentary material accompanied by limited commentary. Next are specialised professional histories on the event, and I would cite as important *La Chute de la Royauté 1792* by Mortimer-Ternaux, *La Révolution du 10 Août* by Philippe Sagnac, *La Commune du Dix Août 1792* by Fritz Braesch, *Le 10 Août 1792* by A. Mathiez, Marcel Reinhard's *La Chute de la Royauté 10 Août 1792*, and Pierre Dominique's *10 Août 1792, la Monarchie est Morte!* From the Swiss side, specifically covering the Swiss Guards, I would mention *Der 10. August 1792* by A. von Gonzenbach, *Das Französische Schweizer Garde-Regiment am 10. August 1792* by W.F. von Mülinen, and *Les Troupes Suisses Capitulées et les Relations Franco-Helvétiques à la Fin du XVIII Siècle* by A.-J. Crouz-Tornare. The first two books are scholarly works written in the second half of the nineteenth century, relating the action fought by the Swiss Guards. Both books were written without Deville's valuable testimony, published later. The last work referred to is a recent major thesis for a doctorate concerning Swiss troops in France at the time of the Revolution. While not detailing the events of 10 August itself, it provides much data concerning the Swiss Guards in the days before and after. In addition to all the above, a number of other general and specialist histories, monographs and correspondence have been read for specific details and to contribute to the overall picture.

CHAPTER 1

The French Revolution

Louis XVI was a benevolent ruler, but he failed to recognise, as did nearly all those around him, the extent of the collapse in popular support for the outmoded political system he had inherited. A financial crisis led to the summoning of a freely elected Estates-General in May 1789, which was soon transformed into a National Assembly. This provided the stage for discontents to be expressed and aspirations to be realised. The Ancien Régime was swept away. The Revolution sought not only to found democratic representative government, but also to establish the principle of social equality. This was an explosive mixture. People from all classes were gripped by enthusiasm for the new order. Throughout France it was felt that an oppressive veil of absolutism and privilege had been rent asunder, revealing a new dawn in which participation in civic responsibilities would develop hand in hand with social regeneration.

The members of the new National Assembly set about making a complete break with the despised past. The whole provincial and local administrative structure was dismantled and replaced by democratically elected authorities for France's 44,000 municipalities and 83 new Departments. The judicial system was transformed, and the centuries-old regional Parlements, non-elective assemblies with judicial powers, disappeared without a trace. Nobles lost their privileges and titles were abolished. The property of the Catholic Church was seized, and priests became state employees by the will of politicians who, in keeping with the Age of Enlightenment, were largely atheists or deists. Soon, only the king and his Royal Council remained of the major institutions of the Ancien Régime, as the legitimacy they embodied was still considered desirable for consolidating the gains of the Revolution. Distrust of the king, however, remained the guiding principle of the revolutionaries and his actual authority was reduced to a shadow of its former self. The half-French American statesman Gouverneur Morris from the State of New York, who was in Paris much of the time from 1789 to 1794, described France at the outset of the Revolution as 'a nation which exists on hopes, prospects, and expectations – the reverence for ancient establishments gone, existing forms shaken to the foundations, and a new order of things about to take place in which even the very name of all former institutions will be disregarded'.

Yet, in one crucial aspect, the Revolution became very much a continuation of the past in demanding political conformity. In trying to establish a democratic constitutional government, the French were taking a giant step where existing political theory, such as the strict division of powers, could only provide inadequate assistance. Practices being developed across the Channel based upon a stable political majority, liberal laws, and legitimate opposition, which in turn might become the majority, were imperfectly understood, if understood at all. These proved to be the real way forward. Instead, falling back on theory, revolutionary politicians were easily seduced by the passionate arguments of Rousseau. Writing some decades before the Revolution on the nature of the ideal state, Rousseau believed that a free people must exercise their sovereignty by what he termed the General Will. This might be tentatively defined as the overall intentions of the community after deducting individual personal differences. How one could easily set about determining the General Will was left unclear. Once decided, however, its authority was incontestable. There was no room for opposition or political parties in Rousseau's system. Naturally, such a concept was particularly attractive to totalitarian-minded politicians who were tempted by Rousseau's dictum that anyone resisting the General Will 'will be forced to be free'. Despite a liberal voting franchise and praiseworthy intentions, the Revolution engendered undemocratic politics, especially as the trappings of political democracy were unsupported by the necessary ingredients of tolerance and experience. The dictates of force, rather than the statutes of constitutional law, became the means for changing governments.

The conformity demanded by the radical revolutionaries, especially after August 1792, required a fundamental rejection of past traditions and beliefs. This led to totalitarian politics and a deeply divided society. Although the Terror was liquidated in the summer of 1794, deep-rooted political instability continued. Napoleon, who dismissed the more extreme ideas of 1789 as being 'nothing but weapons in the hands of malcontents, ambitious men, and ideologues', eventually, with some success, attempted to create a national reconciliation from above. He knew, nevertheless, that the Revolution, while destroying political legitimacy based upon the former Monarchy, had failed to establish a durable substitute. His régime might only last as long as he could continue to dazzle the French people with military conquests.

In September 1791, after much heart-searching, Louis agreed to accept France's first written constitution which had been under consideration for two years. He was given circumscribed executive powers but had no say in legislation, except a temporary veto. The administration over which he presided had no real control over local and regional authorities and no direct command over forces for maintaining public order. It was not that Louis XVI, who had been reigning since 1774, now had difficulty in accepting constitutional government and representative institutions. But he justly believed the weakness of the executive part of the government made the 1791 Constitution unworkable, confronted as it was by a Legislature composed, to borrow Gouverneur Morris's description, of politicians 'new in Power, wild in Theory, raw in Practise'. In sum, the National (Legislative) Assembly had supreme authority without the need or ability to exercise it responsibly, while the national administration headed by the king, called the Executive Power, was supposed to govern France without the means to do so. The general belief that the principal duty of the Legislature was to check and frustrate the Executive, which among other things led to the exclusion of ministers from membership of the Assembly, meant Louis could expect minimal support from the nationally elected representatives in carrying out his duties.

On the right of the political spectrum in France were members of the former nobility who in 1789 may have equalled as much as 1.5 per cent of the total population of 27 million. By 1792, a considerable number had emigrated. For the most part they either wished for a return to the Ancien Régime, or for the establishment of a dictatorial monarchy which could maintain their privileges. A relatively small minority of nobles accepted the Revolution, having played a crucial part in its earlier stages. Some of this aristocratic minority, together with certain bourgeois politicians and journalists, now sought a constitutional monarchy on variations of the British model. They desired enhanced power for the Executive which would place limits on populism and safeguard property. Whether it would include a greater role for the aristocracy was more controversial. The effectiveness of this grouping was limited by lack of consensus on the details of a modified constitution, and the danger and reluctance of being considered counter-revolutionary. However, the majority of the population, in so much as they were politically active, regarded the 1791 Constitution, which still preserved a limited 'paternal' role for the king, as fulfilling its aspirations.

The radicals, whose power rested on activity rather than numbers, sought to take over the Revolution and advance it in the name of liberty and equality. To achieve this end, they aimed at eradicating what remained of the Ancien Régime: the king who still reigned despite being labelled a tyrant, and the former nobles who still retained some influence and position. By the beginning of 1792, the radicals were increasingly divided into two main factions, although it is important to emphasise that the word 'faction' was a term of opprobrium and the idea of organised parties with different political agendas, rejected by Rousseau, was anathema. It was considered that the revolutionary polity must embody the indivisible General Will. Nevertheless, groupings arising from political self-interest, and ideological and personal sympathies, came into existence. Later, the two radical factions acquired the respective labels of Girondins and Jacobins. For convenience, these will be used throughout this text.

The new National (Legislative) Assembly, which replaced the original National (Constituent) Assembly, started sitting at the beginning of October 1791. It had a majority of moderates, but they were divided, and experienced politicians who might have led them had been made ineligible for election due to legislation excluding members of the former Chamber. Radical politicians, for whom ideologically the Revolution was still unfinished business, soon gained a commanding position. This was achieved partly though oratorical skills but largely because they could always promote issues which would allow them to denounce moderates as actual or potential opponents of the Revolution. They were considerably helped in this process by the support of radical claques in the large spectator galleries. The leading revolutionary faction in the Assembly, initially called the Brissotins and later the Girondins, sought to increase their authority by adding 'patriotism' to the powerful rallying cries of 'liberty' and 'equality'. They began to agitate for war in order to export the Revolution abroad. Some radicals initially feared that war would benefit actual and potential counter-revolutionaries. These became the core of the Jacobin faction. The Girondins were helped in promoting their policy by the existence of a vociferous body of external opponents to the new political order, the émigrés, consisting of French princes and nobles based in Coblenz. The king complained about the émigrés' agitation which rendered his own situation more difficult. His pleas fell on deaf ears. The émigrés naturally sought to bolster their position by inciting the reluctant major European powers to intervene to restore the political situation in France as it had existed before the Revolution.

In 1792 Louis was thirty-seven years old. Physically, he was corpulent with poor deportment, and his heavy features produced an appearance of complacency. His virtuous behaviour, consideration, and conscientiousness, however, enabled him to command genuine sympathy and devotion. He was well informed, by no means unintelligent, but lacked imagination and energy. Introverted by nature, he was capable of obstinacy and even petulance. More seriously, an ingrained lack of confidence tended to make him irresolute and distrustful, and unduly reticent. Although receptive to sound judgement, he had difficulty in pursuing a policy against strong opposition. While Louis remained bound to the divinely consecrated responsibility he had inherited for acting as 'father' to the French people, and was a man of strong convictions, he was nevertheless reasonable, prepared to accept change, and had come to have some understanding of the Revolution, and rejected the reactionary politics of the émigrés. Unfortunately, this was not fully appreciated by many of those who surrounded him, including significantly the queen. Louis would probably have made an excellent constitutional king in a political system like the British, which showed respect for monarchical traditions and social status.

On 20 April, much against his will, Louis was forced by his Council into declaring war on Austria. For the first time, despite their incompatible politics, he had chosen a ministry consisting principally of nominees of the radical Girondin faction which dominated the National Assembly. This did not help him with the Legislature, however. The bullying by Girondin politicians continued, now supported by their adherents within the Royal Council. Louis was blackmailed into disbanding his Constitutional Guard and was faced with savagely punitive legislation against priests who refused to renounce the Pope's authority. The king, a sincere Catholic, sought to use his constitutional veto. The Girondin ministers either resigned or were dismissed. The king invited replacements largely from the administrative class. In revenge, the Girondins organised a mass demonstration on 20 June which led to the occupation of the Tuileries, the royal palace in central Paris. The king was subjected to threats and abuse over several hours. There was a short-lived revulsion against this treatment of the monarch, including an attempt by Lafayette, one of the first leaders of the Revolution who had seen himself as a French George Washington, to launch a coup against the radicals. He arrived alone in Paris from his army command in the north, but failed to find support.

While the ideological positions of the Girondin and Jacobin factions then largely overlapped, they were differentiated by their means for driving the Revolution onwards. The Girondins, because of their strong position in the National Assembly, sought to use constitutional measures to carry forward

Posthumous portrait of Louis XVI by Joseph Boze (1745–1826), who was an intimate of the royal family. Louis is wearing the royal orders of Saint Esprit and Saint Louis and the Holy Roman Imperial Order of the Golden Fleece. Louis was born at Versailles on 23 August 1754. Boze is believed to have acted as the channel between the King and leading Girondins in secret negotiations at the end of July and beginning of August.

the Revolution under their auspices. Deterred by the absence of large-scale popular support for a Republic, many, but by no means all, of this faction believed their political objectives might be largely achieved by reducing the king to the status of a puppet. They aimed at bringing his remaining assets – his numinous appeal, administrative resources, patronage, and Civil List funds – under their total control by dominating the Council of Ministers. Choudieu, who was a deputy belonging to the radical Jacobin faction, commented on the Girondins' position before the insurrection of 10 August as follows: 'I cannot say that the Girondins were far from joining us in organising a republican movement, but as they had much more chance of gaining the direction of affairs under a King in his minority, and with a Regent such as the Duke of Orléans, they were only seeking to gain time.' However, establishing a Regency was not without political difficulties, and it seems in the last weeks of Louis' reign, the immediate objective of the Girondins was to control the king. In due course, as Choudieu suggested, this policy might well have led to establishing a Regency, followed by a Republic.

The other radical faction operated substantially through its domination of the Paris Jacobin Club (Club des Jacobins), essentially a middle-class institution of which the Girondin politicians still remained members but without commanding influence. The Paris club had hundreds of affiliates in the provinces as well as connections with popular political societies in the capital, making it a truly national institution. By speeches, the radical press, and inflammatory posters, the Jacobins pursued a vociferous campaign against the Monarchy, culminating in demands for the king's dethronement. Their motivation was complex and varied from individual to individual. Obviously, ideology, fear of counter-revolution, political ambition, and the desire to prevent the Girondins from monopolising power all played a part. Nevertheless, revolutionary ideology of the indivisible 'Nation' decreed that antagonism between the Jacobin and the Girondin factions must remain muted. To have brought it into the open might have undermined the Revolution itself while there were prospects, backed by foreign intervention, of counter-revolution. In essence, however, the coup d'état of 10 August 1792 was at least partly an attempt by the Jacobins to outflank the Girondins, although it would be wrong to suggest that the king was merely a stalking horse in a game of power. For both the Jacobins and Girondins in general, the continuing existence of the Monarchy was an affront to the principles of Liberty and Equality.

By July 1792 there was increasing political polarisation. The war had brought an additional dimension. Patriotic feelings heightened revolutionary fervour. Concerns about counter-revolution grew, especially as French armies suffered initial reverses. The radical press depicted the king not only as a despot, but also unfairly as a traitor owing to his inescapable family connections with the émigré army. While the Jacobins continued to stoke up their campaign of vituperation against the king and Court, and took the first steps towards an insurrection, the Girondins abandoned the idea of repeating the direct action they had employed on 20 June. They had found the king's moral courage a tougher nut to crack than expected and now sought to negotiate his compliance. Increasingly aware of the intentions of the rival Jacobin faction, they began to realise that if the king was to be their puppet, it was necessary to try to preserve his position, at least temporarily. This duly led them to moderate their hostility, and even their demands, the chief of which had been the restoration of the three ministers who lost their portfolios in mid-June. Although Louis was deeply reluctant to seek an accommodation with the Girondins, there is evidence that secret and desultory negotiations continued up to the time when the Girondins were out-trumped by their more ruthless Jacobin rivals on 10 August.

From July onwards, two further channels for influencing the situation became available to the Jacobin faction. The first was units of National Guards arriving in Paris from the provincial departments. These were citizen militia banded together from neighbouring municipalities, called fédérés from the fact that the National Assembly had requested the eighty-three departments to send units of National Guards to Paris to assist in celebrating the Fête de la Fédération on 14 July, the anniversary of the fall of the Bastille. Many of these units arrived late. The Girondins had intended that they should become an armed force under their control as a counter to the generally moderate Paris National Guards. To the fury of the Girondins, the king had vetoed the establishment of a special camp for them just outside Paris. The Jacobin Club now took advantage of the situation by establishing a special committee of forty-three members called the Central Committee of the Fédérés. This committee liaised with arriving units, provided hospitality within Paris, and induced them to petition the National Assembly with the Jacobins' political demands, while also seeking, with limited success, their military support for a coup. The Girondins responded by having the fédérés sent out of Paris to join the armies on the frontiers. The Central Committee provided cover for a splinter group called the Directorate of the Insurrection. Initially only five members, a dozen more were rapidly co-opted who would be useful in organising an insurrection. On the political front, Robespierre, Danton, Manuel, Billaud-Varenne and others heightened tension by speeches attacking the king, and demanding the 'sovereign people' be approached to elect a National Convention for changing the constitution. The agitation escalated into a call for the king's immediate dethronement. The Jacobin leaders were doubtless aware that this would interfere with the Girondins' plans.

The second channel was the forty-eight sections into which Paris' 650,000 inhabitants were divided for voting purposes, roughly equivalent to wards in English towns. As political parties did not then exist, the section was a collective organisation covering all voters. They normally only came to life at election time, but were now persuaded to activate themselves, although hampered by legal restrictions which limited the frequency of their sessions. The Jacobins sought to use the Paris sections as a counterpoise to the provincially dominated National Assembly. Choudieu stated that three of his Jacobin colleagues in the legislature sedulously toured the more proletarian areas of Paris each evening to agitate against the regime. This was not out of ideological sympathy with the working class, as socialist politics were still in the future, but because they were more biddable and less interested in stability than were the bourgeoisie. The moderate General Council of the Paris Municipality was presided over by a Girondin mayor, Jerôme Pétion. French mayors acted as chief executives. However, his deputy, Procureur Général Pierre Manuel, belonged to the Jacobin faction and began to invite the sections to send delegates to the Hôtel de Ville to deliberate on important issues with a view to presenting petitions to the National Assembly. On

Grande Séance aux Jacobins en janvier 1792, ou l'on voit le grand effet intérieur que fit l'annonce de la guerre par le Ministre Linote a la suite de son grand tour qu'il venoit de faire

A cartoon of the Jacobin Club in early January 1792. The government has given an ultimatum to the Elector of Trier and war is threatened. A war policy is supported by Gironde politicians and the Minister for War, Narbonne. The latter is referred to as Minister Linot(t)e, or linnet, meaning feather-brained. One of the officers in the centre is shown as a bird head, the others as stag heads. The Jacobins are largely opposed as they fear war will play into the royalists' hands. Note the conservative dress of the members.

25 July, the National Assembly foolishly accepted a resolution by Deputy Thuriot permitting the sections to meet permanently. Thuriot was close to Danton, and no doubt part of the overall conspiracy. He again played a crucial role on 10 August. Jacobin caucuses, chiefly in the poorer areas of Paris, started to take control of sections, largely by making key decisions late in the evening when moderates were absent. As the sections encapsulated the voters of Paris, the Jacobins hoped to bypass the Municipality's moderate legally elected General Council.

With the arrival of a small but disciplined unit of fédérés from the area of Brest, an insurrection was planned for the night of 26/27 July. Propaganda was prepared, and military objectives were detailed which included a takeover of the Hôtel de Ville as well as an attack on the Tuileries to seize the king. However, the Paris National

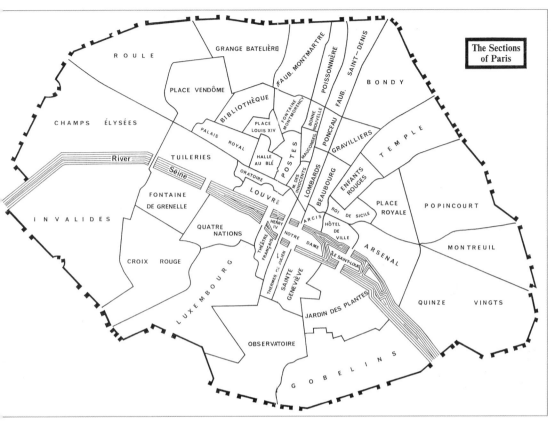

Paris was divided into 48 sections for electoral purposes. Administratively, however, it was divided into 60 districts. The sections became politically active and played a key role in events leading to 10 August 1792. Shortly afterwards the districts were abolished and the sections incorporated their limited administrative functions such as recruiting National Guards and issuing residence papers. Overall, the administration of the Paris Commune remained highly centralised based on the Hôtel de Ville.

Guards remained aloof. The poorer members of the population were still ineligible for recruitment into this part-time citizen militia. The Girondin Pétion, who as mayor had overall control of the 25,000 strong National Guards, appealed for order. But, as a committed republican, he was not prepared to act firmly against the revolutionaries. Another attempt was considered on 30 July after the arrival of the Marseillais fédérés, and was again resisted by the mayor. Likewise, Pétion intervened against the insurrection planned for the night of 4/5 August, aided by the reluctance of the insurrectionist military leader, Santerre, to mobilise his forces.

The agitation of those sections controlled by the Jacobins increasingly dominated the political scene from the beginning of August. Petitions were presented to the National Assembly calling for the king's dethronement. However, these did not yet have the support of the majority of the sections. The Girondin leaders in the National Assembly, such as Vergniaud, Gensonné, and Guadet, continued to temporise. The foremost revolutionary section of Quinze-Vingts in the industrial east of Paris passed resolutions for an uprising if the king was not dethroned by the evening of 9 August. The Assembly agreed to start a debate on the subject by the evening of that day. The Girondins advised the king that if an insurrection took place they would be unable to save him. It turned out to be true, but this warning was primarily a threat to persuade Louis to accept their demands.

As the situation deteriorated, the king came under increasing pressure from his advisers to escape from Paris. Various proposals were made. In one case, the king went so far as to authorise preparations for seeking refuge in a château near Rouen. Ultimately, he turned down all such suggestions for a number of reasons – fear of humiliation if the evasion failed as at Varennes a year previously, promises he had made to the Assembly, desire not to start a civil war, and concern that whatever authority he still retained would be diminished if he left Paris. Fundamentally, the king saw the more extreme revolutionary sentiments as a dangerous fever which must be allowed to run its course. Provocative action might only inflame and prolong it, and probably destroy his dynasty. Thus, he awaited events, which after 3 August included the looming decision on his future by the National Assembly, as well as the continued threats of a popular assault on himself and his family at the Tuileries.

On 30 July, the military equation in Paris was changed adversely for the forces of order by the arrival of the Marseillais. In the previous month, the republican Charles Barbaroux, a handsome lawyer from Marseilles living in Paris, had requested the mayor of his home city to send to Paris 'six hundred men who know how to die'. Marseilles was then under Jacobin control, and had formed an élite unit of National Guards. They were citizen volunteers, and not a band of desperate ruffians, criminals, and cut-throats as depicted by the monarchist press. Their exploits in the south had given them a fearsome reputation. In February 1792, they had participated in forcing the Swiss Bernese Regiment d'Ernst garrisoned in Aix to disarm, and had also helped to crush a counter-revolutionary movement at Arles. They had adopted the new patriotic song composed for the Army of the Rhine by Rouget de Lisle, 'Allons, enfants de la Patrie, le jour de gloire est arrivé' with its rousing chorus, 'Aux armes, citoyens, formez vos bataillons'. As a result of giving frequent renditions when they came to Paris, but ultimately because of the major role they played on 10 August, the song came to be named after them.

The two-battalion unit of Marseillais consisted of a total of 516 men and four cannons. National Guards battalions varied considerably in size. On 29 July, they arrived at Charenton, on the outskirts of Paris at the confluence of the Seine and the Marne. Santerre, a brewer from the Faubourg de Saint Antoine and the leading military figure on the side of the insurrectionists, went out to meet them. He was followed by a delegation of six men from the Jacobin Club who arrived at 6 a.m. on the 30th. Around midday, the Marseillais halted on the Place Bastille with drums beating, standards unfurled, and chanting the Marseillaise. The Jacobin journalist Chaumette described their tanned faces and martial figures in close formation, marching under a red flag, and shouting 'Vive la Liberté!'

Santerre had promised them a general uprising, but all he could muster was some 200 Paris National Guards and 50 fédérés. The Marseillais left the Place

Bastille, and crossed over to the Ile de la Cité to pay their respects to the mayor at his official residence. Santerre went into the Mairie to speak to Pétion. The latter forbade any action, and instructed him to conduct the Marseillais to barracks prepared in the north of Paris. However, Santerre was persuaded by others to allow them to make a demonstration by eating in the wealthy and constitutionalist part of Paris surrounding the Champs Elysées. Messengers were sent ahead to obtain space at a large restaurant surrounded by a garden with the cumbersome name of Au Grand Salon du Couronnement de la Constitution. On the other side of the avenue, some 160 grenadiers belonging to the smart National Guards battalions of the Petits-Pères and Filles Saint-Thomas were dining at Au Jardin Royal belonging to the traiteur [fine provisions supplier] Dubertier. As they left the restaurant, a radical crowd, which had accompanied the Marseillais, insisted that they shout 'Vive la Nation!' The grenadiers countered with cries of 'Vive Lafayette! Vive le Roi! Vive la Reine!' The crowd started to throw hard lumps of sun-baked earth. Some of the National Guards drew their sabres. The Marseillais, who had been observing all this across the avenue, then intervened. They jumped through the windows, wide open because of the summer heat. Leaping over the low palisade surrounding the garden, they put the grenadiers to flight. One of them, a stockbroker named Duhamel, fired his pistol at a Marseillais and missed. Furious, a group of them ran after him, cornered him in the rue Saint-Florentin, and hacked him to death. In panic, a number of the grenadiers, including ten or so lightly wounded, ran across the swing bridge from the Place Louis XV (now the Place de la Concorde) into the Tuileries garden. They made their way to the palace, where they were received by the king and queen in person and had their wounds dressed.

This incident convinced the Court that even élite National Guards could not be relied upon to protect them. The queen wrote to this effect to her friend Count Fersen on 1 August. Concerned, the king summoned the aged Colonel Count d'Affry, the commander of the Regiment of Swiss Guards. They met the next day, but what happened at this meeting is unrecorded. Affry had long followed the principle of full acceptance of the Revolution while minimising the political profile of Swiss mercenary troops in France for which he had overall responsibility. On 20 June, the Swiss Guards had been withdrawn from the Tuileries rather than taking action to protect the king. Affry was now persuaded to be more positive. It must have been agreed to bring the guard at the palace up to full strength. This was provided by the 1st Battalion garrisoned in Paris. The guard was to be further reinforced in an emergency by troops from the three Swiss Guards battalions based just outside the city to the west, with the proviso that the order came from an appropriate French authority. As part of the deal, Pétion was persuaded to grant the necessary laissez-passer for entry into Paris. Such reinforcements marched to the palace during the night of 4/5 August. They returned immediately to barracks when the threat failed to materialise. The radical sections had freely publicised their decision to rise by midnight on Thursday 9 August. To meet this, on the evening of the day before, the Swiss outside Paris were summoned again.

CHAPTER 2

The Tuileries

Sentries in the guardhouse of the barracks of the Swiss Guards 2nd Battalion at Rueil heard the sound of a horse swiftly approaching from Paris. It was around 10 p.m. on Wednesday 8 August, a warm humid night continuing the heat-wave in which Paris had been stewing for the past week. The duty officer was summoned, and the man on horseback, Aide-Major de Glutz, handed him an order signed by Mandat, Commanding General of the Paris National Guards. Reinforcements were requested for the guard at the Tuileries, some 10 km away. They were to arrive there by 3.00 a.m. Glutz then rode on to the nearby barracks at Courbevoie where the 3rd and 4th Battalions were stationed. The men gathered their kit and were mustered. A far from formidable 448 men were selected to strengthen the Swiss Guards already at the palace, leaving some 350 men allocated to guard duties elsewhere, on local leave, or as a skeleton force protecting the sick and rear echelons remaining at the barracks. A further 300 men had departed two days beforehand to act as guard for the king if he should decide, as now constantly urged, to leave Paris for the Château de Gaillon near Rouen in Normandy. The total current strength of the Regiment of Swiss Guards was some 1,450 men, dressed in red coats with blue facings, and white waistcoats and breeches.

Before setting out, cartridges were distributed by company quartermasters. The number seems to have varied, as figures given by witnesses range from 15 to 30. Even the larger figure was inadequate for anything but a relatively short engagement. There were no reserves. The six flags of the three battalions, emblazoned with the Swiss white cross surrounded by a red ground, were buried to safeguard them if disaster struck. The three flags of the 1st Battalion based in Paris were at the Tuileries. These included the special standard belonging to the Compagnie Générale signifying the regiment's relationship with the king, a white flag embroidered with the fleurs de lys of the French Monarchy.

The association between the Regiment of Swiss Guards and the Kings of France went back to the former's formation during the reign of Louis XIII in the early part of the seventeenth century. Their principal duties were guarding the exteriors of royal palaces and certain state institutions, and helping to protect the king on journeys. They formed part of an overall force of some 12,000 Swiss troops in French pay in the summer of 1792. These mercenaries organised in regimental units enjoyed extra-territorial privileges in view of their recruitment under treaties signed with the Swiss cantons. Their employment brought significant economic benefits to Switzerland in the form of pay and pensions, as

The Terrace of the Dauphin from the Place Louis XV. The workmen and blocks of stone are possibly involved in the construction of the Pont Louis XVI across the Seine close by.

well as honours for leading families. They also helped to ensure French political support in Swiss relations with other powers. In order to preserve these advantages, the 78-year-old Colonel d'Affry, mentally alert although physically infirm, worked hard to keep the Swiss troops out of politics, despite the natural royalist sympathies of most of their officers.

According to Constant-Rebecque, a nineteen-year-old second sub-lieutenant, the force only set off at 2 a.m. Strict silence was maintained as instructed, and it was met a short distance away at the Neuilly bridge by Lt-Colonel de Maillardoz and Major Bachmann. These senior officers brought with them a laissez-passer which had been signed by the mayor, permitting the Swiss to enter Paris at the Porte Maillot. The possibility of ambush or resistance had been anticipated. De Gibelin, an under aide-major, commanded an advance guard with flanking units to keep the way clear, and to capture, if necessary, the swing bridge over a water-filled ditch separating the Place Louis XV from the Tuileries garden. The red-coated column marched down the Champs Elysées, traversed the Place Louis XV without incident, crossed the swing bridge, circuited the large octagonal basin, and continued along the ceremonial alley through the garden to the palace some 600 yards away.

What were the feelings within the regiment as the crisis approached? A number of officers' letters written over the previous month have survived. These give some idea of the political atmosphere surrounding the Swiss Guards at that time.

Exit from the Tuileries garden into the Place Louis XV. The Pont Tournant is ahead, and beyond is the equestrian statue of Louis XV. The square was constructed in the latter part of his reign.

On 18 July, First Sub-Lieutenant Forestier Saint-Venant wrote to Madame d'Epinay (the daughter-in-law of Rousseau's patroness) telling how he and three comrades were walking on the terrace overlooking the Seine at the top end of the Tuileries garden. There they saw the little dauphin and the princess royal accompanied by their mother, Marie Antoinette, who was seated on a bench. The seven-year-old prince was amusing himself by chasing his older sister. They noticed around 100 curious onlookers, of whom a few had disrespectfully kept their hats on their heads. Some fédérés arrived also wearing hats, but the Swiss officers made them remove them. Shortly afterwards, when the queen got up, a dozen or so 'scoundrels' ostentatiously paraded in front of her wearing their hats. The four Swiss officers then surrounded the queen and escorted her for several hundred yards back to the palace.

Another Swiss officer, Captain d'Erlach of Berne, who habitually commanded the force of Swiss Guards at the palace, and who was to die on the 10th, wrote to a leading magistrate of his home city on 1 August. 'You can judge, Sir, the terrible situation of the palace in the middle of these troubles. Its only hope rests on the Regiment of Swiss Guards. Let us see, and I trust that it will not be in vain. The other day, the King and the Queen had the goodness to make us understand, to myself and two comrades, the anxiety that they feel for our fate. The Fédérés from Marseilles have declared that their objective is the disarmament of the Swiss Guards;

but we have all decided not to surrender our arms but with our lives.' Here we have one of the principal ingredients in the tragedy which was about to unfold. The Marseillais continued to brag when they arrived in Paris how, at the end of February that year, they had compelled the Bernese Ernst Regiment, garrisoned at Aix-en-Provence, to surrender their arms. The Swiss Guards were repeatedly taunted with receiving a similar humiliation. For a proud and élite regiment, this in itself would be enough to explain the refusal of the Swiss Guards to lay down their arms when confronted by the Marseillais at the Tuileries on the morning of 10 August.

Forestier Saint-Venant wrote his final letter to Madame d'Epinay on 6 August. He told her that there had been the possibility of being posted to Normandy or Champagne, but in neither of these regions would he be able to be useful to the king, whom he had sworn to serve. 'There is more danger in remaining in Paris, therefore I ought to wish to remain here.' He added that the palace was subject to continual alerts and he had had to remain up all night. He mentioned that the 'brigands' would be able to force entry into the Pavillon de Flore at the river end of the Tuileries by coming from the Louvre through the long gallery overlooking the Seine. The king had brought in a building contractor to block the gallery with large beams, and to take up some 20 feet of floorboards. Forestier continued his letter by mentioning that two days before, a grenadier of the National Guards had placed himself in front of their guardhouse in the Cour des Suisses at the Tuileries, and had spoken with relish of the horrors facing them. He added that yesterday, 'we had a mob of three hundred persons under our windows. It was all we could do to retain the fury of our soldiers against this rabble. You can have no idea of the ardour with which our soldiers sharpen their bayonets, and try their flints; all this helps to quicken the blood.' The final paragraph of his letter is typical of the period, when emotion was generously displayed and expected to be received with sympathy. 'Farewell! My soul is wretched. Alas! What is going to become of us? If my life could suffice to restore calm and re-establish that unfortunate [royal] family on which I shed tears, Heaven is my witness that it will cost me only a sigh. I would give my life with all my heart.' He was to give his life on the 10th, one hopes without costing a sigh, but his sacrifice was to be in vain.

The last letter dated 8 August is from a 23-year-old native of Neuchatêl, Georges de Montmollin, who had only arrived in Paris the previous day. Since 1786 he had been an officer with the Regiment of Salis-Samade, but over the past year had been seeking through his father a commission in the more glamorous Swiss Guards. A month earlier, while Georges was on leave in Switzerland, his father had received a letter from Colonel d'Affry saying that the king had authorised him to appoint officers to fill vacancies in the regiment, and asking whether his son was still interested. After hesitating over whether he should join the émigrés at Coblenz instead, Montmollin junior had accepted. The son's scarcely reassuring letter to his father gives an indication of radical political sentiment in France:

I am writing you a few lines, my dear father, in order to assure you of my well-being and my arrival yesterday in Paris. During the journey I suffered only the unpleasantness clearly to be expected; that is to say I was insulted everywhere. At Ornans they simply proposed to throw me into the river, and at Vitteaux they

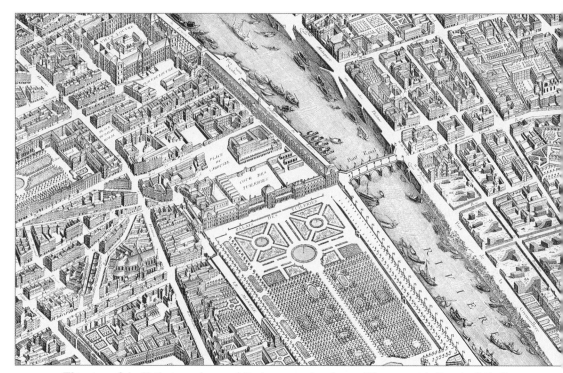

This view of the Tuileries and central Paris was produced some fifteen years before the fall of Louis XVI. The Manège is at the left of the garden at the bottom. It was enlarged when it became the National Assembly by the addition of a surrounding covered passage and offices. The courtyards of the Tuileries can be clearly seen beyond the palace in the centre.

threw wood into my carriage. My entry here has not been happier, for to-day I was molested by five of those scoundrels from Marseilles who seized me by the arms, and have insulted me with the most horrible imprecations, because I had, they said, an aristocratic cockade. Note, that it was in the colours of the Nation. But it was a pretext, perhaps they had seen me leave our guardhouse. At length when I returned, all our officers congratulated me on getting off so lightly. I am making my visits; I will be received tomorrow Thursday at the palace. . . . That day [9 August] is an important day for France and for us! They have to decide on the dethronement of the King, perhaps worse. . . . They will have to disarm us and chase us away; all our Regiment will be at the Tuileries that very day! We are detested in the Faubourgs [newer parts of Paris surrounding the historical central area], above all by the Marseillais who are here, and who are the greatest scoundrels that the world has ever produced. They commit murders with impunity and openly in the streets! In order to go to the palace, we are obliged to have our uniforms sent separately. We would be insulted if we passed along the streets wearing one! Our soldiers have orders not to go out save in groups of five or six, so as to avoid being attacked! Farewell, I embrace you all. . . .

Madame Campan, born Jeanne-Louise Henriette Genet, also had little reason to doubt the hostility of the insurgents. She was forty in 1792 and had enjoyed a long career at Court, starting as reader to Louis XVI's aunts. She was now Lady of the Queen's Bedchamber, administrator of the domestic side of the queen's household, and fiercely devoted to her mistress and the royal family. It was to her that the king entrusted, a few days before his fall, key documents which he wished to preserve. Later she felt it necessary to burn them. In due course, after the end of the Terror, she established a second career even more successful than her first as founder of a prestigious school for girls. In her lively memoirs she describes the atmosphere in the palace where many of the lower servants were extreme Jacobins. She noted on the last Sunday before 10 August that, when the king passed through the palace, half the National Guards said, 'No King! Down with the veto!' At vespers that evening during the Magnificat, republicans in the choir sang loudly 'Deposuit potentes de sede [He hath put down the mighty from their seat].' The royalists countered by emphasising, 'Domine salvum fac regem et reginam [O Lord make safe the king and queen].'

The king and queen could not leave the palace without the risk of being jeered at; even in the Garden of the Tuileries, though it was now closed to the public. Insults shouted from the garden under the royal apartments had become more and more insufferable, which had decided the king on the garden's closure. The National Assembly retaliated by expropriating the Terrace of Les Feuillants along the northern edge of the garden, beyond which was situated the Manège, the former riding school where the National Assembly held its sessions. Along the terrace was placed a tricolour tape on which were fixed taunting notices reading 'Terre Nationale' on the town side, and, according to the Jacobin Deputy Choudieu, 'La Forêt Noire' (the Black Forest) on the garden side, which presumably referred to both its tree-lined alleys and the counter-revolutionary émigrés based around Coblenz in south-west Germany. Extremists threatened death to any citizens who dared to step into the Forêt Noire. A constant crowd now manned the terrace to boo the queen if she tried to use the garden for recreation with her two children.

The queen had become increasingly depressed in recent weeks. She wanted a resolution to the situation, even if it were adverse, rather than to live day by day through continuous alarms where the Court's weakness seemed to foretell an inevitable catastrophe. She deplored her husband's inability to act and told Madame Campan: 'The King is not a coward, he has great passive courage, but he is crushed by an over-tender conscience, and a distrust of himself which comes as much from his education as from his character. He fears to give orders, and dreads more than anything to address a gathering. . . . As for myself, I would like to act, on horseback if necessary. But, if I acted so, it would give weapons to the King's enemies. The outcry against the Austrian women, against the domination of a female, would be general in France. In showing myself, I would destroy the King. A Queen who is not Regent, must, in the present circumstances, remain inactive and prepare herself for death.' Madame Campan's report on the queen's views, in which she may well have mixed some of her own, might be compared with a similar observation by the elderly respected former minister and amateur botanist, Malesherbes. 'The King's extreme sensibility, this tenderness of disposition, so

An angled view from earlier in the eighteenth century of the Tuileries and its garden from above the entrance. Allowance must be made for considerable foreshortening. In reality, the palace would look further away. The trees occupied some two-thirds of the garden length.

amiable in private life and in times of tranquillity, afterwards became, in times of revolution, more fatal to a king, than even certain vices might have been.'

The stage on which were performed many of the main events concerning the fall of the king on 10 August 1792 was the Tuileries and its surroundings. The palace or château of the Tuileries had been started in 1565 by the famous architect Philibert Delorme for Catherine de Médici, the widow of Henry II. Its name derived from the tile-works situated on its site. The main building extended in a line over 300 yards in length, at right angles to the Seine. Its eastern side faced towards the old palace of the Louvre, which had been rebuilt and enlarged. On the other, it looked westwards across an extent of gardens over 700 yards long towards the Place Louis XV and the Champs Elysées.

At the centre of the palace stood the high roofed Pavillon de l'Horloge, or clock tower, where the main entrance to both sides of the palace was situated. The tower contained the Vestibule, a large rectangular hall which was the principal passage between the two fronts of the palace. To the right of this hall, entering

Marie Antoinette (1755–93), Queen of France. During the Revolution she tried to play a semi-independent political role and certainly at times had some influence on the king. Her interventions were generally harmful, being dominated by personal feelings rather than the objectivity of a statesman.

from the Cour Royale, were the Great Stairs which provided ceremonial access to the Royal Chapel on the first landing, and on the landing above the State Apartments, which extended in the opposite direction towards the river. The principal state rooms in order from the landing were the Salle des Suisses, the Salle des Gardes, the audience ante-chamber called the Oeil de Boeuf, the Bed Chamber, and the Council Chamber. Reverting to the external appearance, on either side of the Pavillon de l'Horloge was an architectural unity of two equal façades flanked by wing blocks. The left side from the Cour Royale housed the State Apartments above, with the dauphin's apartments and those of some leading courtiers below. On the right was the chapel, with the apartments of the King's aunts, now living in exile, in the wing block.

This central symmetrical architectural mass was continued on either side by two imposing similar façades. On the south side was the Galerie des Carraches with the Queen's apartments below. On the north side was the Theatre of Servandoni, which was later to become the seat of the National Convention. Finally, this vast edifice was terminated by two further pavilions, that of de Flore on the south or river side which contained the apartments of Madame Elizabeth, the king's sister, and the Pavillon de Marsan at the other end. These two pavilions, largely rebuilt, are all that remain of the palace which was demolished after the Commune of 1871, having been gutted by fire.

The Pavillon de Flore was connected, as it is today, by an immensely long gallery at right angles along the Seine joining up with the Louvre. It was then called the Galerie du Louvre. Facing east, the palace overlooked a number of courtyards. The central one was the Cour Royale and was connected with the Place du Carrousel by the Porte Royale, flanked by guardhouses and small grace-and-favour lodgings for courtiers. The Place du Carrousel gave access to the town via a number of little streets leading to the principal thoroughfare of the rue Saint-Honoré. Only the rue de l'Echelle survives today. On the south side of the Cour Royale was the Cour des Princes which gave access to the Queen's apartments. On the north was a small courtyard, the Cour de Suisses, surrounded by buildings including stables and the guardhouse of the Swiss Guards, with the Hôtel de Brionne on the north side. Beyond this building was a small courtyard in front of the Pavillon de Marsan, and named after it.

On the west or garden front of the palace, a terrace ran along the whole façade, divided from the garden by iron railings with a central gate. At right angles on the river side, access was blocked off to the Pont Royal over the Seine by imposing iron railings called the Grille de la Reine, also with a gate. This barrier was continued by a raised terrace called the Terrasse de l'Eau. This bordered one side of the garden above the Quai des Tuileries along the Seine. The first third of the oblong garden consisted of flower beds with decorative basins and statues. The other two-thirds was made up of tree-lined alleys with a central alley [Grande Allée] running into the Place Louis XV over a swing bridge [Pont-Tournant]. On the left and right of the garden exit were raised terraces overlooking the square. The left-hand terrace was called the Jardin du Dauphin and the right one the Terrasse de l'Orangerie, which linked up with the Terrasse des Feuillants opposite the Terrasse de l'Eau. These terraces were graced by large trees. On the far side of the Terrasse des Feuillants, about two-thirds of the way from the palace, was the Manège, which, enlarged, now housed the National Assembly. There, steps led up to the terrace from the garden, directly opposite a small alley in which the main entrance to the Manège was on the right. These selfsame steps now lead towards the Rue de Castiglione across the Rue de Rivoli.

CHAPTER 3
Defence

The Swiss reinforcements from their barracks to the west of Paris spent much of the day in inactivity billeted a few yards away from the palace in the stables of the Hôtel de Brionne, which the king had rented from Madame de Brionne on 5 August. There, the stolid Swiss soldiers would have quietly amused themselves by playing jass, a traditional card game, and smoking their clay pipes. Food may have been inadequate. Grenadier Fonjallaz complained he had hardly anything to eat on the 9th. We are told there were occasional alarms which may have caused them to check the firing mechanism of their flintlock muskets.

The Swiss were not the only reinforcements. At 10 a.m., the commander of the constitutionalist National Guards battalion of the Filles Saint-Thomas requested twenty men to reinforce the guard at the Tuileries. Grenadier Weber volunteered. His mother had been Marie-Antoinette's wet nurse, and the two had shared her milk. As small children they had been allowed to play together. He had come to France ten years earlier to profit from his foster-brother relationship, and was sincerely attached to the queen. He claimed in his memoirs that the various guard posts had been tripled. Such an increase in strength would not be evident all the time, as it was usual for the citizen militia of blue-coated National Guards to leave their posts to take refreshments.

A radical National Guards captain called Langlade, who commanded a battery of four cannons of the Val de Grâce battalion, arrived to take up his post at 1 p.m. in the Cour Royale, the principal external courtyard of the palace leading to the Place du Carrousel. Some, at least, might have queried the defensive value of this unit in view of its open support for the revolutionary mob on 20 June, when the Tuileries was invaded. Having positioned his guns, Langlade went off to eat with his men. They met two Marseillais fédérés and enjoyed a 'patriotic' (politically radical) conversation. After refreshing themselves, they returned to the Cour Royale. Langlade started to ask a mason why he was placing an obstacle on top of the main gate, when he was struck on the shoulder by a grenadier of the National Guards with a white pompon on his hat, and wearing a ribbon of the Cross of St Louis. The royalist grenadier felt the radical gunner captain needed some political instruction and answered for the mason: 'Valiant captain, it is for those brigands from Marseilles who have come to Paris to pillage everything, and threaten to come and assassinate the King this very night.' Langlade asked him in umbrage if he knew any Marseillais, as he was acquainted with a great number including their commanders, and they were all people of good standing. The grenadier swore that they were a bunch of damned rascals, and in taking their side, Langlade also. The latter replied that he and the grenadier did not seem to belong to the same world, and if they were not on duty, he would know how to make him change his views.

Late in the afternoon, Langlade was told that his hero Pétion, the Mayor of Paris, was going to the National Assembly, and he took time off to visit the spectator galleries to hear what he had to say. He arrived at the moment the mayor was mentioning the formation of two camps of 600 men each in the Place du Carrousel and the Place Louis XV. After Pétion had finished his speech, Langlade returned to his position in the Cour Royale. He was told that during his absence a number of National Guards near his guns had suggested that he deserved to be arrested for the views he had expressed with his gunners over their meal. Langlade replied that he was not apologetic. Gunners, he stated, should have firm opinions, although this did not mean that they should quit their duty. The gunners belonging to the Paris National Guards received pay as specialists, unlike the infantry who provided their services free. Their officers were recruited from former regular army NCOs and artisans with mechanical skills, and were generally strongly revolutionary. The royalist journalist Peltier, who in London that autumn wrote the first major account of 10 August 1792, complained that the professional classes did not like the rough work of manhandling cannons.

While the Swiss and National Guards were fulfilling their guard duties at the palace, the young François–Armand–Frédéric de La Rochefoucauld was attending a matinee at the Comédie Française, when he heard of a large crowd gathering around the Tuileries. A descendant of the famous author of *The Maxims*, he had been born in Paris in September 1765. He had joined the army at the age of fifteen as a cadet, and was soon appointed under-lieutenant. His father, the Duc de Liancourt-Rochefoucauld, who was well known as the founder of a national organisation for the development of arts and crafts, arranged for him to make a series of study tours during the 1780s, first in his native country, and later in England. There he met the well-known agricultural economist Arthur Young and invited him to France. He continued his military career

François–Armand–Frédéric, duc de Liancourt (1765–1848), later de la Rochefoucauld.

and reached the rank of major. His portrait shows a sensitive mouth and a strong aquiline nose in a long serious face surmounted by dark wavy hair.

His father had supported the Revolution from its outset and sat in the National (Constituent) Assembly. It was he who, when asked by Louis XVI at the fall of the Bastille on 14 July whether it was a revolt, replied: 'No Sire, it is a revolution!' He then went on to advise the king to appeal to the National Assembly rather than to flee to Metz, which he had been considering. Louis regretted later that he had listened to this advice, as he came to feel that it had been his last 'window of opportunity' for a successful escape, and an attempt to restore the situation. As the Revolution progressed, Liancourt-Rochefoucauld saw the need to check the radicals, and during the last year of Louis' reign was in frequent attendance at Court, while remaining a strong constitutionalist. He had command of the Sixteenth Military District in Normandy and was involved in the plan for the king to leave Paris for a castle near Rouen. His son, on the other hand, disagreed with the over-sanguine liberalism of his father and uncle, the latter being the family's titular head. He had become a royalist and saw his duty to watch over the lives of the royal family. Given to ardent introspection, he seems a character Stendhal could well have created.

The 26-year-old Liancourt, to give François-Armand-Frédéric his title, had difficulty in believing that anything was wrong, as when he had been at morning Mass with the King, the situation had then seemed tranquil. He believed it would remain so until Sunday, which, he mentioned in his memoirs, was the usual day for demonstrations. Nevertheless, he leapt into his chaise and reached the Place du Petit-Carrousel, leading into the Place du Carrousel, without encountering any difficulties. Then, to his surprise, he found the entrance to the Cour de Marsan, leading to the northern end of the palace, had been blocked by a large timber barrier constructed some distance from the gate. He entered instead through the main gate leading into the Cour Royale, and found it and the two adjacent courtyards very calm, with only a few people in uniform. Some National Guards, however, were gesticulating and talking politics in, he felt, an unpleasant manner. He was told that the king was in the State Apartments, and the queen with the dauphin. A number of people were standing in groups in the Rue de l'Echelle which led into the main thoroughfare, the Rue Saint-Honoré. He was used to seeing them there and they did not seem menacing, especially as there were many women among them. He decided to return to the theatre. Strangely, Liancourt seemed to be unaware of the much publicised threats to start an insurrection that very night.

Captain Viard, commanding an élite Chasseurs unit of the National Guards, was stationed in the Royal Apartments. The allocation of guard posts was for security reasons determined by lot. He relates how around midday he arrested a suspected assassin who claimed to be acting on behalf of the Marseillais. At around 4 p.m. they were advised that there were 3,000 Marseillais in the Faubourg Saint-Antoine, and the tocsin, two rapid bell strokes repeated continuously, would be tolled at 11 that evening. After midnight they would attack the palace and murder everyone. The name Marseillais was frequently given to insurgents in general.

The Marquis de Mandat, the commanding general of the citizen National Guards, set about meeting the crisis. He was staunchly constitutionalist but not particularly bright according to Madame Campan. Moreover, his authority was limited. The Mayor of Paris, Pétion, had recently censured him for over-reacting about the fracas involving the Marseillais in the Champs Elysées. Mandat was told that henceforth units could not be mobilised without the mayor's permission. The previous day, the Royal Council had applied for help to the more amenable Department of Paris. The Council of the Department instructed Roederer, the 36-year-old lawyer from Metz who was their chief executive officer, to write to the mayor to find out what measures he was taking to prevent an insurrection.

The Department of Paris was in a somewhat anomalous position vis-à-vis the Paris Municipality which accounted for 90 per cent of its population. The Department had only supervisory powers over the Paris Commune, and had no direct control over its National Guards which came under the ultimate authority of the mayor. Subject to confirmation by the Minister of the Interior, it had the right of suspending municipal officials who acted illegally or failed to undertake their functions. It had recently exercised this authority against Paris's two leading officials, Pétion and Manuel, following the invasion of the Tuileries on 20 June. The Municipality had failed to safeguard the king and his family despite its responsibility to do so. Pétion had been acting hand in glove with Girondin politicians in the National Assembly to bring pressure to bear on the king to rescind his vetoes of contentious legislation, and restore the three Girondin nominees who had recently quitted the Royal Council. Pétion's and Manuel's suspensions were shortly reversed by the National Assembly.

Pierre Louis Roederer was born at Metz in 1754 into a wealthy family and purchased a senior legal post with the provincial Parlement. He patronised the development of political and social ideas, sponsoring prize essays, one of which was won by Robespierre. He represented Metz in the Estates General and became a member of the National (Constituent) Assembly. Being ineligible for serving in the new National (Legislative) Assembly of October 1791, he stood for the post of chief officer of the Department of Paris, that is Procureur Général Syndic, and was elected. A fine figure, hook-nosed, with bony features and a supercilious expression, he had a not undeserved reputation for being two-faced. He was a political moderate, but was considered an opportunist. Jointly responsible with the Municipality for maintaining order in Paris, he lacked real resources for doing so. At the beginning of August he told Talleyrand, one of the most prominent original aristocratic supporters of the Revolution, that it would be better if the king left Paris. After 10 August, Roederer unsuccessfully tried to exculpate himself with the revolutionaries. He went into hiding and survived the 'Reign of Terror,' resurfacing after the fall of Robespierre. He played a significant role in Napoleon's coup d'état of 18 Brumaire (9 November) 1799, revenging himself on the Jacobins who had humiliated him in 1792. He prospered in high-level civil posts under the Consulate and Empire. Initially supporting the Bourbon restoration in 1814, he made the mistake of reverting to Napoleon during the Hundred Days, and lost his rank as peer, and other dignities, when Louis XVIII returned. These were restored after the 1830 Revolution and the accession of Louis Philippe. It was only then that he felt the time was opportune to publish a detailed account of his activities during the last fifty days of the reign of Louis XVI, derived from copious notes taken at the time.

In the afternoon of the 9th, both Roederer and Pétion were called to the barrier or bar of the National Assembly facing the president (chairman) to report on the situation in

Paris. Roederer arrived first. He explained that the Department had written twice to the Municipality asking for a daily briefing on the sections' intentions and details of the measures being taken to prevent an insurrection that night. He expressed his irritation that Pétion had only replied to one out of these two letters, and had failed to keep an appointment at 9 p.m. the previous day. We know this was because Pétion had had to receive a Jacobin-inspired delegation sent to find out his intentions in the event of an attack on the Tuileries. Roederer told the Assembly that the Council of the Department had invited all citizens to maintain public order. He pointed out that the Department lacked policing resources within Paris. They did not wish to interfere with measures taken by the Municipality, nor to go beyond their legal authority without

Roederer (1754–1835) as Procureur Général Syndic of the Department of Paris failed to show firmness in resisting the insurrection. His memoirs are an essential source of information on events.

consultation with the mayor. In his memoirs, Roederer related that the mayor had replied in his letter, 'with a coolness that was almost mocking', that he had authorised Mandat in the event of insurrection to use 'la générale', the name of the drumbeat the French used for forming up military units. Shortly after receiving the mayor's letter, Roederer met Mandat in the Department's Council Chamber. Mandat told him he had obtained no such authorisation from the mayor. Roederer claimed he was annoyed, and had the Department certify the authenticity of the mayor's letter, handing it over to Mandat as the permission he was seeking. He also added the Department's own sanction to mobilise units provided there was evidence of an uprising.

However, the *Journal des Débats et Decrés*, reporting on the Assembly's proceedings, requires Roederer's account to be considerably amended. It appears Roederer read out the mayor's letter to the Assembly and its contents are given in the newspaper report. These included authority to double the guard posts at the Tuileries and to beat 'le rappel' not 'la générale'. The signal called 'le rappel' only recalled troops to their mustering points, but not to form up. The newspaper report continued that Roederer went on to advise the Assembly, without giving details, that the Department had authorised Mandat to reinforce the troops at the palace that evening. It would seem that Roederer in his memoirs sought to implicate the mayor in authorising 'la générale' when the Department was alone responsible. His motivation for so doing is unclear, unless it was merely an invention to show the mayor was two-faced. Certainly, Roederer may have felt that Pétion let him down badly in failing subsequently to do his utmost to stop the insurrection.

When Roederer returned to his offices, he was rather surprised to find the mayor. He was calling at the Department on his way to the National Assembly, having just visited the palace. They discussed the maintenance of order, and became quite emotional together, swearing to die at their posts. Pétion then went in his turn to the bar to address the Chamber. He explained that for the past eight days the Municipality had been occupied in trying to keep order. Municipal officers and councillors had been repeatedly sent to tour the sections, and police commissioners asked to make reports. He remarked on the problems of keeping the peace when the available security force, the National Guards, was itself politically divided. It was only possible to maintain order by arming one section of the population at the expense of another, an action he was sure the Assembly would not approve. In effect, he meant supplying National Guards in the moderate wealthier parts of Paris with ammunition, while depriving the poorer radical areas. Doubtless, the Jacobins would have claimed that such action favoured a counter-revolution. The National Assembly did not bother to query the mayor's assessment. He continued by advising his audience that two reserves would be established on either side of the palace, but discreetly omitted to mention the doubling of the posts specifically protecting the Tuileries, unaware that Roederer had already revealed this when reading out his letter. It was around 6.30 p.m. when the Assembly adjourned, earlier than usual to allow members to leave in daylight in view of what had happened the previous evening. Deputies had been manhandled and threatened in the streets for acquitting Lafayette of the charge of leaving his command to launch a coup at the end of June.

An anxious Pétion returned to the Hôtel de Ville to make a final appeal for the maintenance of law and order, in accordance with the dictates of his office and the political interests of the Girondins. The past fortnight must have been one of mental turmoil: covertly sympathising with the republican sentiments of the plotters, but fearful their growing strength might undo the Girondins, while at the same time sensitive to his legal obligations, yet determined to ensure his political survival whoever won. Now, on the evening of the 9th, he issued his last call for the sections to keep the peace. It was a cleverly composed entreaty for patience, mixing authority with reason. 'Citizens, one has sometimes wished to undo you by seeking to relax your zeal; today one wishes to undo you by leading you astray. The Assembly is busy at this moment with our greatest interests; let calm surround it so that it may debate in a solemn and imposing manner, and let us wait with confidence the decision which will come forth from its wisdom. I have heard it said that one wishes to fix the day and the moment of its decision. This is intolerable. Never can you tell a judge at what hour he will be able to judge your case; for even greater reason you cannot use this language to an Assembly which is deciding on a great national issue. I believe that the situation is such that citizens must devote themselves to the imperative law of observing the most perfect calm.'

This address was hastily printed and circulated throughout Paris. Pétion, in his reference to the National Assembly, was alluding to the debate on the king's future, supposedly scheduled at the latest for that evening. He was well aware that the

Assembly had not yet even started to consider the issue, despite the promise made on 3 August. On the other hand, the revolutionaries had stated they would rise up if no decision to dethrone the king had been made by the evening of the 9th. He was asking them to stay their hand and await the Assembly's decision which he believed would in due course decree the king's dethronement. Pétion had already acted to prevent an insurrection four times since 26 July. This time his intervention was half-hearted.

Jacobin propagandists made strident claims that the Court was about to launch a bloody counter-revolution. No hard evidence emerged for such a coup during interrogations of royalists after 10 August, nor in subsequent memoirs. Some royalists may have entertained fond hopes of destroying the radicals but, as far as the king and his ministers were concerned, the preparations at the Tuileries against the insurrection promised for the night of 9/10 August were to preserve the royal family, pending a decision on their future by the National Assembly or the arrival of the Austro-Prussian armies in Paris. The Court was awash with rumours about the assassination of the king and the murder of his wife.

Mandat, commanding the National Guards, and his staff were busy making plans and drawing up orders. He had considerably strengthened the normal palace guard by bringing in additional Swiss and National Guards. The total number of the Swiss Guards at the Tuileries cannot be stated exactly, as muster rolls were lost as a result of the insurrection. However, considerable direct and indirect evidence points to a figure approaching 800 men, lower than that given in many histories. The number of reinforced National Guards on duty probably amounted to four or five hundred. There were also some 900-plus troops belonging to the Gendarmerie who were special security troops recruited from the civilian National Guards, and not regular soldiers of the line. These came under the authority of the Department rather than of the Mayor of Paris, but its control over them was weak.

In addition, it is claimed that around 2,000 summonses were sent out to royalist former members of the King's disbanded Gardes du Corps and his Constitutional Guard, and to other supporters of the Monarchy. This, and the action of the Swiss Guards, seems to be the principal evidence for a possible counter-revolution. Jacobin spies claimed that some of these royalists were to be dressed in Swiss uniforms. No credible eyewitness mentions this happening. The turnout from the summons proved disappointing. Peltier's total of 210 seems the likely figure, although some witnesses gave higher numbers. It can be argued that this was 200 or so too many, as their presence was definitely counter-productive in the eyes of most of the National Guards. They arrived stealthily during the evening and night, provided with special identity cards to gain entrance to the palace. Because people in civilian dress carrying arms were subject to arrest, they largely arrived with weapons of indifferent quality which could be easily concealed. Later on, some palace officials and servants also armed themselves. No provision had been made to ensure that they would be adequately equipped. By far the greatest negligence, however, was the failure to ensure an adequate supply of musket ammunition. The palace had no reserves, and the king had resolutely vetoed any plans for remedying this deficiency, which might have involved measures of doubtful legality.

The command structure within the Tuileries was complicated by the existence of two general staffs: that responsible for National Guards, and that of the 17th

Military District, of which Paris was the centre. However, all regular army units belonging to the District had left Paris for the frontiers since 15 July, so the latter consisted of staff officers without troops. As the National Guards were to form the bulk of the defence force, Mandat might be regarded as overall commander. The Swiss too had a general staff, but in accordance with Colonel d'Affry's strict policy they saw their position as auxiliaries, and probably did not play a significant part in organising the defence. D'Affry, suffering badly from gout, left his town residence to visit the Swiss guardhouse at the Tuileries on the evening of 9 August, determined to ensure the Swiss Guards played a subordinate role. He told his officers that the only orders he had to give were to 'neither march nor act for any reason without a written order from the King, or a requisition from the Commanding General [of the National Guards], or from the Municipality, and in all these cases only to serve as auxiliaries or secondary to the National Guards'. He then withdrew and retired to bed. These instructions were inadequate to meet the situation the next morning. Had he remained at the palace, he might have intervened to prevent a battle between the Swiss Guards and the revolutionaries. If bloodshed had been avoided, the revolutionaries might have been thwarted in taking the extreme measures which followed the insurrection.

It seems the over-elaborate plan of defence in depth was conceived by General Vioménil and his regular army staff. Apart from stationing troops within the palace itself, and in the Hôtel de Brionne looking out on to the Place du Carrousel, infantry and cannon were also placed in the exterior courts, and on the garden terrace along the other front of the Château. Strong points were also to be established on the bridges across the Seine to block insurrectionary units from the south attempting to cross to the north side where the Tuileries was situated, and thus to join up with forces from the Faubourg Saint-Antoine to the east. A contingent was also to be posted at the Pont-Tournant, to cover the entrance to the Tuileries long garden from the Place Louis XV. Other contingents were to be posted in the Place Vendôme and on the Place du Palais Royal, to sweep down the Rue Saint-Honoré. A large reserve of nearly six hundred of the Gendarmerie was stationed on the far side of the Louvre palace under its colonnade. It was planned that this contingent, together with a unit of National Guards on duty at the Hôtel de Ville, would attack the insurgents in the rear once they were engaged in assaulting the Tuileries from the Place du Carrousel. Most in the palace, including the king who is reputed to have given orders to avoid bloodshed, as he had done in July 1789 in the events leading up to the storming of the Bastille, must have trusted it would be unnecessary to put these measures to the test. It was hoped that the extent of the defensive preparations would overawe the insurrectionists. However, these ambitious plans depended upon Mandat mobilising substantial contingents of loyal National Guards when the authorisation he had received from the Department permitted him to do so, that is when there was definite evidence that an insurrection was taking place. In the afternoon and early evening of the 9th, there was no such justification. When he was able to mobilise, these elaborate plans proved to be over-ambitious, depending as they did upon commanders and troops prepared to show resolution and willing to risk civil war. These factors were largely absent.

CHAPTER 4

The Mayor

Jerome Pétion was a lawyer from Chartres. He had made his mark early in the National (Constituent) Assembly over which he had from time to time presided. Now thirty-two years old, the Mayor of Paris was well built with a heavy fleshy face, a sensuous mouth, and fine arched eyebrows. He was a complex character; a sensitive man playing at being tough. Madame Roland, who saw Pétion relaxed in domestic surroundings, liked him because of his softness and sensibility. The writer Mercier, perhaps revealing the strain in Pétion's conflicting personality, described his manners as artificial, his eyes shifty, and his complexion having a lustre which repelled confidence. Articulate, and with an understanding of popular psychology, he had considerable demagogic influence over the artisan class in Paris.

Pétion believed that reason left little room for kings whom he considered no different from other men. When it was proposed that the king should be called 'King of the French by the Grace of God', he replied that to title him thus was to insult God. Against the proposal in the 1791 constitution to make the king's person inviolable, he said: 'In order to be inviolable, it is necessary to be impeccable; but, there is not any man who has been endowed with that fine privilege; and it is not in the gift of men to create such a man by a fiction. The King is not an abstract being, he is not power in itself. A judge is not justice. A king is not royal majesty. He is a man, an official, a citizen, whom one can bring to justice.' Pétion had an important role in the Girondin political manoeuvres to bring the king under their control during the month up to his fall. His job was to head off the Jacobin-led insurrection, even though he partially sympathised with its objectives.

The Jacobin Deputy Choudieu confirmed that Pétion was continuing to collaborate with Girondin leaders in preserving the king while they tried to make Louis accede to their demands, principally to appoint their nominees as ministers and to surrender control of the Civil List. On 7 August, Pétion had even visited Robespierre, with whom he was on friendly terms and shared a similar ideology. He asked him to use his influence to moderate attacks on the king at the Jacobin Club, and to control the activities of its conspirators. This alarmed the plotters and a deputation went to the mayor the next evening to ask him what he would do if the palace were attacked. He coolly replied that he would give instructions for force to be resisted with force. He appears to have carried out his promise at the Tuileries on the night of the 9th/10th. More was required. The revolutionary situation was now far developed. It was his duty to maintain order and protect the Tuileries. He had the legal authority, the political prestige, and the oratorical skills to make a difference to

This portrait of Pétion (1756–94) was made just before he became Mayor of Paris in November 1791. The mayor abandoned his responsibility for maintaining order in Paris in the early morning of 10 August.

the course of events. However, although he went through the motions of trying to prevent the insurrection from taking place, this time he did not wish, nor perhaps dare, to visit its focal points as he had on previous occasions. He was unwilling to risk his popularity or even life to try to save the Monarchy, an institution he ultimately regarded as incompatible with the ideology of liberty and equality.

To a letter from the Royal Council mentioning concern about the deteriorating order within Paris and the threat of insurrection, Pétion replied on the 9th that he would do his best, but could promise nothing. This reply was obviously unsatisfactory, and he was asked to come to the palace to discuss the matter further. Earlier that day the Minister of Justice, Dejoly, had written his eighth unanswered letter to the National Assembly, complaining about the political agitation in Paris. When the mayor arrived at 5 p.m., accompanied by a municipal officer called Osselin, the palace had just received confirmation of the planned revolt that night, including specific threats against the royal family. The two members of the Municipality were received by Dejoly and another minister. Information was exchanged, and it was agreed that the means to prevent the insurrection were almost nil. The mayor then went to the Council Chamber of the Department where, as already recounted, he met Roederer who had just returned from the National Assembly. Immediately after this meeting the mayor carried on to the National Assembly and gave his report on the situation in Paris. Next, he returned to the Hôtel de Ville, made the proclamation detailed in the previous chapter, and followed it with the despatch of municipal officials and councillors to disaffected parts of Paris in order to call for calm.

Later that evening Pétion received two letters from Mandat, urging him to come again to the palace for consultations. One read: 'Monsieur le Maire, your presence is necessary, appearances are menacing, and as Magistrate of the people, you are the best person in the circumstances to bring them to reason. I beg you, therefore, to come and join your efforts to mine.' Pétion claimed he was reluctant to go to the palace, since he feared he would be received with hostility by the royalists gathering there. However, members of the Municipal General Council, over which the mayor was presiding, put pressure on him to go. He took the precaution of taking with him several colleagues for support, arriving at the palace somewhere around 11.30 p.m.

Pétion's own mendacious report, in which he was desperate to prove he was not involved in supporting the defence, had him remaining only briefly inside the palace, before going outside and idling for a considerable time on the garden terrace until he was called to the National Assembly. Fortunately, the historian is able to rely on other more informative accounts. By piecing these together and using plausible deductions where necessary, it seems possible to establish a relatively complete picture of events. Let us start with the graphic description of his arrival by the young royalist aristocrat, Liancourt. He had returned to the theatre after the false alarm that the Tuileries was being invested. Later, he went back to the palace and spent the evening with a friend. Apart from the mayor's antipathetic politics, he had even less reason to like him because a few days previously he had been personally interrogated by him after being detained. He gave some support to Pétion's own slanted account, in which the mayor claimed that he was met with angry and furious glances seeming to say: 'At last you are going to pay today for all you have done to us!' Liancourt wrote: 'Towards midnight, I saw Pétion enter the Bedchamber with head held high and a false air. No one moved to make way for him, and I noticed that he took exaggerated care not to bump into anybody. He was followed by three or four others with tricolour sashes. It was the first time I had seen him since 4 August, when I had been taken as a prisoner to the Mairie, to be questioned by him. He went into the Council Chamber, and, as the door remained half open, I slipped inside. I heard him telling the King that the faubourgs were very disturbed, and that considerable crowds were gathered, but he hoped that with care he would be able to restore calm, or at least contain the situation until the morning. The King spoke to him in a firm manner and asked him what the people wanted, to which the Mayor did not make any reply. The King told the Mayor that his function was to keep order, and he hoped that he would go where his presence was necessary. Pétion replied that he would give instructions to repulse force with force. He then left, walking across the rooms.'

The king hoped Pétion would do what he had done on previous occasions and use his personal authority to quell unrest in the disturbed areas of Paris. This time the mayor signally failed to do so. While Pétion suggested that the king was even brusquer to him than Liancourt mentioned, the conciliatory Dejoly, who was also present at the interview, quoted the mayor as saying, 'This is the moment of crisis, and one should not dissimulate the danger. I have hastened to come in person to watch over the safety of the King and the security of his family.' The king, according to Dejoly, thanked the mayor in a most affectionate manner. The conversation continued for several minutes, which the mayor then broke off, saying he wished to inspect the National Guards' posts and go on to the National Assembly.

Neither Liancourt nor Dejoly relate the words Pétion had with Mandat. The latter was apparently standing beside the king, and had interjected, when the mayor announced that he had come to watch over the safety of the king and the royal family, 'That doesn't matter, I am taking care of everything. My measures have been well considered.' Roederer, who reported this remark, continued his account by noting the development of an acerbic interchange. Mandat complained bitterly about his shortage of ammunition. The Police Department at the Municipality had refused to give him a requisition for powder. The mayor replied that it was not policy for him to have it, and asked him if he had any reserves. Mandat told him that his battalions had only around three cartridges per man, and some battalions had none. According to Roederer, the mayor cut the conversation short by saying: 'It's stifling here, I must go into the garden to take some air.'

As reported in the memoirs of the royalist François Huë, it must have been at this juncture that Major General d'Hervilly, second in command of the former Constitutional Guard, intervened with the King to propose ammunition should be seized from the Arsenal. Louis asked Hervilly to take the matter up directly with Pétion and Roederer who must have moved a little way off. They advised against it, and the king refused his permission. This would account for Hervilly's later remark, reported by Madame de Tourzel, that nothing was being done. The lack of ammunition for the National Guards had exercised its general staff and the king's ministers considerably in recent days. It is very likely it played a role in the collapse of the defending National Guards' morale the next morning. Grenadier Weber of the Filles Saint-Thomas expressly stated in his memoirs that his loyalist battalion only received two rounds per man.

The mayor and his entourage went down the Great Stairs. After inspecting some National Guards posts, they walked across the garden to the National Assembly to find out what was going on there, having heard it had recently started an all-night sitting. It was a warm and beautifully calm night, and Pétion remarked that from the terrace the tocsin and other noises of the city could be heard distinctly. On arriving at the Manège, although they probably did not enter the Chamber, they learned that a delegation from the Hôtel de Ville was shortly scheduled to make a report on the situation within Paris. It can be surmised from subsequent events that they left a message for this delegation to join them later on the garden terrace by the palace. The mayor's party was returning to the Tuileries when they were met by Roederer who was taking a stroll in the garden.

Roederer recounted he had received a summons from the king which had reached him at 10.45 p.m. He was at the Tuileries 15 minutes later, about half an hour before the mayor. He stated that he left the palace just after midnight to get some air, and shortly afterwards saw the mayor's party in the garden returning from the Manège accompanied by a group of young National Guards without weapons, walking arm in arm and chattering gaily among themselves. Pétion suggested a tour of the garden together. They walked to the Terrace de l'Eau, overlooking the Seine, still followed by fifteen to twenty young National Guards. Roederer spoke to Pétion about the agitation in the capital and the consequences he feared. The mayor tried to reassure him. 'I hope that nothing will happen,' he said. 'Municipal representatives have been sent to the insurrectionary mustering places. Thomas has told me there will be nothing; Thomas must know what is going on.' This was very likely the person of that name on the Jacobin slate of twenty-four candidates elected to represent Paris in the National Convention at the beginning of September. Roederer mentioned in his memoirs that he had no idea who Thomas was. Not wishing to show his ignorance, Roederer then turned to other members of the mayor's party and discussed different matters. At the palace they heard drums beating, which we know from a Swiss officer's account signalled the changing of the guard at around 12.30 a.m. They decided to return, and were about to mount the Great Stairs to the State Apartments when, according to Roederer, someone came to summon the mayor back to the National Assembly. Roederer was mistaken, as there seems no doubt from other evidence that the mayor remained on the terrace to keep his rendezvous with a three-member delegation from the Municipality that had been reporting to the National Assembly. This delegation included Municipal Officer Leroux who three weeks later wrote a detailed account of the events of 9/10 August.

Leroux was a physician who later in life became a professor at the Paris Faculty of Medicine. In 1790, as a matter of civic duty, he joined the municipal administration. He was a constitutionalist and had made the proclamation of martial law, signed by the previous mayor, on the Champs de Mars on 17 July 1791, when a number of demonstrators were killed. He had taken his wife and children out of Paris on Monday 6 August, and had set his affairs in order, as he expected the worst. He wrote: 'I saw death ahead of me. I was prepared for death in defence of the law.' In his account of the fatal night, he stated that he found the mayor and his party sitting on the edge of the terrace by the Pont Royal. This position was over 100 yards from the main entrance, and must have been an arranged rendezvous. It would have been difficult to find the mayor in the dark unless he knew where to look for him. Leroux and his colleagues told the mayor their latest news. The latter decided to take them up to the State Apartments to make a report. They arrived in the Council Chamber. In Leroux's own words: 'We found there the Queen, the Princess Royal [the daughter of the king], Madame Elizabeth [the king's sister], two ladies whom I knew to be Madame de Lamballe and Madame de Tourzel [respectively the Queen's personal companion, who was also Superintendent of her Household, and the Governess of the seven-year-old dauphin], the six Ministers of

J.-J. Leroux (1749–1832) depicted later in life under the Empire. His report as a municipal officer of the Paris Commune on events of 9 and 10 August is a valuable source of information.

whom I only recognised three former colleagues, Monsieur Mandat, Commanding General of the National Guards, Monsieur Lachesnaye, a Legion commander, some other officers, and about twenty persons without uniforms. The remaining nearby apartments contained 150–200 people, not counting the National Guards and Swiss soldiers. I noted it was around 1 a.m. Having replied for some time to questions from the Queen and Madame Elizabeth, and some other persons, we were told that the Mayor had been summoned by the National Assembly.'

In fact, the mayor had gone there voluntarily. His official summons was to come later. Because his formal summoning to the National Assembly made an important impression on so many at the Tuileries that night, it was easy for those who wrote accounts to anticipate this event. Dejoly's version, although unclear in places, shows that the mayor did not finally leave the Tuileries until probably 2.30 a.m. Aged thirty-seven, Dejoly was a lawyer who came from Montpelier in the south of France. He was a former secretary to Pétion at the Municipality, one of the colleagues mentioned above by Leroux, and had been proposed by the dominant Girondin faction for the new position of Secretary to the Council of Ministers. He only held this position a short while, however, until on 3 July he found himself nominated Minister of Justice and Keeper of the Seal. Unlike the three Girondin ministers, who had been dismissed or resigned in mid-June, Dejoly seemed genuinely concerned about the king's interests. A few days after Louis' fall, he wrote an important account of his brief ministry. This was followed by a memoir on the events of 9 and 10 August. His writings reflect an honest if ineffective personality. Imprisoned briefly, he was released before the September massacres, and survived the Terror. The rest of his life was passed in obscurity.

The three principal people missing from Leroux's list were Roederer, the mayor and the king. The first admitted he was having a nap. Thus, it appears that before going to the Assembly a second time, the mayor had a short private audience with the king. This is confirmed by Dejoly who stated that the mayor left the palace for the Assembly at around 1 a.m. with a request from Louis. He is emphatic about this timing which occurred after the tocsin had been heard at the palace, while he referred to the first meeting with the king, reported above, as occurring before the tocsin. There is also a reference to a 1 a.m. meeting with the king in the evidence presented for Major Bachmann's trial. It seems likely that the meeting largely concerned matters of a confidential nature. If indeed official matters had been discussed, such as the defence of the palace, the king would have required the presence of relevant officials such as Mandat and d'Abancourt, Minister of War.

What passed between the king and Pétion is pure conjecture. Obviously, the mayor would have briefly relayed Leroux's report. A clue to what followed may come from Liancourt's report on the earlier interview, when the king asked the mayor what the people wanted, and received no reply. The king could have understood that the mayor had been reluctant to discuss this sensitive issue in the presence of others, and now sought to speak to him privately. It is reasonable to expect that Louis was reviewing his options. He was well aware that the radicals wanted to be rid of him, but did they intend to be done with the dynasty altogether? As in the summer of 1791, when the Monarchy was also at a low ebb, and Louis' thoughts had turned to securing the position of his son if he himself was unable to rule, the king must again have anxiously debated this issue. There is a report that Malesherbes had broached with Louis the subject of abdication in favour of the dauphin shortly before 10 August. Louis would have realised that, in the eyes of many of his subjects, his association with the Ancien Régime meant that he could never have a clean slate. His young son, however, could start afresh. In view of Pétion's influential position, it might be sensible at this critical juncture to seek his views. What would Pétion have said? He was inclined towards a republic and would have regarded the succession of the dauphin as not in accordance with his principles. On the other hand, the dauphin still had many years to go before he reached his majority. The Girondins might ensure the Regency would be under their control, and a republic could be introduced when the situation was favourable. The king would have been very concerned to exclude the Duke of Orléans from the Regency, even though under the Constitution he was the designated regent. The constitution permitted alternative arrangements in certain circumstances, and the king may have wished to examine Pétion on this matter. The mayor might well have insisted that the 'people' would require the king to forgo any influence over his son's education and future upbringing. The king was prepared to make personal sacrifices for France, but could he as a tender father justify leaving his son entirely to upbringing by others? This would have been difficult for Louis to accept. Nevertheless, the conversation appears to have been reasonably amicable, as immediately after Pétion left him, the king sought out Dejoly and requested him to pursue the mayor. He wanted him to persuade the National Assembly to close the entrances to the Terrasse des Feuillants on the northern edge of the Tuileries garden, and thus prevent the crowd gathering there from growing larger.

Dejoly does not mention that he had any problem finding the mayor, and it is unlikely Louis would have sent a minister to go after him unless he knew where he had gone. A reasonable supposition is that Pétion had gone to National Guards' headquarters in the Salle des Gardes to hand over the requisition he had promised earlier on, authorising force to be used to repel force. François Hüe mentions being told by d'Aubier, a Gentleman of the Bedchamber, that the mayor gave such a requisition to Mandat. D'Aubier, as a Court official, may well have escorted Pétion after he left the king. When Dejoly spoke to the mayor about closing access to the terrace, he found him receptive. Pétion's visit to headquarters also fits in with an incident related much later in Pfyffer d'Altishofen's Swiss account. The mayor found himself well situated to ask for a military escort to enable him to carry out the king's business in safety. It seems more than probable that Pétion was genuinely concerned that some disgruntled aristocrats or loyalist National Guards might attempt to ambush him in the tree-lined alleys of the garden. He was probably far from immune from radical stereotyping that the former nobles were a bunch of assassins. Certainly, his report reflects a growing paranoia as the night wore on. He remarked that he had noticed that there were many gentlemen carrying weapons. He related the personal hostility of former nobles and certain loyalist National Guards. In Altishofen's account, the king instructed Baron de Salis-Zizers, the senior captain of the Swiss Guards, to protect him with a detail of troops. Salis, who survived until 1819 and could well have been the source of the story, is said to have to have told the mayor with black humour: 'Don't worry, Monsieur Pétion, I personally assure you that the first one who kills you will die the moment after!'

The mayor went to the Manège and seems, without formally addressing the Assembly, to have passed on the king's request to some deputies there, since the nearest of the two gates on the terrace to the palace was shortly closed.

Returning promptly to the palace, Pétion resumed a position on the garden terrace. If he had a Swiss escort, it must have left after fulfilling its duties. According to the mayor, a number of well-heeled bourgeois grenadiers of the battalion of the Filles Saint-Thomas came towards him, and deliberately upset the oil lamps on the terrace pavement. Some surrounded him and spoke in menacing and insulting terms. One said, 'Let us seize him, and his head will answer for it [the insurrection].' It seems likely here that Pétion was only echoing the same remark attributed to Mandat by Mouchet, when the commanding general was later interrogated at the Hôtel de Ville. The mayor claimed other National Guards joined in the threats. Preserving his hard-man image, Pétion stated that he kept perfectly composed, but other members of his party showed less sang-froid. Fortunately, we have a less biased witness for this scene. Dejoly had stayed on the terrace while the mayor went to the Manège, and was there when he returned. He heard a grenadier say to the mayor, 'Why do you allow yourself to be dominated by the seditious persons who will destroy us? Why, for example, is that gentleman Santerre always with you? Why, Monsieur Mayor, is he at the Hôtel de Ville at this very moment? Monsieur Mayor, you are responsible for public order, and the preservation of property.' The mayor told his accuser that he was being disrespectful. Some of the grenadier's comrades agreed and told their colleague to shut up.

Dejoly went on to mention that the commander of the Prémontrés battalion accosted the mayor by the main palace entrance at the centre of the terrace. He told him that all was quiet and there was nothing to fear. He continued by saying that section delegates meeting in the Faubourg Saint-Antoine had separated, but would meet early in the morning at the Hôtel de Ville. The mayor seemed delighted at the news. However, some commented that the commander's information might not be up to date as his section of the Croix-Rouge had adjourned its meeting at 11 p.m. Since then the tocsin had been ringing and there had been the sounds of a call to arms in many parts of Paris.

The group was now joined by bandy-legged Mouchet, a Paris magistrate (Juge de Paix), and another person. Mouchet advised them that he had visited the Faubourg Saint-Antoine, and all seemed quiet. The person accompanying him said the exact opposite. The tocsin had sounded and the alarm cannon had been fired. The people were stirring and the crowds becoming menacing. Pétion considered these reports. Their relevance depended upon the timing of the visits, as activity in the Faubourg Saint-Antoine fluctuated considerably during the night. Pétion stated that he wished to leave the palace. No doubt Mouchet, who was in the conspiracy, strongly advised him to do so. However, counter-pressure was brought to bear on him to remain. He said he would stay until there was no danger of an insurrection. Pétion claimed that Dejoly then expressly asked him to go upstairs to see the King, who absolutely needed to speak to him again. But Dejoly denied responsibility, saying the invitation came from others. Pétion replied that he preferred to remain on the terrace for the time being. Dejoly then left.

Pétion's true feelings at this juncture are uncertain. It helped his revolutionary credentials to claim in his report that he was being threatened by the royalists. But it is likely he was uneasy. He may have realised by now that the defensive measures at the Tuileries were in excess of what he had authorised. His continued presence at the palace might be construed by the revolutionaries that he was siding with the Monarchy. He reported: 'It is certain that if I had gone up, I would never have come down.' He related that if he made a move the National Guards around him would have stopped him, and in a few minutes he would have been killed. There is no evidence of any plot to kill him, but in the palace there may well have been those who wished to retain him as a hostage. This would have been strongly disapproved by the king's civil advisers, who were well aware of the likely political repercussions and still hoped the mayor might be able to defuse the situation in the faubourgs.

To extricate himself from this situation, Pétion claimed he hit on the plan of sending Mouchet to the National Assembly, to have him summoned to the bar, and to despatch a unit of its guard to escort him there. He considered no one would dare to dispute the fiat of the legislative body. Mouchet rushed to the Manège. He was fortunate that at the same time representatives had come from the Hôtel de Ville, bringing a document from the Police Department, signed by the Jacobins Panis and Sergent. This stated that there was concern that the mayor was surrounded by treacherous people at the palace who might act against him. It is possible that Mouchet's visit to the National Assembly to have the mayor recalled took place without Pétion's intervention. Obviously, there were fears among the conspirators gathered at the Hôtel de Ville that the mayor might be compelled to act forcefully against the impending insurrection, even to sign an order imposing martial law; and they wanted him out of the hands of the Court.

Reports on the Assembly's proceedings show some members protested against Mouchet's representations, saying that when they had seen the mayor on occasions during the past two hours, he had told them that he was remaining in the vicinity of the king and the National Assembly in order to ensure order. The majority, however, accepted Mouchet's plea: 'If you do not immediately order the Mayor of Paris to your bar, he is going to be assassinated.' Two of the Assembly's ushers together with several National Guards were sent from the Manège to escort him from the palace. Dejoly placed the time of the mayor's final departure to the National Assembly at around 1.45 a.m., which was the same time he gave for Mouchet's arrival. This would allow no space for Mouchet to go the National Assembly and make his plea for the mayor to be summoned to the bar, followed by the despatch of an escort to fetch him. Working back through the events of the night from the time of the mayor's first arrival, which is not disputed, his final departure to the National Assembly could not have been much before 2.30 a.m.

At the Assembly, Pétion authenticated the signatures on the letter from the Hôtel de Ville. He was asked whether the fears on his behalf were justified. Certainly, there was no report of Pétion claiming there had been a plot to detain him. The mayor told the Assembly that when one was concerned with the public good, one forgot personal matters, but it was true that he had not been well received at the palace, and had heard the strongest remarks against him. These would have disconcerted a man who believed himself without enemies but, as one who knew he had a great number and that his love for the public good was well merited, he was in no way frightened. This was a typical performance. In maintaining his reputation for firmness of character, Pétion on at least one occasion exceeded the bounds of good taste. He boasted in his memoirs that, when seated next to the king's virtuous sister in the overcrowded coach returning from Varennes, he felt the close proximity of his charms was strongly exciting her interest and she would succumb 'to the dictates of nature' if the opportunity presented itself. However, he immediately concluded that there might be a Court plot to seduce his revolutionary virtue.

Pétion was asked by the Assembly's president whether he would like to stay on to witness the session. The mayor declined. He said he had to return to his post at the Municipality. He went on foot, but did not stop at the Hôtel de Ville where events were beginning to take a dramatic turn. He carried on home to his official residence on the Ile de la Cité, no doubt exhausted in mind and body. His carriage was left in the Cour des Princes at the Tuileries. He did not dare to pick it up. Justice of the Peace Mouchet, who was with Pétion at the Assembly when he made his address, did not accompany him back towards the Hôtel de Ville. Instead, he returned to the palace where he was questioned by Dejoly who was concerned about the consequences of rumours of a plot to kidnap the mayor. Mouchet was asked whether Pétion had mentioned any such conspiracy. In fact, it is almost certain that Mouchet expressly returned to the palace in order to find evidence for such a plot. He claimed to have found it, with fatal consequences for Mandat. His accusation became an important component in the republican version of events immediately preceding the fall of the king. A notice was later to be posted above the main entrance of the Tuileries stating that on the night of 9/10 August, Pétion had there escaped death.

The mayor was placed under house arrest upon the usurpation of the Municipality by the insurrectionists. However, the victors were aware of their debt towards Pétion, although he had played no direct role in overthrowing the king. As soon as the authority of the new Municipal Council was established beyond doubt, they acceded to the demand of the National Assembly to allow him to resume his functions. If the insurrection had failed, Pétion had not compromised himself, and might still be in a position to offer assistance to beaten republicans. This was no doubt a consideration in the minds of their leaders when they confirmed him in office on taking over the Town Hall, although they rendered him temporarily powerless. Pétion had been in the position at least to damage the insurrectionists' plans if he had thrown himself body and soul into saving the Constitution. By not doing so, he helped to ensure the success of the coup d'état which was to have far-reaching repercussions on European history. Later, he summed up his thoughts about 10 August 1792, exaggerating his revolutionary sympathies. He wrote: 'I desired the insurrection, but I trembled that it would not succeed. My position was critical. It was necessary to do my duty as citizen, without neglecting that of magistrate. It was necessary to maintain all outward appearances, and not to neglect the formal requirements of my duties. There was a combat to the death between the Court and Liberty, one or the other must necessarily succumb.'

Pétion became a member of the National Convention, resigning from the Mayoralty of Paris. Later, he remonstrated with Robespierre over his growing dictatorship and, as one of the defeated Girondin faction, was proscribed in the late spring of 1793. He was on the run for a year. In June 1794, his body, and that of his fellow Girondin Buzot, were found in a wood near Bordeaux, partly eaten by wolves.

CHAPTER 5

Insurrection

The National Assembly had promised the Paris sections to start debating the dethronement of the king by the evening of 9 August. Deputies Lamarque and Isnard made a limited attempt that day to have the issue discussed, but received no encouragement from the mainline Girondin leaders. This is evidence in itself that they were still hoping to do a deal with the king. Instead, the president of the Assembly called speaker after speaker to express indignation at the treatment meted out the previous evening to those deputies who had voted in favour of acquitting Lafayette by a convincing majority of two to one. He had been charged with leaving his military command at the end of June to come to Paris in the hope of launching a coup against the radicals.

Many of the complainants did not dare to attend the current session, but sent letters to be read out instead. A Deputy Denzi wrote: 'I believe it is my duty to report to the Assembly the bad treatment I received on leaving the building. Having been subjected to insults by a crowd of people posted at each street corner, the worst outrages and threats happened in the Rue Saint-Louis. I was struck from behind by a man who said that he recognised me for having urged a motion against the people in the Chamber's galleries. Immediately I was attacked with stones, several of which hit me in the back, and twice a sabre was raised against my head, but it was parried by a man who protected me. Eventually, I arrived at the guardhouse of the Palais Royal [the palace of the Duc d'Orléans], where I found several of my colleagues. Seeing that the door of the guardhouse was about to be forced, we escaped by a window at the back. If the Assembly does not take effective measures to ensure our liberty, I will absent myself from its sittings until I can vote freely and without compromising the dignity of being a national representative.' The reference to the Chamber's galleries reveals one of the most pernicious aspects of the political populism of the Revolution. The large space available for crowds of citizens to barrack politicians as they spoke led easily to intimidation. The Jacobin Club used this opportunity to introduce hired claques.

A bolder deputy who had turned up to complain in person addressed the Chair: 'Monsieur le Président, I left yesterday with Monsieur Lacuée. Arriving at the gate of the Rue Saint-Honoré, I found myself surrounded by a multitude of men in National Guards uniform with red bonnets on their heads. I heard them say distinctly that they would string me up on a lamp-post. I promptly claimed my inviolability as deputy and showed them my ribbon. They replied that it was for that very reason that they were going to hang me. At that moment, a man wearing a jacket took hold of me from behind and led me away. Then a grenadier of the Sainte-Opportune battalion arrived, named Lavilette, who, sabre in hand and aided by several of his brave comrades, freed me from the situation, and conducted me to the offices of the Department, from whence a detachment escorted me back home. I cannot bear to think about it. I can no longer attend Assembly sittings. I will instruct my electors of my decision.' There were similar protests from other deputies, including one who gave evidence that the Jacobin Club was involved in organising the general molestation.

While many at the palace may have felt their cause was lost, the insurgents were no more confident that *their* cause was won, surprisingly so in view of the relative ease with which the Monarchy collapsed the next day. Genuine republicans, however, were still in a small minority, while the better-off classes were natural supporters of the Constitution, being alarmed by the idea of rampaging mobs emerging from the working-class areas of Paris. Lucile Desmoulins, wife of the radical journalist Camille Desmoulins, has left an emotional account of the tension on 9 August in one corner of the conspiracy. She and her husband were neighbours of the Dantons who occupied a house in the Rue des Cordeliers in the Section Théâtre Français on the left bank of the Seine. The Dantons had just returned that morning from the country. Lucile wrote:

> After dining [in the afternoon] we passed the time well enough. We were all at the Dantons. His mother wept, she was very distressed. His father seemed in a daze. But Danton was resolute. As for myself, I laughed like a madwoman. They feared that the insurrection would not happen. Although I was uncertain myself, I told them that I knew it would take place. 'But how can you laugh in such a way?' asked Madame Danton. Alas, I replied, that warns me that I shall shed many tears this evening. I was not mistaken. Towards evening we took Madame Charpentier back home. It was very fine. We walked up and down the street. There were quite a lot of people about. We sat down beside the café. Several Sans-culottes passed by shouting 'Vive la Nation', followed by trumpeters on horseback. At last, in full sight of everyone, fear took hold of me. I told Madame Danton we should go. She made fun of my fear, but in doing so she became frightened herself. We left. . . . Arriving back at the Dantons' apartment, I saw Madame Robert and many others. Danton was nervous. I rushed up to Madame Robert and asked whether they would sound the tocsin. She replied yes, but in the evening.

The Directorate of the Insurrection, which had been meeting spasmodically over the past three weeks, had decided to split itself into three for the uprising planned to start that night. One part operated in the Faubourg Saint-Antoine, another in the Section Théâtre Français with the Marseillais, and the third in the Gobelins Section of the Faubourg Saint-Marceau. It was hoped to overcome the lack of co-ordination in the previous attempts. Contact would be maintained by a series of messengers. Paris was to be criss-crossed by a great many on errands that night. There were messengers to all the other sections from the Section Quinze-Vingts which initially played the leading role in the insurrection; there were couriers passing to and fro keeping half a dozen or so of the leading revolutionary sections in direct touch with each other, and there were representatives going back and forth after midnight between section delegates at the Hôtel de Ville and their respective section meetings. On the government side, there were the Department's police agents, and spies commissioned by the Ministry of the Interior bringing back reports to the Tuileries every half hour on activities in the Section Théâtre Français where the dreaded Marseillais were stationed.

Representatives of the fédérés at the Jacobin Club on the Rue Saint-Honoré were reluctant to make a final decision about joining in the coup d'état. They wished to present one more petition to the National Assembly. According to Fournier, a member of the insurrectionary Directorate, he dissuaded them. 'You have already presented a thousand,' he said, 'but they have not taken notice of any. I will propose the following which will be the last. It is to go immediately and cut off six hundred conspirators' heads in the royalist den. We will carry them to the National Assembly and will say: "Here are your masterpieces, legislators!"' The last remark indicates the revolutionaries saw the Legislature as friendly to the Court, especially following the acquittal of Lafayette the previous day. However, apart from the Brestois and the Marseillais, there were only some 500 other fédérés remaining in Paris. It was the sections that now took the lead in making the revolution, not the Jacobin Club and its Directorate.

It was known by the politically aware in Paris that the Section Quinze-Vingts in the Faubourg Saint-Antoine had resolved the insurrection would begin at midnight. During the day, the Battalion of the Filles Saint-Thomas sent out agents to the Faubourgs Saint-Antoine and Saint-Marceau to find out what was going on. They reported back that there was every sign of preparations for an uprising. Activists were running from house to house calling on the occupants to participate in the forthcoming insurrection. Nevertheless, at 9 p.m. the mayor's appeal for order seemed to be having some success, save in Quinze-Vingts. Even the sections of Montreuil and Popincourt, also in the Faubourg Saint-Antoine, appeared calm. The centre of the insurrection, the Section Quinze-Vingts, only represented a third of the faubourg. This one section out of forty-eight was responsible for setting in motion the avalanche of revolution. Its strange name derived from a residential institution for three hundred indigent blind, 'fifteen-twenties', originally established in the Middle Ages by Louis IX (St Louis). An hour or so later, the agitation in Quinze-Vingts was joined by some other areas. But most of Paris remained calm, above all in the middle-class areas. In some cases, revolutionary activists delayed putting on the pressure until after general meetings of section citizens were adjourned around 10 to 11 p.m., leaving executive committees dominated by radicals to continue to act in their name. Many of these were small compact bodies; the Committee of the Arsenal Section was reduced to three. Sections in the more moderate parts of Paris closed down altogether.

Around 11 p.m., an officer associated with the Tuileries' defence, probably Langlade, reported to the National Guards headquarters stationed in the palace that there was a crowd of between twelve and fifteen hundred on the Place Bastille. This triggered a prompt response. The Adjutant-General of the National Guards was instructed to have le rappel beaten in all quarters of Paris to summon guardsmen to their mustering points. Orders were despatched to selected

National Guards battalions to send reinforcements to the palace, but these did not start to arrive until the small hours of the morning. The Scottish traveller, Dr John Moore, wrote in his journal: 'Between eleven and twelve at night, I was disturbed by a great noise in the streets from the beating of drums and repeated huzzas. The landlord informs me that orders have been given to all the citizens to illuminate their windows, that there is reason to apprehend an attack on the Château of the Tuileries, that the drum was beating to arms, and that the National Guards are all at the posts of their respective departments. I went into the streets, which are all illuminated – the Pont Neuf is covered with soldiers under arms – a large party of National Guards are also in possession of the Pont Royal – nobody is allowed to pass: yet all seems to be conducted with so much regularity, that whatever mischief may have been intended, will, I hope, be prevented.' These units, of course, belonged to Mandat's defence.

When summoning troops to reinforce the guard at the Tuileries, some discrimination was made between reliable and unreliable battalions. Peltier mentions that sixteen had been selected because of their probable loyalty to the King and Constitution. For forming up these battalions, Mandat may have authorised the use of la générale, as agreed by the Department of Paris. It certainly appears the use of la générale was widespread throughout Paris. It is unknown whether all this was due to Mandat's orders, or resulted from initiatives by individual battalion commanders. It must have been believed at this juncture that the great majority of National Guards officers, with the exception of the gunners, were loyal to the constitution, of which the king was an integral part. The National Guards' headquarters staff might well have hoped that full mobilisation would be beneficial in combating the insurrection, especially if martial law were to be declared. It appears that a half-hearted attempt was made to obtain such a declaration from Roederer. However, he refused on the grounds that the mayor was responsible.

A cacophony of alarming noises reigned on and off in Paris throughout the night. National Guards battalions, of which there were sixty, sought to recall their members to stand to, and then to muster them under arms. Apart from the drum beats of le rappel and la générale, more impressive and far carrying, as Madame de Staël described, was the monotonous, lugubrious, and rapid tolling of church bells sounding the tocsin throughout much of the insurrectionary central, northern, and eastern parts of Paris. This sound, causing alarm and despondency in the hearts of the royalists, appears to have been intermittent. From time to time the night air was punctuated by the sharp report of an 'alarm' cannon. An observer noted that it was only when this was fired around 10.30 p.m. in Quinze-Vingts that the situation really began to heat up. Desbouillons, the informative commander of the Brestois fédérés, writing on the 11th to his Department's Directorate in western Brittany, stated: 'Yesterday at the stroke of midnight, "la générale" was beaten and tocsin sounded in almost all the quarters of the town. We immediately took up our arms, and after a written order from the Gobelins Section, we went to join the St Marcel Battalion. The commander of this battalion (Alexandre) sent observers to the different quarters to find out what was happening. We knew that all the battalions remained under arms at their barracks.' Desbouillons' use of the word midnight must be regarded as more figurative than precise.

Earlier that evening, Santerre had conferred with the coup's military leaders, and fellow members of the insurrectionary directorate. He first met Westermann and Rossignol in Saint-Antoine, before going to the Marseillais' barracks on the Left Bank to see Alexandre from Saint-Marceau. Santerre features in all the memoirs, by conspirators and royalists alike, as the key figure in the insurrection. He was born in 1752 and ran a successful brewery in the Faubourg Saint-Antoine. He was a tall powerful man with a commanding voice, noted for his liberality towards his employees, and as a promoter of horse racing, importing English thoroughbreds. He probably indulged in his own product as he is described as having a fleshy face and double chin. Interestingly enough, he had a brother who was likewise a brewer, but in the Faubourg Saint-Marceau. Although his brother appears to have played no direct role in the Revolution, he may have helped to provide the contacts which led to the close relationship between these two faubourgs in preparing and carrying out the insurrection. Believed to have been brought into politics by the Duke of Orleans in June 1789 to provide working-class muscle for a coup against the Monarchy, Santerre had impeccable revolutionary credentials. He and his workmen had played a leading part in taking the Bastille, and Santerre was the secretary of an association of those who had participated in the action (Les Vainqueurs). He was one of the first politicians to attack Lafayette, and had been involved in organising the anti-monarchist demonstration in the fatal episode of the Champs de Mars of July 1791. He had been prosecuted as a result. As colonel of the National Guards battalion of Les Enfants-Trouvés, he controlled one of the few military assets of which the conspirators could be absolutely sure. In effect, it seems to have been accepted that the proposed insurrection could not take place without his participation. It was up to him, as it were, to fire the starting pistol. The apogee of his career was 10 August 1792. Appointed General of Division in 1793 to fight against the Vendéeans in western France, he was not a success, leading to a cruel rhyme: 'Here lies General Santerre, who of Mars had only the beer.' He died paralysed and in poverty in 1809.

The Quinze-Vingts' Section minutes for the night of 9/10 August report that by around 10 p.m. thirteen sections had confirmed they would be ready to march at midnight. A letter was read from two fédéré units seeking to join the people of Quinze-Vingts and march under their flags. The offer of a citizen to supply guns was received with much approbation. And then, around 11 p.m., the key decision was taken to delay the insurrection. 'It has been decided, in order to save the Country, and on the proposal of a Paris Section, that three delegates shall be nominated by each Section to meet together at the Hôtel de Ville, and consider the immediate actions needed to save the public interest. Following on this decision, it is agreed that no orders will be accepted save that from the majority of delegates meeting together at the Hôtel de Ville. Messieurs Rossignol, Huguenin and Balin are nominated to represent the Section.' The proposal of a Paris section referred to was that passed on 7 August by Mauconseil. The authority of the Quinze-Vingts Section meeting for starting the insurrection was now transferred to the Hôtel de Ville where Huguenin was to preside over the meeting of insurrectionary delegates, thus continuing his section's leading role. He was a former army deserter and customs clerk who had played the part of the demonstrators'

The brewer Santerre (1752–1809) was the overall military leader of the insurrection. His image in National Guards uniform is heavily romanticised. Two heroic Sans-culotte National Guards stand in the background. Note the symbolic officer's silver breastplate suspended on Santerre's chest. Swiss officers were similarly accoutred.

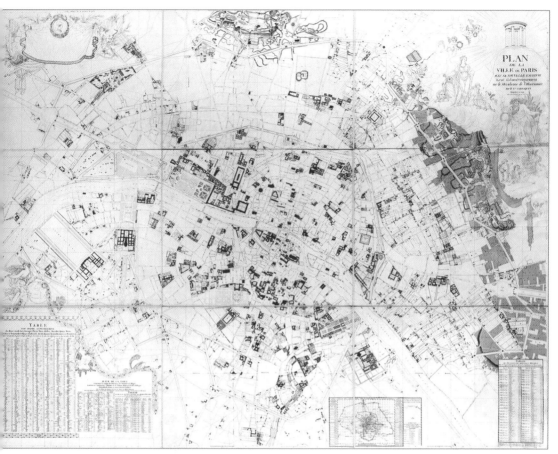

Map of Paris in 1791. The revolutionary Faubourg Saint-Antoine is on the right of the city with the Section Quinze-Vingts between the river and the large circular Place du Trône.

spokesman at the National Assembly on 20 June. The conspirators at the Hôtel de Ville had obviously ensured that a suitable room would be available. Immediately, messengers were despatched calling on all sections to nominate delegates.

It seems that the leadership at Quinze-Vingts had decided that the support of just over one-quarter of the sections was insufficient, and the insurrection should be put on hold until greater backing was received. Nevertheless, the decision to ring the tocsin at midnight was not cancelled. In fact, it may have been rung in Quinze-Vingts as early as 11.15 p.m. Not to ring the tocsin might have badly damaged the morale of potential insurgents who had been expecting this signal. The Tuileries also was waiting for the tocsin, but with trepidation, and the revolutionaries were doubtless loath to disappoint them.

In the Rue des Cordeliers, Lucile Desmoulins carried on her account of events in the Dantons' flat. 'Soon, I saw each man arm himself. My husband reassured me that he would not leave Danton's side. I have learned since that he took risks. . . .' Danton went to the Cordeliers Club to engage in inflammatory propaganda, an exercise in which both camps indulged. 'The People can only rely upon itself, as the Constitution is insufficient. Nothing remains for you but to save yourselves. Hasten then, as this very night, henchmen hidden in the palace must come out to attack the people and cut their throats, before leaving Paris to rejoin their friends in Coblenz. To arms! To arms!' The Cordeliers Club, dominated by Danton, was in alliance with the much more important Jacobin Club. Lucile continued: 'Danton returned to lie down. He did not seem much concerned. He hardly stirred. Midnight approached. People came to fetch him several times. At last he left for the Commune. The bell of the Cordeliers tolled.'

It is commonly believed that Danton, who was Second Substitute Procureur Général in the Commune, played the major role in orchestrating the insurrection. This is not the case. He had been away in the country since the beginning of August. His pre-eminence after the success of the coup d'état was due to the prestige he had long held among the non-Girondin radicals. While he participated in events leading to the takeover of the Commune on the morning of the 10th, his usefulness to the conspirators at the Hôtel de Ville was inferior to that of Manuel, who as Procureur Général was second in rank to the mayor.

Following the lead of Quinze-Vingts, the minutes of the meeting, attended by some 2,000 of the revolutionary Section Mauconseil in a working-class area north of Les Halles in central Paris, reported the nomination of three delegates for the Hôtel de Ville. The section meeting included the refinement of appointing three additional people to ensure communication with the Town Hall, making up the six proposed in their resolution of 7 August. Up to then, they had been prepared to march at midnight, and had with them delegates representing the working-class faubourgs of northern Paris. When the tocsin started to ring around midnight, Mauconseil's chairman Lulier was reported as saying that: 'before the sun next reaches the middle of its course, it will shine on a free France or an enslaved France.' The Section Théâtre Français on the South Bank, where Danton lived together with a considerable proportion of the republican intelligentsia, was said to have nominated delegates for the Hôtel de Ville as early as 10 p.m., although only two. Either there is a mistake in the reported timing, or they were independently following up Mauconseil's proposal of 7 August. More probably, they were privy to knowledge that Quinze-Vingts would pass a formal resolution to send delegates to the Hôtel de Ville. It is obvious that sending delegates to the Town Hall was part of the conspirators' overall plan, whether or not the armed insurrection started at midnight.

As a means of following the confused development of the insurrection during the night of 9/10 August, it is suggested using the more comprehensive minutes of the Section Poissonnière in the north of Paris as pegs for specific activities. The minutes begin: 'Today, 9 August 1792, year IV of Liberty, at eight in the evening, the citizens of the Rue Poissonnière met together in continuous session in the church of Saint-Lazare, in order to discuss measures for saving the public interest [chose publique], and notably the resolutions of Quinze-Vingts as voted on the 4th and 7th of this month.' These resolutions, of course, refer to leading an insurrection if the National Assembly failed to depose the king by the evening of

Manuel (1751–93) rose from humble origins to be Procurer Général of the Paris Commune and used his important position to play a key role in the success of the insurrection. A member of the Convention, he left politics after the execution of the king and retired to the country where he was persecuted and attacked by Jacobin agents. Subsequently arrested, he was eventually guillotined in November 1793, refusing in the previous month to give evidence against the queen at her trial.

the 9th. The minutes continue: 'The meeting not wishing to leave anything to chance, and in the circumstances only following the dictates of prudence and patriotism, named 15 representatives to go immediately to the Sections of the Gobelins, the Théâtre Français, the Quinze-Vingts, the Gravilliers, the Lombards, Mauconseil, Croix-Rouge, Fontaine de Grenelle, the Innocents, the Tuileries [the section, not the palace], Sainte-Geneviève, and the Halle-au-blé, to observe their deliberations, and to report back to the Section here. . . .' Before the days of telephone or radio, keeping in close touch with action elsewhere in Paris required lavish human resources. Only those sections with well-attended meetings were able to remain in contact with the overall situation. These happened to be the insurrectionary sections.

The minutes resume: 'The Chairman told the meeting that he had just received a letter from the Mayor, and this was read to the assembled citizens by the Section Committee Secretary.' This was the notice calling for order drafted by Pétion after returning from addressing the National Assembly. The meeting decided that it should await the views of other sections before considering the matter further. The section's representatives were now beginning to return to report back. The minutes continued: 'The representatives who went to the Théatre-Français reported that that Section is standing firm to its previous resolutions, and it will march at midnight with its brothers from the Section Quinze-Vingts. The messengers sent similarly to the Gravilliers Section reported that they had the same intention. Those coming back from the Fontaine-de-Grenelle likewise stated that the said Section would prefer a thousand deaths to the torture of being in opposition to their brothers of the Faubourgs Saint-Marcel [Marceau] and Saint-Antoine, and they would always march beside these valiant patriots. The Tuileries Section resolved that, when the situation arose, they would march as an armed Section, not as part of [National Guards] battalions. Nevertheless, they would await the return of representatives sent to the Quinze-Vingts in order to ascertain their latest decision. Information was then received from the Gobelins Section which declared that, in conformity with its previous resolutions, it was going to arm itself and march.' These minutes show that the intention to march at midnight was then still firm. The 11 p.m. resolution by Quinze-Vingts to await a decision by delegates at the Hôtel de Ville represented a major change of plan.

Municipal Officer Leroux accompanied by Councillor André and Substitute Procureur Général Desmousseux came to the National Assembly at midnight to report on the situation in Paris. When admitted to the bar of the Chamber, they told the relatively few deputies present that a considerable concentration of armed people had been observed in the Faubourg Saint-Antoine and that they were threatening to march on the Assembly to demand the suspension of the king. On the other hand, the streets in central Paris between the Hôtel de Ville and the Manège were quiet. However, they reported that as they were arriving they had heard the tocsin commence, probably from the large bells of the churches of the Cordeliers and Saint-André des Arcs which started to ring about 11.45 p.m. The churches in Saint-Antoine and Saint-Marceau might have been too far away to hear. They advised the Assembly that the Municipal General Council had sent representatives to various sections, but the greater part of these had been detained, and it was reported that one section had resolved that it would no longer accept the authority of the Municipality, the Department, nor even the National Assembly itself. Obviously, the Municipality was failing to overawe the sections, and reporting this to Pétion later may well have influenced him in his decision not to intervene personally to stop the insurrection. At around the same time as the Municipality was informing the National Assembly, an official report from the Department of Paris to Roederer at the Tuileries also stated that Saint-Antoine was in a fever, the main streets were lit up, and numerous armed groups were formed up around the church of Les Enfants-Trouvés. It must be remembered that the centre of the Faubourg Saint-Antoine was nearly 5 kilometres from the Tuileries, and the information being reported was considerably out of date.

Around midnight, the observers sent from the Section Poissonnière to the Section Quinze-Vingts reported back, 'that the said Section at eleven in the evening had resolved to appoint three delegates to go to the Hôtel de Ville, and that they invited the 47 other Sections to do likewise, in order to save the "chose publique", and it would only take orders from the delegates assembled there.' The insurrection was on hold pending directions from delegates at the Hôtel de Ville. Other sections would have received similar instructions, and the movement began to go into reverse. Armed units went back to their guardhouses in the case of National Guards battalions, while individuals in irregular units were sent home, though they frequently stood in readiness outside their respective doorways. After 1 a.m. Paris was much quieter and hopes rose at the Tuileries. The tocsin, except at the Cordeliers, must generally have stopped ringing, but started to ring again after 3 a.m.

It is reported that at about 1 a.m., Quinze-Vingts received a message from one of its delegates at the Hôtel de Ville proposing the tocsin should be stopped until further notice. The Section Committee accepted this suggestion and ordered the terrible signal, as they called it, to cease. A deputation was sent to the neighbouring Section of Montreuil, in the same faubourg, to 'express its astonishment at the alarm signal being rung by all the churches of the quarter and "la générale" being beaten in all the streets of the Faubourg Saint-Antoine, and wished to be assured that the Section meeting was in no way involved'. Montreuil resisted the suggestion of its bossy neighbour for a while, but soon the tocsin ceased.

The General Council of the Commune had carried on trying to maintain order in the absence of the mayor, and sent municipal officers to the sections Gravilliers, Mauconseil, Lombards, Ponceau, and Théâtre Français, all relatively close by, to stop the tocsin. On arriving at the section meeting of the latter, they said 'that in consequence of a resolution of the Council, they had already visited several Sections with the result that the tocsin had ceased'. The chairman Lebois replied: 'We fully respect the Paris Municipality, and will do everything for it, but you ask us to grant the impossible. Instead of stopping the tocsin, I order, in my capacity as Section chairman, that it continue, because it is no longer a question of turning back, rather it is time to destroy the tyrants.'

Lucile Desmoulins reported events at around this time in the Dantons' flat nearby. 'Danton returned,' she wrote. 'Madame Robert was very anxious for her husband who had gone as a Section representative to the Faubourg Saint-Antoine. He now returned in a hurry to see Danton who gave him a very uninformative reply. Messengers came from time to time to give us good and bad news. . . . Danton continued to lie on his bed, he who was at the centre of the insurrection! If my husband perished, I was wife enough to murder him! . . . Camille returned at 1 a.m. and went to lie down.' He probably brought a message for Danton, as the latter then got up and returned to the Hôtel de Ville. The Desmoulins hero-worshipped Danton, an ugly barrel of a man, with a powerful orator's voice, and considerable charisma.

During the early hours of the morning, the Mauconseil Section Committee decided to send four gunners to seize the alarm cannon permanently stationed on the Pont Neuf, a few hundred yards due south. The timing of this important event is uncertain. The section minutes suggest 4.30 a.m., but Roederer at the Tuileries puts the event up to two hours earlier. The circumstantial evidence suggests that it is unlikely that Mauconseil's gunners arrived much later than 2.30 a.m. at the Pont Neuf. They found additional cannons posted there, together with a strong unit of National Guards belonging to the Battalion Henri IV. Mauconseil's gunners were promptly arrested by the post commander. The Council of the Commune was informed and sent municipal officers to obtain their release. The commander refused. The conspirators at the Hôtel de Ville pointed out that the positioning of cannons on the bridge impeded communications between the two halves of Paris, which of course was the intention. They managed to obtain a signed order from the General Council to withdraw them. Official representatives were sent to execute it. The document stated: 'The General Council, being advised of the current disposition of cannons on the Pont Neuf, revokes and cancels all orders that may have been given by the Commanding General, and charges Messieurs Osselin, Huë [not the royalist memoirist], and Baudouin to ensure the order is carried out, and commands that all the cannon be withdrawn to the artillery park.' At a stroke, one of the key components of Mandat's defensive strategy was eliminated. The Pont Neuf was the most important bridge linking the two banks of the Seine, and led directly to the Rue des Cordeliers where the Marseillais were stationed. When the news arrived at the Tuileries of the withdrawal of the cannons on the Pont Neuf, there was consternation followed by much discussion on how they might be restored. Meanwhile, the gunners from the Section Mauconseil were released, and returned at 5.30 a.m. to report that the National Guards battalion Henri IV stationed around the Pont Neuf was unfavourably disposed towards the insurrection.

The minutes of the Section Poissonnière state that their three nominated delegates with plenary powers only left for the Hôtel de Ville at 3 a.m. At this time there were delegates from nineteen sections, all with full authority, at the Town Hall. There were many moderates among them, but these were easily swayed by the fierce determination of the insurrectionists. Nineteen was still six short of a majority of the forty-eight Paris sections. Nevertheless, it was probably around 3.30 a.m. that the conspirators among the section delegates at the Municipality made the decision that the insurrection would go ahead, and sent instructions to the insurrectionist sections for their forces to be ready to march towards the Tuileries at daybreak. It was decided that north bank units should concentrate in the Faubourg Saint-Antoine, and that Quinze-Vingts was to take the lead in signalling the general advance. On the south bank, the insurgent units would concentrate in the Faubourg Saint-Marceau, but the Brestois fédérés were specifically detailed to join up with the Marseillais in the Rue des Cordeliers, and march as a separate column with the local National Guards battalion of the Théâtre Français. The latter battalion refused to co-operate and had to be replaced by Alexandre's battalion from the Faubourg Saint-Marceau. Activity in the revolutionary sections now began to wind up. The insurrection was back on course. The meeting at the Section Poissonnière in the north of Paris started to take preparatory measures. They passed a resolution dismissing the existing officers of the National Guards battalion Saint-Lazare, and nominated replacements supporting the insurrection. They began to issue arms to citizens who wished to join in the attack, and also to the fédérés of the Department of the Basses-Alpes lodged in the barracks on the Rue Poissonnière. At 4 a.m. the minutes claimed that the section's armed units left for the Faubourg Saint-Antoine. This timing may be on the early side as their arrival is not mentioned when Santerre started his advance near 6 a.m.

Reports on the National Assembly proceedings give an account of two municipal officials who visited the Faubourg Saint-Antoine, probably around 3 a.m. They had found everything relatively quiet. They were going back to the Hôtel de Ville when they heard the tocsin beginning to toll again in the Faubourg Saint-Antoine, and turned round. When they arrived back they found the faubourg buzzing with activity. They asked on whose authority the tocsin was being rung and 'la générale' beaten. They were told that it was on Mandat's authority. It seems unlikely, though not impossible, that he would have given orders to mobilise the National Guards in this strongly revolutionary part of Paris. The tocsin was not under his control. This was probably black propaganda, and the revolutionaries had decided to place the blame on Mandat for their own mobilisation. Whatever the truth, the municipal officers reported back to the Municipal General Council which was either in the dark about the extent of Mandat's defensive preparations, or had decided to turn a blind eye unless challenged. Certainly, Mandat had received no official authorisation from the Municipality for beating 'la générale'. It was decided to summon Mandat to the Hôtel de Ville to explain. It seems probable that the conspirators were involved in prompting this decision.

At the Section Quinze-Vingts, Santerre had had his own National Guards battalion of Les Enfants-Trouvés under arms and ready to march by around 5 a.m. He had resolved not to advance until he had at least three battalions of National Guards under his command. He waited. At last the Battalion des Minimes arrived under its commander Laboureur from the Section Roi de Sicille, 2–3 kilometres to the west near the Hôtel de Ville. Laboureur, who was a Chevalier of Saint-Louis and a royalist, announced that on instructions from his section he was opposing the insurrection. This was bravado. According to the royalist journalist Peltier, the gunners of this battalion had persuaded the men to go and join the insurgents in the Faubourg Saint-Antoine. Santerre had little difficulty in rallying this battalion to his side. The Battalion Montreuil from next door then arrived. Its commander, Bonnard, had made it known beforehand that he had sworn to defend the Constitution, and would do so unless he was compelled otherwise. This was to be the standard reaction of so many Frenchman that day. He now found himself under the required degree of compulsion and joined the insurrection. Santerre had his three battalions. Towards 6 a.m., he at last gave the order to march. Messengers were hurriedly despatched with the news to the Rue des Cordeliers and the Faubourg Saint-Marceau, and with the request that the insurrectionist forces undertake a concerted advance towards the Place du Carrousel.

CHAPTER 6

Vigil

As night was falling on the 9th, it is said that a Swiss sentinel in the Cour Marsan was approached by an insurgent in a white shirt and brandishing a naked sword. 'Wretch,' he shouted, 'this is the last guard you will mount, we are going to exterminate you.' Meanwhile, Madame Campan was attending their majesties at supper. She reported an unseemly fracas at the doorway when two National Guards started arguing about the Constitution. One supported it, but the other said it needed to be replaced by one worthy of a free people, and to do so, it would be necessary to cut some throats.

The 26-year-old Norman aristocrat Liancourt did not take supper in town as was his wont, but returned early to the palace. He was increasingly worried about the situation. He went to the room of the young Marquis de Tourzel, whose mother was governess to the dauphin. Tourzel, however, did not believe that there would be a great alarm. They remained together and had a glass of punch. Time passed. Towards 11 p.m. Monsieur de Fleurieu, the dauphin's governor and inventor of an advanced marine chronometer as well as a former navy minister, brought a note from Tourzel's mother stating that there was strong reason to believe in an attack that night. She wrote that her son should go up to the queen's apartments by an interior staircase if armed groups came to the palace. After that, a succession of people came to their room with vague and alarming news. Liancourt and Tourzel tried to make sense of it all. They wondered whether the agitation had not been instigated by the constitutionalist faction in order to frighten the king into escaping from Paris. This had been pressed upon him by certain ministers and advisers for several days now. Their belief increased when they learned that, for the first time in his reign, there would be no Coucher du Roi [the king's formal retirement to bed]. They expected to be booted in half an hour's time and ready to mount their horses as part of the king's escort. Liancourt, who had been sleeping at the Tuileries over the past month, had a horse ready at riverside stables by the new Louis XVI Bridge (now the Pont de la Concorde).

The 33-year-old Jean-Baptiste Cléry, the dauphin's valet, became the sole remaining servant of the royal family after François Huë was jailed at the beginning of September. He managed to keep notes on their imprisonment which he later made into a journal. In his introduction he wrote: 'Although I have been induced since to arrange these notes in the form of a Journal, my design is rather to furnish materials for those who may in the future write the history of the melancholy end of the unfortunate Louis XVI, rather than to compose memoirs myself which is above my talents and pretensions.' He underestimated his capabilities. In his journal he created a moving historical document. Beginning on 9 August, he wrote: 'In the evening of the ninth at 8.30, after having been present at the Dauphin's going to bed, I went out of the palace with a view to learning the feelings of the public. . . . I made my way to the Palais-Royal, where I found almost all the approaches blocked. Some of the National Guards were under arms, ready to march to the Tuileries in order to support the battalions that had gone before them. But a mob, set in motion by revolutionary leaders, filled the adjacent streets, and rent the air on all sides with their clamour.' At that time the palace had yet to receive major reinforcements. Cléry must have seen the battalion of Saint-Roche which was then stationed at the Palais Royal. It formed part of Vioménil's elaborate defence plan, and was under orders to attack the revolutionaries in the rear when they reached the Place du Carrousel.

'At about 11 p.m. I returned to the palace by the King's Apartments,' Cléry continued. 'The attendants of the Court, and those in waiting on His Majesty, were gathered together showing much anxiety. I passed to the Dauphin's room, which I had scarcely entered when I heard the tocsin ringing, and drums beating to arms in every quarter of the town.' There are conflicting times given for when the tocsin first sounded. Madame Campan, Cléry, and Leroux suggest the tocsin was first heard towards midnight. It may have then ceased. The buzz of activity in the interior of the State Apartments could have drowned out the sound there, as Roederer claimed he did not remark it until around 12.45 a.m.

Again, as darkness fell on the Cour Royale, a Monsieur Agate arrived from the Arsenal with a wagon-load of tents for the camps proposed by the mayor. He entered the palace to report to the general staff of the National Guards. They had been resisting the establishment of temporary camps on the Place du Carrousel and Place Louis XV over the past two days for political and administrative reasons. They had refused to accept tents, demanding more substantial structures instead. The tents were once more declined. Captain Langlade accosted Agate when he was leaving the palace and was furious to learn the tents had been refused. He regarded this as an insult to his hero, Pétion, whom he had heard speaking about the camps that very afternoon in the Assembly. Langlade rushed inside the palace to tell the staff the error of their ways. He was advised the tents were unacceptable. Langlade then asked for the provision of one for him and his men only. He was refused. They countered by asking him if he had brought his ammunition. He answered that he had. He stormed back to his guns and told his comrades to keep them safe while he went to obtain his own requisition for a tent from the Hôtel de Ville. There he found Sergent and obtained the necessary document. He continued onwards to the Arsenal. While returning with his tent, he saw a great many people in the Place Bastille, though mainly without arms. Back in the Cour Royale, he erected the tent beside his guns and was then asked by an officer to make a report at headquarters. He told them what he had seen. Captain Viard claimed it was a Gendarmerie officer who made the report, but he was probably mistaken. Langlade added that an orderly was despatched on horseback to check the truth of his account.

Under the Constitution the seven-year-old dauphin should have succeeded the king. He ostensibly died in June 1795 as a result of neglect, although there are many stories backed by circumstantial evidence that he was spirited away. Later there were many pretenders claiming to be the dauphin, but none could produce conclusive proof of their identity.

Returning shortly afterwards towards 11 p.m., the orderly reported that he had been turned back by the crowd before he could reach the Place Bastille and had been threatened with arrest. Doucet, who was Adjutant of the 6th Legion but was acting as Adjutant General that night, was instructed to give general orders for men to be recalled to their respective mustering points throughout Paris and for certain units to be summoned to defend the Tuileries. Captain Viard mentioned he was instructed to ensure these orders were passed to his own battalion commander. Up to then, the palace was only being defended by a strengthened guard, double or triple its normal complement. Apart from the 800 or so Gendarmerie dispersed away from the palace to provide defence in depth, the number of troops within and close by the palace may have only been about 1,350, of whom 800 were Swiss and the remainder National Guards with some Gendarmerie.

According to Lieutenant Deluze of the Swiss Guards, the first wave of these reinforcements started to arrive between midnight and 1 a.m., and several detachments joined the Swiss at their posts. These included men from the battalion of the Filles Saint-Thomas who were probably the first to come. Their Adjutant-Major, Monsieur Tassin, had received an order to muster this constitutionalist battalion on La Place de la Comédie Italienne as early as 10.30 p.m. He confirmed, when interrogated later, that the order to go to the Tuileries only arrived between 11 and 11.30 p.m. The French historian Marcel Reinhard, who has researched the military situation in Paris that night, states that some dozen or fifteen battalions responded to Mandat's appeal between around midnight and 6 a.m. Some of these split into factions in making their decisions. The Grenadier companies, whose more expensive clothing and equipment resulted in their ranks being filled by the better off, tended to favour the Monarchy. Battalions, which varied in size, did not send their full strength, often much less. The battalion Saint-André-des-Arts only supplied 150 men who were placed on the palace terrace. Battalion commanders took the view that part of their manpower had to be retained for local defence in case of a breakdown of law and order in Paris. Even the loyalist Filles Saint-Thomas kept back 100 men at their guardhouse near the Place Vendôme.

Langlade must have spent some time inside the palace as he heard that the mayor had gone to walk in the garden, which as we know was around midnight. In fact, Langlade may not have left the palace for his position in the Cour Royale until around 2 a.m. He recounted that some officers at headquarters expressed hostile remarks about the mayor, whom they called an unspeakable wretch, on a par with the Marseillais and the gunners. It seems possible they were deliberately riling him. Meanwhile, the threat from the area of the Place Bastille disappeared.

Liancourt expressed his astonishment at finding the palace so well garrisoned when he left Tourzel's room sometime after 11 p.m. Normally, the units on guard duty melted away as the night progressed. 'This evening,' he wrote, 'I went around the palace and was very surprised to find a very numerous guard, many persons loyal to the King, many ex-Gardes de Corps and Constitutional Guards in civilian dress, in fact a great number of gentlemen. The gossip I received spoke of an attack on the palace, but others spoke of small gatherings which would shortly disappear. I went up to the State Bedchamber, and found a great many people, though few in court dress. I myself was in a frock coat. . . . All the public officials were there, Messieurs Carle, Mandat, Borie and Leroux, Municipal Officers with their sashes, and two members from the Department; some Swiss and National Guards officers, and the best known among the nobility. . . . It seemed that all were aware of a great danger; and little by little, each had come armed as best he could, some with swords, others with hunting knives, almost everyone with pistols. I had my sword at my side, although I was in a frock-coat, and two pistols concealed under my shirt. Our armament was distinctly grotesque.' Liancourt mistakenly included Leroux and the members of the Department who arrived later.

Madame Campan was impressed by the impassive disciplined silence of the Swiss Guards, who were ranged in line like actual walls, comparing them favourably with the National Guards and their continuous chattering. She was near the king when she heard him explain the plan of defence prepared by General Vioménil of the 17th Military District. This officer later advised her to fill her pockets with money and jewels. He told her that the danger they faced was inescapable and that the means of defence were nil. The king needed to be vigorous, and this was the single virtue he lacked. The Foreign Minister, Bigot de Sainte-Croix, was occupied in arranging the printing of details of the conspirators' plans which had been obtained that afternoon. These included parading the queen through Paris in an iron cage, then placing her in the female section of the prison in the Hôtel de la Force whose inmates included prostitutes, while the king would be taken to the Hôtel de Ville for interrogation, and then to the Temple. It was expected the insurgents would attack during the night, and it was intended to harden resistance by reading these plans to the defending troops by torchlight and then to distribute printed copies. Lieutenant Deluze of the Swiss Guards obtained a different version on the 'grapevine'. This proposed that the royal family be incarcerated in the fortress of Vincennes to serve as hostages if the Austrians and Prussians reached Paris. The Swiss and all supporters of the king in the palace were to be eliminated.

J.B. Cléry (1759–1809), the dauphin's valet and later sole servant with the royal family, when imprisoned in the Temple. This portrait was published in England in 1798.

When Roederer returned from the garden at around 12.30 a.m., after leaving the mayor and his entourage on the terrace, he received a note from his office saying there was much movement in the Faubourg Saint-Antoine, but no armed gathering. It must be borne in mind that such information concerning the distant faubourg would be over an hour late by the time he received it. He read the contents of the note to the king, the queen, Madame Elizabeth, and the ministers, who were gathered together in the Council Chamber. Altogether there were 20 to 30 people in the room. The tocsin sounded and Roederer graphically described how everyone rushed to the open windows to try and guess from where it was coming by identifying the distinctive sound emitted by each church bell. Roederer then retired to take a nap, but this was of short duration. He was at the centre of affairs that night. A little after 1 a.m., another message arrived from the Department stating that there were now some 1,500 to 2,000 armed men in the Faubourg Saint-Antoine, together with some cannon. Roederer was awakened. It would seem that the king was not present when he passed on these details; further evidence that Louis was having a private meeting with Pétion at that time.

A minister asked whether martial law should be declared as a result of this information. Roederer replied that the Law of 3 August 1791 permitted martial law when the public peace was threatened with continued disturbance. But he added somewhat cryptically that the situation was beyond such a remedy. In any case, it was the responsibility of the Municipality rather than the Department to declare martial law. The minister suggested that the Department could tell the Municipality to do so. Roederer disagreed. However, to show willing, he went to a lamp to read the text of the law in a book with a tricolour binding. The king's sister, Madame Elizabeth, noticed and enquired what he was doing. He told her that he was looking to see whether the Department could declare martial law. She asked him whether it could. He replied that he thought not. He explained that the Paris Commune [Municipality] represented nine-tenths of the population of the Department and could not be subjected to its will. Roederer's frank reporting of his disingenuous response failed to mention that he and the Department owed their authority to virtually the same electorate.

In effect, he resisted taking action which might lead, at least briefly, to civil war. The last time martial law had been declared in Paris was on 17 July 1791, as a result of a major demonstration in the Champ de Mars. There had been some fifty dead whom the radicals regarded as martyrs. The present situation was graver as the radicals were better organised and more determined. Roederer felt circumspection was essential. Neither he, nor the king and his ministers, seemed ready to consider the logic of the situation. Civil war could only be avoided if one side or the other was prepared to back down. The king had no room for manoeuvre to do so. The revolutionaries on the surface appeared less hard pressed, but in fact their recent abortive coups, and the detailed threats they had made, had also pushed them into a corner. The king and his civil advisers failed to appreciate that a stand-off was no longer a practical outcome. The situation had to be resolved one way or another. Feebleness gained the day at the palace, and reliance was placed upon the mayor's lesser authorisation to 'oppose force with force'. In effect, this rendered the defence passive. It allowed the insurgents to utilise their greater ability to operate at the psychological level and suborn their opponents in the knowledge that they could act unchecked, as long as they did not fire first.

Ignoring etiquette, Roederer was seated on a stool by the door of the State Bedchamber when the queen passed by, accompanied by ladies of the Court. Roederer specifically mentioned that a tall thin lady attracted his attention. Despite or perhaps because of the perilous situation, did he feel a frisson of attraction? He was brought down to earth by the queen asking whether the

Marseillais would go away. Roederer replied: 'In the morning.' He related that the Department had authorised the Municipality to provide 20,000 livres to the Marseillais for expenses, and a loan for this purpose had been agreed by the Ministers of Justice and the Interior. The mayor had advised him that the Marseillais were anxious to leave Paris. Pétion and other Girondins had connections with Barbaroux, who had been instrumental in inviting the Marseillais to Paris. It should be noted that the Marseillais had stipulated that they would not take part in the insurrection unless specifically supported by at least one Paris National Guards battalion. It seems likely that if the uprising had not gone ahead this time, the Marseillais would have departed in disgust, and possibly well paid. Louis' advisers were involved in a plot to bribe the Marseillais. For the insurrectionists, 10 August may have represented the last chance. Historical events are frequently determined by a much finer balance than first appears.

When Captain Langlade left the National Guards headquarters, he found his four guns had been ordered up close to the gateway of the Cour Royale, and platoons of infantry were stationed beside them and behind. While crossing the court, he had heard words to the effect that, 'if we did not want to fire our guns, they would make us do it at bayonet point'. He questioned his men and found they had heard similar threats. Weber in his memoirs confirms that he and his fellow grenadiers had noted the disaffection of the gunners, who had threatened to exterminate all in the palace with the exception of the king. Weber and his comrades had discussed measures for taking possession of the cannons. Apart from feeling that he and his men were being coerced, Langlade realised his guns had been positioned for offensive use. He kicked up a fuss. Doucet, the Adjutant General, was sent for. The latter advised Langlade that it was he who had given the order. The guns had to remain where they were. Langlade countered that there was a staff officer responsible for artillery at the Tuileries and he intended to appeal to him. The guns had to be placed in positions where they could be defended. Doucet went to complain to the nearby commander of a National Guards battalion and asked him to remonstrate with Langlade. The commander replied that he knew Langlade's way of thinking and that he should be left alone.

At this moment two municipal officers arrived beside the guns. According to Langlade, they began to insult the Marseillais by saying that many had been branded as robbers, but had had operations to remove the brand marks. A gunner denied their claims. Langlade clipped him on the shoulder, telling him to keep his mouth shut as it was he who would answer for his unit. The municipal officers departed shortly afterwards saying the gunners knew and trusted their captain. Langlade claimed that it was around 2 a.m., but the evidence of Leroux' account, who must have been one of the unnamed municipal officers concerned, places the time perhaps an hour later.

The ministers and Roederer remained on duty to meet emergencies. These occurred at intervals throughout the early hours. The royal family, however, were permitted some repose, although not untroubled. Madame Campan suggested in her memoirs that the queen and Madame Elizabeth retired at around 1 a.m., but from Roederer's and Leroux' accounts, it was more likely 1.30 a.m., or even later.

They went to recline on a sofa in a small room on a mezzanine floor. The queen asked Madame Campan to sit nearby. They were unable to sleep. They spoke sadly of the situation. Madame Elizabeth showed Madame Campan a pin with a large carnelian head with an inscription: 'Forget affronts, pardon insults.' The king's devout, stout, and unmarried 28-year-old sister sententiously remarked: 'I very much fear that this maxim has little influence among our enemies, but for us it must not remain less dear.' Sometime after 4 a.m., a shot was discharged by accident in the Cour Royale. The queen said: 'There is the first shot, it will not be the last.' They decided to go to where the king was resting in a room on the ground floor, looking on to the garden.

Others tried to obtain some rest, but were equally restless. Madame de Tourzel watched over the dauphin. She wrote: 'I and my daughter Pauline [aged sixteen] passed the night by the side of Monseigneur le Dauphin, whose calm and peaceful slumbers were in striking contrast with the agitation which reigned in every mind. About 4 a.m., I went to the State Apartments to find out what was going on, and what we had to hope or fear. "Today," said Monsieur d'Hervilly to me, "I anticipate the worst; the worst thing to do is to do nothing and, in actual fact, nothing is being done."' Liancourt spent the night sitting on the balustrade around the state bed in the king's Bedchamber. Because of the excitement of the previous week, when he had been arrested twice, he could not relax. From time to time he left the Bedchamber to seek out his friend Charles de Chabot and exchange news. For the past month they had been sharing a room at the Tuileries. He related that the number of people in the king's apartments continued to increase, and by the middle of the night all the chairs were occupied and people were sitting on tables and even the floor, or leaning against anything which could provide some support. At the beginning, some members of the palace staff protested that it was against etiquette to sit down in the king's rooms. Liancourt commented that some people were unable to adjust their minds to new circumstances. Viard mentioned in his report that the Royal Apartments were so packed that it was difficult to reach the Council Chamber.

During these small hours of the night, in lamp and shadow chiaroscuro, there must have occurred many earnest conversations in hushed voices, some on trivial matters, some idly speculating about the threatening future, some of a more practical nature. The account of one such conversation was published 30 years later by an anonymous bourgeois member of the Paris National Guards. He related that he spoke to Frédéric Deluze, a lieutenant in the Swiss Guards from Neuchâtel. Deluze explained how easy it was to approach the palace under cover. If the Swiss had been in open country, they would have formed a square and placed the royal family within. However, they were under strength having sent 300 men to Normandy and left others behind at Courbevoie. They also lacked cannons. The regiment had had twelve. Deluze continued: 'We shall be faithful to our obligations. Whatever inferiority is presented by our actual position, perhaps we shall counter it by our courage, by our resolution, and by the skill of our manoeuvres. I spoke to you just now that for some time the Regiment no longer has its own artillery, but the commander of your National Guards has had half a dozen field pieces placed in the courtyards. If your gunners, who are generally badly disposed, do not act as they should, we will decide to use force to take over the guns, and we will man them ourselves as we still have trained artillery men in the Regiment and know who they are. In a word, we understand our duty and will fulfil it to the utmost, rather than lose our honour, and betray the sanctity of our oaths.' The Swiss were not able to seize the artillery until too late, and exploit the advantage earlier possession would have given them.

According to Roederer, the king was still up towards 2.30 a.m., as he had then given Louis another verbal report on the situation within Paris. It was improving. He was told by his staff at the Department that the gatherings of armed men appeared to be dwindling. Now that the leadership of the insurrection had decided to postpone action until daybreak, units had dispersed to gain a few hours' rest. Shortly after Roederer had made his report, a municipal deputation arrived from the Town Hall to investigate whether the mayor had been forcibly detained. They were advised that he had recently gone to the National Assembly and the party followed him. Rumours of plots against the mayor agitated the palace for the next hour.

At around 3.45 a.m., the ministers were faced with a more concrete emergency. They received the unpleasant news that cannons placed on the Pont Neuf had been ordered away by the Municipality. The plan to prevent a junction of insurgent forces divided by the Seine was unravelling. A minister promptly asked Roederer if the order could be rescinded. Roederer refused to take any responsibility for annulling the order, but agreed to send a written message to the Council of the Department, which was in session, to ask for their opinion. He explained that he was unable to take up the matter directly with the mayor, as he was now understood to be returning to the Hôtel de Ville from the National Assembly. The Department's Council agreed to send two members of its Directorate, Messieurs Levieillard and Faucompret, to join the discussions at the palace on action that might be taken to restore the guns. When they arrived, they decided with Roederer that the Department's entire Directorate should be summoned to the Tuileries, but this would need a formal request from the king.

With the ministers, they went down to a small room belonging to the king's valet de chambre, Thierry. This looked out on the courtyard side of the palace and connected with the king's private bedroom, which gave on to the garden terrace. They asked that Louis be awakened and waited for him to appear. At this juncture, Roederer distinctly remembered hearing the noise of the mayor's carriage leaving the Cour Royale. It must have been around 4.15 a.m. Municipal Officer Leroux mentioned that he had noticed the carriage during his extensive tour of inspection of the National Guards posts protecting the palace. When he learned Pétion had left the National Assembly for the Hôtel de Ville, he had given orders for the carriage to be sent back. While on this tour, he claimed he had helped to mollify the feelings of some National Guards who were upset by rumours that there had been an attempt to hold the mayor at the palace against his will. He had also organised a messenger link between the Tuileries and the General Council at the Hôtel de Ville.

Outside in the Cour Royale, Captain Langlade had remained quiescent since the departure of the two municipal officers, but he continued to fume inwardly about the positioning of his guns. Daylight was now approaching and he decided it was necessary to rectify the situation. He gave the order to withdraw his guns from near the Porte Royale. The comedy resumed. He was immediately reported. Doucet promptly reappeared on the scene and brusquely countermanded the order. Langlade related:

> I told him he did not know about artillery and would not speak to me in that manner if he knew. At that moment Monsieur Lachesnaye approached, a Legion commander, and another individual with his blue coat embroidered in gold and decorated with the Cross of St Louis. He told me that it was unimportant whether I was right or wrong in this matter, but to be in agreement to defend ourselves against the brigands who had already pillaged several shops in the Saint-Denis and Saint-Martin streets, and also in the Faubourg Saint-Antoine, and who would soon be here to assassinate the King and Queen. I replied that it would be impossible for me to defend the gate, because I was too close to it and unable to manoeuvre. Earlier on, I had succeeded in persuading the platoons immediately behind me, which had threatened my men, to withdraw. They now returned and took up a position immediately to the rear of my guns. I told them that I must have space to position my ammunition limbers. I went to look for them, something I had been unable to do in the middle of the night as they were hidden to the rear of the battalion behind us. Then, the gentleman Carle, Colonel of the National Gendarmerie, appeared on the scene. He repeated that it was necessary for us all to agree with each other and not to be divided. He did not believe the grenadiers were angry with us, and he himself would move the chairs on which they had been sitting at our back.

Carle, who was a goldsmith, was to be murdered that afternoon. The picture of the citizen militia occupying their position on chairs is slightly risible. More important is the desire shown by senior officers to be conciliatory at all costs to prevent division and possible defection.

The queen and Madame Elizabeth had joined the ministers and Roederer in the downstairs room while they waited for the king to appear. The shutters were thrown open and Madame Elizabeth went to admire the dawn which was just beginning. She invited the queen to join her. The king came out of his bedroom at about 4.30 a.m., since Roederer wrote that it was not yet daylight. He keenly noted that Louis looked a sight. His dressed and curled hair from the previous evening was flattened on one side where he had been lying. They asked him to give an order to summon the Department's Directorate. The king replied that he would do so when the minister concerned returned. The counter-signature of Champion, Minister of the Interior, was necessary.

None of the witnesses at the Tuileries mentioned that Champion had gone to the National Assembly alone that night. We know from a report of the Assembly's proceedings that he addressed the Chamber some time after Pétion had left for the Mairie. Champion had spoken about the anxieties of the king and the disturbances in the Faubourg Saint-Antoine, remarking that the public authorities had so far done nothing, but should now take prompt measures. He was rebuked and told that the Legislature only made laws, while it was the responsibility of the Executive power to maintain order. There was no discussion on the inadequate means at the monarch's disposal. Champion's visit was a personal initiative. He must have decided to find out what Pétion had said to the National Assembly about plots to kidnap him. Champion seems to have had an adventurous nature. He had indulged in an individual reconnaissance of the insurrectionist gathering of 26 July on the Place Bastille and barely escaped a lynching.

While awaiting Champion's return, the king and ministers continued to discuss the withdrawal of the cannons on the Pont Neuf. Then Roederer and Dejoly were called away to deal with a new crisis. The General Council of the Commune had summoned Mandat, the commanding General of the National Guards, to report to them at the Hôtel de Ville. Liancourt described how a National Guard came to seek Mandat, who was sitting close to him on the balustrade in the State Bedchamber. He saw Mandat go as white as a sheet, and say in an alarmed voice: 'I will not return from there.' Liancourt gave the time as 2 a.m., but he was obviously mistaken. It must have been about 2½ hours later. Accounts of events at the Tuileries and elsewhere reveal much erratic timing. While people usually had a clear memory of physical activities, and of telling remarks, presumably as notes were made shortly afterwards, ideas of timing were more uncertain. It would be helpful if eyewitnesses specifically mentioned that they had consulted their watch, but this seldom occurs. One must assume that times given were frequently an afterthought. The historian may be in the fortunate position of having more than one account, and is able to create a chronology based upon cross-referencing the estimated duration of specific activities.

Roederer and Dejoly met Mandat in the Council Chamber. Mandat was strongly against obeying the summons from the Hôtel de Ville. As it turned out, he had very good reason. Leroux and his colleague Borie arrived when the argument was in full swing. They added their weight to Roederer's contention that Mandat was under the authority of the Municipality and should obey its instructions. Moreover, the mayor would want Mandat to accompany him on visits to the insurrectionary sectors and to help him restore obedience to units of National Guards wavering in their duty. Roederer was still unaware that Pétion had withdrawn from the fray by retiring to his residence. Dejoly, on the other hand, claimed that Mandat was needed for the defence of the palace and could not be spared. Roederer countered by suggesting that Mandat could investigate the instructions to remove the guns from the Pont Neuf. Mandat may have been conscious that a few hours previously the Municipal Council had supported his request that the mayor come to the Tuileries. Could he now justly refuse a return visit? A second summons arrived. Roederer's arguments prevailed. Reluctantly, Mandat departed and promised to send back any news. De Lachesnaye, commander of one of the six legions into which the Paris National Guards were divided, was nominated as his temporary replacement. Afterwards, Roederer naturally regretted his intervention. He defended himself by blaming Mandat's death on being unpopular, a situation which he did not know about at the time.

He also complained that Mandat should have taken a proper bodyguard with him. But this could have led to Mandat being accused of attempting to intimidate the Commune.

After this discussion, it seems Roederer left the Council Chamber and entered the State Bedchamber next door. Liancourt saw him there near the fireplace. The news of Mandat's departure had already spread, causing alarm and despondency. Roederer sought to alleviate it by saying: 'Messieurs, do not be concerned. I have here an order from Monsieur Pétion to repulse force with force; but even if I did not have it, I myself would command, as a member of the Department, that the troops defend their positions.' It must be assumed that, before departing to the Hôtel de Ville, Mandat had handed over the mayor's requisition to Roederer for safe keeping. What happened to this authorisation will be discussed later.

One of Lachesnaye's first orders was to instruct Viard commanding a unit in the Salle des Cent Gardes Suisses to supply 12 to 20 men for a post at the top of the Great Stairs. Viard demurred at supplying soldiers to this post currently being manned by a detachment from the Compagnie Colonelle of the 1st Battalion of the Swiss Guards. Major Bachmann of the Swiss Guards wanted to ensure that all Swiss units were brigaded with National Guards in pursuit of Affry's orders that the Swiss should only act as auxiliaries. Viard was finally persuaded to comply after replacements had been found for his detached men, and he himself was put in command of the post with the Swiss serving under him.

Roederer had been summoned to the queen's apartments, but he failed to note the time. The internal evidence points to it being a little after 5 a.m. The king was now with his confessor, l'Abbé Hébert. After signing the order on Champion's return requesting the presence of the Department's Directorate, Louis spent up to half an hour making his peace with God. A devout man, he believed this was a greater priority than trying to invigorate the defence. The queen, who was with the ministers, took the lead for her absent husband. She asked Roederer what was to be done. He replied that the royal family ought to go and seek the protection of the National Assembly. Why this major change in policy? He had not hinted at such a course of action in his commentary up to then, despite many contacts during the preceding hours with the king and ministers. Roederer provided no explanation in his memoirs. It is possible that the cold light of day had led to a reassessment of the situation. He had been disturbed by the withdrawal of the guns from the Pont Neuf, followed by the summoning of Mandat to the Hôtel de Ville. More probably, he had just heard from the Department's staff that the mayor had not returned to the Hôtel de Ville after all, but had gone straight back to his official residence on the Ile de la Cité. His hopes that the mayor was working somehow to defuse the situation, as he had done in the past, were now dashed. But if he had received such information, why did he not mention it as justification for his proposal to seek the protection of the National Assembly? A likely reason is Roederer's guilty feelings at having insisted that Mandat go to the Hôtel de Ville to help the mayor when in fact he was not there. Stating in his memoirs that he learned of Pétion's absence shortly afterwards would underline his responsibility.

The queen was surprised by Roederer's advice. So was Dubouchage, the Minister for the Navy, who retorted: 'You propose to send the King to his enemy!' 'Not so,' replied Roederer, 'there were 400 votes in favour of Lafayette against 200. Besides, it is the least danger.' The Queen intervened: 'Here we have forces. It is time to find out who is going to overcome, the King and the Constitution, or the [revolutionary] faction.' 'Madame,' Roederer replied, 'in that case let us see. I propose we summon Monsieur Lachesnaye, the officer in command in the absence of Monsieur Mandat.' When Lachesnaye arrived, he gave a résumé of the defensive arrangements. He did not support Roederer by implying the palace was defenceless. However, he then turned specifically towards the queen, and said: 'Madame, I cannot let you remain ignorant of the fact that the rooms are full of people who greatly irritate the National Guards and prevent them from being close to the King. They find this very discouraging.' The queen tartly rebutted Lachesnaye. She told him his remarks were inappropriate and the people concerned could be counted on. Nevertheless, the presence of numerous aristocrats had awoken feelings of class enmity. Perhaps some of them had not been altogether discreet. Viard, in his report to the National Assembly a few days later, emphasised his great indignation at seeing so many of the former nobility while on guard duty in the king's apartments. Undoubtedly, class divisions were an important contributory factor in lowering morale among the National Guards defending the palace.

Some with republican sympathies, together with monarchists who deplored the king's lack of spirit, have found it tempting to depict the queen as Lady Macbeth egging on a phlegmatic and indecisive husband during the final hours of his reign. A number of anecdotes lend credence to this view. Although since 1787 Marie Antoinette had played a political role, she lacked real discrimination and objectivity, and the limited effect she had on the king's decisions tended to be negative rather than positive. While the queen certainly had a more lively temperament than her husband, she was also highly strung and no Amazon. In these critical hours of extreme peril for her family and the Monarchy, she would not have considered otherwise as wife and queen than to defer to her husband's rank and position. Roederer commenting on her attitude during the fateful hours of the night of 9/10 August, reported: 'The Queen showed nothing unwomanly, nothing heroic, nothing unnatural nor romantic. I did not see in her either passion or despair, or a desire for vengeance.'

CHAPTER 7

Review

Exhausted by the night's activities, Leroux sat down at the council table and, leaning on his elbow, had briefly gone to sleep. He was awoken towards 5.30 a.m. by the entry of the king, whose coiffure was still unattended since he had left his bedroom nearly an hour earlier. Down in the main courtyard, Captain Langlade was about to retrieve his ammunition limbers when several battalion units arrived at the Tuileries with their cannons. Some entered by the Cour des Princes, and others went on to the garden terrace, having passed through the Grille de la Reine opposite the Pont Royal. One of these battalions brought two guns through the passageway under the Clock Tower into the Cour Royale and placed them alongside Langlade's four cannons by the main gate. Meanwhile, senior officers had decided that the king should make a grand review of the forces defending the palace. It was hoped that his presence would inspire the troops.

Dejoly wrote that he had noticed considerable activity in the interior and around the palace. The National Guards and Swiss were called to their posts, the Great Stairs and the Vestibule were lined with troops, the units in the courts were reorganised, and more cannons were placed in position; all of this indicated preparation for a resolute defence. Despite this, Dejoly commented that he had few doubts about the overwhelming strength of the revolutionaries, although here there may have been an element of retrospection. He added that he trembled because of the threatened bloodshed and deaths without number. He believed that the defence was criminal and an extravagant waste of effort, as he 'was convinced in advance that there was no dike powerful enough to stop this impetuous torrent'. As a civilian Dejoly was frightened, and as a Girondin he understood the ideological impetus behind the insurrection.

As part of these preparations, Langlade was commanded to load his guns. He refused to comply with the order because he had been told by staff officers that the insurgents would march with women and children shielding their front. However, his second in command gave the order to load and was obeyed after persuading the men that they could fire on the flank, always providing they were fired on first. This incident among many shows the state of insubordination and indiscipline among the National Guards, where the need to cajole and persuade superseded the prerogatives of command. It also hints that determined leadership among the defenders might have achieved something. It was against the king's nature to provide it. Nor could it be provided by aristocratic senior officers out of tune with the bourgeois and artisans who composed the National Guards.

Langlade next reported that the king appeared on the balcony overlooking the Cour Royale. He was surrounded by grenadiers and also several people dressed in different colours, predominantly green. The courtyard resounded with cries of 'Vive le Roi!' Weber, posted in the Cour Royale near Langlade's gunners, described how the king was acclaimed with ardour the whole time he was on the balcony. Soldiers placed their hats on the points of their sabres and bayonets. The cheers continued for some moments after Louis withdrew. Weber commented that this was the last burst of genuine enthusiasm the king was to receive.

The king was still wearing the violet evening dress in which he had appeared from his bedroom when awakened at dawn. With his coiffure crushed on one side, his outré appearance must have created a far from flattering impression to many who saw him during the review. His hat under his arm, the corpulent and well-meaning king had started first on a tour of the posts in the interior of the palace accompanied initially by the queen, their children, and the Princesse de Lamballe, the Director of the Queen's Household and her close personal friend. Witnesses say the king looked distressed and anxious, but tried to conceal his concern with a smile and the frank expression of his eyes. He made halting remarks such as: 'Ah well, it is said that they are coming.' ' I will not do what they want.' 'For this once, I consent that my friends defend me; we will perish, or we will save ourselves together.' The queen had difficulty in repressing tears, but nevertheless held herself erect with a steadfast air. After a little while, she and her entourage left the king and retired to her apartments. The ministers again accompanied her. The interior inspection seemed to go well, and the king then descended the Great Stairs into the Cour Royale towards 6 a.m. He was accompanied by the senior officers of the 17th Military District, the National Guards, and the Swiss Guards. He entered the courtyard to the sound of beating drums and cries of 'Vive le Roi!'

According to Langlade, Louis started his inspection on the right side of the Cour Royale with a unit which had only just arrived, indifferently armed with all sorts of weapons. His suite of officers was encouraging the troops to echo them in crying 'Vive le Roi!' Municipal officer Leroux heard the great commotion in the Cour Royale from within the palace. Prompted by those with him, he felt it was his duty as an official of the Paris Commune to go down into the courtyard to gauge the feelings of the National Guards towards the king. He registered cries of: 'Vive le Roi!' 'Vive Louis XVI!' 'Vive le Roi et la Constitution!' 'It is he who is our King, and we want no other, and we wish it so!' 'Down with the Faction!' 'Down with the Jacobins!' 'We will defend him to the end, let him put himself at our head!' 'Long live the Nation, the Law, the Constitution and the King, all are but one!' Leroux added that these cries only came from the National Guards infantry units, while the gunners and Swiss Guards did not make a sound.

One must assume that Leroux was so busy writing notes on the political sentiments of the Paris militia that he failed to notice what others report, that both the Swiss Guards and the gunners joined in the clamour, the first in favour of the king and the second against. Langlade stated that he waved his hat in his hand and shouted with all his might: 'Vive la Nation!' when the king passed by. This cry was taken up several times by all the gunners present, who added that they did not recognise any master but the Nation. Peltier stated that there were also hostile cries of 'Vive la Nation!'

from the battalion Croix-Rouge which was probably the unit Langlade mentioned entering with its guns from the garden side of the palace around 5.30 a.m. Weber agreed with Leroux that the king was generally welcomed with favourable cries. He also corroborated Langlade's account; and said that Louis, who according to Liancourt had remained generally silent, was moved to expostulate with the gunners: 'Yes, my children, the Nation and your King make and will make only one.'

Langlade reported that the gunners' behaviour infuriated some grenadiers who rushed forward and placed their fists under their noses after the king had departed. Langlade was livid and aimed a sabre blow at one of them. Weber telling the story from his side omitted mentioning any antagonistic gestures towards the gunners. 'Hardly', Weber wrote, 'had the King re-entered the palace, when several Gendarmes and National Guards began to provoke us with their insults. They were joined by the gunners who drew their sabres and derisively called us 'royal' grenadiers. Turning round their cannons ten paces away from us, they cried out in rage that the Filles Saint-Thomas alone were sold to the Court and that the Commander Mandat had sent only aristocrats to the palace. They made us the most atrocious menaces. We tried to appease them, remonstrating with the most outraged among them that they had been deceived and that our conduct was irreproachable. We were only there on the instructions of the Hôtel de Ville to provide twenty men from each battalion to reinforce the guard. We had come to protect the King's residence, and it was not the moment to be bitter and quarrel over a misunderstanding. Instead we were all friends and should mutually support each other rather than cut each other's throats.' Weber seems to have forgotten the hostility of his comrades towards the gunners during the night. The National Guards who joined in with the gunners would appear to have come from the battalion which arrived in the Cour Royale shortly before the king began his inspection there.

Continuing his account, Langlade went on to say that this battalion with two guns felt so indignant at the behaviour of the grenadiers that it promptly left through the gate into the Place du Carrousel. Peltier claimed that it dispersed there except for the two guns and a detachment. At this time, the main gate into the Cour Royale was left open to let in reinforcements. It was only closed shortly before the arrival of the Marseillais towards 7.30 a.m. The hot-headed Langlade decided that he would follow the departing unit. Unlike their guns, his were unlimbered and needed to be recombined with their ammunition caissons. While he was organising this, the ever-watchful Adjutant General Doucet descended on him again and shouted: 'What the hell are you doing! You are leaving your position. You are a damned coward!' Langlade replied in kind, and continued: 'You accuse me of leaving my post. You have allowed my fellow gunners to go. You wish me to have my throat cut by forcing me to fire on my brothers.' Doucet reiterated that he was leaving his post out of cowardice. This put Langlade on the defensive. He started to exculpate himself, claiming that he had never acted dishonourably since he had joined the service three years before. Peltier wrote that it required the energies of de Boissieu, the senior officer of the 17th Military District, to sort the situation out in the Cour Royale, and to despatch two ill-equipped newly arrived recalcitrant battalions out of harm's way on to the Water Terrace.

View of the Hôtel de Ville and Place de Grève in 1753. The church of St Gervais and St Protais, Roman soldiers martyred by Nero, is to the right.

When the queen reached her apartments with the ministers, she again summoned Roederer. He repeated what he had told her before the start of the review, that the royal family ought to go to the National Assembly. This was not acceptable to most present. As a compromise, both Dejoly and Roederer claimed to have proposed that the king write a letter to the National Assembly asking for help. Dubouchage and some other ministers disliked the idea of the king begging for assistance from the National Assembly. They talked about the royal dignity being wounded, and that writing personally was unworthy of the throne's majesty. A letter from the Minister of the Interior, Champion, would suffice. Roederer suggested a further compromise: 'If my idea is unacceptable, at least two Ministers should go to the Assembly to let them know the state of affairs and to ask them to send some of their members as representatives.' This was acceptable to Dubouchage and his supporters. It was agreed that Dejoly and Champion should undertake the mission.

The two ministers set off across the Tuileries garden at about 6.30 a.m. It was the second visit Champion had made to the Manège in the last few hours. It was now Dejoly's turn to address the Chamber. He wrote that he informed the Assembly that the palace was already invested, entry would be forced, and the king's safety could no longer be guaranteed. But his memory had failed him. The insurgents had not yet arrived on the Carrousel. A report on the Assembly's proceedings mentions the Minister of Justice saying that movements were increasing, that units of troops were advancing towards the palace, and that it was very urgent to take effective measures. The king had required the ministers to witness his desire that the Assembly send a deputation to safeguard not only the palace but order throughout the capital. A leading moderate, Bigot-Préameneu, proposed a motion that a deputation be nominated immediately.

However, news was beginning to filter through of the takeover at the Hôtel de Ville, and the atmosphere began to change. It was observed by a deputy that there was less than the quorum of 200 present required to pass a motion. Such a consideration had not prevented the Assembly during the night from passing a resolution summoning the mayor from the Tuileries. It was further suggested that the proposed measure was delicate in the circumstances. It was better that the king should come to the Assembly. Another member rejected this proposal by pointing out that the Constitution forbade the National Assembly to debate in the king's presence. It was important at this juncture that there were no restrictions on the ability of the Assembly to act. Dejoly was thoroughly disillusioned. He might have expected more support, especially in view of his Girondin connections. The ministers decided to leave and let the debate continue.

Around the same time as the ministers left for the Assembly, Louis and his entourage began to review the posts on the garden side of the Tuileries. First, they inspected the posts along the palace terrace on which were stationed the constitutional loyalist battalions of the Petits-Pères and the Filles Saint-Thomas. Next, they went towards the units, partly armed with pikes, which had just been stationed on the Water Terrace. Liancourt reported: 'This post was composed of very badly turned out soldiers, and they cried strongly, "Vive la Nation! Down with the Veto!" The King did not stop. As he advanced towards the unit posted by the Swing Bridge, a frightful horde of brigands who were on the terrace of the Feuillants, that they call the land of Liberty, went along at a distance shouting all possible horrors against the King. They were very numerous and armed with pikes.'

At the palace, Dubouchage was standing in front of an open window in the queen's apartments looking over the garden. Suddenly, he exclaimed: 'Great Heavens! They are booing the King. What the devil is he going to do down there? Let us go quickly and bring him back.' Roederer noticed that the queen was silently crying. Immediately, Bigot de Sainte-Croix rushed out to rescue the king. Leroux was sitting in a room where the rest of the nine-member Directorate of the Department's Council had just arrived. He was advising them on the palace defences and the morale of the National Guards, when he too heard the discordant noises in the garden. He was pressed as a municipal officer to go out and try to calm the populace. He hurriedly left the palace towards the Swing Bridge, some 700 or so yards away at the end of the garden.

Liancourt wrote that when the king reached the Swing Bridge, his inspection passed off quietly. The situation then deteriorated. 'On leaving,' he wrote, 'we had a moment of great fright, since several of the Sans-culottes, who were on the terrace, came down and advanced towards the King. Then those who were escorting him formed two rings around him with interlocked arms. One consisted of National Guards whom we knew to be brave and honest men, and the second was composed of Messieurs de Sainte-Croix, de Lajard, de Maillardoz, Bachmann, de Boissieu, de Briges, and several others, because at moments like this, one does not busy oneself

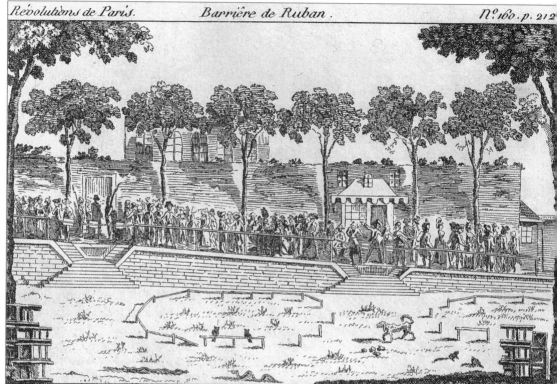

Révolutions de Paris.   Barrière de Ruban.   N.º 160. p. 212

*Pour séparer le jardin des thuileries de la terrasse des feuillans, le Peuple tendit le lon
de cette terrasse un simple ruban; cette barrière fut respectée, Personne ne la franchie*

*Cartoon showing the ribbon on the Terrasse des Feuillants dividing Paris from the Tuileries
garden. The steps, surmounted with difficulty by the royal family and later the Swiss Guards,
which led to the iron grille gate giving access to the Manège and the Convent des Feuillants, can be
seen on the left. The top of the Manège looms over the wall. The steps on the right lead up to the
Café Holtot and the Rue du Dauphin. In reality, the two pairs of steps are some 250 yards apart.*

with examining one's companions. I was in that chain. Monsieur de Menou walked
beside me. Monsieur de Poix was in front of the King who had near him several
officers of the National Guards, Monsieur Guinguerlot among others, to whom he
spoke.' Liancourt was not the person to suppress the aristocratic particle 'de' for
the sake of revolutionary orthodoxy. It is interesting to note that the circle nearest
the king consisted of National Guards, and not former nobles.

As they retired back along the Grande Allée, they were confronted by a man
flourishing a long pike, and displaying a pistol. 'Vive Pétion! Vive la Nation!' he
cried. 'I also,' replied the king. 'I have never wished anything but its happiness.'
Leroux had joined the king near the Swing Bridge. His narrative, regaining its
earlier fluency, described how they were followed by some dozen men as far as the
flower beds, 'among whom were five or six gunners, who rushed after the King,

absolutely like flies who pursue an animal they are determined to torment'. Again Leroux noted the slogans including 'Down with the fat pig!' No doubt the loyal Liancourt felt them too indelicate to repeat. The latter recounted that the withdrawal back to the palace seemed so uncertain that a grenadier anxiously said to the king: 'Sire, you ought to regain the palace immediately', meaning they should break into a run rather than walking as fast as their cumbersome formation would permit. The king looked at him coldly and replied: 'It is singular that I have less fear than a brave grenadier.'

When they arrived near the palace, many people had assembled close by, some with very unpleasant-looking faces, according to Liancourt. Major General de Menou advanced ahead of the party, and ordered the Swiss post by the central entrance in the iron railings to open only one side of the gate, and to close it immediately after Louis and his suite had passed through. This was achieved with difficulty. Many hostile people had pressed close to the king's entourage and sought to follow him. Madame Campan looking out of a window saw some gunners posted on the terrace leave their cannons and rush up to him, putting their fists under his nose as he was entering the palace and insulting him with gross remarks. The king blanched. Messieurs de Salvert and de Briges pushed them aside. Louis mounted to the Royal Apartments, perspiring and out of breath after his precipitate return through the garden. Roederer mentioned, however, that he did not seem unduly disturbed by what had happened. Meanwhile, the recalcitrant battalions quitted their position on the Water Terrace, and left the garden by the Queen's Gate opposite the Pont Royal. Some two hours later they joined the insurgents.

The pessimistic queen spoke privately to Madame Campan that all was lost, that the king had lacked energy, and that the review had done more harm than good. The collapse of the morale of the National Guards at the palace was in no small part due to the king's failure to arouse any real enthusiasm. Although Louis possessed the sympathy and interest necessary for relating to ordinary people, he lacked the eloquence and personal magnetism to exploit this to his advantage.

CHAPTER 8

The Commune

When Mandat arrived at the Hôtel de Ville accompanied by a few officers including his son, his worst fears must have been confirmed. Contrary to expectations, he found the mayor was not there. It seems possible that Mandat had heard during the night about the gathering of delegates from the insurrectionary sections. There was also the news of the cannons being withdrawn from the Pont Neuf. All this must have contributed to his reluctance to leave the palace. The revolutionaries tried to compel him to go directly to the room where they were meeting, presided over by Huguenin of Quinze-Vingts. Mandat resisted, saying his orders were to report to the General Council, composed, he added, of decent people. Danton is said to have grabbed him by the collar, shouting melodramatically: 'Traitor! This Commune is saving the People and will force you to obey, since you betray and conspire with the tyrant against it. Tremble, your crime is discovered and soon you and your infamous accomplices will receive their due.' Mandat shook him off and entered the room where the Municipal General Council was in session, presided over by the elderly Cousin, Professor of the College de France.

Mandat, a former senior officer of the Gardes Françaises, was a simple soldier and no orator. His was not the role to convince the council that the Constitution was in danger and that there was not a moment to lose if order was to be maintained. Instead, he sought to parry questions on his conduct as best he could. He was asked why he had allowed the drums to beat 'la générale', leading to an increase in tension and the prospect of strife in the capital. He replied that he had only ordered 'le rappel' which merely required National Guards to report to their mustering places, but not to form up as fighting units. Although the Department had conditionally authorised him to utilise 'la générale' the previous afternoon, he was aware that the Municipal Council via the mayor had only instructed him to use 'le rappel'. Mandat was then asked why the size of guard posts had been doubled at the palace. He answered that he had received an authorisation from the mayor to this effect but had left it behind at the palace. The council was satisfied with Mandat's replies and he was allowed to leave.

The General Council's interrogation had been relatively perfunctory. Moderates were in a majority. The revolutionaries, on the other hand, were determined to neutralise Mandat. Pétion wrote that if Mandat had refused to obey the summons to come to the Hôtel de Ville, a messenger would have attempted to assassinate him at the Tuileries. On leaving the Municipal Council, the conspirators waylaid Mandat to face a much more hostile questioning. Manuel, part of the conspiracy and Procureur Général, made himself available to sanction the proceedings when required. Huguenin asked Mandat again about doubling the guard. Once more he mentioned the mayor's authorisation. He was asked to show the order. 'If I had been warned,' he replied, 'I would have brought the Mayor's order with me rather than leaving it behind among my papers.' Huguenin unjustly doubted he had really received the order. Mandat tried to change the subject by referring to his visit to the Department the previous afternoon. 'There was a general request,' he said tentatively, 'that I made to the Department. If a Commanding General cannot take expeditious action to meet an unforeseen event, it is not possible to command.' Huguenin ignored this remark. It is obvious he was not fully aware of the scope of Mandat's preparations to defend the Tuileries. He again reverted to the mayor's authorisation to double the guard. It was decided to send a deputation of five members led by Tronchon to the Mairie to obtain a direct explanation from Pétion. According to François Huë, this document survived and was offered to Malesherbes for the king's defence at his trial in December. Typically, Louis refused to use it as he did not wish to implicate Pétion.

Mandat was next asked if he had given a formal order for cannons to be brought to the palace and also to be placed on the Seine bridges. He waffled by replying that since the time of Lafayette, it was regulations that when a battalion marched it should be accompanied by its guns. Huguenin tried to focus the issue. He asked specifically about the stationing of the cannons on the Pont Neuf. Mandat replied even more pedantically: 'Orders are given like this; the Commanding General gives an order to a Legion Commander who then passes it down to his battalions. As for the stationed cannons, I have neither given nor not given orders, the cannons are part of the battalions.'

Huguenin, realising that this line of questioning was getting nowhere, started to lead up to a carefully prepared coup de théâtre. He asked him about plans to detain the mayor at the palace. Mandat replied: 'The National Guards have shown great respect for the Mayor. He was certainly not detained; and as for myself, I greeted him and then withdrew.' Huguenin then asked him the apparently innocuous question of who wrote Mandat's letters to the mayor the previous evening. Mandat replied that it was his secretary. This question was a prearranged prompt. Mouchet, the Justice of the Peace who had gone to the National Assembly to ask them to extricate Pétion from the Tuileries, now intervened. In general the Municipal Justices of the Peace were moderate, but Mouchet was a major exception. The Justices were to be purged a few days later. 'Mandat's secretary,' Mouchet said, 'informed me that Monsieur Mandat had told the grenadiers of the Gravilliers Battalion, speaking of Pétion, that they were to go and bring him back, saying: "His head will answer to you for any breach of the peace."' The Gravilliers, of course, were unable to comply. One cannot know for certain whether Mouchet was bearing false witness or not, but his accusation is not implausible. Dejoly independently confirmed that Mouchet returned to the palace after the mayor had finished addressing the National Assembly, and that pressure had been put on the mayor beforehand to go up to the State Apartments. When the mayor's reluctance was reported, and there was news that he had been summoned by the Assembly, it is reasonable to suggest that Mandat might well have said it was

Sulpice Huguenin Pétitionaire du 20 Juin,
Elu Président de la Révolution du 10 Août,
estampe-Gérard Sculp, Mallet Del. -, coll. Ste Vinck, B.N.
reprod. au tome 3 de l'Inventaire de la collection

Huguenin from the radical Faubourg Saint-Antoine presided over the Revolutionary Commune on 10 August, and led their triumphant delegation to the National Assembly.

important to detain the mayor. How peremptory he was cannot be known, and Mouchet may well have embroidered his remarks.

It was agreed that the mayor again be approached for his comments and be asked to make a report on the matter to the National Assembly and the Municipal Council. The revolutionary meeting decided to adjourn the interrogation briefly and carry out another stage in their putsch. They now believed they had sufficient grounds to justify dismissing Mandat and to purge the aristocrat-tainted command structure of the National Guards. They had no legal authority to do so, but everything was possible if one freely appropriated the name of the People. Redolent with a lawyer's midnight oil, the following pronouncement was made: 'Considering that one can no longer leave the control of the armed force to the cruellest enemies of the people; that the lives of the people can only be preserved by an officer who has earned the right to merit their confidence, who loves them and is loved by them, that also this officer is sufficiently experienced to lead the public forces and to direct them only against the Country's enemies and not against fellow citizens, it is decided unanimously that Citizen Santerre will be nominated from this moment as provisional Commanding General, due to his patriotism and the important services that he has given to the Revolution.' The meeting then revoked the commands of battalions from the Sections Gravilliers and Poissonnière and authorised all sections to nominate commanders of their choice.

The interrogation then resumed. Huguenin asked Mandat for exact details of the defences of the palace. He replied that there were only some 1,200 men including 600 Swiss, and eight cannons, with 100 National Guards in reserve. He went on to say that he had requested ammunition but had been refused. Historians have suggested that Mandat gave this underestimate of the number of troops defending the Tuileries as a deliberate attempt to mislead and entrap the revolutionaries. Taking into account Mandat's mention of the lack of ammunition, which was vital military information, it seems more likely he did not wish to be accused of grossly exceeding his authority on the number of troops posted to protect the palace. Then Rossignol, another section delegate from Quinze-Vingts, intervened. He was an ex-soldier, jeweller's assistant, and member of the insurrectionary Directorate. He reported that the commander of the National Guards battalion posted outside the Hôtel de Ville had revealed an order signed by Mandat. This was to attack the insurgents in the rear as they passed by on the way to the Tuileries. The commander had given the order to the Chairman of the General Council. After reading it out loud, and having a copy made, Cousin had returned it to the officer concerned. Huguenin promptly turned on Mandat and commanded him to give orders for half the forces defending the palace to withdraw. To his credit Mandat refused.

A certified copy of Mandat's order dated 9 August to the commander of the battalion at the Hôtel de Ville was brought to the meeting. It said: 'The Commanding General orders the commander of the National Guards battalion on duty outside the Hôtel de Ville, to scatter the column of troops marching to the palace, in conjunction with the Gendarmerie, whether foot or horse, by attacking from behind. (Signed) Mandat.' The delegates promptly ordered Mandat's arrest and he was sent to the prison cells located within the Town Hall. The legally constituted General Council tried to intervene. They pointed out that only justices of the peace had power to make arrests, which must be carried out by due process. Manuel responded by signing the order. It must have been around 6.30 a.m. The time had come to terminate the moderate-dominated General Council. It seems probable that the insurrectionists had just learned Santerre had started his advance. Moreover, the number of sections represented at the meeting chaired by Huguenin could have now reached 50 per cent of the total. It was certainly recorded at 7 a.m. that delegates from 28 out of 48 sections formed the new insurrectionary Commune.

Huguenin entered the Council Chamber accompanied by armed men and drew the text of a carefully phrased resolution from his pocket. This copybook example of illegality dressed up as legality with its lawyer's convoluted phrasing was as follows: 'The Meeting of Delegates from a majority of the Sections, united with the full authority to save the public interest, have decreed that the first measure required by the public welfare, is to take possession of all the powers delegated by the Commune, and to deprive the General Staff [National Guards] of the woeful influence it has exercised until this moment on the destiny of Liberty. Considering that this can only take place in as much as the Municipality, which can only act according to established procedures, would need to be suspended provisionally from its functions, it is resolved that the General Council of the Commune shall be so suspended, but that the Mayor and the Procureur Général of the Commune, and the sixteen executive officers should continue their administrative functions.' It was signed by Huguenin and Martin, respectively chairman and secretary of the putschist gathering. The duly elected members of the General Council were advised that their suspension was necessary as they were bound by legality, which the revolutionaries needed to ignore. The authority for this was the 'People', united in the Paris sections.

Councillors protested against Huguenin's decree, but were told that when the 'People' revolt, they withdraw their delegated authority to use it themselves. They considered refusing to accept their dismissal, pending an appeal to the

National Assembly. But they were threatened with armed force provided by some of the revolutionary sections, of which Mauconseil was one. It must be assumed that by this time the National Guards unit posted outside the Hôtel de Ville had been neutralised. The red flag used to signal the declaration of martial law on the Champ de Mars on 17 July 1791 was seized. The radicals showed that they had avenged their humiliation at the hands of the politically moderate Municipality on that fateful day. After a short interval, the legal councillors found themselves herded out of the Chamber and replaced by the section delegates. Three representatives of the legitimate Municipality hastened first to the Tuileries and then on to the National Assembly to report and object to the diktat.

The first act of the new council was to have a roll call. The eighty-two delegates were made up of constitutional priests, lawyers, actors, writers, artisans, and even well-to-do bourgeois who had retained the reputation of ardent 'patriots'. It also included the infamous journalist Hébert who was to become a major revolutionary figure. Although there were a number of moderates among the delegates, they could be expected to acquiesce as usual to radical intimidation. The new rulers busied themselves with taking over the reins of power. Later that morning it was decreed that Mandat should be transferred to the Abbaye prison. The most plausible time would be towards 10.30 a.m., when news would have arrived of the initially successful Swiss counter-attack and momentarily the Hôtel de Ville might be considered insecure. No chances were taken. As he was led down the steps of the Hôtel de Ville, he was shot through the head, it is believed by Rossignol. Mandat's body was then hacked and stabbed in full view of his son and thrown into the Seine close by.

After passing by the Tuileries, the delegation of ousted members of the Municipality reached the National Assembly shortly after the departure of Dejoly and Champion. The following account is taken from the issue of the newspaper *Journal des Débats et Decréts*, reporting on the Assembly's proceedings up to 9 a.m. on the 10th which would seem to have escaped the self-censorship suffered by the next issue. The spokesman for the ousted Municipality, probably Desmousseux, announced that anarchy had arrived, and there was now a dual municipality. He described how Mandat had been seized by the meeting of section delegates. He brought with him a copy of the decree deposing the General Council and read it out to the National Assembly. He remarked that Mandat had been arrested without due process until Manuel, who he may not have realised was hand in glove with the insurgents, had signed the warrant. They had then committed an illegal act by sending a force of National Guards to seize the Arsenal under pretence that it was under attack. It is not too much to say that here was invented the blueprint of the modern revolutionary coup d'état.

The report of the municipal representatives promptly started a debate, the urgency of which was reinforced by news that insurgent forces had reached the Carrousel. The right-wing constitutionalist deputy, Dalmas, who after the success of the insurrection hid in Rouen until the end of the Terror, demanded that the National Assembly annul the decree deposing the legally elected General Council of the Commune and that it be re-established in its functions. 'It is not because our enemies wish to force us by these criminal manoeuvres to allow anarchy to rule, that we must legalise it. This illegal act of the Paris Sections will bring joy to

Coblenz [the royalist émigrés]. If this city [Paris] is discontented with the Municipal Council, it could complain to the Legislative Body, for what prevents our enemies from placing in the Municipal Council those sold out to them? Let us maintain the law if we wish it to be respected; courage and principles will save the country.' Thuriot, Danton's accomplice, tried to halt the debate on this issue by demanding to return to the matter of sending a delegation to the palace to assist the king. 'It is not', he added, 'by violent measures that you bring back the people; it is by such means that in the past one has succeeded in antagonising them.' The reporter mentioned that this observation met with murmurs of disapproval. Several members demanded to speak. 'It is not the moment,' cried Monsieur Cambon, 'to give oneself up to discussion. The public interest is at risk. It is not a matter of knowing who specifically stands to lose. In a moment of crisis, such as that where we are now, all divisions must end. Let us reunite ourselves; let us give to the executive power, that is the [legal] Municipal Authority, the power to give the law the force that is necessary. If the Municipality is not in the position to respond to your wishes, it is necessary to change it. In a word, messieurs, let us take definite measures to save the public interest.' Monsieur Voysin supported the proposal to annul the decree made by the section delegates. 'At least,' he added, 'I have done my duty, I have acquitted my conscience. May this situation not justify my fears!'

The Girondin Vergniaud, who was presiding, failed to support a motion for the restoration of the legal General Council of the Commune, or alternative measures. He might have been distracted by having to consider three major issues at the same time: that is, sending a deputation to the palace, providing a refuge for the king, and now the expulsion of the legal Municipal Council. Political indecision and weakness is a fairer explanation. A member reverted to the debate on sending a delegation of deputies to the palace. He said that the matter was pressing, and there was no time to lose. The Jacobin Choudieu intervened to say his electors had not chosen him to take part in delegations, but to remain at his post in the Assembly. A Monsieur Emmery agreed, but said a place

The Girondin leader Vergniaud (1752–93) presiding over the National Assembly. He failed to react to news of the takeover of the Paris Commune, and later presented the decree setting aside the king. Note the president's bell.

Deputy Cambon (1752–1820) tried to intervene against the takeover of the legitimate Municipality of Paris by the insurgents. He was ignored by Vergniaud who was presiding over the sitting.

must be found in the Assembly precincts for safeguarding the royal family. At that moment, there was further distraction with the news that a number of people who had been arrested nearby were about to be lynched, accused of being a patrol of counter-revolutionaries. The Assembly instructed the commander of its guard to intervene. On his way to the guardhouse, where the prisoners were being kept, he was briefly held up by a person armed with a musket and bayonet, and wearing civilian clothes. Reporting this incident to the Assembly, the commander said: 'I told him I was going to the guardhouse in the alley. I was followed there by a crowd. I found our guardhouse had been stormed, and someone had dismissed the soldiers who were in it. I do not know where they are.'

Another deputy rose to say that he had seen a head on a pike in the Cour de Manège. He asked in the name of humanity that a serious effort be made to save further victims. There were murmurs of horror in the Assembly. Deputy Cambon, who was to manage the finances of France during the Reign of Terror and to clash with Robespierre in the Convention on his last day in power, rose again to insist that a motion about the Commune be put to the vote. Vergniaud ignored him. Ideological sympathy with revolutionaries may have left him undecided whether they should be confronted or not. Besides, did the Assembly have the physical means? He signalled for Deputy Laporte to speak on the pressing but safer issue of receiving the King within the National Assembly. This was perhaps the last real chance to take resolute action to save the Constitution. Over the next hour or so, the National Assembly let time slip through its fingers without confronting the subversion of order and legality. When fighting haphazardly broke out between the insurgents and the Swiss, the resultant indignation over French casualties rendered any intervention increasingly unrealistic. Yet, if Vergniaud had but known, henceforth the Paris Commune was to belong to his faction's political rivals. In some nine months' time, the forces of the Commune would be brutally used by the Jacobins to bring about the political destruction of the Girondins, leading in due course to their execution. Vergniaud's passage to the guillotine began at this very moment.

CHAPTER 9

Decision

When he arrived back with the king from the Tuileries garden, Liancourt sought out his friend Charles de Chabot, with whom he was sharing a room at the palace. He was unable to find him. Someone told him that a column of pikes was advancing with the Marseillais at their head, and he decided to see for himself. He crossed the courtyard and went through the Swiss officers' quarters in the Hôtel de Brionne, where he left his sword. It would have been dangerous to be found armed in civilian clothes. He passed on to the Place du Carrousel, went behind a small mounted unit belonging to the Maréchausée du Département, and arrived at the exit which went under the long Galerie du Louvre on to the quay bordering the Seine. He distinctly saw the column advancing slowly towards him along the river embankment. It appeared very dense. He returned to pick up his sword and relate what he had seen. The evidence strongly suggests the king finished his review at about 7 a.m. Thus, one can establish a plausible time of towards 7.30 a.m. for the arrival of the first insurgent units on the Place du Carrousel.

Jean-Baptiste Cléry also witnessed the approach of the Marseillais. He mentioned that since the Tuileries did not appear to be in immediate danger of attack, he left the palace to walk along the river towards the Pont Neuf. He gave no time but it must have been somewhat earlier than Liancourt's sortie. He wrote: 'I again went out, and walked along the quays as far as the Pont Neuf, everywhere meeting bands of armed men, whose evil intentions were very evident; some had pikes, others had pitchforks, hatchets, or iron bars. The battalion of the Marseillais was marching in the greatest order, with their cannon and lighted matches, inviting the people to follow them and to take part, as they said, in dislodging the tyrant and proclaiming his deposition to the National Assembly.' He hastened back to the palace along the river embankment and witnessed the recalcitrant battalions, which had chanted anti-royalist slogans on the Water Terrace, streaming in disorder out of the Queen's Gate opposite the Pont Royal. Cléry noted that the troops in these units were by no means all hostile to the king. He wrote: 'Sorrow was visible on the countenances of most of them, and several were heard to say, "we swore this morning to defend the King, and in the moment of his greatest danger we are deserting him". Others, in the interests of the conspirators, were abusing and threatening their fellow soldiers whom they forced away. Thus did the well disposed suffer themselves to be overawed by the seditious, and that culpable weakness, which had all along been productive of the evils of the Revolution, gave birth to the calamities of this day.' Cléry's eloquent observations might well form the leitmotiv for 10 August, when moderates throughout Paris, who had little wish to dethrone their king, allowed themselves to be cowed by the vociferous and menacing agitation of the revolutionaries.

The force seen by Liancourt and Cléry would have consisted of at least 450 Marseillais, allowing for sick and guards left at the barracks, and nearly 200 Brestois fédérés. These were supported by the Saint-Marcel National Guards battalion from the Gobelins Section in the Faubourg Saint-Marceau consisting of 200 men and two cannons under the command of Alexandre. Together with a number of pikemen enrolled during the past two weeks by the revolutionaries in the Section Théâtre Français, the total which stationed itself on the Carrousel was probably at the most some 1,100 men. This would have included the gunners and a detachment remaining from the battalion which left the Cour Royale precipitately after the king's review.

The insurgent column had brushed aside the National Guards battalions of the Grands-Augustins and Henri IV guarding respectively the Pont Saint-Michel and Pont Neuf. The Saint-Marcel battalion had received strict instructions not to fire first on other Frenchmen. The distaste for fratricidal bloodshed was not unique to the king but was a common factor throughout Paris, reinforced by the knowledge that death was the legal penalty for inciting civil war. It was the general intention of the insurrectionists to succeed with minimum force and to rely on 'patriotic' sentiments and revolutionary agitation to dissolve opposition.

The Brestois commander, Desbouillons, described his participation in events in a letter dated the next day. He wrote that they arrived on the Place du Carrousel, drew up in battle order, and then remained inactive. He continued: 'There was no formal plan, no recognised overall commander. With several of my comrades, I did everything possible to bring the commanders of the different units together, so that they might choose a commanding general. The individual commanders met, but our efforts were in vain, as they separated again almost immediately. Without having a definite plan we knew we had to attack the Tuileries palace filled with armed men and behind closed gates. . . . However, we continued to remain inactive; we were only in small numbers on the Place du Carrousel, and we did not know if the other side was in greater strength.' Fortunately for the insurgents, inability to identify and clarify the real political issues at stake, to motivate the troops and prepare them for offensive action, left the defence in no position to take the initiative.

The size of the force immediately defending the Tuileries when the first organised insurgent troops arrived is debatable. It was probably less than 2,500, consisting of some 800 Swiss, a guestimate of 1,250 or so National Guards, 200–plus former Gardes du Corps and Constitutional Guards, 50 or so Gendarmerie à Pied under Colonel Carle in the Cour Royale, and 100 dismounted Gendarmerie à Cheval stationed in the stables by the Cour des Suisses. The major uncertainty is the number of National Guards. Captain Durler and another Swiss officer estimated in all 2,000 reinforcements arrived during the night. If we assume the likely figure of some 400–500 National Guards being on duty before midnight when reinforcements started to arrive, then Durler's figure accords well with Peltier's detail of 2,400 National Guards being present at 6 a.m. This figure probably excludes the disordered troops who arrived in the Cour Royale as the review there was ending and were promptly sent to the Water Terrace. Weber mentions that defections started as early as 4 a.m. According to Cléry, desertions increased markedly after 7 a.m. It seems likely that when the Marseillais arrived, National Guards strength at the Tuileries was well below 2,000. Cléry suggested only 400 to 500, but this seems on the low side, and possibly referred only to troops inside the palace. After 7 a.m., there is no mention of any significantly sized units except in the Cour Royale.

The main strength of the Gendarmerie, which was devoted to providing defence in depth and not strictly part of the forces directly defending the palace itself, has not been included in the above totals. The bulk of the Gendarmerie was posted on the other side of the Louvre, that is some 600, with additional units of 100 men each guarding the Pont Royal and the Place de Grève by the Hôtel de Ville. There was a small mounted unit of 25 men on the Place du Carrousel which was noted by Liancourt. All the Gendarmerie ultimately defected. There is also uncertainty over the number of cannons available for the defence. Peltier gives an overall figure of eleven. The number given by different witnesses ranges from three to six in the Cour Royale, with four very likely the correct figure, and two to five on the garden terrace by the central entrance. There is also mention of single cannons at the extremes of the palace terrace and in the Cour Marsan.

The other major prong of the revolutionary advance coming from the Faubourg Saint-Antoine had further to travel. Santerre had started off at around 6 a.m. with three National Guards battalions, accompanied by revolutionary levies. The Montmartre battalion was waiting to rendezvous with him at the Place Bastille. He divided his command into three parts. One to protect his left flank marched along the quays of the Seine to head off possible attacks from the battalions of the Ile Saint-Louis and the university area of Saint-Etienne du Mont and the Thermes-de-Julien on the Left Bank. The right flank was to protect the central column against potentially hostile forces from west central Paris. His principal force marched down the Rue Saint-Antoine. It continued along the line of the current Rue de Rivoli, which did not then exist, eventually joining the Rue Saint-Honoré. About 7 a.m., Santerre was advised that he was replacing Mandat as the new commander of the Paris National Guards. He was reluctant to accept this responsibility. Eventually, he agreed to take on the position provisionally for six weeks and handed over his operational command to François Joseph Westermann, aged forty-one, who came from Molsheim near Strasbourg in Alsace. A former soldier, he was to campaign successfully against the Vendéans in 1793, unlike his superior, Santerre. He was guillotined with Danton in April 1794.

Santerre set off for the Hôtel de Ville where he had been summoned to issue instructions to all the National Guards battalions to bring them over to the revolutionary side. He also set in hand measures for preserving order and protecting key institutions and commercial property which might be tempting to pillage. It was too late to protect gun shops. These were systematically looted of their weapons by unarmed citizens who wished to participate in the insurrection, or indulge in murder and robbery. The handover of Santerre's command probably delayed his columns by half an hour or more. Certainly, these forces advanced cautiously and only reached the Carrousel towards 9 a.m. The size of this force was grossly exaggerated by contemporaries. It may have been not more than 1,500 after detachments. For instance, a substantial unit had been seconded to guard the mayor at the Mairie, to ensure he was not rescued by the Girondins. A larger number would make it difficult to explain the ability of the insurgents to abandon the Cour Royale and Place du Carrousel rapidly when the Swiss counter-attacked.

Meanwhile the arrival of the Marseillais and other units began to affect morale among the civilians and defending troops at the palace. Dejoly wrote: 'I had thought that after all the day would end with negotiations but now I lost all hope.' The desertion of National Guards increased. They had the ready excuse to leave the palace in search of breakfast. As local militia, they were expected to provide their own nourishment or use public eating places. Efforts were improvised within the palace to try and provide food on the spot. A more sinister explanation for defection may arise from an incident related by Leroux. He was accosted by a man who claimed to be an official representative of the insurrectionary Section of the Tuileries. He showed Leroux one of the laissez-passers that he and Borie had issued earlier on to two National Guards for keeping in touch with the Hôtel de Ville. The man asked Leroux to authenticate his signature. When Leroux asked how he had obtained the laissez-passer, he was told to keep silent if he did not wish the original bearer to come to harm. Leroux weakly consented to collaborate, even agreeing that he would be unable to identify the guardsman to whom he had first given the document. He failed to comment on the obvious fact that the revolutionaries were inserting an agent within the palace defences.

In the meantime, the defenders took a number of unhelpful initiatives. Langlade proposed that a deputation should be formed from units in the courtyard to find out the insurgents' intentions. This idea was accepted by senior officers, and a sergeant-major and two grenadiers were selected. They returned with subversive propaganda. They stated that the armed gathering on the Carrousel consisted of fellow citizens representing all the sections of Paris, who wished to counter the Court's plots and to disarm the Swiss. Dupont de Nemours, a well known economist, one of the king's occasional advisers and a National Guards battalion commander, was well aware that there were mixed feelings in Paris over the provincial fédérés, including the Marseillais. He drafted a petition for the National Assembly urging that they should be made to leave immediately. This was promptly covered with signatures by National Guards of the battalions Saint-Roche and Palais Royal, who had no wish to enter into combat with the fearsome Marseillais. Needless to say, there was no time to present this petition. Foreign Minister Bigot de Sainte-Croix took the opportunity to release the printed statement he had been preparing since the previous afternoon on the dastardly intentions of the revolutionaries towards the royal family. Nothing more was heard of it.

The king briefly saw the queen and his ministers in the Council Chamber after his precipitate retirement through the garden, and then left to change his clothes and have his hair dressed. After he went, the debate dragged on about the best course of action. The discussion was rudely interrupted by news brought by the First Substitute Procureur Général and two municipal officers from the Hôtel de Ville. They announced that the Municipal Council had been overthrown and that the revolutionaries were marching on the Tuileries, including the dreaded Marseillais. Roederer immediately seized the opportunity to press once again the necessity of escorting the royal family to the National Assembly. The sceptical Dubouchage replied that the threats experienced by the king showed the garden could not be crossed safely, so it would be better to remain where they were. Roederer then offered to go with his Directorate to the National Assembly to ask for help and advice. It did not seem to strike him, or if it did he kept it to himself, that the Commune was answerable to the Department within the law, and that the illegal overthrow of its General Council could have provided grounds for suspending the Commune as a whole and taking over the government of Paris.

Leroux related that he and Borie waylaid the Directorate when it was setting out in order to ask its opinion and authorisation for proclaiming the statutory right of self-defence to the troops. They believed the situation was desperate but their duty required them to try and maintain the law if possible. They found the Directorate in favour of their project. It seems more logical, however, that Roederer rather than the municipal officers took the initiative in this matter. While the members of the Department carried on towards the National Assembly, Borie and Leroux went to a guardhouse situated at the side of the Cour Royale. They carefully checked the legal position, reading all the relevant articles from the law books they were carrying. It was as if by invoking the law in detail they might make it prevail. Leroux wrote pedantically in his memoir: 'Our duty, in the situation in which we found ourselves, and the manner of carrying it out, were laid down in the statute of 3 August 1791 in articles 13, 20, 21, and 22; and followed by articles 26, 27, and 28. We had no need to pay attention to articles 32, 33, and 36, as the Directorate of the Department was present, and we were acting under their eyes, and following its advice, and in any case it would always have been in a position to arrest us if we had acted unlawfully.'

Seemingly satisfied that even if the palace might prove indefensible their legal position was invulnerable to attack, they summoned Lachesnaye, and in accordance with article 22 they presented him with the following document: 'We, Municipal Officers, require, by virtue of the law against armed gatherings, given in Paris the 3rd of August 1791, that Monsieur Lachesnaye, Legion Commander, Commanding General of the National Guards, constitute the regular troops [the Swiss], the National Gendarmerie, or the National Guards necessary for repulsing the armed gathering menacing the palace, and to repulse force with force, and we have signed: J.-J. Leroux, Philibert Borie.' In fact, as will be discussed, this rigmarole was very likely an elaborate subterfuge to protect the mayor.

As for Lachesnaye, he seems to have been feeling thoroughly discouraged. Around this time he met Viard stationed at the head of the Great Stairs. 'I was unable,' reported Viard, 'to obtain any orders from Monsieur Lachesnaye, who replied that I should leave him in peace as he had a headache. He seemed [presumably afterwards] no longer to be at his post [headquarters], which decided me to act with considerable circumspection.' Lachesnaye was now accompanying the two municipal officers around the palace courtyards facing the Place du Carrousel.

Halfway towards the National Assembly, by the Café Holtot on the Feuillants' terrace, Roederer and his Council Directorate met Champion and Dejoly returning from their unsuccessful mission. They were told that they had barely received an audience. In any case, there was no quorum for passing a resolution. Fearing to be

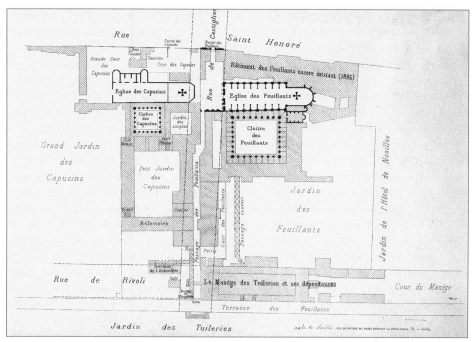

Plan of the Manège and the Convent of the Feuillants. The steps from the garden and the gateway to the Terrace of the Feuillants can be seen at the bottom left centre. To the left of the gateway is the Bureau des Inspecteurs where twelve Swiss officers were held. The narrow passageway leads up to the Rue St Honoré via the Cour des Feuillants opposite the church where the Swiss were imprisoned.

cut off by a gathering hostile crowd, Roederer and his companions decided to withdraw to the palace. They were stopped at the entrance to the Clock Tower by some gunners, who asked whether they would be obliged to fire on their brothers. Roederer replied that they only needed to fire if they were fired on first, in which case those who had fired on them would no longer be their brothers. The gunners suggested that he should repeat this advice to their colleagues in the Cour Royale, who were tormented by the idea that they would have to fire on the 'People'.

It is to Leroux and Roederer that we owe a clear picture of events in the courtyards between the palace and the Carrousel, where the armed insurgents were now drawn up in some strength. 'Conforming to article 21,' wrote Leroux, 'we went with Monsieur Lachesnaye into the Cour Marsan in order to read the order we had drafted to the assembled soldiers, of which each platoon [post] was composed of National Guards and Swiss.' Units were mixed except in the Cour Royale, where the Swiss and French were drawn up separately. 'Our intention was to go successively into the Cour Royale, the Cour des Princes, then through the Vestibule on to the garden terrace where more troops were stationed. While I was undertaking the proclamation in the Cour Royale, we were advised that citizens [armed revolutionaries] assembled in the Carrousel were seeking to make a petition. Monsieur Borie went there while I continued giving my instructions.' In fact, Borie did not go into the Place du Carrousel, but stayed with Roederer at the wicket gate in the Porte Royale talking to a small deputation of insurgents.

When Roederer entered the Cour Royale, he found the National Guards battalion of the Filles Saint-Thomas, which had recently been ordered into the courtyard from the garden terrace, ranged on the right. On the left was a substantial unit of Swiss, while the gunners with their four cannons were in the centre between the two units. He noticed the main gate was now closed. He went up to the gunners and told them not to attack, but to stand firm and make a strong defence. One gunner, tall and fine looking according to Roederer, looked him fully in the face and asked whether he would still be there when the fighting began. Roederer claimed to have replied that he would not be behind the guns, but in front in order to die first. This vainglorious response annoyed the gunner, who withdrew the charge from his gun and put out his slow match.

Langlade, in his account, reported that Roederer came into the Cour Royale but first addressed other units on the law of legitimate defence before coming to his guns. When he read the law to Langlade and asked if he would defend, Langlade replied he would do so provided Roederer ordered the opening of the main gate and addressed the insurgents outside. Roederer promised to do so. Instead, together with Borie, he harangued them from the safety of the wicket gate. For some reason, Langlade made no mention of unloading his guns at this juncture, although this action is related by other reports. This is surprising in view of Langlade's tendency throughout his account to show that his heart lay with the revolutionaries. The earlier accusation of cowardice may still have rankled when he made his report two days later. Confirming Roederer's account, Leroux wrote: 'I was at the end of the semi-circle [of Swiss troops] drawn up on the Cour Marsan side of the courtyard, when the Directorate and Monsieur the Procureur Général Syndic returned from the National Assembly.' We know, of course, they had not gone there after meeting Dejoly and Champion on the way. 'They [Roederer and the Directorate] were witnesses of two of my readings', Leroux continued. 'I went to make one to the gunners who occupied the middle of the courtyard, but we had difficulty in getting them together. In response, despite remarks made by Monsieur Roederer, they unloaded their cannons in our presence.'

'Monsieur Borie returned from the Carrousel,' Leroux went on to say, 'and confirmed the wish of the citizens on the Carrousel to make a petition. We stopped making our proclamation, the great gate was partly opened, and seven or eight citizens entered without weapons saying they wished to require the National Assembly to decree the dethronement of the king. Monsieur Roederer pointed out that the proper path to the National Assembly did not lie through the palace.' In Roederer's own account, he mentioned that he spoke to one of them, an insurgent gunner officer who told him that they had twelve cannons in the Place du Carrousel, which impressed him considerably. Roederer detailed a serious conversation. The insurgent officer explained: 'We do not wish to do harm to the King. We wish only to secure him. However, it is not to restrict his liberty. That is not what we wish. On the contrary, we understand that he must be free, but the conspirators at the palace must remain afraid.' The claim to have twelve cannons was possibly a bluff. It is likely that the insurgents then had only two-thirds that number.

'But we magistrates', Roederer replied, 'have to be obedient to the law. It forbids armed gatherings. Do you wish to send twenty persons without arms to the palace? You are the masters, and we cannot grant you less,' he added ingratiatingly. 'Certainly,' replied the officer, 'we do not wish to do you any harm. We are all citizens together, Monsieur Roederer, and we know you to be such.' 'Ah well, in God's name, be reasonable and withdraw,' Roederer retorted. The insurgent officer answered that he could not make a decision himself and asked Roederer and Borie to enter the Carrousel. They demurred because they were concerned that they might be detained. Borie countered that the officer should bring some people to the wicket gate. The officer said that he would try to bring his six commanders.

The gate was closed and hammering recommenced. Some insurgents climbed up on top of the wall and started to try and make contact with the National Guards stationed within the courtyard. Roederer consulted with Beaumetz, the senior member of his Directorate. It was agreed that while the Directorate waited there in case negotiators arrived from the revolutionary forces in the Carrousel, Roederer would return to the palace and explain to the king the necessity of going with his family to the National Assembly. Nevertheless, Roederer could not resist lingering in the hope of playing a leading role in meaningful negotiations. In his account Dejoly, who must have seen what was happening in the distance out of a window, mentioned Leroux' and Borie's activities there, but reserved his main praise for Roederer who he believed alone had spoken to the insurgents. 'One must praise Roederer,' he wrote. 'He did everything possible. Although at length he was not able to triumph over the anger of the people, he nevertheless gained half an hour's respite.' Dejoly was wrong. The insurgents had no intention of making a serious move until Westermann's forces arrived.

Leroux continued: 'Monsieur Borie left a second time to speak to the people assembled in the Carrousel. During this time, I went to a little barred window in the guardhouse at the left of the Royal Gate. Several fédérés and citizens armed with pikes and other weapons demanded that the gate be opened and that the royal family be handed over to them. They protested that their intentions were honourable. I wanted to caution them in the name of the law, but I only made them angry. They started to make insulting remarks, gestures, and menaces which made me realise that the weak and widely spaced bars would not guarantee me against their assaults. Already they were thrusting their pikes through the window, and soon they would have touched my badge of office and the person who wore it. I left the guardhouse for the courtyard.' Leroux went on to claim that it was he rather than Roederer who took the initiative about returning to the palace. He spoke to Roederer and members of the Directorate, saying that he believed an attack was imminent, and that the only way to save the King and his family, and prevent the spilling of blood, was to take them to the National Assembly. This view was generally accepted. He asked Roederer to try to persuade the king, while he would explain the proposal to the ministers. Leroux briefed Borie on what he had discussed with the representatives of the Department.

However, Leroux likewise did not return to the palace immediately. He noticed that the National Guards detachment on the south side of the Cour Royale was in disorder. Several National Guards exclaimed that they were not in sufficient number to resist. Leroux was of the same opinion. He said aloud that it would be folly to seek to oppose such a considerable and well-armed force. He complained about the unfortunate obligation of having to be obedient to the law, which had compelled him to proclaim a dangerous order. A member of the citizen militia said that it was all very well for him to agree with them about the danger, but he was able to retire to a position of safety. Leroux now felt a little ashamed about the panic he was creating, and replied: 'No, Messieurs, no, my brothers, if it comes to the worst, and in support of the law you form up in columns, I will march at the head of one of these columns. If you remain in a semicircle I will place myself at your centre. My post will be where peril is most certain. But I repeat, it seems to me senseless to think of resisting. I only ask you to stand firm a little while longer. I hope that we will be able to persuade the King to withdraw to the National Assembly. Once he is there, resistance will become pointless, as much as it is already dangerous and murderous.' It is not impossible that Leroux inserted this speech into his account to prove he was not in favour of resistance, despite having promulgated the law to that effect. He then left the Cour Royale to find the ministers. It seems Borie and Lachesnaye were left to continue, in view of what Leroux may have just said, their now rather pointless visits to the troops. In the next courtyard, the Cour des Princes, Baudin, an under-lieutenant in the grenadiers of the Notre-Dame battalion, later reported that a municipal officer came to harangue them about repelling force with force. He had scathingly replied that with only five men and no cartridges, it was impossible to use force.

'In effect,' Leroux wrote in his graphic account, 'I returned to the King's Apartments looking for the Ministers. I found them in the King's Bedchamber, which I entered after first having told some senior officers I met in the Council Chamber to assemble a secure escort for the King on the garden terrace or in the Vestibule, as he would probably be going to the National Assembly. The King was seated between the alcove where his bed was placed and a chest of drawers which was near the entrance. Around him were the Queen, the Royal Prince, the Princess Royal, Madame Elizabeth, Madame de Lamballe, Madame de Tourzel and the Ministers. Several other people came in at the same time as myself.' Other eyewitnesses only mention a discussion between Louis and the better-known Roederer, but Leroux' account is backed by Peltier who wrote that a municipal officer saw the king first. Peltier only reported one item of conversation, a question from Dejoly. Leroux was asked what the people wanted. The municipal officer replied: 'Dethronement.'

The king, his family, and his ministers would appear to have moved back next door to the Council Chamber, where it would be more appropriate to make a decision. A little time before, Weber had left the Cour Royale to see how Marie Antoinette was faring. He found her holding the young dauphin in her arms. She protested that he had left his post. Despite her attempts to discourage him, he eventually succeeded in persuading eighteen of his comrades to join him in the palace. They took up a position in the Council Chamber where they were welcomed

Duchesse de Tourzel (1749–1832) was the royal children's governess and left useful details concerning the fall of the Monarchy. The portrait would seem to show her later in life. She was forty-three in 1792.

by the group of armed gentlemen already there. A spokesman of the latter declared that they would jointly defend their majesties to their last breath. The queen entered the Council Chamber, reported Madame Tourzel, where she saw some twenty grenadiers of the National Guards on one side of the room and a group of gentlemen in civilian attire, former officers of the disbanded King's Bodyguard and his Constitutional Guard, on the other side. The grenadiers were, of course, Weber's group, and knowing their loyalty the queen took the opportunity to make an emotional appeal. 'Gentlemen, all that you hold dear, your wives and children, depend upon your resistance; our interests are one.' Then, pointing to the former officers of the King's Guard, she added: 'You cannot distrust these brave men, who will share your danger, and will defend you with their last breath.' Madame Tourzel said the grenadiers were moved to tears and swore to die if necessary in defence of their majesties.

Leroux continued: 'I made a report to the King on what I had done, observed, and understood, and ended by advising him to withdraw with his family to the heart of the National Assembly. I assured him that it was the only option available to him. There was not even time to discuss it, for perhaps within a half an hour the palace would be attacked with cannon, and this attack would engender resistance, which would only further exasperate the insurgents. In the disorder which would necessarily follow, nobody would be able to answer for the lives of the King and the royal family. It was true that they were not specifically menaced, but an unforeseen incident might place them in danger. In effect, they ought to leave on the spot.'

Leroux wrote that the king asked him whether he was certain. He reiterated that it was the only course of action to take. To say otherwise would be to betray him. The queen then intervened and suggested there might be drawbacks in putting themselves in the hands of the National Assembly. Leroux replied that it was the only institution respected at that moment by the people. He then appealed to her emotions by offering to take personal charge of her son. She accepted his offer. Overwhelmed by the situation, she took hold of her husband's hand and rubbed it against her eyes which were wet with tears. The king broke down too, followed by the dauphin and Madame Elizabeth. Leroux said there was hardly a single onlooker who was not obliged to wipe their eyes.

The 26-year-old Liancourt continued his story after returning from his reconnaissance:

> While going up to the King's Apartments, I found the Swiss drawn up evenly on the Great Stairs, their officers at their head, the National Guards in good enough order in the antechambers; and then all the gentlemen ranked three in depth in the room of the Oeil de Boeuf, the majority having drawn their arms. They believed themselves to be there to die in front of the King, and at his feet. How I felt relieved in this desperate situation to join such a force. Perhaps our valour would triumph over number? I did not know, at that moment, either who was commanding us, or what were the plans of defence. Ashamed at not yet having taken my place, I joined the unit nearest to me. My part of our little force was sent [after some time] into the gallery [des Carraches] situated between the King's and the Queen's apartments.
>
> We passed by the King and the Queen who were standing at the door of the Council Chamber. [Presumably they were about to enter with Leroux and the ministers]. We were placed against the wall in the gallery facing the windows opposite. Soon a detachment of National Guards arrived and drew up with their backs to the windows, leaving a passage between us. They said that they regarded us as their comrades and would support us. We responded almost person to person, saying unanimously that we had been annoyed by the suspicions that the National Guards had entertained against us, that we never had any other plans but the defence of the King, and that we would join ourselves with pleasure to all those Frenchmen who shared our love for the King. We embraced each other as comrades.

Liancourt's unit, numbering some 110, was under the orders of Lieutenant General Vioménil, with Major General d'Hervilly as second in command. The other half of the small aristocratic force, save for the small detachment in the Council Chamber, remained in the Oeil de Boeuf, under the command of Lieutenant General Puységur and Major General Pont de l'Abbé. The French Army still retained its Ancien Régime superfluity of senior officers. In 1789 there was one general per 157 ordinary soldiers and NCOs.

Liancourt strained his ears in the gallery to hear what was going on in the Council Chamber. The billiards room was in between but the connecting doors were wide open. 'I heard the King and Queen speaking loudly in the Council Chamber,' he said, 'without being able to understand what they were saying. Someone cried, "Vive le Roi", and we repeated it while drawing our weapons. The National Guards loaded their muskets. We were given the order not to act unless the bandits reached the room we were in. Our unit was divided into platoons of fifteen men, each platoon being commanded by a senior officer; mine was by the Chevalier d'Allonville, former governor of the first Dauphin [who died in 1789]. Monsieur d'Hervilly went ceaselessly from our position to the Council

Chamber to bring us orders. Hardly had we been five minutes in our position, when I saw the National Guards facing us start to turn round, and look out of the windows where they saw the tops of the pikes of the Sans-culottes over the wall and buildings fencing off the courtyards. That sight appeared to unsettle them. They observed that the formation bristled impressively.' The pikes were particularly intimidating for loyalist National Guards supplied with very limited ammunition. An unloaded musket, even with a bayonet, would be a poor match for the longer reach of the pike, although training would make a difference. Pikes were in the hands of poorer people, who were feared on social grounds. A Swiss soldier interrogated after the battle mentioned that his officers had instructed him and his comrades to concentrate their fire on those armed with pikes.

'Worried by the dejection that started to grow among the National Guards,' Liancourt wrote, 'I left my position to go and ask the King for an order to close the lower half of the shutters. The remaining half would continue to provide us with enough light. When entering the Council Chamber I found my friend Charles de Chabot. He said softly in my ear: "It's finished. We will be killed." I saw the King, the Queen, and the royal family standing near the desk. Roederer was persuading them to go to the National Assembly.'

Eventually, the Procureur Général Syndic with his Directorate had left the Cour Royale. Roederer typically ignored Leroux in his own account. He wrote that he tried to speak to Louis alone. He first asked the courtiers to withdraw, which many did. It seems that Madame Tourzel and possibly Madame Campan remained to witness what happened. He then asked the same thing of the ministers, no doubt concerned about opposition to his proposal. They refused. He had to carry on in their presence, and claimed to have said: 'Sire, Your Majesty has not five minutes to lose. There is no safety except in the National Assembly. The opinion of the Department is that you go immediately. You do not have sufficient men in the courtyards to defend the palace, and besides they are not well disposed. The gunners have unloaded their guns.' It is uncertain whether the king was irritated by hearing the same story twice over, but he was sufficiently stirred to remonstrate that he had not seen all that many insurgents in the Place du Carrousel. Roederer then pulled out his trump card, the threat of the twelve cannons, and added that an immense mass of people was converging on the Tuileries from the faubourgs. The queen tried to resist the pressure, and so did some of the ministers, although Roederer could depend upon Dejoly's support. It may be here that Marie Antoinette made the famous aside that she wished to be nailed to the walls of the palace rather than go to the Assembly. This is not reported by any of the leading witnesses and was denied by Roederer. He admitted, however, she strongly queried whether they really lacked forces to resist. She sharply rebuked a Monsieur Gerdiot, a member of the Department's Directorate, who tried to intervene on Roederer's behalf. Madame Tourzel said the queen remarked to her husband that it was impossible to abandon the brave men who had come to the palace solely to defend the king.

Roederer's reply to the queen according to Madame Tourzel was minatory: 'If you oppose this measure, you will be responsible, Madame, for the lives of your husband and your children.' She said the queen went silent and experienced such a revulsion of feeling that her face and neck became suffused with colour. Roederer denied he said such words, but it seems very likely he did. Madame Campan also reported the same threat. If she was not present, she was close by and could have heard it directly from Madame Tourzel or others. The Marquis de Ferrières, although he was not at the palace, supported the dauphin's governess in his memoirs. Commenting on Louis' state of mind, he wrote: 'Firm in his principles to consider death without fear when it only threatened himself, he was unable to sustain the prospect when it menaced the Queen and their children.' Weber wrote that Louis was concerned to avoid bloodshed. Dejoly claimed to have made the final exhortation: 'Let us leave and not discuss the matter further. It is honour which commands us. It is the good of the State which requires it. Let us go to the National Assembly; this step should have been taken a long time ago.' It was now around 8.15 a.m. The king made up his mind. Various accounts were given of his acceptance. Roederer and Dejoly both agreed he raised his right hand. Bigot related that Louis said: 'Let us start. Since we are going to the Assembly, there is nothing further to do here.' Dejoly reported a more positive note to his decision. 'Let us go, and give this final token of devotion [presumably to the Constitution], since it is still necessary to do so.' Madame Elizabeth, with typical sisterly solicitude, had the last word. Turning to Roederer, she said: 'Can you guarantee the King's life?' 'Yes, Madame, with my own,' he replied.

CHAPTER 10

Refuge

After making the decision to go the National Assembly, the king and the royal family passed through the State Rooms led by the self-important Roederer who announced: 'The King and his family are going to the National Assembly alone without any following, except the Department, the Ministers, and a guard. Please make way.' In going through the audience chamber called the Oeil de Boeuf, the king removed a hat with a tricolour cockade from the head of a National Guard and placed it on his own, exchanging it for one he was wearing with white feathers. The embarrassed soldier took it off and put it under his arm. It is likely that Louis wished to show solidarity with the National Guards. Madame Tourzel said Roederer tried to sweeten the pill by holding out hope that the royal family's stay in the Manège would be short. She said the queen did not really believe him because of her natural pessimism. However, she pretended to accept his remarks since Liancourt heard her say to her ladies that she would soon see them again back at the palace. The king is also reported to have mentioned returning. It would have been in character for him to make the remark ascribed to him by Madame Tourzel: 'Gentlemen, I beg of you to withdraw and abandon a pointless defence; there is nothing more to be done here for either you or me.' More prosaically, Roederer described the tongue-tied king going round a circle of courtiers mumbling: 'I am going to the National Assembly.' Senior members of his entourage explained that the king was leaving in order to request personally that some deputies come to the Tuileries to disperse the insurgents.

Faced with a situation beyond his capacity to resolve, the fatalistic side of Louis' character would have given him some protection against the agonising emotions that others might have felt. He would have consoled himself with the thought that bloodshed was being avoided and that the responsibility for defending the Constitution, which he saw as deficient, was no longer his concern. If the National Assembly failed to save it, at least he would have the bitter satisfaction of being proved right. What were his immediate political intentions? The issue of dethronement had been raised during Leroux' attempt to persuade the king to withdraw to the Assembly. Liancourt was later told that the king had said that he would accept his dethronement if the Assembly decreed it, although he would not abdicate voluntarily. Knowing the king's resigned character, it seems highly probable that he went to the Assembly that morning with few real hopes of saving his constitutional functions, but with expectation that a delegation from the Assembly could disperse the armed gatherings which threatened the Tuileries.

As they were descending the Great Stairs, the king remembered the royalist gentlemen he was leaving behind. 'What is going to become of all those who remain upstairs?' he asked. Roederer replied: 'Sire, they appear to me to be in civilian clothes. Those who are wearing swords have only to take them off, and leave by the garden.' The king was still having some regrets about his decision. He turned to Roederer for reassurance, repeating the issue he had raised before. 'There do not appear to be a great many people in the Carrousel,' he said. It was too late for backsliding. Roederer reiterated his arguments as if to a slow-witted child. 'Sire,' he replied, 'the people from the faubourgs are about to arrive. All the sections are armed and they have met together at the Town Hall. Moreover, there is not a sufficient number of men, nor a strong enough will, to resist even the present armed force in the Carrousel. Besides, they have twelve cannons.'

The king's repeated observation that there were not many people in the Carrousel deserves examination. The force which had arrived around an hour earlier probably amounted to no more than 1,100 men. Since then, there would have been a trickle of revolutionary adherents, but the main forces from the right bank of the Seine had yet to arrive. Nevertheless, the Place du Carrousel at that time was not particularly extensive, being hemmed in by buildings on all sides which no longer exist, including the palace and its courtyards. An assembly of 1,100 men would have looked relatively impressive in the area concerned. It seems likely the king had looked out on the Carrousel when the insurgents had temporarily redeployed some of their forces out of sight of the palace. This is supported by Peltier who mentioned that around 8 a.m. the insurgents placed cannon in the Rue de l'Echelle and the Rue Saint Niçaise to seal off the Carrousel against the movement of the significant force of unmounted Gendarmerie stationed under the colonnade of the Louvre, towards the Place du Palais Royal. The rank and file of the Gendarmerie were disaffected and this unit was in no position to attack the insurgents.

While still in the Royal Apartments, Leroux argued with Roederer about the right to look after the seven-year-old dauphin. In detailing this almost farcical scene of bourgeois pretension, Leroux recounted: 'Monsieur Roederer also wanted, like me, to carry the royal Prince. "I will carry him on my breast," he said. I reminded the Queen of the promise she had made me, but at the instant I took the hand of the Prince, a person that I had not noticed up to then, and who I presume was his teacher, took hold of him. We started on our progress. It was around 8.30 a.m. I offered my arm to the Queen, telling her that I was unaware of court etiquette, but dressed in my sash of office, it would perhaps be to her advantage that I was her equerry. The Queen accepted my hand only for crossing the Council Chamber. She then let go to take care of her children, which she did not leave off doing until she reached the Assembly.'

'While passing through the apartments, the staircase, and the Vestibule,' Leroux continued, 'I told the troops: "The King is leaving the palace; he will be in safety at the National Assembly. All resistance is useless." It was excessive caution on my part, as Monsieur Lachesnaye, who possessed the only order, that I had signed, was with us and commanded the King's escort.' Leroux' remarks were not only to exonerate himself from encouraging the defence, but to emphasise that Lachesnaye held his authorisation to oppose force with force.

For, at the end of August, the timid Leroux produced a report in four copies of his activities on 10 August, which included the frank admission of responsibility for drafting the order recounted in the previous chapter. Of these copies, he kept one, and sent the remaining three respectively to the Municipality, to the Extraordinary Committee of the National Assembly, and to his Section Committee. This action was tantamount to placing one's head in the lion's den. It seems highly likely that he had been blackmailed into producing his report with the express purpose of exculpating the mayor. By going on public record that he and Borie, after consulting with the Department, were responsible for authorising the use of force to resist force, it may have been hoped to protect the mayor from any embarrassing revelations during the anticipated forthcoming trials of officers who had been at the Tuileries on 10 August. Leroux' pointed mention that Lachesnaye held the *only* order authorising resistance, which was signed by him and Borie, would distract attention from any reference to an earlier authorisation signed by Pétion. All that rigmarole in the previous chapter detailing the relevant clauses in the statute book was to highlight Leroux' and Borie's initiative. A warrant for Leroux' arrest was issued a day later on 1 September. Leroux was not found. Presumably he was allowed to escape. As it turned out, this exercise was unnecessary: with the exception of Bachmann, the officers concerned were given summary rather than formal justice, and the matter of legal instructions from the Municipality to resist was easily suppressed. The historian, however, benefits from Leroux' valuable account.

Weber, who was imprisoned in the same cell as Lachesnaye, stated that the latter held a letter from the Municipality authorising the use of force. Unfortunately, Weber omitted to say who signed it, although he cryptically remarked that the document turned out to be the signal for Lachesnaye's death rather than for his justification. It cannot be ruled out that Leroux' order was a figment. If so, and no doubt as part of his collaboration, an *ex post facto* document would have been produced to confuse the matter if anyone attempted to reveal an authorisation written and signed by Pétion. The royalist journalist Peltier confirmed that the mayor had, in fact, given such an authorisation, although we do not know his source. At the opposite political pole, the Jacobin Choudieu related that Pétion had told the insurrectionist plotters that he would do so. More importantly, we have Liancourt's eyewitness account of Pétion promising the king to draft such an order and of Roederer stating that he held the document in his pocket. It is true Liancourt disliked the mayor, but it would have been out of character, and possibly beyond his interest in radical politics, for him deliberately to produce a fictitious detail of this kind. If his intention was to damage the mayor's revolutionary reputation, it is odd that he failed to publish his account during his long life. There is also François Huë's hearsay information mentioned previously, obtained from Aubier, a Gentleman of the Bedchamber, that the mayor had given an order to resist force to Mandat that night. After careful consideration, it must be concluded that definitely Pétion produced an authorisation, but Leroux' claim to have done likewise is more doubtful, although certainly a smoke screen.

While witnesses disagree about when the royal party with its military escort started out across the garden, a time of around 8.30 a.m. is supported, and fits in with subsequent events. There was an ongoing argument about who should be allowed in the procession. At first the officious Roederer had wished to confine it to as few people as possible, the king and his immediate family accompanied of course by himself and his Directorate. He claimed he was worried that the National Assembly might refuse entry altogether if it included persons without specific constitutional right of access. It seems more likely he was motivated by self-importance. Dejoly had from the outset insisted that the ministers be allowed to join, since they had the right to sit in the Assembly if invited. The queen was able to persuade Roederer to allow the inclusion of Madame Tourzel and the Princesse de Lamballe. Roederer also tried to insist that the accompanying escort of National Guards should exclude the less politically acceptable grenadiers with their distinctive headgear. Weber, as a grenadier of the Filles Saint-Thomas, was told: 'Grenadiers, you are going to get the King killed. Such an escort can only irritate and add to the fury of the people.' Roederer was ignored and Weber with his fellow grenadiers managed to slip into the escort on the Great Stairs. The foreign Swiss might have been considered even less acceptable. But their commanders must have insisted on the traditional right of the Swiss to guard the king.

The size of the escort is not known for certain. Liancourt, who was part of the procession, gave a figure of 200 for the red-coated Swiss on the left, and 300 for the blue-uniformed National Guards on the right, composed of units from the two loyalist battalions of Filles Saint-Thomas and Petits-Pères. The figure of 300 men for the National Guards is confirmed by another source. The Swiss part of the escort consisted of a detachment of fusiliers and a company of grenadiers. Ensign Deville, who commanded the fusiliers, stated that the strength of his unit was 60. It seems unlikely that the grenadier company commanded by Captain d'Erlach would have been near full strength to make up the balance of 200. The Swiss muster rolls disappeared during the sacking of their barracks, but it is certain the Swiss companies at the Tuileries were considerably below strength, bearing in mind detachments elsewhere and under-recruitment. Weber mentions 100 Swiss grenadiers, without referring to the fusiliers who would have had different headgear. It can be postulated that Liancourt's figure of 200 Swiss is on the high side, and a figure of around 150 may be more accurate. This is supported by a Fribourgeois lawyer living in Paris, François N-C. Blanc, who sent a carefully drafted report to his cantonal authorities on 25 September. He put the figure at 150. Erlach and Deville appear to have been the only company officers in this escort, which as will be seen later was too few for effective command. The fact that the Swiss troops were accompanied by most of the regiment's staff officers may have concealed this officer deficiency.

Ensign Gabriel-Denis Deville was nineteen years old and the son of a wealthy Parisian banker of Swiss origin with solid royal connections. Born in Neuchatel in January 1772, he had an Irish grandmother belonging to the Celtic-Irish nobility which helped when, in due course, he joined the British Army. His passport described him as being, after converting to English measurements, 5 feet 6 inches tall, with chestnut hair and eyebrows, grey eyes, a small forehead, a medium-sized nose, and a round chin. He was commissioned into the Swiss Guards on 12 March 1791 as a result of his father's influence. The latter had by then emigrated to Coblenz to provide banking services for the émigrés. The young Deville wrote a most informative account of his experiences on 10 August and his subsequent

A fusilier in the Swiss Guards armed with a sabre as well as a musket and bayonet.

escape to England. He described the king's passage to the National Assembly as follows: 'The King came down dressed in a grey coat without any decoration. He was sad and pale. The Queen accompanied him, red and crying. They were followed by Madame Elizabeth, Monsieur le Dauphin, Madame Royale, Madame la Princesse de Lamballe, and Madame de Tourzel. A great many gentlemen preceded them. My detachment was joined to a company of grenadiers, the whole commanded by Monsieur d'Erlach. We crossed the garden at the left of Their Majesties with the National Guards of the Filles Saint-Thomas on their right. The sun was so hot that Madame de Tourzel held a white handkerchief on the head of Monsieur le Dauphin. The journey to the National Assembly took half an hour.' This length of time was due to a hold-up below the Terrace of the Feuillants which will be described later.

Liancourt wrote that a great crowd in the palace wanted to follow Louis' party. He was borne along by the people seeking to accompany him despite Roederer's admonitions. In his own words:

We descended the Great Stairs by the chapel through the regiment of Swiss and went into the garden by the central gate in the railings. There we ceased to be hemmed in, and were able to recognise each other. Monsieur de Bachmann, Major of the Swiss, marched at the head of two ranks of his soldiers. Monsieur de Poix followed him, at some distance, and marched immediately in front of the King. The Queen followed the King and held her son by the hand. Madame Elizabeth gave her arm to Madame Royale, daughter of the King. Madame la Princesse de Lamballe and Madame de Tourzel followed them, and were surrounded on all sides by Ministers, and representatives of the Department and the Municipality, and by some persons attached to the King, Messieurs Montmorin, Brézé, Hervilly, Tourzel (the son), Nantouillet, Fleurieu, Rochedragon, Charles Chabot, and myself [the particles of nobility have been dropped in the translation]. I found that I was next to Madame de Lamballe, and offered her my arm, which she accepted, as she was very distressed and fearful. [The Princess of Lamballe's nerves were notorious.] The King walked straight, with an assured look, although he was unable to conceal his misfortune. The Queen was tearful, but from time to time she tried to make herself appear cheerful which lasted some minutes. However, leaning by chance against my arm, I felt her trembling all over. Monsieur le Dauphin did not seem particularly frightened.

In fact, the dauphin was too young to understand what was going on. According to Roederer, he amused himself by kicking up piles of leaves heaped up by a gardener into the person in front of him. 'Madame Elizabeth was the calmest,' stated Liancourt. 'She was resigned to everything. It was religion which inspired her. She said, on seeing the ferocious people [presumably on the Terrasse des Feuillants]: "All these people have been led astray; I would wish for their conversion, but not their punishment." I was unable to prevent myself from remarking to her that I was far from her virtue, and it was the desire for vengeance which possessed me the most.' Liancourt continued: 'The little Madame [Princesse Royale] wept

much. Madame de Lamballe said to me: "We will never return to the palace."
Dreadful prescience!'

There are many accounts of this journey of some 500 yards across the grounds
of the Tuileries garden which in the telling seems to last almost an age. For the
royal family and many others in the group, it was indeed a Via Dolorosa.
Humiliation, imprisonment, and death were awaiting them, in some cases such as
the Princess Lamballe after only a few weeks. 'The people, the bandits, the Sans-
culottes,' wrote Liancourt, 'who were on the Terrasse des Feuillants, seeing the
King leave the Tuileries, had rushed along the terrace towards the steps leading
up from the garden to the passageway of the Convent of the Feuillants. They were
there in such a great number that it was impossible to mount up to the terrace.
The King stopped at the bottom of the steps. The most furious among them
overwhelmed him with insults. They menaced him from above with their pikes. I
was afraid that any moment I might see him massacred under the eyes and in the
midst of his family. We remained stuck there for ten minutes. In the end Roederer

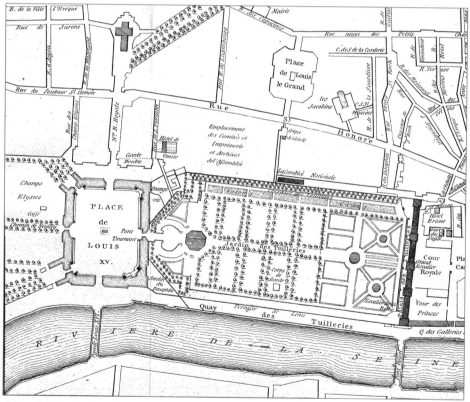

*Plan of the Tuileries garden and its surroundings which was published with Peltier's history in 1792.
The National Assembly building is the black oblong on the northern edge of the garden. The space
between it and the Rue St Honoré was occupied by the Convent of the Feuillants and an extensive
closed garden. The palace is to the right of the Tuileries garden and the Place Louis XV on the left.*

and another persuaded them to give way. They enabled the King and his family to enter the Assembly.' Both Bigot and Weber claimed a delay of a quarter of an hour at the steps leading up to the terrace and the Manège beyond.

The other person mentioned by Liancourt must have been Captain Viard, who was at the head of the escort of National Guards. He reported: 'We marched until 50 paces from the terrace where people were demonstrating their just discontent. I spoke to the King. "Sire, the people appear to be very upset: I believe it will be prudent to proceed softly." The King agreed with me. I then took everything on myself. I ordered the head of the column to halt, and I advanced alone towards the crowd, my sabre in its scabbard, and I said to them: "My friends, the National Assembly has passed a resolution which summons the King to be among them, and at the same time orders me to protect his passage. I am, like you, a good citizen, and I know how to respect the soil of liberty where you are standing, and no soldier will pass the first step leading to the terrace. I will bring the King to the beginning of the gap you are going to make for him, and from that moment you will be his guardians. If you are capable of forgetting for a moment the responsibility I am placing in your hands, think that the entire Nation will have the right to hold you to account. But, I speak to free men, and there is no need to say more." These good citizens opened the way for me.'

The National Assembly had been advised by a Justice of the Peace that the king and his family were coming to the Assembly. A resolution had been passed to receive them. Following protocol procedures established in the Constitution, a deputation of twenty-four members was standing on the terrace to welcome the king. But the passage of the royal party was blocked. The terrace had been decreed part of the precincts of the National Assembly, and it would have been illegal, as well as impolitic, for the escorting troops to try and force a passage without permission. Many of the crowd were prepared to let the king come up, but not the queen. There were cries of 'Down with them', and even threats to finish them off on the spot. A large man thrust a long pole down the steps towards Louis and his entourage, and Roederer took the opportunity to grab hold of it and haul himself up. He harangued the crowd. 'You seem disposed to prevent the entry of the King and his family into the National Assembly. You are not in the right to place any obstacle there. The King has his place by virtue of the Constitution, and his family, who do not have the authorisation of the law, have just been summoned by a resolution to go there. Here are the Deputies of the National Assembly sent to welcome the King. They will attest that this decree exists.' The welcoming deputies acknowledged what Roederer had said. He then grabbed the pole from the man and threw it into the garden. The mass of people gave way, but there were further delays in the crowded narrow passageway in front of the Manège where the Assembly sat. Roederer obtained permission for a few unarmed National Guards from the king's escort to clear the way. One of them, a man of considerable height and ferocious aspect, lifted the dauphin to save him from being trampled by the press. The queen cried out, thinking he was being kidnapped. Weber related that this National Guard was in fact a devoted royalist. Returning to his comrades after leaving the dauphin in the National Assembly, he exclaimed with rapture: 'I have just carried the son of my masters, the entire universe in my arms, long live Monseigneur le Dauphin.' The poor young dauphin was to die in 1795, brutally treated and neglected, one of the more unpleasant crimes of the Revolution.

It was by the passageway that a National Guard with a strong Provençal accent accosted the king with remarks which may well have reflected the feelings of the common people. They suggest how adroit action by the king and his advisers might possibly have countered republican propaganda. 'Don't be frightened, Sire,' he said. 'We are decent people, but we don't want any more plots. Be a good citizen, Sire, and don't forget to chase your sainted priests from the palace.' The king seemed to take it in good part. Eventually, Louis and his family, some members of the Royal Household and nobles, together with the ministers, members of the Department, and Leroux, succeeded in entering the Chamber. Louis took his constitutional position beside the President of the Legislature, while the immediate royal family were allocated the seats reserved for ministers when called to address the Assembly. The latter were placed above and to the left of the king. Choudieu claimed that the queen and Madame Tourzel had become separated from the party in the crush and came in afterwards. According to Madame Campan, the queen was robbed of her fob watch and purse.

After being seated, the king made a brief statement. 'I am come here in order to avoid a great crime which might be committed, and I believe myself in safety – I, my family, and my children – when I am among the representatives of the Nation. I will stay here with my Ministers until calm is established.' This is Dejoly's version which differs a little from other versions, particularly the last sentence. As it seems probable that Dejoly may have drafted the king's statement, this could be the most authentic. It was the last public statement he was to make. Within a short while, he was to be imprisoned under the total control of those who were currently mounting their insurrection against the legitimate authorities.

CHAPTER 11

Parley

It seems likely the king believed that he had relinquished his right of self-defence in quitting the Tuileries, and if there were any fighting, he would not be held directly responsible. The reverse was to happen. The king was held accountable for his Swiss Guards' resistance which led to the killing of French citizens. Regrettably we know little of Louis' thoughts and intentions during the night and early morning of 9/10 August, above all on military matters. At the beginning of the military review, the king is reported to have acquiesced to the idea of defending if attacked. However, he regarded any prospect of civil war with great reluctance. It seems certain he hoped for a peaceful stand-off leading eventually to the retirement of the insurgents. Only scant details are available of advice from senior officers. We have seen he rejected Hervilly's proposal to seize cartridges from the Arsenal. He apparently took no notice of a final attempt by a leading French officer, General Vioménil, to persuade him to escape from Paris. He ignored advice from Major Bachmann, overheard by Under Aide-Major Gibelin, that he should not go to the National Assembly. It is claimed that Minister Dubouchage, who was a professional soldier before going into administration, proposed at some stage to lead the Swiss against the insurgents. His offer was refused. Roederer stated that while he was persuading the king to leave the Tuileries with his family, the military personnel present kept silent. Afterwards, he sounded out some of them and claimed they agreed he had given the right advice.

Although Louis had abandoned the idea of resistance, it seems probable that he hoped to come back to the palace. He accepted that there was a likelihood that he would be dethroned, and any return might be short term while consideration was given to providing a more appropriate residence or decreeing his exile. Nevertheless, it was natural for him to want to keep the Tuileries inviolate, not least in order to protect the lives and property of loyal retainers living there. But it is unlikely he saw his palace as an overt symbol of royal power as suggested by Bigot de Sainte-Croix, who wrote: 'The King was no longer King when the brigands had forced an entry, and they knew it.' The king was prepared to sacrifice the Tuileries if necessary, as events were to show. Bigot was the only witness to raise the specific issue of orders for the troops remaining at the Tuileries. He was unaware of any being given. If they were, he was convinced that they would have been couched in purely defensive terms. The evidence from Swiss officer sources is that the king did give some kind of order to exclude the insurgents from the palace. It seems highly likely that it was formulated as a request rather than a formal written command. No thought seems to have been expended on the problem of excluding the insurgents without risking bloodshed.

Roederer excused the lack of consideration on what would happen at the Tuileries after the king and his family departed by referring to the events of 20 June. On that occasion the mob had shown little interest in pillage. He presumed that once the king had quitted the palace, all motives for attacking it would disappear. Yet Roederer, during his presence in the Cour Royale, ought to have become aware of the insurgents' hostility towards the Swiss and of their intention to disarm them. It was a careless assumption that the revolutionaries would lose interest in the Tuileries and its Swiss defenders once Louis departed. If the insurgents were to persist, there was a definite risk of fighting. The solution to this mystery, however, may lie in the belief that the National Assembly would rapidly despatch a mission to calm the situation. In fact, such a mission *was* despatched in due course, but too late. Events might have turned out differently if Roederer had not wasted the Assembly's time by insisting on making a lengthy report without raising the issue of sending a delegation.

Baron Bachmann (1733–92), painted against an Alpine background. Although only third in command of the Swiss Guards, he was held responsible for their resistance on 10 August and was guillotined after formal trial on 3 September.

The king might be partially excused for not giving detailed consideration to these issues as the safety of his family was very much on his mind. It is less easy to exonerate his senior officers, particularly the two Swiss commanding officers, Lt Colonel Maillardoz and Major Bachmann, who remained with the king's escort near the National Assembly. They left no instructions with their subordinates back at the palace, not even bothering to inform them whom the king had left in overall command. Although the Regiment of Swiss Guards was divided into four battalions, there were no battalion commanders. Operational command was at the company level. The Swiss remaining in the Tuileries, amounting to some 80 per cent of the force, were commanded by a number of company captains, lacking a regimental officer of superior rank to direct their actions.

This should have been the imposing Major Bachmann. It is difficult to explain this extraordinary state of affairs apart from the assumption that nothing would happen. Another possible explanation, unsupported by evidence as the officers concerned failed to survive, is that Maillardoz insisted that Bachmann accompany him with the king's escort to prevent him from acting rashly. Maillardoz was d'Affry's nephew, and had been made Lieutenant Colonel of the regiment over Bachmann's head because of the latter's more reactionary politics. Despite not being at the palace when the action began, Bachmann was indeed made the principal scapegoat for the hostilities, because of his known enmity to the Revolution.

In effect, the Swiss at the Tuileries were deserted by their senior commanders, as no subsequent attempt was made to lead them, although the officers concerned were only some 500 yards away. At least one messenger arrived from the Tuileries to advise that the insurgents had entered the courtyards; apparently there was no response. It seems possible that Bachmann and Maillardoz were at odds and were unable to agree on a course of action. Now that Louis had chosen to place his safety in the hands of the Assembly, rather than rely on his Swiss Guards, it is difficult to believe that he would have refused a definite request by their commanders to withdraw the Swiss at the palace back to their barracks. No such approach seems to have been made. When the fighting began, the king took the initiative and ordered the Swiss to retire. By then it was too late.

There are a number of eyewitness accounts from both sides about events before hostilities began at the Tuileries, probably some minutes after 9.45 a.m. There is no fundamental dispute over the order of activities, which may be summarised as follows: after the king's departure at about 8.30 a.m., the National Guards remaining at the palace deserted even more rapidly. The gunners' unloaded guns were dragged next to the palace. Half an hour later, around 9 a.m., the forces from the Faubourg Saint-Antoine and elsewhere arrived to support the insurgent units which had been on the Place du Carrousel for more than an hour and a half. This led to the redeployment of Alexandre's Saint-Marceau Battalion to the Cour du Manège on the other side of the palace via the Rue Saint-Honoré and the Rue du Dauphin. The arrival of substantial insurgent reinforcements, and the desertion of most of the remaining National Guards, caused a decision to abandon the forecourts of the palace facing the Carrousel. Constant-Rebecque, a nineteen-year-old Swiss junior officer who later in life was to play an important role in the Waterloo campaign as Chief of Staff to the young Prince of Orange, estimated only 200 National Guards stayed at their posts. Made aware of the evacuation of the Royal Court by their lookouts on the roofs of the small lodgings forming the front edge of the courtyard, the insurgents decided to force an entry. There was no need to do this. The wicket in the main gate was opened for them at around 9.10 a.m. They then entered the Cour Royale led by the Marseillais, at first very hesitantly. They embraced a group of National Guards who had been sent to parley with Langlade's gunners. The latter had remained alone in the courtyard after the rest of the troops withdrew to the palace. With the help of the Marseillais, the gunners repossessed their guns placed next to the palace and withdrew them to the Carrousel. Signs of friendship were made to the defenders in the palace and they were exhorted to yield. A small contingent of Gendarmerie à Pied came over immediately. They were followed by some Swiss when the insurgents occupied the Vestibule at the bottom of the Clock Tower. The insurgents mounted the Great Stairs. They were stopped at the first landing by a barrier. After clamouring and confusion, a senior insurgent commander arrived to negotiate with the Swiss. Positions were stated. A strenuous attempt to persuade the Swiss to surrender failed, and fighting commenced.

The principal issue behind the various versions of events was the responsibility for starting hostilities. It was essential for the revolutionaries to assert that the royalists were deliberately responsible for the carnage in order to establish the reality of a plot against the 'People'. The so-called plot provided retrospective justification for the coup d'état which overthrew the king and the Constitution. It also helped to excuse the extreme measures which followed against political opponents. Insurgent witnesses would wish to prove that the revolutionaries were victims of a premeditated, unprovoked, and treacherous assault, while French royalists including the Swiss would seek to blame the start of hostilities on the insurrectionary forces. An official enquiry by the revolutionary Commune into who started the fighting was headed by the police chief Sergent. Responsibility was finally placed upon 100 aristocrats disguised as Swiss Guards who had slipped into the country from abroad. They were accused of opening fire from the top of the Great Stairs, hitting friend and foe alike. The existence of these pretended Swiss Guards was almost an article of faith among the radicals. But there is no evidence to support their reality. Sergent's report was a political document where truth was a secondary consideration. Let us return to the primary sources.

Pétion, in his report to the National Assembly of events on 9 and 10 August, provided a lucid account of what happened between the king's flight to the Assembly and the commencement of fighting. Although Pétion was not an eyewitness of the event, he is believed to have obtained information directly from Westermann and Granier, the latter commanding one of the Marseillais battalions. Neither of these left written statements of their own. As the mayor's political reputation was not directly involved in what happened, it seems likely he accurately relayed what he was told. Before beginning his account, it would be useful to recapitulate a description of the Great Stairs given in Chapter 2. These were situated in an opening on the right side of the Vestibule when entered from the Cour Royale. A single broad flight led up to a first landing giving access to the Royal Chapel. Two parallel flights in the opposite direction then led to the next landing, giving access to the State Apartments.

Pétion began his version by making a scathing and not unreasonable comment on the king's decision to leave the palace. 'Those who had come,' he said, 'to make him a rampart with their bodies were furious at this desertion which they regarded as contemptible cowardice. They were convinced that if the King had remained and shown himself, he would have rallied around him many citizens.' Undoubtedly, most National Guards did see the king's move to the National Assembly as absolving them of any responsibility to defend the palace. An anonymous Swiss officer, who gave a lengthy written account to a fellow officer who was not present on the 10th, castigated the adverse consequences of the king's withdrawal. He wrote: 'In less than half an hour, all the reinforcements, even the ordinary guard of the Tuileries, had slipped away.' Lieutenant Deluze from Neuchâtel confirmed the decline in morale after the king left for the Assembly. 'From that moment,' he wrote, 'the National Guards, in the interior of the palace and in the courts, began to sidle away and abandon the Swiss in a frightful and treacherous manner. . . . I except some persons of this guard to whom I do not cease to offer the justice they merit. From that moment the Swiss were very clearly going to be sacrificed, but they did not lose courage for all that. Monsieur de Boissieu came at 9 a.m. to all the exterior posts to order us to withdraw into the palace; that it was necessary, he said, to defend to the last breath.' Peltier was also critical. 'The departure to the National Assembly had made a bad impression on the National Guards. Some said they were betrayed, left with the aristocrats on one side and the Swiss on the other, as between two fires. The Swiss themselves seemed violently affected. . . . Soon there was no real order in the Great Gallery [des Carraches]. For a while the palace resembled more the foyer of a theatre than a guardhouse, and nobody gave orders.'

Pétion's report continued with a brief summary. 'At 9.30 a.m. the new Municipality gave its orders. The palace was surrounded by armed and non-armed citizens. Towards 10 a.m. the battle began.' He then reverted to what happened after first entering the Cour Royale.

The Marseillais advanced first. They had waited a long time for the troops of the Faubourg Saint-Antoine. The Swiss threw out their cartridges [from the windows], and gave signs of friendship. Several people mounted the Great Stairs, and reaching the top, were preparing to enter the Royal Apartments. They saw everything ready for vigorous defence. Barriers were placed at the doorways to prevent entry. [In fact, they were at the first landing.] Cannons were positioned to fire down the staircase. [There is no evidence for this.] One of these barriers was opened for negotiations. Westermann advanced, spoke to the Swiss officers, and asked them to yield the palace. He told them that they had no one to guard since the King had left, that they would be able to leave with all the honours of war, and that the Swiss and French were brothers. The Swiss officers refused to listen. Westermann turned to the ordinary soldiers and addressed them in German. The officers wanted to fight, but the men wavered. A young Swiss officer went out to join the people. Westermann withdrew with the brave Marseillais who had accompanied him. The bold Granier, commander of the second battalion of Marseillais, remained the last. He chatted in a friendly manner with two Swiss who held him by the arms. He saw he was going to be killed. One of the Swiss drew his sabre to plunge it into his heart, and an officer gave the signal to fire on the Marseillais who were pressed against each other as they sought to escape the expected musket balls. Fortunately, Granier thrust himself free and threw himself to the bottom of the staircase on to the crowd beneath. He was unhurt. The Swiss had the advantage of being under cover. Some Swiss stationed in the Gallery des Carraches threw their guns, cartridge pouches, sabres, uniforms and hats out of the windows. "My friends," they said, "we are with you, we are French, we are with the Nation." [This last detail is out of order, belonging to the period before firing commenced. Some of them may have been actually French due to the recorded shortage of genuine Swiss recruits.] They were nevertheless killed [later in the action].

While Pétion was reporting at second-hand, the irrepressible Langlade of the Gunners of Val de Grâce was certainly present. After the king went to the Assembly he recounted: 'My lieutenant and I approached the Swiss. We told them that there were more than 100,000 men outside, and that it would be a good idea to lay down their arms, and not to fire. They replied that they had been told to fire but would not do so. [Presumably they were referring to the instruction to repel force with force.] They begged my lieutenant to go and speak to their commanders, which he did. The reply of the officers was to send us back to our posts to do our duty; for they themselves feared nothing, and they would know well how to deal with the canaille out there. We returned to our guns, hooked up our limbers and placed them against the wall of the Poste d'Honneur backing on to the Cour des Suisses towards the Cour Marsan.' Some Swiss officers had suggested earlier that these guns be seized, but they were overruled. No attempt was made to seize them now, although there were further suggestions that they should be. 'After half an hour,' continued Langlade, 'a senior officer of the Military Division of Paris [Boissieu] gave an order by a signal for the Swiss and the Gendarmes à Pied to withdraw to the palace, which they did. Some moments later the liveried porter at the Royal Gate raised the bar which closed the wicket gate in the door and ran off. Then our friends who were in the Carrousel and who had patiently waited two hours, although often beating on the gate to make it open, advanced while crying: "Brothers, come with us." Seeing that we were without defence, they opened the two battens of the main gate, and came to help us take out our guns.' The French historian Mortimer-Ternaux plausibly added that the porter was made to open the wicket door by threats from the gunners.

Langlade continued:

Immediately, many of the Gendarmes left the palace, their hats on the point of their bayonets, while crying 'Vive la Nation!' They came to join us. We then dragged our guns into the centre of the Place du Carrousel, and aimed them at the palace. From that position, always hoping to unite the Swiss with us, I turned back to the palace where I saw our people in the Cour Royale ranged in battle order from right to left, making signals for the Swiss to surrender. By the signs that the latter made, we understood that they desired it. Immediately, with confidence, we entered into the palace, went up the staircase till the chapel door on the first landing. We saw the two sides of the staircase, and also the steps above, filled with Swiss and National Guards grenadiers. We summoned them, in the name of the Nation, to surrender without fear for their future. I was recognised by two Swiss who took me by my arms, while weeping and telling me that they hoped their comrades would do the same [would surrender]. We went down together into the courtyard, where their weapons were taken away and they were embraced. While turning around to re-enter the palace, in order to persuade others to come, I noticed that on the balcony some Swiss were throwing down their cartridges. I made a sign for them to stop in order to prevent a stampede to pick them up. [The insurgents were also short of musket ammunition.] I went up to the chapel landing with several comrades. I took hold of two other Swiss, and heard their officers forbidding them to follow us.

I persisted in leading these Swiss down the stairs to go outside. I had the frightful spectacle of one of these Swiss being killed at my side, and the other wounded. Terror, rage, and despair took possession of my soul. I fled across the courtyard, passing over dead bodies with balls whistling in my ears. I flew to my guns, which had remained in the Carrousel, to revenge my brothers assassinated by monsters who had drawn them in with the appearance of joining their side.

There is no essential element in Langlade's graphic account which disagrees with Pétion's. Unfortunately, this is the end of Langlade's lengthy, lively and coherent report, which on the whole cross-checks with other accounts from royalist sympathisers and is a principal source of information for events in the Cour Royale so far. It is a great pity that it does not continue to the end of the action, but the revolutionary politicians were not interested in details of the battle itself.

Desbouillons, the Brestois fédérés commander, gave an account of activities prior to hostilities which is particularly valuable because it was not produced to support a revolutionary version of events as in the case of Langlade and Pétion. In fact his correspondence only came to light some 150 years later. There is little indignation and a considerable feel of objectivity. After remarking that the wicket gate had been opened and closed several times to let people in and out, he continued: 'Several hotheads decided to force the main gate. Axes were raised, breaking it and knocking it wide open immediately.' [Possibly Desbouillons' attention had been momentarily distracted, and he assumed the axes had done their work, when in fact it had been opened from the other side.] 'Several risked entering the courtyard,' continued Desbouillons. 'Some Gendarmes advanced towards us raising their hats. We embraced them and led them out. We tried several times to persuade the National Guards defending the palace to imitate them. We succeeded in part and they joined us in taking away the cannons which were in the courtyard. I omitted to tell you that immediately the gate was opened, some gunners had the audacity to enter with one of their guns, which they dragged to the middle of the courtyard, and aimed at the main entrance to the palace. There still remained some guns in the Vestibule, but we did not try to remove them. However, we entered it immediately and went up part of the stairs to where the Swiss were barricaded. We did everything to persuade them to quit their position and unite with us. We had no instructions but to disarm them.'

This, of course, is a crucial issue. Pétion talked about Westermann offering the Swiss 'all the honours of war' if they left their position. This would have meant that they would have been able to march off as an intact unit with their flags and commanded by their officers. It did not imply they would be able to retire fully armed. For an élite and proud regiment to surrender its arms without having satisfied its honour by making at least token resistance was difficult to accept. It is possible that many of the insurgent militia did not appreciate this, but Westermann who had been in the regular army should have. 'They constantly refused to agree to our pressing solicitations,' Desbouillons continued. 'A single person among them decided to come and speak to the National Guards and descended the staircase, when some men, no doubt posted there and paid to put the match to the fire, tried to stab him. He immediately rejoined his comrades. Negotiations continued. A musket was discharged without causing the business to begin. The commanders of the Swiss and other generals persisted in telling us that without an order from the king, they would not abandon their positions. "You wish therefore all to die?" they were asked. "Yes," they replied, "we will all perish rather than abandon them without an order from the King." The bottom of the staircase was filled with citizens, most of whom were only armed with sabres. One of the Swiss officers received, in the jostling, a light cut and immediately a general discharge crushed these citizens.' While the incident of the shot being fired at the palace is referred to in Altishofen's publication, there is no mention elsewhere of any Swiss officer receiving a light cut. Nevertheless, Desbouillons' account generally agrees remarkably with Durler's report which is considered next.

The Swiss Captain Jost Durler came from Lucerne and died in British service in 1801 at the battle of Alexandria. He was in his late forties on 10 August and had been given command of the Cour Royale and the Swiss Reserve. He appears to have been a humane man and a brave though not particularly enterprising officer. On returning to Switzerland in February 1793, he wrote the principal eyewitness account from the Swiss side, confined to those incidents in which he had directly participated. It appears there was more than one draft and the last was signed by a number of his fellow officers who were involved in the same events. Despite this, what Durler wrote is a personal statement reflecting his naïve vanity. He stated that at 9 a.m. Santerre's troops began to appear on the Carrousel:

Immediately, Monsieur de Boissieu gave me the order to abandon all the posts in the courtyards and to retire into the interior of the palace, which was immediately executed. I placed the major part of my people along the staircase, on the right and the left. The first landing was already occupied by some grenadiers of the Filles Saint-Thomas and other National Guards. I posted a platoon behind them near the door of the chapel. I sent up the remainder to the first room facing the staircase, where were situated Messieurs le Maréchal de Mailly and Lieutenant of Grenadiers Zimmermann, and other officers and many soldiers of the Regiment posted previously in the interior of the palace. [The room Durler referred to was La Salle des Cent Suisses.] I was busy arranging my forces when Monsieur le Maréchal de Mailly sent Monsieur Joseph de Zimmermann to me, to tell me to report to him. I went to find him [Mailly], and he told me that he had been placed in command of the palace by command of the King. I then asked for his orders, which were not to allow myself to be forced. I told him that he could count on us. While I spoke to him, I saw through the windows that the porter was opening the Royal Gate. Some Marseillais appeared under the gateway, making a sign to us with their hats, and crying out for us to join them. At first, they dared not enter the courtyard, but soon they took the decision to enter by columns, and bolder ones penetrated the Vestibule and mounted in a crowd up the staircase to the first landing, occupied by the grenadiers of the Filles Saint-Thomas, other National Guards, and our men. I ran there immediately with Captain Reding, Joseph de Zimmermann and Aide-Major de Glutz, to erect a wooden barrier across the stairway. Monsieur de Boissieu came, placed himself beside me, and wished to speak to the assailants. But they made yells and piercing cries so that he

The Great Stairs of the Tuileries where the battle began. The Vestibule can be seen below. The landing in the foreground leads to the chapel, and the landing above to the State Apartments. The incident depicted occurred one and a half years earlier when National Guards were called out to arrest a gathering of royalists ostensibly come to defend the King against a possible attack on the Tuileries.

was unable to make himself heard. The intrepid Adjutant Roullin [he was actually an under officer at the time but one of the signatories of Durler's account] proposed to go and see what was happening outside, and find out if there were any means to appease the madmen. I told him that he could do so. He went down and was seized by them. They took away his watch, started to take off his clothes, and pushed down his head in order to kill him, when he was delivered by our brave soldiers who rushed to his rescue.

Durler undoubtedly needed to contact a senior insurgent commander with whom it would be possible to negotiate. Roullin was very likely the person referred to by Desbouillons. Durler continued:

An instant afterwards, the Commander of Santerre's troops, who was a former French Guard [he was a former soldier but not of the French Guards], came up close to the wooden barrier and asked to speak to the Swiss Commander. I was close to the banisters with Monsieur de Boissieu and told him that it was me. I had my right hand on the top of the banisters; he seized it saying to me: 'Join us, you will be satisfied and well treated, you must give yourselves up to the Nation.' I replied to him vehemently that we would believe ourselves dishonoured if we surrendered to them and asked him to leave us alone at our posts. I told him that we would do him no harm, but if we were attacked, we would defend ourselves to the last extremity. He threatened me, and I added that I was responsible for my conduct to the cantons, my sovereigns, and never would I surrender, and never would I lay down my arms. At these words he raised his sabre, uttered all kinds of insults, and exclaimed that I would pay with my head for the infamy of not wishing to surrender to the Nation. As he held my [right] hand strongly while he had raised his sabre, I said to one my soldiers in German that, if he gave me a cut with his sabre, he was to lay him low with a musket shot. Hearing me speak German, he lowered his sabre, and in a moment another former French Guard lunged at me with his pike, which I parried with my left hand, while freeing my right hand that the Commander of Santerre's troops was still holding.

Westermann may have seized Durler's hand as a sign of friendship when he first mounted the stairs, but it makes no sense that he held on to it all the time. Durler gives the unreasonable impression that discussions with Westermann were brief, and he omits that the latter spoke to the Swiss soldiers in German over his head. This very likely caused Durler to remonstrate by pushing him. Westermann retaliated by drawing his sabre while grasping his hand. Durler's mention that he gave an order in German, to kill Westermann if the latter should strike him, shows that he had been made aware the insurgent commander would understand. At the same time, he wished to avoid provocation by concealing his menace from the French-speaking insurgents on the stairs. Durler went on:

Messieurs Joseph de Zimmermann, and de Glutz, always at my side, noticed that on the other side of the staircase, a leader of Santerre's forces sought to persuade our people to join him, and already two bad lots had just been taken away by him. Monsieur Joseph de Zimmermann with Adjutant Roullin rushed there, and placed themselves in front of them, and succeeded by cool firmness in preventing the seduction. They spoke for some time with this leader, who exhorted them to put down their arms. I joined them, and this leader spoke to me in the same terms. [The leader seems to be a composite of Langlade and Granier.] The commander and the other leader, seeing that all seduction was useless, went down the stairs into the Vestibule with all their followers, except two Marseillais who slipped between the legs of grenadiers of the Filles Saint-Thomas. My soldiers wished to put an end to them. I saved their lives and told them to hide away in the chapel. Immediately afterwards, Santerre's forces in the Vestibule opened fire. They wounded and killed several soldiers. The fine grenadiers of the Filles Saint-Thomas replied and our men followed their example. Hardly had the attack begun in the Vestibule than Santerre's artillery placed in the Place du Carrousel and the Cour Royale played on the windows of the palace, and musket shots followed.

Other Swiss officer accounts expressed their indignation over the excitable behaviour of the Marseillais and their demands to surrender. Durler, however, was the only one who mentioned defections by the Swiss rank and file. The officers expected the troops under their command to do their duty. To report such desertions would reflect adversely on their own professional performance. Yet it is almost certain that such defections did take place. The testimonies of captured Swiss soldiers, although perhaps coloured by a desire to propitiate their captors, make it clear that the desire to resist was far from

Captain Durler (1744–1801), who commanded the Swiss reserve at the Tuileries, and who wrote a major account of the action. This portrait was published in an Italian translation of Altishofen's work.

being rock solid. Sergeant Din declared on 21 August that the withdrawal from the courtyards had been fatal, as it had taken away the easy means of communicating with the attackers. He commented: '. . . with the opening of the gate, one would not have failed to fraternise, as had happened on several occasions in the past.' Another soldier, Vassenat, testified that he and several comrades threw their arms out of the windows and fled with some National Guards. Even the patriotic Altishofen refers to a number of Swiss soldiers who deserted before the action, claiming they were bribed by being offered pay of 3 francs a day in the French Army. A municipal officer from Marseilles named Jean-Baptiste Loys, closely connected with the Marsaillais fédérés, stated that around forty Swiss had deserted and come down into the Cour Royale, where they were embraced like brothers. Others threw away their cartridges. François N.-C. Blanc, the already mentioned Swiss lawyer from Gruyère living in Paris, told of twelve Swiss stationed inside the guardhouses at the main gate who gave up their arms immediately and joined the Marseillais.

Finally, many years later after the Bourbon restoration, a former royalist member of the National Guards who was present on the Great Stairs, cited a particularity which he would have preferred to pass over in silence. He wrote: 'At the sight of this overflowing torrent [the insurgents], the company of Swiss grenadiers placed on the first landing of the great staircase, no longer hearing the voices of their officers, hastened to throw their arms over the balustrade. . . . Soon, I saw the greater part of these unfortunate soldiers entirely disarmed, raise their hands in the air, and respond to cries of the rabble with their favourite slogans. Useless and fatal submission! They would be no less massacred than those of their comrades who at least by courageous combat had known how to sell dearly their arms and their lives.' No doubt these quotations may exaggerate the degree of disaffection, but its existence is undeniable. Peltier tried to deny it by writing that the gestures of friendship made from the windows were really misinterpreted signs for the revolutionaries to withdraw.

The insurgents expected the Swiss to surrender their weapons. J.B. Jardin, Adjutant of the Filles Saint-Thomas, recalled that the Marseillais entered the courtyard as he was about to speak to Langlade's gunners. He was embraced by one of the insurgents and told that it was certain that the Swiss would give up their arms, and he was going into the palace to invite them to join their side. It seems the insurgents believed there was no need to offer special terms, and the Swiss Guards would give up their arms like the Regiment Ernst at Arles earlier that year. They assumed, with some reason, that even if the officers proved recalcitrant, the rank and file would ultimately go over individually and in groups to their side. It was a question of time. If there was no formal surrender, the Swiss Guards would be eradicated as a fighting force by erosion. The insurgents strongly felt the justice of their cause. The Nation must triumph.

Initially, the insurgents would have been encouraged in their hopes by propitiatory signs on the part of the Swiss. Many of these have already been related. Viard reported that a sergeant in his command, left behind at the Tuileries, was asked by the Swiss to lead a deputation to tell the Marseillais in the courtyard that they had no wish to kill French citizens. But the determination of the officers and many of the men to resist humiliation was underestimated. As a result both sides were at cross-purposes. The Swiss may have hoped to receive honourable terms which would have enabled them at least to keep their weapons, but the revolutionaries believed that all they needed to offer was fair treatment after surrender. Sergeant Blazer's famous reply to Westermann's demand that they lay down their arms summed up the situation: 'We are Swiss, and the Swiss only abandon their arms with their lives. We do not believe we have merited such an insult. If our regiment is no longer required, then let it be properly discharged; but we will not leave our position nor let ourselves be disarmed.'

An essential element is missing from all the accounts of the negotiations for the Swiss surrender, the need to refer to their senior commanders, Major Bachmann and Lt Colonel Maillardoz. The insurgents' lack of concern about dealing with proper authority may have been partly due to ignorance, as well as their haste to obtain a quick solution. Durler, who in the heat of the moment referred to himself as being answerable to the distant Swiss Cantons, failed to mention that authority lay closer at hand, a mere 500 yards away in the garden below the Manège. Durler's failure to refer to his commanders in his report is all the more remarkable as he knew he did not command all the Swiss Guards left at the Tuileries. Captain Salis for certain had an independent command on the garden side of the palace, and there were probably others. To negotiate surrender without instructions for part of the forces holding a position would be a gross breach of military conduct, certainly subject to court martial.

Durler's failure to seek instructions from his commanders or to consult with other officers commanding contingents elsewhere in the Tuileries can only be explained by incipient panic. Despite the apparent impression of soldierly imperturbability shown in his account, it seems plausible that he had been seriously unnerved by the tendency to defect. He must have been alarmed that any appreciable delay resulting from seeking orders from higher authority, or even the opinion of fellow officers posted elsewhere in the palace, while his soldiers and the insurgents remained in close proximity, might lead to the agonising shame of the forces under his command melting away. He held on as best he could. He was almost certainly relieved when hostilities commenced. It is an irony that if the Swiss had shown more discipline, Durler might have been better able to ensure a peaceful outcome. It appears very likely that if the Swiss senior commanders had been approached for fresh orders before hostilities began, they would have gone to the king who would have authorised withdrawal, and even surrender if it were explained that there was a serious prospect of bloodshed.

The majority of eyewitness sources from both sides agree that the engagement began in the Vestibule. Those who wrote that the action started with cannon-fire from the Cour Royale, such as Deluze and Constant-Rebecque, or the six eyewitnesses mentioned by Peltier probably including Deluze, were assuredly not in a position to see or hear what was happening on the Great Stairs. The extreme agitation of insurgent gunners in the Cour Royale immediately before they fired, noted by Constant-Rebecque from a window, which he attributed to drunkenness, can be better explained by the sight of their comrades fleeing with many wounded out of the Vestibule. When shooting started, escalation to a general engagement was rapid. Both sides may have genuinely believed that the other began the fight, but the balance of probabilities suggests that the Swiss fired first, albeit under compelling provocation. The Swiss lawyer Blanc, who undoubtedly had opportunities to speak to eyewitnesses, was of this opinion. He wrote that the Swiss on the stairway were persuaded to remove their bayonets and cry 'Vive la Nation!' This they did. He continued: 'A few Marseillais then passed under the barriers and sought to disarm the Swiss. Some handed over their muskets, others refused. This resulted in a confused struggle. After weapons were brought to bear several times, and knocked down by the sergeants, a shot was loosed. Immediately, firing became general on the stairway and everywhere.'

Reaching the complete truth on the matter of how the battle started is perhaps insuperable. A careful reader might notice that neither Pétion nor Langlade expressly said the Swiss and their allies fired first, but they strongly suggested it. Desbouillons did state it, and gave a believable description of how the fighting started. He implied that he was an eyewitness, but he employed the more impersonal plural pronoun 'we' rather than the direct first person singular. He was probably not in the Vestibule nor on the Great Stairs as he makes no mention of having to flee from Swiss fire. Nevertheless, the story of the slight wounding of a Swiss officer as the immediate cause for the beginning of hostilities has the ring of truth. Unfortunately, there is no support for this story elsewhere. Swiss officers were strongly motivated to suppress any idea that their side first gave an order to fire. But there is a candidate for this slightly injured officer, namely Second Lieutenant Castelburg, who some captured Swiss soldiers claimed gave the first command to fire. Castelburg was mortally wounded in the Vestibule by a cannon ball shortly afterwards and his evidence died with him.

After the Swiss later withdrew to the Assembly, on Hervilly's misrepresentation of the king's orders, and laid down their arms at Louis' command, some dozen Swiss officers who fought at the Tuileries were confined together for several hours. It is easy to imagine a bitter post-mortem. Their part of an élite regiment with a proud history had had to surrender, and the rest was probably destroyed. Were they to blame? They were all aware that they had received strict instructions from their aged colonel not to fire first, and only to act in support of the National Guards. While discussing the situation, they must have attempted to set at rest any doubts on whether they or the insurgents started the action. Deluze managed to escape abroad immediately afterwards and drafted the first Swiss account three days later. This was published in the *Leyden Gazette*, an international news bulletin. It ended: 'I swear by all that is most sacred that we did not begin the fire.' When Durler came to write his report some six months afterwards, he expressly described, as already quoted, the start of the action as if it had occurred in accordance with the Municipality's order to return fire if fired on first, and d'Affry's to act only in support of the National Guards. To reiterate, he wrote: 'The instant after, Santerre's forces fired in the Vestibule. They killed and wounded some soldiers. The brave grenadiers of the Filles Saint-Thomas replied and our troops followed their example.' If it happened like that, the Swiss had properly obeyed orders. Durler's version can be discounted.

While the revolutionaries had their treacherous plot, the royalists had their atrocity stories. Before the action began, it was claimed that the insurgents murdered a number of Swiss who had either surrendered voluntarily or who had been seized in isolated positions. Bigot, Peltier, Weber, and Ruault were among those who made these allegations at second hand. Such murders were also mentioned by Madame Campan who was in the Tuileries at the time, but it seems unlikely she specifically saw them. They do not feature in any of the six relevant eyewitness accounts by Swiss officers. If they did occur, why did none of these six officers mention them? It is difficult to believe they were all unaware of such happenings. There may, however, have been a certain shame in having failed to ensure their soldiers' safety, or if Swiss Guards had actually deserted before being murdered, an unwillingness to admit such indiscipline. Nevertheless, if such murders did occur, it is surprising they failed to mention them.

One primary Swiss source, however, does support the atrocity stories. This is from the only non-officer witness who wrote an account, namely Grenadier Fonjallaz. He composed a remarkable memoir of his experiences in the Regiment of Swiss Guards over four and a half years, dwelling particularly on the aftermath of 10 August which will be related later. Fonjallaz seems to have been posted on the first landing of the Great Stairs when the Marseillais and others entered the Vestibule. He wrote: 'Those of the Swiss who were at the bottom of the stairs cried out all was finished and went out with the Marseillais. When they were outside in the courtyard, they were told to give up their arms as prisoners of war. They were deprived of their arms, and then larded with pikes. [He employed the graphic culinary term where fat is inserted into meat by a sharp knife before cooking.] We on the stairway were curious to look out of the windows in order to see how they had treated our comrades. But by God, when we saw how they had treated them, we all started to weep. We told the others not to go down as our comrades were being murdered. Those near the bottom of the stairs mounted hastily. The Marseillais came up the stairs to make us go down by force. We let them climb the stairs, and then when it was full, we made a rolling fire on them which knocked down nearly all.' The last sentence should not be construed as an intention to entice the insurgents to enter a trap, but merely that the Swiss did not physically prevent them from mounting the stairway. Fonjallaz, with limited formal education, frequently did not allow for time intervals in his description of events. Moreover, he felt no need to mention the negotiations as he was not involved in them. After taking these factors into account, his brief statement on events up to the commencement of fire is not contradicted by other reports. However, in suggesting the Swiss and their allies fired first, he hardly supports the authorised view presented by his officers.

CHAPTER 12

Battle

When firing broke out somewhere around 9.50 a.m. on the Great Stairs, the action spread rapidly. The insurgents recoiled in confusion down the stairs and streamed out of the Vestibule into the Cour Royale. Their cannons replied. Orders were given by the 84-year-old Maréchal de Mailly to fire from the palace windows into the courtyards, while Captain Durler mobilised a force to drive the revolutionaries out of the Cour Royale. In Durler's own words: 'I repulsed the Marseillais in the Vestibule. I went down with my force, and judging that in the long run we could not hold the palace against an immense amount of artillery, I put myself at the head of all those around me, in all about 200 men, to go out and seize their cannons. I swept the courtyard with fire, and made myself master of it in an instant, as well as four guns which I found unloaded and without ammunition. Some grenadiers of the Filles Saint-Thomas, or the Petits-Pères, realising that this artillery was of no use to us, took the ramrods from their muskets, and broke them in the touch holes of the cannons. Several were even killed on the same guns. Monsieur de Mailly, observing the battle in the Cour Royale from the windows, ordered a cease-fire [by those within the palace].'

Durler gave the impression that the occupation of the Cour Royale was a very brief affair. This was correct from Durler's viewpoint once he had succeeded in deploying his troops in the courtyard beyond the Vestibule. He failed to mention what happened beforehand. His sortie was initially blocked by cannon and musket-fire concentrated on the exit from the Vestibule, and his eventual deployment was not without difficulty and loss. Second Lieutenant Castelberg had a leg shattered by a cannon ball and subsequently died. Second Lieutenant Philippe de Glutz was killed outright. Constant-Rebecque, who was stationed in the Salle des Cent Suisses overlooking the Vestibule and had an excellent view of what was happening below in the courtyard, was quite clear that Durler's initial sorties were held up. He said up to three attempts were made to deploy without success. However, the downward raking fire from Swiss soldiers stationed behind the window embrasures of the palace was demoralising for the insurgents and would have forced the gunners to abandon their pieces. Some of the shots went as far as the Carrousel where Choudieu, a Jacobin deputy, had stationed himself. Aide-Major Glutz described the fire as murderous. The insurgent commanders were rapidly forced to order a retreat. But the evacuation of the courtyard could not be carried out all at once.

During the period of forty minutes or so between the first entry into the Cour Royale and the start of the action, it is obvious from accounts that the courtyard had become crowded with insurgent forces. These probably numbered over a thousand. Constant-Rebecque mentioned that two battalions were lined up against the palace in battle formation, almost certainly the Marseillais, followed by many more units. In addition, three cannons were placed some fifty paces from the Vestibule. It was not possible for this mass to disappear instantaneously through the narrow bottleneck represented by the Porte Royale. While insurgent officers at the back would have been trying to organise some semblance of order in exiting from the courtyard, those nearer the palace had little alternative but to return fire until it was their turn to leave. Among these were the Marseillais who took the most casualties of all the insurgent units. Glutz mentioned the heavy fire of the insurgents, while Deluze suggested that it took a quarter of an hour to clear the Cour Royale, which must have included the time spent bottled up in the Vestibule.

The shock of being caught in an exposed position, from which escape could not be effected immediately, caused the revolutionaries to fulminate against the treachery of the Swiss in particular and the royalists in general, and fuelled the myth that a trap had been deliberately set. Robespierre, writing an article in his newspaper, described how the 'citizens' gave themselves up to the sweet illusion that the Swiss would accept their offers of friendship when '. . . cannon fired from the palace ploughed into the army of the people; among whom were counted a considerable number of the Marseillais, and one hundred fell on the pavement. This horrible treachery must be less imputed to the Swiss in general than to the execrable trickery of their aristocrat leaders and to the Court who, for several days, had not ceased to influence the Swiss in order to prepare them for this assassination.' The Swiss and their remaining National Guards allies did not have any cannon for firing on the Cour Royale, but the devastating nature of the revolutionaries' repulse was made more acceptable and explicable by pretending they had. It is possible the brief use of captured guns by the Swiss later on gave the impression they had possessed cannon all along.

Altishofen gave the size of Durler's force when he broke out into the Cour Royale as 120 Swiss. To this number should be added those loyalist National Guards stationed on the Great Stairs and landings. This would roughly tie in with Durler's initial overall figure of 200 before losses from insurgent fire. The Swiss advanced in textbook fashion, moving forward and firing by platoons. At length the insurgents withdrew through the Porte Royale, leaving the courtyard speckled with the dead and wounded. Unfortunately for the historian, Constant-Rebecque failed to witness the ultimate success of Durler's deployment from the Vestibule. A cannon ball crashed through a window into the room where he was posted, ricocheted about, killing and maiming many in the confined space. This caused a panic in which he was caught up, and he found himself on the opposite side of the palace overlooking the garden.

The number of guns captured is uncertain; a likely figure is three rather than the four mentioned by Durler. These cannon had been brought into the Cour Royale at the time of the insurgents' entry, while Langlade's guns were taken outside. The insurgent gunners had run off with the powder charges, ramrods, and slow matches. Finding them useless must have been a great blow to the Swiss officers. Some sources, however, insist that they were loaded with grapeshot when

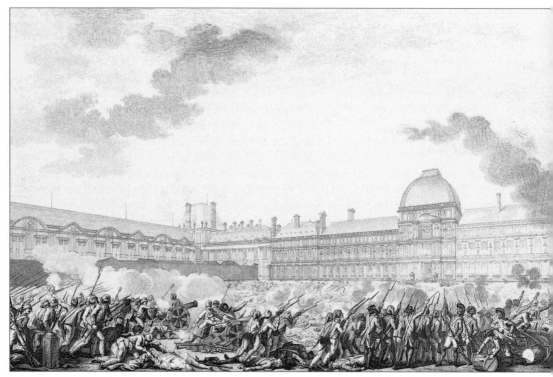

The battle raging in the Cour Royale. Note the Swiss fire from the palace windows and the three insurgent cannons in action. Half the courtyard is already empty except for casualties on the pavement and it seems the artist is depicting the insurgents' rearguard. Those behind (not in the picture) are retiring through the Porte Royale. They are not shown for propaganda reasons.

captured, and the Swiss succeeded in firing a single round utilising their personal tinder boxes. There is a possible confusion in reporting with the guns captured shortly afterwards on the Carrousel. It cannot be over-emphasised that lack of artillery was the major weakness of the defence. Langlade's guns together with their ammunition could have been seized at any time before the gate into the Cour Royale was opened, and it is unlikely there would have been significant objections from the few remaining loyalist National Guards units who were well aware of the gunners' disaffection. However, senior officers had wished to be conciliatory at all costs, and the Swiss now paid the price. The attempts related by Durler to spike the cannons proved unavailing, and they were later dragged back next to the palace when the Swiss withdrew from the Porte Royale.

Once in the courtyard, the Swiss suffered a single casualty from the retreating enemy. But when they took up position by its main entrance, they began to take further losses. 'The Marseillais,' wrote Durler, 'driven back into the Carrousel, continued to fire strongly on us from opposite the Porte Royale. Many soldiers were killed, and Aide-Major Glutz, always at my side by the gate, had just had his sword broken by a musket ball when a sergeant of the Colonelle Company discovered a unit of 15 to 20 Marseillais who were hiding in the angle of the wall behind the cavalry guardhouse flanking the gate, and were lying on the ground. At first I believed them dead; but on approaching them, they begged me for their lives. I threw myself between them and my soldiers, who heated by the fight and carried away by anger, did not wish to spare them. I succeeded in calming them down. I ordered the Marseillais to surrender their weapons and their cartridges. I led them myself to the passageway behind the Swiss barracks, and showed them the route by which they would be able to escape; after which I returned to the main gate of the Cour Royale.' The incident of saving the Marseillais made a powerful impression on Durler, which he dwelled upon when he wrote to his wife three days later. Glutz also mentioned this incident, but was more positive about the action at the Porte Royale. 'We took possession of the Porte Royale, from whence we made a cross fire on the Carrousel, which extended death and dread among the multitude of men . . .'. While Durler and his soldiers had been mopping up in the Cour Royale, First Lieutenant Zimmermann and his son Alexander led a force which chased the insurgents from the Cour des Suisses and captured a loaded cannon.

The garden side of the palace was under the command of an officer from the Grisons, Captain Baron Henri de Salis-Zizers, a name French clerks found difficult to transcribe. He was the officer reputed to have escorted Pétion to the Manège during the night. While Durler was clearing the Cour Royale, Salis led an attack on either two or three cannons situated at the northern end of the terrace by the gate leading to the Cour de Manège. These guns were able to exercise a deadly crossfire on any Swiss on the terrace or moving into the garden. Salis's attack was successful and the guns were seized at the cost of some thirty casualties. Many of these resulted from rebel musket fire on the Terrace des Feuillants close by, probably from the Battalion Saint-Marceau. These captured cannons were found loaded and were dragged back to the centre of the terrace under the Pavillon de l'Horloge. After securing the garden terrace, Salis then moved his force, according to one source of a little under 100 men, through the palace into the Cour des Princes. This appears to have been evacuated by the insurgents save for a gun positioned towards the gate leading into the Carrousel. Grapeshot was discharged against the Swiss. They rapidly deployed and caught the gunners in a crossfire, killing them or forcing them to flee. The Swiss followed them up to the exit, and then withdrew into the adjacent Cour Royale.

When he returned to the Porte Royale after dealing with the captured Marseillais, Durler decided that the only course of action was to advance into the Place du Carrousel in the hope of seizing more of the enemy artillery. 'At length,' he wrote, 'I decided to pursue some other enemy units in order to gain possession of their cannon. I went out of the Porte Royale, and directed my fire to the left along the outside of the Swiss barracks [Hôtel de Brionne], where the Marseillais and others defended vigorously.' It would seem the insurgents were intent on retreating further. The anonymous Swiss officer summed up the overall action so far in one sentence. 'The platoons which were made to advance successively from their positions towards the Carrousel, saluted with their fire the tail of the columns which fled in rout by the streets of l'Echelle, Saint-Niçaise, and towards the Galleries of the Louvre.'

This was the high-water mark of the Swiss success. It was witnessed by the ultimate beneficiary of 10 August, the young Napoleon Bonaparte; then an artillery captain on leave, just a few days short of his twenty-third birthday. No doubt the rapid collapse of legitimate authority came to his mind when seven years later he contemplated his own coup d'état of 18 Brumaire. A long time afterwards, he recounted to Roederer that on 10 August he had been interested in finding out what was happening at the Tuileries. He went to a furniture shop, owned by the brother of his friend Bourrienne, which looked out onto the Place du Carrousel. 'The Swiss served their artillery vigorously,' he said. 'In ten minutes the Marseillais were chased up to the Rue de l'Echelle, and the Swiss only retreated by order of the King.'

It is strange that Durler makes no mention in his account of taking and using enemy artillery, despite having stated his intention to capture it. However, Napoleon's observation may be supported by Grenadier Fonjallaz who stated: 'We fired on the gunners, we had taken their six guns, and fired on the Carrousel, as long as our ammunition lasted.' He continued with the words: 'No more powder bags for guns, no more cartridges . . .', implying the Swiss were employing cannons as well as muskets. Fonjallaz also added the information that the insurgents closed the twin doors of the Porte Royale and tried to barricade them from the outside, possibly by placing a pike through the handle loops. The Swiss broke open the doors with the butts of their muskets.

Writing his account of the battle in London that autumn, the royalist journalist Peltier had been able to question Swiss and other witnesses. Describing the Swiss foray into the Place du Carrousel, he wrote that a detachment of sixty placed themselves in square formation at the Porte Royale and subjected the insurgents to rolling fire which soon cleared the place. It would not have been realistic to adopt this formation unless first the gunners had been made to abandon their pieces by aimed musket fire from the partial cover of the gateway. Adopting the square formation would have provided protection against any cavalry in the vicinity. When this threat did not materialise, they then deployed into line and advanced, with their flank against the courtyard wall towards the Rue de l'Echelle, pushing the insurgents ahead of them. Peltier also said that four guns were abandoned in the centre of the Carrousel, opposite the Hôtel de Longueville, although he did not mention them being fired by the Swiss.

At the Committee Room of the Section Poissonnière in the north of Paris, the minutes related that two citizens arrived at 10.30 a.m. to report on the Swiss attack, direct from the Place du Carrousel. At the same time a delegate arrived from the Hôtel de Ville stating that orders had been given to besiege the palace and even to demolish it. No mercy was to be shown to anyone, whoever they were, as being the only way to be rid of the enemies of the 'People'. We know from Pétion's account that this resolution had been made at 9.30 a.m. On the Left Bank, Lucile Desmoulins wrote that the distant noise of the fighting caused Danton's wife to faint. They wished to leave the Cour du Commerce where the Dantons' flat was situated, but no one would open their doors for exiting the courtyard. A neighbour yelled that the fighting was all Danton's fault.

News of the revolutionaries' discomfiture was now reaching the new Municipality at the Hôtel de Ville. Immediately, it made a desperate demand for reinforcements from outside Paris: 'The General Council entreats, in the name of the Country, in the name of the most sincere brotherhood, to our brothers, the citizens of Sèvres and their surrounding neighbourhoods, to send as many armed men as possible. The Carrousel is covered with the corpses of "patriots". To arms, come to us, citizens!' At roughly the same time, Panis and Sergent in the Police Department signed a note which read: 'Powder! Powder for different units at the Mairie. . . . Nothing is more urgent than powder and that we are informed who now holds the Arsenal in order that in the name of the Commune we may send it there [to the Mairie] immediately.' Presumably the Mairie on the Ile de la Cité was being used as a concentration point for reinforcements. Shortly afterwards, instructions were passed on to send all available munitions to the Tuileries. It should be noted that for the first hour or so of the battle, the revolutionaries, as well as the loyalist Swiss and National Guards, were short of musket ammunition, although the cannons were better provided. This tended to reduce the level of battle casualties. It seems probable that the insurgent force sent to seize the Arsenal had been dilatory, perhaps sitting on the fence until the action began.

Dr John Moore, the 63-year-old Scottish writer and physician accompanying Lord Lauderdale, gave an account of the battle from another vantage-point across the Seine. He wrote in his diary that he had not gone to bed until 3 a.m., and was awakened at 9 by the firing of cannon. The evidence is that the battle began over three-quarters of an hour later, and that he must have been mistaken about the time. They were told the Château was being attacked. 'Soon after,' he continued:

we heard the cry of 'To arms, citizens, to arms! They slaughter your parents, your brethren, your sons!' We saw men running half frantic through the streets, exclaiming in that manner. Lord Lauderdale, being still indisposed, could not go out; and my son remained in the hotel with him. As soon as I was dressed I went into the streets; a party of National Guards, with a number of citizens armed, were marching towards the Tuileries – another body of men followed soon after, dragging several cannons along the Quai de Mazarin to the Pont Royal. Some men, flying from the Tuileries along this bridge, were killed by the National Guards before they reached that end to which the cannon were advancing. Those cannon being mounted on the bridge, were repeatedly discharged against that part of the Château which looks to the Seine. Some women who stood near me on the Quai de Voltaire, as soon as they heard the first discharge, fell a-clapping their hands, and cried, Bravo! Bravo! In the meantime there was some firing of musketry along the windows of the Louvre facing the river – a few people were killed and wounded on the quays. Those who were on the side next to the Louvre had run from the quay to the brink of the river that they might be sheltered from the shot by the parapet. A party of National Guards who marched along the Quai Mazarin, as often as they saw a group of people conversing together, called out 'bas les motions!' [no politics!] and dispersed them – an officer at the same time advising all who were without arms to retire to their houses.

'A little after,' Moore continued, 'as a body of pikemen hurried past, one of them in a very decisive style pointed me out as an aristocrat. Such an accusation in the

The aftermath of the battle for the Tuileries. The outbuildings are on fire and the palace has been entered. The Cour Royale and the Carrousel are strewn with corpses, but it is interesting to note that the carnage is limited, which provides some support for the casualty figures in the final chapter.

streets of Paris, any time these four years, would have exposed a man to insult: in the present circumstances, when execution is the immediate consequence of accusation, it might have proved fatal; but the hotel servant, who accompanied me, declared, that far from being an aristocrat, or anything like it, I was "un Anglais." "Bon!" cried the pikemen, and continued their course.' The men shot running across the Pont Royal were probably part of a unit of 100 Gendarmerie mentioned by Peltier who had been stationed in the stables off the Cour des Suisses containing the Court carriages, and who were now abandoning their post, not without cost. In referring to the Louvre, Moore meant the long gallery which bordered the Seine eastwards from the Pavillon de Flore.

From the first shots inside the Tuileries until the Swiss clearance of the palace courtyards, probably not much more than fifteen minutes elapsed. The Swiss action to possess the Carrousel may have lasted another ten minutes or so. It was ended in the insurgents' favour when they regrouped and succeeded in placing two cannons which subjected the Swiss to enfilading fire, causing them to retreat after taking many casualties. Following the successful intervention of their cannon, it is at this juncture that the charge of a small number of insurgent cavalry probably occurred. This incident is lauded in the weekly *Les Revolutions de Paris* of 11 August. Horsemen, probably the Maréchaussée Liancourt had seen earlier, attacked a building facing the Carrousel by the Cour de Suisse, from where some soldiers were providing covering fire for Durler's withdrawal. An insurrectionist leader, Fournier, mentioned this fire was suppressed by throwing fused powder bags into window openings.

Describing the setback, Durler wrote: 'During this fight, two cannons were manoeuvred on our right in the corner of a little garden facing the Swiss barracks, and fired on us with grapeshot. After some rounds my unfortunate force lay stretched on the paving stones. I remained alone with a sergeant and some soldiers. We withdrew to the Porte Royale where we found Captain de Salis and Under Aide-Major Gibelin. The forces that Monsieur de Salis had been able to bring up to the Porte Royale being soon killed, others of the Colonelle Company came to our assistance, and they had almost the same fate.' Fonjallaz also mentioned two guns being involved in the Swiss retreat. Durler probably exaggerated the proportion of Swiss casualties to excuse his retreat, but they were relatively severe, and his position on the Place du Carrousel had become untenable owing to his small strength, lack of support, and shortage of ammunition. Fonjallaz wrote that he and others had already run out of cartridges, had disabled their muskets, and were resorting to their sabres.

Surprisingly, lack of ammunition does not feature in this part of Durler's report, but other Swiss accounts make it clear that it was now the determining factor, certainly for those who had been actively engaged in the courtyards and on the Carrousel. Their own and their opponents' dead and wounded had been ransacked for any remaining cartridges. Possibly conserving a few rounds for a final stand, Durler and Salis moved their units away from the Porte Royale back to the columned entrance of the Vestibule where they could be covered by troops firing from the windows of the palace, who were still a little better supplied. Deluze mentions the three cannons originally captured in the Cour Royale being hauled back towards the Vestibule by around fifty soldiers and some officers. These cannons were useless from lack of powder, and the objective was to deny their employment by the enemy. There now appears to have been a period of standoff, when the insurgents trying to re-occupy the Cour Royale were kept in check by the Swiss fire from the palace windows, and perhaps occasional sallies by Durler's men with fixed bayonets and sabres. This may have lasted ten minutes or so. One Swiss officer claimed that the insurgents had been successfully repulsed, when suddenly the *deus ex machina* of Major General D'Hervilly arrived on the scene from the Manège with an order from the king. In Durler's words: '. . . Major General d'Hervilly, unarmed and without a hat, ran towards me through the musket shots, and cried out to us: "On behalf of the King, I order you to cease fire and to withdraw to the National Assembly." He repeated the same order further off, wherever Swiss were fighting in the courtyards against the Marseillais.'

If the gallant Swiss were able to clear the courtyards and garden terrace, and briefly occupy the Place du Carrousel, with an overall force engaged, after allowing for defections, of about 600 men together with a few loyal National

Guards, how much more could have been achieved earlier on before the king went
to the National Assembly? Then they could have had the support of probably
over a thousand National Guards, plus the full complement of 800 Swiss
commanded by their senior officers. This was the view of a former member of the
Constituent Assembly, the Marquis de Ferrières, who believed the Court could
have carried the day.

Certainly, those who adhered to the Constitution did not receive the leadership
their cause deserved. The fatalistic and phlegmatic king did not provide it. The
risk-averse and politically hesitant Procureur Général Syndic failed to react
effectively by declaring martial law when the ousting of the legitimate Commune
was known around 7.15 a.m. If firmness and determination had been present, if
the king and his ministers had possessed true confidence in the legitimacy of their
position rather than conceding it to the revolutionaries, if they had believed in
restoring order instead of only contemplating being massacred, might not the
initial insurgent force, then arriving on the Place du Carrousel, have been swept
aside by the Swiss and loyal National Guards long before the forces from the
Faubourg Saint-Antoine arrived? Their rout could immediately have been
followed up by a successful advance on the Hôtel de Ville, to restore order under
the legal authority of the Department. The overthrow of the properly constituted
General Council provided justification for its intervention. With the Department
controlling the Hôtel de Ville, followed by the possible restoration of the
legitimate General Council, the moderate sections might have rallied to the cause
of constitutional legitimacy, rather than opting out or joining the insurgent
bandwagon. Apart from the Marseillais, the revolutionary forces were of limited
quality, perhaps most not much more than rabble.

Looking back, the triumph of the insurrection can seem inevitable, but the
French historian Marcel Reinhard in *La Chute de la Royauté*, published in 1969,
emphasised the imponderables in determining who was the stronger on the eve of
10 August. Pétion himself affirmed in his memoirs that those on the republican
side who participated in the action, '. . . could not prevent themselves from
repeating often, in truth, "it is a miracle that we have succeeded".' Seldom was
there greater confirmation of Napoleon's dictum that in war moral considerations
greatly outweigh material numbers than when Louis XVI lost his throne.

CHAPTER 13

The Manège

The great nineteenth-century French historian Jules Michelet wrote: 'I do not know any event in ancient and modern times that has been more completely disfigured than 10 August, more changed in its essential details, more altered and obscured by accessory lies or legends. All parties, deliberately, seem to have conspired here to obliterate history, to make it impossible, to conceal it, to bury it, to such an extent that one can no longer find it.' Michelet concluded by stating that the task of finding the truth must be left to others. The epochal events of the day the king's reign ended were promptly distorted by royalist and republican supporters alike, while those less politically committed were largely overcome by a sense of shock which numbed reasoned analysis and the capacity for accurate description. Ideology continued to hinder objectivity down the generations.

One example of an attempted falsification of history was to utilise the Assembly's own minutes to alter the content of Vergniaud's reply to the address the king made on entering the Chamber. Fortunately, his real words survived in other reports on the proceedings. He actually replied: 'You can count, Sire, on the firmness of the National Assembly; its members have sworn to die in support of the people and the legitimate authorities.' The minutes, on the other hand, excluded any reference to dying for legitimate authorities, which included the king and the legally elected Municipality. Not wishing, however, to pass up the heroic gesture of dying, Vergniaud was claimed to have said that 'the Assembly feared no danger, and moreover, it knew if necessary how to die at its post'. When Louis and his family arrived, the Girondins still probably believed the king might be used as their route to power. They had not instigated the insurrection, but the king, in coming to the Assembly asking for protection, had fallen into their hands, and they hoped to dictate terms. But whatever expectations they had, they were soon to be undeceived by their own failure of nerve, and the Assembly as a whole was to show anything but the firmness claimed by its President.

The Assembly's proceedings were reported by four publications: the *Logographe*, the *Journal des Débats et Décrets* (the *Journal*), the *Moniteur*, and the Assembly's own *Procès-Verbal* or minutes. The first two tended to report in greater detail than the *Moniteur* and the *Procès-Verbal*. Freedom of the press was one of the major victims of the new revolution. The *Logographe* was closed down within a week, and the *Journal* ceased publication later. On 10 August, editors must have been wary about what to print. In the case of the *Logographe* and the *Journal*, the distortion is subtle as the appearance of full reporting is maintained.

The *Moniteur*'s account is sketchy during the morning, but contains some revealing titbits not given elsewhere. The *Procès-Verbal*, as the mouthpiece of the Assembly, manipulated its report on proceedings partly to conceal the extent of its humiliation. Generally, all publications must have felt it expedient to suppress evidence of significant opposition to the republican takeover. The *Journal* was alone in remarking that all the deputies on the political right of the Assembly were absent, and in recording that one deputy, a Monsieur Chéron, asked the Assembly to proclaim its support for the Constitution. It subtly emphasised this point by describing Chéron as 'faithful'; the only speaker it distinguished by an epithet. The absence of right-wing deputies was also mentioned by the Jacobin deputy Choudieu who said they disappeared at the first cannon shots.

The most glaring gap in reporting is the failure to mention the arrival at the Assembly of Swiss Guards from the Tuileries, towards 11 a.m. The silence on this event is so complete that one begins to wonder whether it was only a dream. There are five independent eyewitness accounts by Swiss officers attesting their arrival with soldiers at the Manège, of which one was published only a week after the battle. It is almost inconceivable that they all invented it. Apart from a considerable amount of circumstantial evidence, there is secondary support from Peltier's history and Bertrand de Molleville's memoirs. Choudieu also wrote of seeing Swiss with white handkerchiefs attached to their muskets in the Assembly's corridors. One must conclude, for reasons that will be mentioned later, that it was felt too embarrassing to admit that a significant number of Swiss officers and men had actually penetrated the Assembly building, and some probably even the Chamber itself. Unfortunately, the Swiss accounts were written by officers uninterested in what the politicians were doing within the Chamber when they got there. This compounds the inability to link the arrival of the Swiss with a specific point in the Assembly's proceedings.

After Vergniaud's reply to Louis, a member pointed out that the Assembly needed to be active in the present situation, but the Constitution prohibited them from debating in the king's presence. It was first proposed that he move to one of the ministers' seats on the other side of the bar, but eventually it was agreed to place the twelve persons of the king, his family, and immediate retainers in the Logographie, a reporters' box about 11 feet square to the right behind the President, and separated from the Chamber by a grille. The stifling heat-wave Paris was experiencing added considerably to discomfort in the constricted space available. Onlookers noted Louis took a keen interest in proceedings, surveying the Assembly with a lorgnette because of his myopia.

Roederer was called to the bar to make a statement on the recent events which had led the king to come to the National Assembly. His address was reported in detail, and with a few friendly interruptions he must have spoken for twenty minutes or so. Rightly anticipating future criticism, he made a long legal defence of his instructions to the troops over exercising the right to repel force. At this stage he was applauded since the insurgents were not yet the masters. Roederer failed to mention similar activities by the municipal officers. This might have undermined the alibi Leroux was seeking to establish for Pétion. In his report, Leroux rectified the matter by praising Roederer for not inculpating them, while emphasising that he and Borie were equally guilty. The Procureur Général

Syndic's admission of responsibility was used by Swiss officers when interrogated a few days later. They claimed the Swiss had only been acting on his instructions.

In his memoirs, Roederer wrote that he feared his statement would not satisfy everybody, and he tried to sidle away. Before he could do so, he was invited to remain in the Chamber for the remainder of the session, and felt he had to comply. However, the *Logographe* clearly states that Roederer asked to stay close to the Assembly, no doubt believing there was greater safety there. Roederer might also have explained why he failed to ask the Assembly to send a delegation to the palace to maintain order, either before or after his lengthy speech. A constitutionalist must conclude that Roederer's overall performance during the course of events was less than adequate and he betrayed the trust his office conferred upon him. From 16 August, with the Department of Paris abolished until recreated in an emasculated form, Roederer went into hiding. He immediately published a defence of his activities in the Cour Royale, toning down the measures he had taken to defend the rule of law, and resolutely denying any connection with the Swiss. This apologia caused him to be held in opprobrium by the Swiss, and by royalists such as Liancourt, who mentioned his disgust.

After Roederer had completed his report, Municipal Officer Borie, who had remained behind at the Tuileries when his colleague Leroux accompanied the king to the Manège, arrived at the bar with Adjutant Doucet of the 6th Legion. The minutes reported: 'It was announced that the palace was about to be attacked, that cannons were aimed at it, and the insurgents proposed to demolish it with cannon fire.' Adjutant Doucet added that he was commanding the National Guards remaining at the Tuileries, and their positions had been entered. He demanded that the Assembly should decide what he must do. 'There are citizens there', he exclaimed, 'about to have their throats cut.' Deputy Lamarque promptly proposed that the Assembly appoint ten members to go to the scene to try and separate the potential combatants. Another member asked that the people of Paris should be held responsible for the security of persons and property. A resolution was passed: 'The National Assembly places the safety of all persons and properties under the safeguard of the people of Paris. It appoints twenty members to go to the place of the gathering [of insurgents], to communicate this decree to the people, and to employ all means of persuasion to restore order.' At the same time, on a motion of the leading Girondin Guadet, another mission of twelve members was proposed to go to the Hôtel de Ville to free Mandat, the official commander of the National Guards. The proposed objective of this mission was suppressed in the minutes, and instead a more politically acceptable version based upon an intervention by Deputy Thuriot was inserted: 'The mission was established to confer with the Section delegates, and other persons invested with the confidence of the people, on measures to restore order.' It is uncertain whether this second mission ever set forth. Following these resolutions, Vergniaud ceded the chair to Guadet, who was to preside over the Assembly during the interval which saw the triumph of the insurgents.

These two resolutions exposed the palpable weakness of the National Assembly. Apart from a limited force of National Guards guarding its precincts, it had no armed forces under its own control. The Assembly had stripped the Executive Power of all

The Chamber of the National Assembly in the Manège. This picture does not do justice to the narrowness of the room relative to its length. It does illustrate the considerable space available for spectators.

regular troops in Paris except for the Swiss Guards, which it had been unable to prise away from the king despite efforts to do so. The attempt of the Girondins to establish a dependent force of provincial fédérés had failed. Fearful of a counter-revolution from the right, they had failed to take seriously a revolution from the left. There is a parallel with the Russian Revolution where Kerensky's obsession with counter-revolution led by Kornilov caused him to lower his guard against the Bolsheviks under Lenin. The revolutionary credentials of the right were naturally suspect; while the Jacobin republicans, although politically extreme, were undoubtedly on the side of the angels as far as the basic tenets of the Revolution were concerned. Moreover, not only were military forces lacking, but support within the Chamber for the Constitution was reduced by the general absence of the more moderate and conservative members who were intimidated into staying away. Towards the end of the day when there was a roll-call vote on the appointment of new ministers, less than half the number of deputies were present than had voted for or against Lafayette on the 8th. The Jacobins, making appropriate threats, had placarded Paris with a list of the 400 or so deputies who had voted for the acquittal of Lafayette.

Some time after the despatch of the first mission, a cannon shot was heard. Consternation reigned. Spectators stood up and cried: 'Long live the National Assembly! Long live liberty and equality! Long live the Nation!' The cannon-fire continued, and there was agitation outside on the terrace. While this was happening, the mission sent to the Tuileries returned. They informed the Assembly that it had proved impossible to reach the seat of the fighting. The mob had pressed around them and blocked the way. They had been told that they could not be permitted to expose themselves to the assassins stationed in the palace and should return to the National Assembly which required their presence, and where they would be defended. It is uncertain whether the mob was acting out of genuine concern for the safety of the deputies, or whether the Jacobins had taken measures to ensure that the Legislature would be unable to intervene against an attempt to occupy the Tuileries. The latter seems probable. An officer of the National Guards contingent protecting the Manège rushed in to say the entrance had been stormed. The President placed his hat on his head to call the Assembly to order. He asked for silence, demanded calm in the name of the country, and reminded members that they were at their post. The *Moniteur* alone reported the arrival of a group of 'armed citizens' within the Chamber, a description commonly used to describe National Guards. It seems almost certain that these belonged to the king's escort. Madame de Tourzel in her memoirs referred to this incident, and stated that the Assembly believed they might be trying to rescue Louis.

Over an hour earlier, Liancourt had led Madame Elizabeth and the Princesse de Lamballe into the Assembly Chamber, and had sat down on the spectator benches with M. de Fleurieu and M. de Rochedragon, who like him had also followed the royal party. They were sitting near the entrance, at the foot of the 'Mountain', where the Jacobin deputies sat. Liancourt still had his sword sheathed in its scabbard. Hardly were they seated than they were denounced by members, including Lacroix, as being hirelings of the Civil List, vile mercenaries, and so on. The minutes stated: 'Some armed people introduced themselves into the interior of the Chamber at the same time as the King. It was resolved that no armed force would be allowed in. These persons went out.' Fearing to excite feelings against the king, Liancourt and his companions went quickly into the corridors surrounding the Chamber, which he described as being full of grenadiers of the National Guards who had accompanied the king. He must have misread his notes, however, as at this stage these National Guards were still below the terrace in the garden. What he reported next was definitely pertinent. 'At that moment, a women of around thirty appeared covered in blood. She told us that eight heads were being paraded on the Place Vendôme, of which one was the unfortunate journalist Suleau, together with others who had taken part in what was known as the false patrol.' Liancourt and his companions said quietly to each other that it was going to be a very 'hot' day.

Peltier, a friend of Suleau, gave a detailed account of the incident of the so-called false patrol. This was the first atrocity of the day. According to Peltier, some twenty-two people had been arrested during the night, mostly armed. They had been wandering about the streets in the vicinity of the National Assembly out of curiosity, although some, including Suleau, who was in the National Guards, were involved in obtaining intelligence. Peltier said that the largest grouping was three people. The 'false patrol' rapidly became a republican myth in support of a royalist conspiracy. The arrested were taken to the guardhouse of the District des Feuillants. They were placed in two rooms. Eleven managed to escape from one of them by jumping into the garden and breaking down a gate. Paris was then divided into 60 districts which formed the geographical basis for National Guards battalions. Districts had an office with limited administrative functions. They should not be confused with the 48 sections which were electoral units. Shortly afterwards, local administration was aligned on the sections.

Peltier wrote:

The District was presided over by an ex-Navy clerk called Bonjour, an ultra
Jacobin. At 8.30 a.m. [more likely 7.30 a.m.] they led before him a man of thirty
[actually thirty-five], in a National Guards' uniform, of which the crispness
and the shine of his weapons had made him noticed on the Feuillants' Terrace.
He was Suleau, a royalist well known for his pamphlets against the Duke of
Orleans, and according to the journal *Les Revolutions de Paris*, a protégé of the
Queen. He carried an order which said: 'The bearer will verify the state of
things and make a report to the Procureur Général Syndic of the Department.'
It was signed by Municipal Officers Leroux and Borie. He was taken to the
guardhouse where the signatures were contested, although subsequently
authenticated at the Tuileries. Since 7 a.m. a crowd had amassed on the
Feuillants' Terrace. A Municipal Officer had mounted on a trestle table to ask
them to disperse and promised that the guilty would be subjected to the full
rigour of the law. He was denounced and told to withdraw. The prostitute
Théroigne de Mericourt was there, dressed as an Amazon with sabre and
bandoleer; Théroigne de Mericourt, native of Luxembourg, small, skinny,
wasted by debauchery, having nothing but the Revolution for a living.

Peltier was understandably ungallant. Others found her alluring and she was
known as La Belle Liégeoise. An actual witness of the scene recounted to his
surprise that she was pretty, very pretty, and that her excitement enhanced her
attraction. He remarked that she was overcome by an exaltation difficult to
describe. Théroigne was thirty years old; an adventuress who had travelled widely
in Europe and performed as a singer. At the outbreak of the Revolution she was
being kept by an elderly aristocrat. She counted Pétion and Desmoulins among
her acquaintances. She was a noted orator, and although women did not have the
vote and were excluded from office, she commanded a part of the mob which took
over the Tuileries on 20 June. Her revolutionary attire included a riding habit, a
plumed hat, a pistol in her belt, and a sabre at her side. In 1793 she espoused the
cause of the losing Girondins. Towards the end of May that year, a Jacobin mob
of women seized her, stripped her naked, and flogged her in the Tuileries garden
in sight of her present triumph. The following year she went insane.

Despite a resolution by the National Assembly nearby that the arrested people
should be safeguarded, the mob was determined to have blood. 'She formed a
committee from the crowd', Peltier continued, 'and put herself at its head.
Bonjour forbade the National Guards to intervene against the People.' We know
from the report in the *Journal* that the guardhouse was actually stormed, and the
National Guards within dispersed. The first victim was the Abbé Bougon, a
colossal man, who after fierce resistance was cut to pieces. Peltier gave the time as
9 a.m., which would be about the moment the king was entering the National
Assembly. However, Assembly reports show the killing began before the king's
arrival. The next victim to be lynched was a Monsieur de Solminiac, and then
another, followed by Suleau, whom Théroigne seized personally by the collar.
Suleau had unfortunately written insulting epigrams about Théroigne, and now

was her chance for revenge. A Monsieur de Vigier, a former royal bodyguard, was able to put up a stout fight. Two of the intended victims managed to escape in the confusion, and one of these was Peltier's eyewitness. Peltier had spoken to Suleau on the previous day, and little thought when he left his house on the 10th that one of his first sights would be his friend's head on a pike. Suleau had married two months previously, and left a beautiful young wife with child.

It seems necessary here to give a brief description of the approaches to the Assembly building and the Chamber itself, Le Manège. The public could reach the main entrance from only two directions, from the Terrasse des Feuillants to the south or from the Rue Saint-Honoré to the north. From the latter, one entered through a covered gateway, on the site of the present Rue de Castiglione, into a short passage which opened out into a little square with the Church of the Convent of the Feuillants to the left. On the far side was the guardhouse of the National Guards responsible for the Assembly's security. Leaving the square going south towards the Tuileries gardens, one entered a narrow alley which continued for about 100 yards until an opening to the left provided access to the 'Small Courtyard of the Feuillants', with convent buildings on three sides now appropriated for the Assembly's use. The alley continued for another 30 yards or so until a grilled iron gate gave access to the Terrasse de Feuillants. Halfway along this alley, again on the left, was the main entrance of the Assembly building, the former Manège which, enlarged, now functioned as the seat of the Legislature.

The side of the Assembly building abutting the terrace was without doors. In fact, all along the town side of the terrace, there was a high wall which was broken by only two exits, one of which has just been mentioned. The other break in the wall was about 200 yards further east towards the Tuileries, by the Café Holtot, which led to the Rue du Dauphin. The tree-lined terrace was about 6–8 yards wide – and accessible from the garden of the Tuileries by flights of steps opposite the two gates. It could also be entered at either end: by the palace, or past the Orangerie overlooking the Place Louis XV. The terrace today, with its two sets of steps leading up from the Tuileries garden, is very much the same, but the Rue de Rivoli now occupies the site along its northern edge, including that of the Assembly building. The Chamber itself, situated in the original Manège, was a long and narrow space, decorated in classical style with plaster busts, low reliefs, and imitation marble and draperies painted on the walls. On the south side, that is nearest the Tuileries garden, the deputies sat on six banked rows of seats with the President or Chairman in the middle on a dais. Opposite was an entrance and the bar from which outsiders addressed the Assembly. Facing the deputies were benches for spectators together with a tribune for orators. At either end were nine banked rows of seats for spectators, partly occupied at the west end by Jacobin deputies. There was considerable additional space for visitors in galleries above, running all around the room. Access to these was via an enclosed space running around the exterior of the Chamber, as in a Roman amphitheatre. Contemporaries referred to this ambulatory space as the corridors [couloirs] of the Assembly. As the building was rectangular rather than circular, the plural was used.

Grenadier Weber down below in the garden recounted that the king had hardly entered the Assembly when they saw a spiral of dust on the terrace, and a crowd

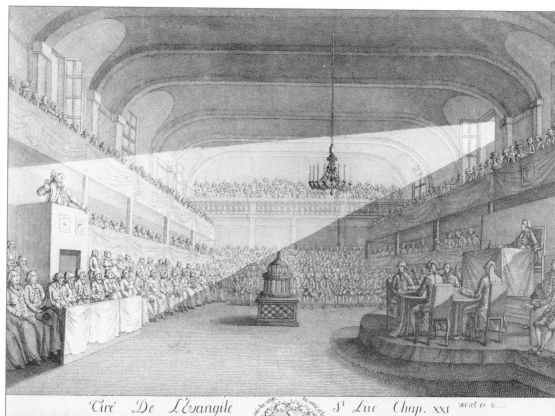

Tiré De L'Évangile   Sᵗ Luc Chap. XXI versets D à....

The Chamber of the National Assembly facing east showing its president seated on a dais on the right with clerks below. Deputies sat on either side. The galleries, and part of the floor of the house, are reserved for spectators. The orators' tribune is on the left. Below is the bar of the Chamber at which petitioners presented themselves. The entrance is on the north side of the building. A stove is in the centre. The breadth of the building is greatly exaggerated.

of people armed with pikes running with shouts of joy. They came up to the gate leading to the National Assembly and stopped to show the heads of two of Weber's comrades in the Filles Saint-Thomas, Suleau and Vigier. 'We had much trouble', Weber wrote, 'in restraining one of our comrades, who seeing the head of Suleau, cried out continuously, while weeping and gesticulating with rage: "Do not let me down, let us kill the assassins, let us revenge our comrades!" They replied by shaking the heads on the pikes and menacing us with the same fate. This horrible spectacle made us more angry than frightened, and we would have attacked if the royal family were not hostages in the Assembly. At the same moment, one of the Swiss in the guard which had accompanied the king from the palace came to add to our fury and consternation. "The Marseillais," he said with an accent of despair, "informed that three-quarters of the National Guard reinforcements at the palace have withdrawn or gone over to the insurgents, have forced the gate in the main courtyard, and have already killed several persons."' Presumably the latter were troops murdered before firing commenced.

'At a little before 10 a.m.', Liancourt related, 'we heard musket fire from the garden and the palace of the Tuileries, and then some cannon. The fire was irregular.' Weber recounted that he heard '. . . a frightful noise, echoing towards them, of the rolling fire of musketry, and very shortly afterwards, the reports of cannon, all of which showed that the palace of our masters had been attacked.' In passing, it should be noted that both these reports, although by witnesses some 500 yards away, support the view that musket-fire preceded the cannons, and not the other way round as suggested by Constant-Rebecque, Deluze, and Peltier in their accounts. Liancourt's time of a little before 10 a.m. for the commencement of hostilities accords well with a best estimate of around 9.50 a.m.

Weber wrote that the populace on the terrace armed with pikes and pitchforks threatened to attack them, while National Guards brought up cannon, and fired blanks. 'We ranged ourselves in battle formation in two columns,' Weber continued, 'rushed up the terrace steps, and seized the passageway leading to the entrance of the National Assembly from the army of pikes. This on our side was the business of a moment. When we reached the entrance doors, we tried to go into the Chamber, with the idea of surrounding the royal family and saving it, while at the same time reassuring the Assembly members. We cried out to two guards to open the doors, but they replied it was impossible as the doors were barricaded from inside, and they ended by asking for our protection.' Weber's description of his colleagues' motivation was probably over-simplified. Many must have seen the Assembly building as a refuge. It seems highly likely that Weber was at the rear of the columns which entered the narrow alley in front of the main entrance to the Manège. As reported by Madame de Tourzel, Peltier, and seemingly Deville, the leading group succeeded in penetrating inside, but by the time Weber arrived, the door had been barricaded. Weber must have been unaware that some of his comrades had partly succeeded in their enterprise.

'The danger facing the royal family redoubled our efforts', Weber continued. 'We threw ourselves a dozen times on the great door. It began to move, but for want of sappers, all our efforts were unavailing.' Weber's group of National Guards abandoned their efforts and moved up along the alley towards the Rue Saint-Honoré, possibly to try and rally support, or to disperse. However, they were blocked by gunners from the guardhouse in the Cour des Feuillants. 'Deliberating what to do in this terrible moment', Weber wrote, 'I saw the gunners of the guardhouse in the Cour des Feuillants, running here and there, sabres in hand, with great agitation. Their gestures and convulsive movements made me anxious. I cried out and gesticulated to my comrades that the alley was too narrow, unless we wished to be attacked on two sides as the actions of the gunners seemed to foretell. We had in fact only time to get out and form up

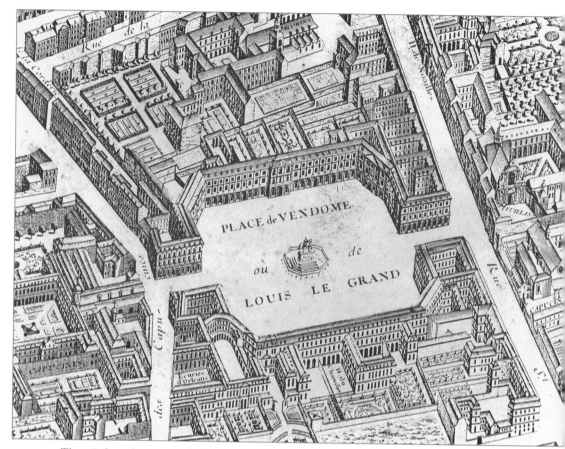

The exit from the courtyard of the Feuillants is on the far right facing the Place Vendôme. The church of the Feuillants where Durler's Swiss were imprisoned can be seen facing the courtyard with the cloisters on one side.

against the wall to face the multitude, when they dragged a cannon with such speed that the wheels passed over the chest of a gunner who was pulled away dead. The cannon was charged with grapeshot and aimed at our position, in order to exterminate, they said, anyone who dared to follow the royal family, against the wishes of the Commune and the Department.' It was obviously not possible to deploy in the narrow alley, and they were frightened of being trapped. The grenadiers of the Filles Saint-Thomas had very limited ammunition, and this probably coloured their actions. But even if they had had more, they would have been reluctant to use it and risk starting a civil war. They had pushed through to the Manège without firing. The gunners, who were part of the National Guards, saw the king's escort as a potential counter-revolutionary force, had been equally concerned not to shoot first at fellow Frenchmen and instead had fired blanks.

We also have a first-hand account from Second sub-Lieutenant Deville on the experiences of the Swiss part of the guard which had accompanied the king to the

Assembly. They waited drawn up below the terrace to the west of their National Guards colleagues. They also saw the heads on the pikes. They heard the murmur of voices in the Manège, and the president's bell frequently calling for order. Deville omitted any mention of the outbreak of fighting at the Tuileries but recounted three blank cannon shots fired at Weber and his comrades. The cannon placed by the gate leading to the Manège now directed blank cannon-fire against the Swiss. Up to then, according to an eyewitness on the terrace, the Swiss below in the garden had been well disposed. However, a small post of Swiss left near the steps now opened fire, probably just to frighten the gunners into running away. A unit of National Guards engaged the Swiss post and after some ten minutes the Swiss were nearly all dead. 'Our brave Swiss', wrote Deville in his account, 'cried out that they were betrayed by the National Guards. They trembled with rage and only waited the command to charge. We put ourselves in battle order facing the terrace; and the crowd, believing that we were going to fire on them, fled at full speed [westward along the terrace] through the cul-de-sac of the Orangerie. While we were in battle order, our generals Maillardoz and Bachmann walked along our front and went to rejoin their Majesties.' It was probably around 10.15 a.m.

The Jacobin Deputy Choudieu, writing 40 years after the event, confirmed Bachmann's visit to the Manège. Although his memory appears uneven, he had good reason to remember confronting Bachmann at this juncture as the latter asked him later to testify to his good behaviour then for his trial. It appears that Choudieu, supported by fellow Jacobins Chabot and Merlin de Thionville, together with some 25 to 30 National Guards belonging to the Assembly's defence force, stopped Bachmann on the terrace steps to prevent him from entering the Assembly. The king had been made aware of the threatened hostilities on the terrace and had sent instructions via d'Abancourt, his War Minister, for the Swiss to withdraw. The Swiss commanders had insisted they receive the order in person from the king. Choudieu and his colleagues eventually let them pass.

Deville continued: 'I then pointed out to Monsieur de Salis, Aide-Major, that our position was very bad, and we should place our backs to the wall of the Manège in order to be in a position where we could see what was coming from the Tuileries Garden.' [Deville was ignoring the fact that the terrace was part of the Assembly's precincts and that they needed permission to station themselves there.] 'We were going to execute this movement when a grenadier of the Filles Saint-Thomas cried out: "Let us go up to the Assembly to defend our King." This voice electrified our officers and our men. We were ordered to turn right and marched off to follow the grenadiers of the Filles Saint-Thomas, by mounting the Feuillants' Terrace. Arriving there, we saw a crowd of armed men coming at us. I saw one who aimed at me.' [Deville, as an ensign carrying the regimental flag, was an obvious target.] 'My comrades and I', continued Deville, 'ordered three rounds of rolling fire. Then we crossed the terrace in order to enter into the Assembly. The grenadiers of the Filles Saint-Thomas, who were in the lead, broke open the two doors and penetrated inside. As soon as members of the Assembly saw them, many fled.' The three rounds fired by the Swiss may have been aimed over the insurgents' heads. The *Journal* mentioned musket balls striking the Assembly's windows, which were high up. Deville very likely could not have been in the position personally to see the entry of some members of the Filles Saint-Thomas and must have obtained this detail from hearsay. As for people fleeing from the Assembly, the *Logographe* referred to some deputies rising up and trying to go out but being restrained by their colleagues.

After careful consideration of the available texts and the overall situation, it is possible to summarise what was actually happening. Witnessing the Swiss fire from the Tuileries, Choudieu rushed back to the Assembly and, as a member of its Military Committee, helped to organise defensive measures against a possible attack from the garden. In his memoirs, Choudieu emphasised his fears of a royalist takeover of the Assembly. A cannon was brought up to intimidate the king's escort in the garden below the Terrasse des Feuillants. Blanks were fired which caused a small Swiss post near the steps leading up to the terrace to shoot back. This post was shot to pieces. The commotion caused the king, not wishing bloodshed, to summon the Swiss to withdraw. Bachmann and Maillardoz went to the Manège to obtain a personal order from Louis. The National Guards of his escort, exasperated and alarmed by the menaces against them, mounted the terrace to try and enter the Assembly. A few succeeded, but the doors were closed on the rest. The Swiss followed after dispersing resistance with three rounds.

Meanwhile, from the outset of the fighting at the Tuileries the king had been under pressure from members of the Assembly to give assurances that he had not ordered the Swiss to open fire. According to Madame de Tourzel, who as the dauphin's governess was with the royal family in the Logographie, the king made a verbal assurance that he had not given orders for any combat. Peltier quoted him as saying: 'I have given orders not to fire.' This is confirmed by the *Moniteur*. However, Louis was unsure. It appears that when firing began, the king enquired from his ministers what precise orders had been given to the Swiss. They too were uncertain. One source had the king repeating to the Assembly the instructions the Swiss had received from Roederer and the municipal officers – that is, to repel force with force.

Madame de Tourzel also wrote of messengers coming to the king from time to time bringing news of what was happening at the Tuileries. The early news would have reported success for the Swiss. Did the king hold off giving definite orders for the Swiss to withdraw until the tide of battle began to go against them? This was claimed by the French historian Marcel Reinhard. The king may have dithered momentarily, but his failure to take any military initiative during the night and early morning showed he was very much aware that accusations of starting a civil war might prove politically fatal. His cause in the Assembly would not then have appeared completely lost, and there is no evidence that he placed any hope in a victory for Swiss arms. He decided to send an order to the Swiss at the Tuileries to withdraw. Circumstantial evidence points to this decision being taken within ten minutes of the battle commencing. This timing seems to be supported by a comment in the *Moniteur* which said the king told the president that he had *just* given an order for the Swiss not to fire, shortly after firing commenced and before the twenty-member mission sent out to keep the peace returned. There is also ambiguous support for this early timing from the official minutes. At around 10.30 a.m., the President of the Assembly announced that he had sent an order for the Swiss at the palace to withdraw to their barracks, and

Dubouchage had chimed in that a similar order sent by Louis had already been received there. In the probable space of ten minutes or so, the king gave two separate orders for different groups of Swiss to withdraw. This must have caused considerable confusion for those editing reports on the Assembly's proceedings.

Madame de Tourzel stated that the king was provided with pen, ink, and paper. The written order sent to the Swiss at the Tuileries has almost certainly survived and must not be confused with the better-known one given by the king to Captain Durler at the Assembly, now in the Carnavalet museum. The Tuileries' order was apparently given to Captain Salis and was inspected by von Mülinen, who wrote a scholarly work on the fate of the Swiss Guards to commemorate the hundredth anniversary of 10 August 1792. Written in ink, the order followed the terms indicated in the Assembly's minutes.

The king sought someone to take the order. It might have been preferable to choose a senior officer of the Swiss Guards from the escort below the terrace who could have gone rapidly across the garden. However, they were not then involved in any confrontation, and it is possible the king in the agitation of the moment may have even forgotten about them. He decided to send a senior regular French officer already present in the Manège, the Comte d'Hervilly, who near midnight had proposed the seizure of ammunition from the Arsenal. He was a Breton nobleman who was to die three years later in an abortive royalist invasion. Hervilly was well known to Louis as second-in-command of his recently disbanded Constitutional Guard. Despite Roederer's admonitions, he had accompanied the king to the National Assembly.

Bertrand de Molleville, a former navy minister and one of Louis' closest advisers, met Hervilly in London in the autumn of 1792. The latter told him that he had offered to carry the order, 'determined at the same time to make use of it in the manner most conducive to the safety of the royal family'. Bertrand went on to overdo the description of what he no doubt felt was a touching scene. He depicted the king and queen imploring Hervilly, as one of their most valuable and faithful servants, not to expose his life; while the latter entreated their majesties to think nothing of it, sententiously adding: 'My post is with the guns, and if I feared them, I should be unworthy of the name of soldier.' Bearing in mind the time to write the order and brief Hervilly, and the length of the journey to the Tuileries, it seems probable that the king decided on the order around 10 a.m., shortly after hostilities had begun and before Swiss successes against the revolutionaries had reached their zenith. Hervilly went via the Rue Saint-Honoré and the Place du Carrousel. This approximately doubled the distance compared with crossing the garden. Allowing for pauses to evade patrols, it must have taken some twenty minutes to reach the palace. The evidence points to Hervilly arriving at the Tuileries towards 10.30 a.m., which means he would have left the Manège not later than 10.10, long before the king could have known about any Swiss reverses at the Tuileries. Moreover, an early timing explains why the king did not use Bachmann and Maillardoz to send an order for the Swiss to withdraw from the palace when shortly afterwards he separately instructed them to lay down their arms and lead the Swiss of his escort back to barracks. By that time, Hervilly was on his way.

According to Bertrand, a Monsieur de Vauzlemont, a National Guards officer formerly under Hervilly's command, insisted upon accompanying him, despite the latter's protests. It was just as well, since Hervilly was splendidly dressed as a

Maréchal-de-Camp in the uniform of the king's former Constitutional Guard, while Vauzlemont wore the more acceptable uniform of a grenadier in the National Guards. No doubt Vauzlemont had been briefed to get him through the post of National Guards blocking the exit to the Rue Saint-Honoré. Hervilly was duly stopped by this post, but Vauzlemont was able to vouch for him, explaining that he was carrying an order for the Swiss Guards to cease fire. 'Look sharp after him, comrade', they replied, 'for you shall answer for him.' Hervilly now became separated from Vauzlemont. It must be concluded that the latter returned to the Assembly to tell Dubouchage that his charge had successfully negotiated the first obstacle. Hardly had Hervilly reached the Rue Saint-Honoré, when he met a detachment of insurgents who fired at him and missed. Two hundred paces further on he was fired upon again, with the same result. On entering the Place du Carrousel via the Rue de l'Echelle, he was grasped by two National Guards. He claimed to have knocked one to the ground, but the other thrust a hand-held bayonet into his thigh, and then ran off. Hervilly extracted the bayonet. It was obviously only a superficial wound, since he was able to keep on running. He entered through the gateway into the Cour des Suisses and passed into the Cour Royale, where as Durler reported: 'Monsieur d'Hervilly, Maréchal de Camp, ran up to me through the musket balls, unarmed and without a hat, and called to us on behalf of the King to cease fire, and withdraw to the National Assembly.'

Bertrand claimed, however, that Hervilly did not at first mention the king's order, but instead began to study whether the defence of the palace might be prolonged. He hoped to gain time for royalists and well-disposed National Guards to join together in repulsing the insurgents and rescuing the king. He concluded against prolonged defence, but for the erroneous reason that the Tuileries was being invaded by insurgents entering from the long Galerie du Louvre. Glutz's account implies that such a military appreciation was carried out, but other reports also make it clear that Hervilly's review of the military situation was rapid, and he quickly gave the order he claimed to have received from the king. No one was actually shown the document. According to the Swiss historian Mülinen it read: 'The King orders the Swiss to withdraw to their barracks; he is within the National Assembly. Paris 10 August 1792 Louis.' Neither Hervilly's version, nor the king's actual written order, mentioned anything about the Swiss laying down their arms as historians frequently repeat.

Mülinen stated that the word 'barracks' was written above a crossed-out word which can be deciphered as 'posts'. The king had first thought the Swiss might withdraw into the palace, but he realised this was unrealistic, and had decided they should retire to their barracks; not the National Assembly as ordered by Hervilly. Bertrand wrote that Hervilly deliberately misled the Swiss in the hope of using them to rescue the king, and had not misread the order. A Swiss officer present, Gibelin, gave a more emphatic version of Hervilly's command, substituting 'next to the person of the Monarch' for 'to the National Assembly'. He also claimed that some people thought they heard Hervilly say, 'with your captured cannons'. Peltier supports this version. Whatever the truth of the matter, Hervilly's erroneous order, unlike that of Captain Nolan at Balaclava, was not to lead to such a glorious episode in the annals of military history, although it was perhaps equally bloody, as the Swiss seem to have suffered a similar percentage of casualties.

CHAPTER 14

Surrender

While the Swiss Guards who had escorted the king to the National Assembly were by the Manège, and the loyalist National Guards were pinned down by a cannon in the Cour des Feuillants, the barricaded doors of the Manège were opened to let out a senior Swiss officer accompanied by a deputy. Deville failed to give the officer's name, but it must have been either Bachmann or Maillardoz. The *Journal* and the *Logographe* report that, following the firing by the terrace, Navy Minister Dubouchage told the Assembly that he had ordered the Swiss on behalf of the king not to use their weapons and to return to their barracks, and had asked for municipal officers to escort them back. Deville wrote: 'The King, who had understood our desire to go and save him, this unfortunate prince who has sacrificed his life – [Deville was writing after the subsequent execution of Louis] – at the horror he felt at sacrificing the blood of his subjects, sent one of our senior officers to us together with a member of the Assembly, to leave the spot, and lay down our arms. We obeyed, and let it please God that we had not done so! We would perhaps have saved our unfortunate master, or we would have perished gloriously in his defence.' This was the second command the king gave that morning for the Swiss to withdraw, following the one despatched with Hervilly to the Tuileries.

Naturally reluctant to surrender loaded weapons to potential enemies, the Swiss discharged their muzzle-loading muskets into the air, preparatory to handing them over. This discharge made a loud noise and was reported in the Assembly proceedings. The Swiss then moved along the alley towards the Rue Saint-Honoré, presumably with instructions to hand over their weapons in the courtyard or little square at the end called the 'Cour des Feuillants'. When they reached it, with the Feuillants' church on the right, Deville noted a six-pounder cannon situated at the end under the Porte des Feuillants leading to the Rue Saint-Honoré. This no doubt was the same gun that Weber mentioned. However, the tail of the Swiss detachment came under fire from insurgents who must have followed them up the alley. The rear Swiss platoons halted, reloaded, and returned fire, and soon caused the skirmishers who had fired at them to withdraw. Carried away by élan, they went in pursuit. In doing so, they became separated from their comrades who had remained in the Cour des Feuillants. Deville wrote that two men were lost in the action, killed at his side.

In relating this incident, Deville omitted to mention that the Swiss were supposed to be surrendering their weapons, which is what the front portion of the force did. When the skirmishing began, nineteen-year-old Deville was leading the Swiss red-coated column with his unit of fusiliers into the Cour des Feuillants. Besides being a unit commander, however, he was also an ensign bearing the regimental flag, white embroidered with fleurs de lys. The flag needed to be near the scene of fighting to inspire the troops. The youthful Deville must have been delighted to find an excuse for not surrendering, and, abandoning his unit without orders, he dashed back with his flag to where Captain d'Erlach and his grenadiers were engaging the skirmishers. He joined them in rushing down the alley towards the Terrace of the Feuillants. By the time the action was over, it would have been difficult to regain his unit without an escort. This whole incident reveals a deep reluctance on the part of the Swiss to give up their arms, and the rear platoons used the excuse of the shots fired at them to disobey the order they had received from the king.

In the confusion, other Swiss also got away in the opposite direction into the Rue Saint-Honoré, including the assistant Regimental Quarter Master, Joseph de Forestier. According to Altishofen, some were caught, but Forestier managed to escape. Constant-Rebecque related that he was chased into the Seine and concealed himself between two boats. The Swiss group commanded by Captain d'Erlach, which Deville had joined, took up a position along the Terrasse des Feuillants towards the Orangerie, where they were left undisturbed for around half an hour. They reciprocated by also doing nothing, when they could have played a critical part. Deville mentioned that they managed to regain a few of their comrades. Presumably some Swiss avoided surrender and went to join their fellow soldiers on the terrace.

It is due to Municipal Officer Leroux that we know what happened to the other part of the escort detachment. When they had finished handing over their weapons and had reached the Porte des Feuillants in order to withdraw to their barracks, they found themselves confronted by armed insurgents in the Rue Saint-Honoré. The formalities of surrendering their weapons had allowed time for a revolutionary force to gather. They were led back into the courtyard by escorting National Guards. On the report that the Swiss had been threatened when trying to exit into the Rue Saint-Honoré, the Assembly resolved that municipal officers Borie and Leroux, who had remained in their midst, should escort the Swiss back to their barracks, thus fulfilling Dubouchage's earlier request. The two municipal officers regarded this as a dangerous assignment, and accepted it with some reluctance. They went to harangue the crowd by the Porte des Feuillants, while the Swiss were reassembled for another attempt at returning to their barracks.

Their efforts to persuade the people to let the Swiss pass were initially successful, according to Leroux. He wrote: 'The considerable crowd which surrounded the gateway were very angry and threatened to perpetrate the greatest violence against the soldiers. We assured the citizens what had been said in the Assembly, that we were charged to lead back these soldiers, who, instead of firing on the people, had fired in the air and surrendered their weapons.' He continued: 'We read the Assembly's resolution, and asked for obedience to the law. The citizens who surrounded us were persuaded, and promised not to attack the Swiss, but demanded that they be disarmed. We insisted that they had no weapons, and several people confirmed this with us, and showed as proof the weapons the Swiss had surrendered. Then we received their word that no harm would be done to these soldiers, placed under the safeguard of the law; and they themselves would organise an escort from the armed citizens [National Guards] who were in the courtyard in front of the gateway.'

It was intended that Leroux and Borie, professional colleagues in medicine as well as municipal officers together, should form part of this escort. Over the past twelve hours, except briefly, they had been inseparable, and if Shakespeare had been alive to write a tragedy on 10 August they might have become as linked in playgoers' minds as Rosencrantz and Guildenstern. They also almost shared the Danes' fate for their pains. No sooner had they obtained some agreement for the Swiss to be escorted peaceably than they were threatened for having collaborated with the Court at the Tuileries during the night and early morning. Leroux had a bayonet thrust against his side, and they were menaced with loaded muskets aimed almost at arm's length. They were roughly told to clear off promptly, if they did not wish to meet their end. Both fled back to the Assembly and took off their tricolour sashes, their emblems of office. The Swiss were not to have their escort back to their barracks and remained within the confines of the Convent of the Feuillants.

Meanwhile, as reported, Hervilly had arrived in the Cour Royale of the Tuileries towards 10.30 a.m., giving orders for the Swiss to withdraw to the National Assembly, rather than to their barracks as intended. The officers grouped around Durler and Salis immediately set about assembling a force. Drummers were found to beat the 'générale' for forming up on the garden terrace of the palace. While the men were being put in line by their sergeants, Durler and other officers spent their time in moving some captured cannons to cover the withdrawal from the palace. A loaded gun found in the Vestibule was pointed at the Porte Royale to deter pursuit. This activity was carried out under fire, and Durler was saved from injury by a grenadier who pushed him violently against a fellow officer when he saw him being aimed at. An instant later, the step on which he had been standing under the columned entrance was hit. The placing of cannons under the Vestibule aimed at the Porte Royale is good evidence that significant revolutionary forces had not yet succeeded in taking up a major position within the Cour Royale. However, there was a certain amount of infiltration, some of which Durler claimed consisted of insurgents who had remained in hiding by the palace from the beginning of the Swiss counter-attack.

Captain Baron Rudolphe de Reding from Schwitz, helping to move another cannon under the Vestibule from the garden terrace, was less fortunate than Durler, and had the top of his arm shattered by a musket ball. Under Aide-Major Gibelin, who had been helping Reding, took the backpack from a dead soldier nearby and placed it under his head. While lying there, he later received three sabre cuts on the head when the palace was overrun, and presumably was left for dead. He was rescued by a tailor in the National Guards who knew him and was smuggled into the Hôtel de Malte, close by in the Rue de l'Echelle. Kayser de Frauenstein, the regiment's Magistrate, who did not participate in the actual battle and because of his quasi-diplomatic position seems to have had immunity from arrest, wrote on 20 August: 'I have only been able to see two officers; one is Reding whom I found that same dreadful Friday in bed in the evening, and very badly treated, having an arm

The advance of the revolutionaries through the Vestibule. The Great Stairs can be glimpsed in the centre of the picture. In reality, the insurgents entered after organised resistance had ceased.

broken by a musket ball, and receiving three sabre cuts in the head. Since the Hôtel de Malte where he is staying is known as a lodging place for Swiss officers, I advised him to have himself taken to a less well-known residence. But he was discovered last Wednesday, and carried off to the Abbaye.' While suffering considerable pain from his wounds in the notorious prison of the former Abbaye of Saint Germain des Prés, Reding's last hours, before he was murdered on 2 September, were recorded for posterity by Journiac de Saint-Méard who was fortunate in being set at liberty.

The number of men formed up on the garden terrace was given by one source as 400, but this figure is not supported by other witnesses or by inference. Glutz claimed the number was 150, while Deluze, who wrote the earliest account, said this number arrived at the Assembly after casualties, which Peltier gave at around 30. Durler wrote that he had 100 men with him when at the National Assembly. Hervilly, who accompanied the Swiss, said he arrived with only around 60. Weber gave a precise figure of 86 for disarmed Swiss grenadiers at the National Assembly, possibly because he was able to count their muskets piled up inside near the entrance. The journalist Peltier wrote that only 100 men and a few National Guards set off through the garden. The inclusion of token National Guards shows that the Swiss were still trying to adhere to the pretence that they were acting as auxiliaries of the municipal militia.

The confusion over the size of this Swiss force which went to the National Assembly may have resulted from the existence of two separate commands, one under Durler and the other under Salis. There is some evidence that informants from one command tended to ignore details relating to the other, although it seems very probable that Durler considered himself in overall command. *Post facto*, this idea was reinforced because Salis failed to write his own account. Thus, Peltier's source may have referred only to Durler's unit. Hervilly's low figure, on the other hand, might be from a need to explain the failure of his efforts to create a situation whereby the Swiss could take over the National Assembly. Any calculation, however, will have to bear in mind that the official count of Swiss prisoners held the next day in the precincts of the convent was only 112. The greater part of these prisoners derived from the surrender of Durler's and Salis' men, but may have included a few from Louis' escort who had not taken advantage of the opportunity offered them to escape during the previous evening. In addition, it is reported that men captured around the Place Louis XV were sent in driblets to the central collecting point of the Feuillants' church. Against this, the French historian Mortimer-Ternaux claimed that some soldiers were extracted from the church in the afternoon and massacred en route to the Hôtel de Ville. This is doubtful. After due consideration, the number of Swiss officers and men who set out with Durler and Salis from the central section of the palace terrace under the Clock Tower was around 150, possibly a little higher if Mortimer-Ternaux was correct.

It is difficult to explain the mystery of why sixteen officers went with this force to the Manège, leaving only nine back at the palace, excluding medical officers, to command some 350 or more men, after allowing for estimated casualties so far and initial defectors. This gave rise to complaints of desertion by their officers, as Peltier reports. There seems no simple explanation for this peculiar situation which must have left large numbers of the rank and file without adequate leadership. It reflects on the lack of a proper command structure among the Swiss at the palace after their senior officers accompanied the king to the National Assembly. One can only surmise that at the time of Hervilly's arrival, the majority of officers had gravitated to the Vestibule to concert a future course of action now that ammunition was running out.

Durler and his colleagues, in their haste to reach the Manège holding the king, were obviously unwilling to delay their departure by trying to extract more troops from defensive positions spread throughout the palace. Thus, it seems likely that they advanced with only the troops they had already to hand, and may have even excluded some like Grenadier Fonjallaz, who were no longer properly armed. Yet if they had waited five or ten minutes, they could have marched with at least double their number. They may have been encouraged to act hastily by skirmishers subjecting the Swiss to harassing fire as they formed up. Their lack of ammunition made them unable to make an effective response. It is probable that the Swiss were also subject to enfilading fire from the cannons posted at the far end of the Pont Royal, as well as from guns stationed on the Terrasse des Feuillants. A Sergeant Fridolin Heffti from the canton of Glaris, described as a man of prodigious strength, had his thigh smashed by a cannon ball as the troops were about to form up on the terrace.

Aide-Major Glutz believed that the king was calling on the Swiss to deliver him from the hands of his enemies, and felt at last something useful was being done. He was probably far from being alone in this sentiment. The Swiss were encouraged as they started off by Baron de Vioménil, brother of the general, who reminded them how they had helped previous kings of France in a critical situation. 'Hurrah! brave Swiss, go and save the King; your ancestors have done so more than once.' Once they had negotiated the gate in the railings leading to the Grande Allée, they marched rapidly in a broad formation diagonally across the garden, probably arriving at the Assembly some minutes before 11 a.m. During this passage they were subjected to heavy crossfire, as well as direct fire from the Terrasse des Feuillants. It was reported that the Swiss did not return fire as they had little or no ammunition left. Second Sub-lieutenant Gros was fatally wounded, and Repond was hit in the leg. Durler had a musket ball through his hat. Two Swiss officers present on the march mentioned severe casualties among the rank and file. The next morning, Dr John Moore reported on the number of casualties on the garden side of the Tuileries: 'The naked bodies of the Swiss', he wrote, 'for they were already stripped, lay exposed on the ground. I saw a great number on the terrace, immediately before the palace of the Tuileries; some lying singly in different parts of the gardens; and some in heaps, one above another, particularly near the terrace of the Feuillants.'

The Swiss were able to mount the terrace and enter the corridors of the Manège. Sword in hand, Captain Salis led a group of officers directly into the Chamber itself. Gibelin, who was with them, wrote: 'I remember that at the side of the Assembly called the "left" side, they rose precipitately crying "the Swiss!" and tried to get out of the windows.' It was in the seating arrangements of the French National Assembly at the Manège that deputies sitting on the left of the president, and hence the left figuratively, became associated with radical politics ever afterwards.

Salis was promptly told that armed men were not allowed in the Chamber. The Swiss eyewitness reports, except Durler's, are generally confused at this stage. It seems likely that Salis and his officer companions withdrew from the Chamber accompanied by deputies. One or more of these spoke to Durler, who was then in the corridors. He was told the Swiss must leave the Assembly precincts and lay down their arms. Durler replied that he had been asked to do this before at the Tuileries, but he was unwilling to obey unless he received a direct order from the king, and only from the king. He was then told by a senior army officer, de Menou, that Louis was in the Logographie of the Assembly. Durler asked a deputy to lead him to the king, which he did. All this may have taken ten minutes or so. He was admitted to the crammed box itself where, he wrote, he found the entire royal family, and Messieurs de Choiseul, Hervilly, the Prince de Guise, and other members of the Court. He related that he said to the king: 'Sire, they want me to lay down my arms. Despite the few who remain with me, I will only do it with your orders. The King replied: "Lay down your weapons, but it is understood only into the hands of the National Guards; I do not want brave people such as you all to perish." The Queen, Madame Elizabeth, and others who were in the box with the King, enquired with much interest whether I was wounded.' The king made a careful distinction between National Guards subject to some discipline, and insurgent volunteers only too ready to take the law into their own hands. His meaning, however, was probably more precise. He could well have been aware that at least part of the National Guards then guarding the Manège belonged to the loyalist citizen militia which had formed part of his escort.

Durler clearly stated next that he went out of the box back into the Chamber, where there were several of his officers and around 100 men. It seems difficult to comprehend that all these men had been allowed not only into the National Assembly building, but into the Chamber itself. No account contradicts Durler's statement, although none supports it, except in so much as, later, six of the officers present signed Durler's account. Even so, it would have made little difference whether they were in the actual Chamber or outside in the surrounding passageway. There can be no argument that the Swiss had come beyond the main entrance doors into the corridors, and there was nothing to stop them from entering the Chamber itself. None of these happenings, from the arrival of this Swiss force at the Manège to their disarming, are even hinted at in reports on the Assembly's proceedings. On the other hand, the shots fired some three-quarters of an hour earlier by the Swiss of the king's escort on the terrace were fully reported. But they had not entered the Assembly building.

It seems more than likely that it was considered best to draw a discreet veil over the fact that the Swiss had been allowed to occupy the Manège, where they might have made things very difficult. It is pertinent to ask why the doors leading into the Assembly precincts had not been barricaded, as they were earlier on to exclude the National Guards belonging to the king's escort. The answer is to be found in Weber's memoirs. It was these self-same troops who were now guarding the entrance to the Manège. He stated that they had no intention of firing on the Swiss. Liancourt independently confirmed the presence of National Guards from the king's escort circulating within the Assembly's corridors.

Fortunately for the revolutionaries, the king could be relied upon to do nothing. Still not wishing to compromise himself and concerned to avoid bloodshed, he had ordered Durler to command the Swiss to lay down their arms and retire to their barracks. What could the Swiss have done if the king had been a desperate gambler and promptly told them to try and restore his position by seizing the Manège, regrouping as many of their comrades as possible, and holding out until the citizens of Paris fulfilled their obligations to the law and the Constitution? The situation would have become interesting, to say the least. If, before entering the Assembly building, the Swiss had briefly reconnoitred the terrace, they could have found the unit under Erlach and Deville a short way along towards the Orangerie. These troops were still relatively well supplied with ammunition. The two forces combined would have been strong enough to control the terrace temporarily as well as occupy the Manège. They would then have been able to add to their ranks the second wave of Swiss coming from the palace, and to release the remainder of the king's escort being held in the convent buildings. One Swiss officer in his account mentioned having seen the surrendered soldiers who had formed part of the king's escort. This would have given them a force of around 450 Swiss Guards to hold the Manège and the convent buildings, which were relatively defensible, to overawe the Jacobins in the galleries, and to inspire a majority of deputies favouring the Constitution. The stationing of loyalist citizen militia at the entrance and within the Manège might have provided the means for rallying National Guards in the surrounding middle-class districts to the cause of legality.

Naturally, this is all very hypothetical. For any chance of real success, constitutionalists interested in preserving the Monarchy would have had to obtain the effective support of the National Assembly. This would have meant preparations for mobilising orators capable of appealing to the right sentiments, and able to obtain decrees for condemning the insurrection and regaining control of the National Guards. There was no such planning, not even by the royalists, despite a strong Jacobin belief that the Court intended to take over the National Assembly. The passivity and self-distrust of the king, the poor calibre of his ministers and advisers, together with the indecision, to say the least, of the National Assembly politicians and the Department, made certain the triumph of the revolutionaries on 10 August 1792.

Although Durler did not mention having done so, it seems likely he asked Louis for a written order to satisfy his commanding officers and the cantonal authorities

The note given by the king to Captain Durler of the Swiss Guards, ordering him to surrender. This was the last act of Louis' reign.

that he had acted properly. Durler's report continued: 'Hardly had I returned to the Chamber when the King had the goodness to send me a note signed in his own hand, of which the words were as follows: "The King orders the Swiss to lay down their arms immediately and to withdraw to their barracks."' The Durler family later sold this document, the last written order the king was to give, to the Carnavalet Museum in Paris. After an interval, the Swiss deposited their weapons behind the main entrance doors of the Manège. This was not without some reluctance. There were protests from soldiers who said that despite lacking ammunition, they would be able to fight on with their bayonets. Durler was instructed to take his men to the Church of the Feuillants along the passage 100 yards or so to the north. He was also advised to tell his soldiers to remove their conspicuous scarlet uniform coats with their blue facings, as otherwise they might be attacked. Some accepted this advice. Durler complained that his force was overwhelmed with insults and threats on the way to the church. On entering the building, four guards told him that he was most guilty, as were the other officers, and that they were going to be taken immediately to the Hôtel de Ville. 'I told the Deputy leading us', wrote Durler, 'that the church was a death-trap, and that I would not remain there. I recalled the officers. Messieurs Aide-Major de Glutz, Deluze, de la Corbière, Ignace de Maillardoz followed me. However, Monsieur Joseph de Zimmermann was too advanced in the church to see me. The Deputy said some hard things, but finished by assuring us that he wished to take us to a place where we would be safe.'

Glutz mentioned that the progress back through the alley was perilous, and they were accused of being criminals who had fired on 'our brothers,' and should be punished and delivered to the people. The deputy accompanying them persuaded the accusers to give way. Deluze wrote in his account that the officers wished to enter the Chamber to receive the direct protection of the National Assembly, but this was regretfully refused. The place of safety chosen for the officers was the Bureau des Inspecteurs which was situated just by the gate leading to the Terrasse des Feuillants, and opposite the Manège. Gibelin described it as a kind of cellar which had been transformed into an Assembly office. When Durler arrived there, he found a number of Swiss officers already present who were not in the party which had been with him when he started to enter the church. This group, which consisted of officers in Salis' force, must have gone beforehand to the Cour des Feuillants, and they had had the same experience as Durler. Gibelin, who was one of them, reported: 'Our soldiers were disarmed in the courtyard of the Feuillants and stripped of their uniforms, and those who tried to resist were murdered.' This statement contradicts Durler who stated that his men laid down their arms in the Assembly corridors, and makes no mention of any mistreatment of his men apart from insults. When Gibelin wrote of disarming 'our soldiers', he was referring to Salis' command, thus indicating there were two separate surrenders.

Hervilly told Bertrand that he had deliberately held on to the order for the Swiss to withdraw to their barracks when he went to the Tuileries. He intended to utilise it to exonerate the king in the event of the latter being accused of trying to organise a coup when the Swiss Guards arrived at the Assembly. But the king's failure to react meant that there was now no need to protect his innocence. It seems certain that Salis was presented with Hervilly's order when he insisted on having his own written order from the king, after Durler had received his, in view of his independent command. Hervilly must have believed he was fulfilling his soldierly duty to provide his ultimate commander, the king, with military means to use as he thought fit. Nevertheless, he probably also saw his action as a triumph of hope over experience. He had deplored the king's inactivity a few hours previously, and very likely did not expect any change now. However, he had done his best, and may have even obtained some bitter pleasure from putting the king on the spot.

As for the Swiss officers, did they record any thoughts apart from deploring the king's orders to surrender? Only one Swiss officer present went so far as to make a reasoned comment on what might have happened if they had not departed for the National Assembly. This is the anonymous account found among the papers of Baron Conrad de Billieux, who was an officer in the detachment which went to Normandy. It was published in 1893, and the author has never been identified. He suggested that if the Swiss had been allowed to prolong their resistance at the Tuileries effectively, which he believed was possible, the insurgents might well have cracked, as although they were much superior in numbers, their military capacity was poor. This would have caused the majority of the National Guard units, who up to then had remained neutral, to come over to the side of legality. Dr John Moore, who was a keen observer of what was happening in Paris that August, made a similar observation. But it is a question of timing. It was probably too late by 10.30 a.m. when Hervilly reached the Tuileries, and found the Swiss almost out of ammunition. As previously argued, the best time for a military solution, assuming the troops could have been motivated for aggressive action, was some three hours earlier when the insurgents first arrived on the Carrousel.

CHAPTER 15

Evacuation

Colonel Karl Pfyffer von Altishofen of Lucerne had been interested for some time in writing an account of the destruction of his regiment on 10 August 1792. In 1818, the matter took on some urgency as plans were afoot to erect a monument, the famous Lion of Lucerne, for the Swiss Guards who fell in the battle or were murdered afterwards. He was not an eyewitness himself as he had been on leave in Switzerland when the action was fought. He now sought assistance from Nicolas de Gady, Colonel General of the Swiss in France. He received the following rather petulant reply: 'Swiss and other persons that I have been able to consult in Paris have always referred me to Peltier. It is truly surprising, as well as irritating, that the surviving participants of that horrible and honourable event for the Swiss, have not during twenty-six years of leisure occupied themselves in producing an exact and substantiated account of the business of 10 August, and of what preceded it and what followed it. It is to be hoped that you will obtain some fragments from each of them, and that you will be able to add them together to make an exact picture.' It seems fair to say that Altishofen only partially succeeded in fulfilling this task.

This book has frequently cited Jean Gabriel Peltier, who published his account in London in autumn 1792 under the title *Dernier Tableau de Paris*. He remains the primary source for what happened to the defenders at the Tuileries after the force under Durler and Salis withdrew to the Manège. The historian may well grimace at the concluding paragraph of Durler's restricted account written in 1793. 'Such is the summary of the principal facts that I saw with the officers here below [seven signatures], who were found under my command. Other officers with our brave soldiers fought and perished, arms in hand, be it at the palace, in the garden, and on the Place Louis XV; many eyewitnesses would be able to give the details.' It is possible that Durler was referring to specific eyewitnesses of whom he was aware, but whose accounts were never taken down at the time. Durler himself died in action in 1801 fighting for the British at Alexandria in Egypt. When Altishofen came to write his account in 1818, memories were fading and it was largely too late to produce the exact picture Gady proposed.

Peltier related that the aristocrats, who had been positioned in the State Apartments, debated what to do while the Swiss were fighting in the courtyards. Few, if any, were equipped for regular combat. At length they saw Durler's and Salis's force drawn up in the centre of the garden terrace and learned that they were preparing to march to the National Assembly. The account given by Swiss sources

A view of the Lion of Lucerne commemorating the Swiss Guards who fought at the Tuileries on 10 August 1792. The monument is carved into the rock face.

of Baron de Vioménil's salutation confirms their awareness of the situation. They decided they should try and follow. Not all the 200 or so gentlemen who had been formed into three units around 7.30 a.m. were still in the palace. Some had left at the time the king went to the Manège, including the young Liancourt. The remainder now went on to the terrace in front of the queen's apartments, with the exception of a few who successfully escaped with some loyal National Guards by bridging the gap made in the floor of the Galerie du Louvre, the exit from which had been left unguarded. The number of these royalist supporters was enhanced by some even more indifferently armed retainers and courtiers living in the palace and its dependencies, together with the headquarters officers from the 17th Military Division. They were joined by those Swiss principally posted in the State Apartments and the Galerie des Carraches, from which they had directed fire on the Cour Royale. They assembled on the garden terrace towards the river. The bookseller Nicholas Ruault, who was in Paris on 10 August, but not present at the Tuileries, gave the size of the force as 500–600. Peltier does not give the starting figure, but later refers to some 300 who went towards the Place Louis XV. A calculated guess is that the force probably consisted of around 200 or so partly armed nobles, officers, retainers and servants, and a roughly equal number of Swiss.

It is unknown whether there was any organised command, but only the Swiss represented any military value. The latter, however, had too few officers, probably six, and limited ammunition. After leaving the terrace, they had to break through the railings below the queen's apartments. They could only pass through the gap in single file, and according to Peltier, the first two Swiss soldiers were killed by a unit of hostile National Guards only thirty paces away. It was decided to march close up to the Terrasse de l'Eau, and then to turn right and cross the garden to approach the Assembly at right angles. The decision to reach the Assembly in this manner, rather than directly by an oblique march, may have come from a desire to keep out of close range of the guns and troops posted on the Terrasse des Feuillants, until the trees in the western two-thirds of the garden provided some cover. Despite being shot at from many directions, casualties in passing through the first part of the garden were relatively light.

Half-way down the garden under the Terrasse de l'Eau, there was a guardhouse manned by National Guards. They fired on the column and the Swiss replied, suffering some ten casualties. Possibly led by the Duc de Choiseul, the column then turned right as planned, and crossed the garden towards the steps leading to the National Assembly. Although partly under cover of the trees, the opposing fire was relatively fierce when they approached the Terrasse des Feuillants. Realising that mounting the steps would force them to attack on a narrow front, and that they had little ammunition to provide covering fire, the troops wavered and abandoned the attempt to 'rescue' the king. Instead, they sought to retire, the Swiss to their barracks to the west of Paris, and the gentlemen and courtiers to their homes or to friends. According to Peltier, some Swiss, having fired off all their ammunition and thrown away their muskets, now also jettisoned their sabres and cartridge pouches with the intention of disbanding.

The young Choiseul, who the year before had failed to provide an escort for the king on his flight to Varennes, tried to rally the force. Believing he had succeeded, he rushed forward sword in hand, mounted the steps, evaded the defenders on the terrace, and succeeded in entering the National Assembly unscathed, expecting to be followed. Charging with upraised weapon, he was stopped by a Jacobin deputy, Merlin de Thionville, who said: 'Wretched man, what are you doing here! You're finished. Put down your sword.' Bewildered by his isolation, Choiseul went meekly to the king and his party in the Logographie. In order for Choiseul to be with Louis when Durler saw him, the time gap between the withdrawal of the first and second groups of Swiss from the palace must have been relatively small, less than ten minutes.

There is a linkage between Peltier's account and the eyewitness reports provided by Liancourt and Deville. The latter stated: 'We saw coming towards us a group whose uniforms we did not recognise, so much were they covered in dust. We were getting ready to fire on them when we saw that they were our brave comrades who were coming from the palace. They like us had received the King's order to withdraw and lower their arms. They had carried it out, and that is what had ruined us. They were covered with blood and smoke. They came to our position and we helped them to climb the wall on to the terrace. They were only a small number, the greater part having been killed, be it in the courtyards, in the interior of the palace, or be it during their retreat.' It seems very probable that these were the unarmed Swiss, mentioned by Peltier, who intended to disband. Moving up the garden towards the Place Louis XV, they had seen Deville's unit formed up on the terrace. Without an officer, they had decided to join their comrades. As they arrived unarmed, it would be natural for Deville to assume they had surrendered their weapons after receiving orders similar to those given to the king's escort.

A military tactician will see that a considerable opportunity was missed by Erlach's unit on the terrace. If their view had not been obscured by the smoke and trees, they might have seen the approach of the main body of Swiss and others across the garden, and have used their still relatively plentiful supply of ammunition to clear the terrace by enfilading fire. This would have enabled these forces to mount the steps leading to the Manège, where they could have found Durler's and Salis' men still operational. In fact, Deville stated that they now dispersed some National Guards above the steps when the latter fired on them after seeing them assisting the band of unarmed Swiss from the garden. This action was too late. Captain d'Erlach had failed to show any initiative, and to try to keep in touch with what was happening elsewhere. If he had, he might have transformed the situation. Shortly afterwards, he was to complain that he had received no orders.

The 26-year-old Liancourt, seething with rage and despair, described his feelings at the time of the repulse of the Swiss:

> I cannot describe the disgust, the anger, and the desire for vengeance I felt. However, it was necessary, for my own safety, to dissimulate them. The result was a feeling of horror and even desire to get myself killed, which is surely not a reasonable attitude; one that I had never experienced before, and did not believe possible to experience. But at that moment, when I wanted to get myself killed, though desiring at least to render my death useful, and going to the entrance of the Feuillant's Passage which gave on to the garden of the Tuileries, I saw

through the wrought-iron gate a man knocked down on the terrace steps. It was an old man dressed in black whose face was hidden by blood. A murderer, standing on the terrace above, hit him with blows from his pike. The crowd was immense. The old man raised himself up and fainted. I threw myself forward, took him in my arms, and carried him into the passageway. I wounded the assassin with a stroke from my sword, and then threw it away in order not to be recognised. The old man was the Vicomte de Maillé, who sometime before had been nominated as Governor of Saint-Domingue. I drew him into the alley approaching the Assembly. A National Guard there went to fetch some water. I washed his wounds. He had three in the head, and a light one in his side. I mopped him with my handkerchief, and finding a Deputy whose expression showed that he was not participating in the crimes of that day, I asked him if he had enough humanity to take the wounded man to his family. He replied that he had and gripped my hand. I trusted him, being unable to do better, and I was right, for he himself took him into a safe place as I learned that evening when I went to take his valuables, still stained with his blood, back to his family.

Separately, Peltier added a gloss to this incident, saying the wounded Vicomte de Maillé was taken to the Bureau des Inspecteurs where many Swiss officers had been placed for their safety. Unfortunately, while the fate of the majority of these officers had a happy outcome, de Maillé was arrested and taken to the Abbaye prison where in due course he was massacred. More fortunate was the similarly named 84-year-old Maréchal de Mailly, whom the king had left in command at the Tuileries. He had been wounded in the thigh. An artisan took pity on him hobbling along, and diverted his comrades' attention by telling them to chase another aristocrat while he 'took care' of this one. Mailly later recounted that the workman said: 'Brave old man, you have difficulty in walking. Give me your arm and do not fear. Do you live far from here?'

The majority of the Swiss and gentlemen appear to have marched towards the Pont-Tournant with the intention of crossing over and debouching on to the Place Louis XV. However, they found the position manned, and the swing bridge turned away. Instead, they moved across its front to the other side of the garden, and mounted the Terrasse de l'Eau to enter the Jardin du Dauphin. Many casualties were suffered from the fire of the National Guards including cannon stationed at the Pont-Tournant. Officers Waldener, Muller and Simon de Maillardoz lost their lives then or shortly afterwards. From the Jardin du Dauphin it was possible to reach the Place Louis XV, from which the Swiss hoped to reach their barracks to the west of Paris via the Avenue des Champs-Elysées, and whence the nobles hoped to disperse. This reconstruction is based upon Peltier's account, but is supported by a brief eyewitness statement in a letter written by Father Secundus Loretan from the Valais. He was probably towards the rear of the column. 'We turned to go the National Assembly', he wrote, 'but there was considerable fire from the terrace and many fell. We next turned to go to the Swing Bridge, but it was closed. There we found the garden strewn with our grenadiers. We changed direction and went to the Dauphin's Garden, and came on to the street which went to Versailles.' Thanks to having exchanged his priest's costume for bourgeois clothes supplied by Simon de Maillardoz, Loretan was able to merge into the crowd and escape.

Peltier's account of events after the Place Louis XV was reached degenerates into a series of anecdotes about happenings to individuals and small detachments. The reliable Desbouillons, however, does refer to a report of the Swiss forming a square there, and inflicting a number of casualties before being overwhelmed by cannon fire. This was almost certainly the main body of Swiss which Father Loretan was accompanying and which formed a square to confront cavalry. 'Then we arrived on the Place Louis XV,' he continued, 'where we were attacked by cavalry [mounted Gendarmerie]. These fell on my comrades like lions and sabred them down. Also some cannons were wondrously effective. The Swiss were assaulted on all sides. A great number of them were killed on this battlefield.' The cannon-fire would seem to have caused the Swiss to break their square and to divide into smaller units. These now began to lose cohesion. Some soldiers escaped up the Champs-Elysées to the west, and others exited the Place Louis XV on the north side via the Rue des Champs-Elysées, the Rue Royale, and the Rue Saint Florentin. Before reverting to these attempts to escape, it would seem best to relate the one substantial known eyewitness account of events in this area, that produced by Ensign Deville.

Deville had recounted that his group had helped a number of unarmed Swiss soldiers to climb the wall of the terrace. 'While we were taking them into our ranks', he continued, 'some National Guards fired on us from the gateway leading towards the Manège. We replied, and having killed some, the remainder took flight. We then went towards the cul-de-sac of the Orangerie terrace [above the northwestern corner of the garden]. Several of our soldiers then left their ranks and went down [via some steps] towards the Place Louis XV, which soon led to the remainder of the detachment following suit.' Deville was disturbed by this development and went up to his commander, Captain d'Erlach. He pointed out that they had a good position on the terrace and should stay there. He implored Erlach to give orders to call them back. Erlach was temporarily in a state of shock. He rounded on Deville in a temper, and said: 'Well! What orders should I give since I have received none whatever myself.' Erlach reconsidered and accepted Deville's suggestion. They both rushed down to the square. Deville cried out as loud as he could: 'How is it possible that the Swiss disband without orders?'

Unfortunately, they were already too far away to hear him. He ran after a file of grenadiers which was now entering the Champs-Elysées. He caught up with them and pointed out that there were many troops in the side streets, including cavalry and concealed cannon. Erlach came to join him, sword in hand. But they had left the remainder of their detachment behind to its own devices. It was now moving up the Rue Royale to reach the Rue Saint-Honoré, from which it would be easier to disperse and hide. Immediately, Deville set off again to rally this force, leaving Erlach behind in the Champs-Elysées. When he succeeded in reaching them, he found himself in the middle of a firefight with a group of insurgents. This did not go all one way for the Swiss, and a number were killed by musket-fire and by a cannon placed among masonry assembled on the Place Louis XV for finishing the construction of the then Pont Louis XVI, now the Pont de la Concorde. It is possible to identify this action with details in Peltier's account.

Deville was unsuccessful in rallying this group and turned back towards the Champs-Elysées. He met some of the royalist gentlemen and general officers of the 17th Military Division, who had been at the Tuileries and now seemed to be wandering aimlessly. He tried to rejoin Erlach, but could not see him anywhere. He was told later that he had gone farther up the Champs-Elysées and was killed by one of the two pieces of cannon situated at the Pont-Tournant. As we shall see later, Erlach may have had an even more unpleasant fate. Continuing up the Champs-Elysées himself, Deville was fired on several times and decided it would be safer to return to the Terrasse des Feuillants. While going there he met Louis de Zimmermann, First Lieutenant of Grenadiers, who was later to be massacred at the Conciergerie on 2 September. Zimmermann suggested that they should try and return to the Manège where the King was. Deville mentioned that cannon fire coming from guns on the Pont Louis XVI was frequent.

He and Zimmermann went back on to the Feuillants' terrace via the Orangerie, while discussing the disastrous turn of events of that unfortunate day. As they reached the gate which led to the Manège and the Convent of the Feuillants, a crowd of National Guards and people came out of the alley by the Assembly, and advanced towards them. Several took aim, and even fired. Deville wrote: 'I said in a low voice to Zimmermann: "Let us defend ourselves and sell our lives dearly." At that moment several men threw themselves on me to seize my sabre.' Continuing his account, Deville related that a colossal pioneer with a false moustache boasted to his comrades that he would break Deville's head with his axe. Deville let go of his sabre and, holding his flagstaff with both hands, thrust the sharp point at the pioneer's chest, threatening to drive it in if he tried to carry out his threat. The pioneer moved away. The National Guards cried out for Deville to surrender. They said that they would do him no harm. His standard was then taken from his hands after a vain struggle.

In fact, once they had been disarmed, Deville and Zimmermann were left to their own devices. They thought to look for their commanding officers, Maillardoz and Bachmann, at the Assembly. Deville took a bourgeois by the arm and asked him to take them inside the building, but they were refused entry and told that their commanders were at the church of the Feuillants. On the way, they came across Second Under Lieutenant de la Corbière from Geneva, who had only been with the Swiss Guards for three days as a volunteer. He had been in Durler's group sent to the church of the Feuillants, and had become separated from the other officers, perhaps trying to escape. Four National Guards were attempting to drag him away. Deville told him not to resist. However, a National Guard gave him a sabre cut on the head which floored him. This incident was also recounted by Corbière himself three months later near Geneva when speaking to a French soldier. According to Altishofen, who probably obtained the information directly, Corbière was threatened with an axe before he was cut to the ground, but an unknown woman protected him with her body. Together with Joseph de Zimmermann, whom Durler had been unable to recall from the church, and possibly Ignace de Maillardoz, they were saved by a supply clerk attached to the National Assembly who hid them in his office until midnight. He obtained a surgeon for Corbière's wounds. All escaped.

Reverting to Peltier, one platoon of Swiss was cornered by the Ministry of the Marine in the Rue Royale, and most were killed. Five managed to hide in the cellar of a neighbouring house where the concierge took pity on them. Another group took refuge in the Venetian embassy on the Rue Saint-Florentin. First Under-Lieutenant Forestier Saint-Venant, the brother of the Deputy Regimental Quartermaster, led a platoon towards the Champs-Elysées, of which the first part, as today, was lined with trees and gardens on either side. Looking back, he saw a similar-sized platoon fleeing up the Rue Royale together with some gentlemen. Like Deville, he decided to try and rally it. He left an officer in charge whom Peltier mysteriously referred to as Monsieur de Mon—. This is the only name that Peltier concealed in his account, unless he genuinely did not know its ending. On returning with some men to where he had left de Mon—, Saint-Venant could no longer find him. Up to this moment, this account so parallels Deville's experiences as part of Erlach's group that some confusion must be suspected. But the sequel is different. Peltier wrote that Saint-Venant, finding himself with only a few troops, wished at least to perish gloriously. This is the officer whose letter is quoted in Chapter 2. 'If my life could suffice to restore calm and re-establish that unfortunate family on which I shed tears, Heaven is my witness that it will cost me only a sigh. I would give my life with all my heart.' He charged a body of insurgent forces stationed by the equestrian statue of Louis XV in the centre of the square. He is recounted as driving it back three times, but, having lost half his men, he felt obliged to fall back towards the Rue des Champs-Elysées, at right angles to the avenue. He reached the Café des Ambassadeurs, when a mounted gendarme saw him. The gendarme leapt with his horse over the ditch which separated the park from the highway and shot him dead with a pistol shot in the back.

Altishofen obviously used Peltier as a source for some of his anecdotes, such as Forestier Saint-Venant's death on the Champs-Elysées, but also has additional stories of heroic and possibly mythical deeds. One such is of Sergeant Stalder from Lucerne, Altishofen's canton, who with two men defended the cannons positioned by Durler in the Vestibule of the Tuileries to cover his retreat. After killing seven of the enemy, he was left to fight on alone. When he had exhausted his ammunition, he resorted to using his sabre with his left hand after his right arm had been disabled by an axe blow. There is the doubtful report of the young ensign de Montmollin who died near the statue of Louis XV. Fighting heroically, he was stabbed from behind. He fell, wrapping his flag around him, supported by a faithful corporal. This event will be examined in Chapter 22.

However, the most famous story of all derives from Peltier, although it was considerably embellished by Altishofen. Comte Hubert de Diesbach, First Lieutenant of Grenadiers, with 80 of his men, defended the Great Stairs at the palace for a quarter of an hour, killing 400 of the enemy. When only seven of his company remained alive, Diesbach said to them, in their local Fribourgeois dialect, that it would be unworthy to survive so many brave men. He seized a musket from a dead soldier and threw himself into the enemy mass with his bayonet. His companions followed his example; all perished save for one who 'miraculously escaped' to report the event! Careful research in the cantonal archives has shown that there could have been no such mass death of Fribourgeois grenadiers. Eyewitnesses, such as Fonjallaz and Moore who were on the staircase after the battle, made no allusion to heaps of Swiss corpses, although they mention where they saw dead bodies elsewhere. Constant-Rebecque, who remained in the Tuileries until the insurgents entered, also failed to refer to a battle on the Great Stairs, although he seems to have left the palace down them. He briefly related Diesbach's murder while wounded together with that of the surgeon Böcking who was attending him. He was probably not an eyewitness, however. Finally, there is no indication of such an action in the sketchy revolutionary accounts, and certainly official French casualty figures are totally unable to accommodate such a mass death of insurgents. Desbouillons, who was present at the final assault on the Tuileries, briefly wrote that the French entered the palace after resistance ended in the courtyards, and killed any survivors. In all, it seems more than probable that Peltier's source was a Fribourgeois soldier seeking a tip. The heroic defence on the Great Stairs was still recently being commemorated in Switzerland, but there is perhaps a growing realisation that it is little more than a glorious myth. How many similar stories distort battlefield accounts down the ages?

Of the remaining Swiss at the palace after the departure of the major groups, about eighty or so who were posted in the northern part of the palace and the Hôtel de Brionne escaped towards the Rue Saint-Honoré via the Rue de l'Echelle. The latter street became a significant killing ground. The substantial number of corpses left lying there was mentioned by several sources, including young Constant-Rebecque who succeeded in escaping from the palace as the insurrectionists were entering, and who faced death several times until he reached a place of safety. He had left the palace by the main entrance, and was fired at as he crossed the Cour Royal which was covered in smoke. Reaching the Hôtel de Brionne he was confronted by an insurgent. 'He wished to fire on me', Constant wrote, 'but he misfired, and lunged to lance me with his bayonet, crying out "will I then be unable to kill one of them?" I warded off his blow with my sword, and he fled.' He saw his fellow officer, Jean de Maillardoz, son of the Lieutenant Colonel of the Regiment, murdered in the Rue de l'Echelle trying to escape in civilian clothes.

Of the remainder, a unit made a belated escape from the Pavillon de Flore along the Water Terrace. Probably under fifty remained isolated in the palace and its outbuildings, intent on hiding rather than resistance. Peltier gave a time of about midday for the ending of organised resistance, both in the palace and elsewhere. This seems on the late side for the palace which was probably first entered around 11 a.m., when resistance from a few Swiss manning cannons in front of the Vestibule were overcome. The insurgents had a brief setback when a group of fifteen Swiss led by Sergeant Jacob Stoffel from Mels in the Canton of St Gallen briefly reoccupied the Vestibule before making their escape through the garden.

CHAPTER 16

Massacre

When the last shots ceased from the palace, the insurgents began to enter, probably with considerable caution in case of ambush. It seems likely the number who proceeded to cleanse the palace of its occupants was relatively few. These would have been the boldest and the most bloodthirsty, not to mention looters out to make a quick fortune. The mass of insurgents and National Guards, who had gone over to the side of the Revolution, seem to have contented themselves, according to eyewitness accounts, with firing a now plentiful supply of ammunition indiscriminately against the palace from the safety of the courtyards and the garden. A radical weekly, *Les Révolutions de Paris*, published an account next day of the sanctioned murder of the very largely defenceless male palace inmates:

> At the same moment, the people inundated the Vestibule, the Great Stairs, the Chapel, the ante-chambers, the corridors, the Throne Room, the Council Chamber, all splattered with the blood of the Swiss and the King's domestics. The colour of the coats of the former and the livery of the latter helped to condemn them guilty of the most unworthy treachery. They were treated without pity. The justice of the people showed itself in all its cruelty and penetrated everywhere to discover the traitors. An Abbé, preceptor of the Dauphin, had hidden eight fugitives at the back of a large closet which he revealed in his fright. He was killed along with the persons he had tried to conceal from public vengeance. . . . Marks of generosity would be lost on the cadaverous souls of the Court. They only deserve terror. The people gave it them; they showed mercy to no one in the palace. The Swiss and others hidden in the attics were brought down and slaughtered, others were caught in the latrines, others in the kitchens where the cooks were killed down to the meanest scullery boy; all accomplices of their master [the King] and strangers to the Nation. Even the cellars were searched where torches were found to burn down Paris at the signal of the modern Nero.

Women were generally spared. The quality of mercy also survived in the case of two Swiss drummer boys. A National Guard called Tasset recounted how he came across a crowd of two hundred finishing off wounded Swiss near their guardhouse, and about to murder two terrified drummer boys, brothers, of whom the eldest was fifteen. He rushed indignantly at the killers with his drawn sabre. His energetic intervention was able to save them, and he took them to the guardhouse by the Pont Neuf where they would be safely looked after by the people of this middle-class district. Not all Swiss were found. For instance, Fonjallaz survived, as will be related later. One is said to have only surfaced after three days when the fury of the mob had abated.

If the revolutionaries could be so frank, it is not surprising that royalist authors did not hesitate to depict scenes of horror in and around the palace, as for example seven corpses displayed on the chapel altar. Naturally concentrating on the fate of his comrades, the anonymous Swiss officer wrote: 'Among the soldiers fallen into the hands of the brigands, some were mutilated and put to death slowly, others were thrown living into the fire, or from the highest windows on to a forest of pikes, and received below with cannibal cries. Even the dead became the object of the people's rage. They were cut in pieces, their palpitating limbs torn from them and spiked on the top of a pike, or dragged through the dirt of the streets.'

The behaviour of female insurgents greatly struck contemporaries. It is well known that Napoleon, then a young officer with no combat experience, was shocked by women committing the grossest indecencies on the corpses of dead soldiers. Another witness reported a common prostitute flattening some brains with her foot in the Rue Fromenteau. It is reasonable to suppose that many of the outrages were committed by fellow members of her profession. Unlike Napoleon, the anonymous Swiss officer could not have been an eyewitness, but was no less graphic in describing what went on: 'Women showed the greatest degree of ferocity and savagery, and distinguished themselves in these unparalleled horrors. All that the most filthy debauchery and the most considered cruelty could suggest that was disgusting and atrocious . . . was inflicted on the cold corpses.' It was the desecration of the dead which so horrified many contemporaries and added an extra dimension to the atrocities committed by the more depraved supporters of the revolution.

A photograph of Joseph Jost, who had been a drummer boy in the Swiss Guards present at the Tuileries on 10 August 1792, here aged 90.

Not all the male domestics of the royal family were immolated in the Tuileries. Jean-Baptiste Cléry, the dauphin's valet, was enrolled as part of the defence of the palace with other like-minded servants in the early morning. He had sworn to defend the king to the last drop of blood. Depressed by the king's decision to seek safety in the National Assembly, he looked gloomily out of the windows on the garden side. He saw the heads on pikes paraded in the distance on the Terrasse des Feuillants, after the lynching of the 'false patrol'. Immediately afterwards, he said, he heard the noise of cannons and musketry as the battle began on the courtyard side. 'The palace was everywhere pierced with balls and bullets,' he wrote. 'As the King was gone, every man endeavoured to take care of himself, but all routes out of the palace were blocked by the fighting, and certain death seemed to await us. I ran from place to place, and finding the rooms and staircases already strewn with dead, decided to leap on to the terrace from one of the windows in the Queen's rooms on the ground floor. I rushed across the parterre as fast as possible towards the Pont-Tournant. A body of Swiss who had gone before me were rallying under the trees. Finding myself between two fires, I ran back to gain the new flight of steps leading up to the terrace on the waterside, intending to throw myself over the wall on to the quay, but was prevented by the constant fire kept up from the Pont Royal.' Cléry failed to indicate that an hour must have elapsed between the first firing and his jumping from the window. This account seems to confirm Peltier's reference to a firefight between the Swiss and National Guards half-way down the garden.

'I went along the terrace until I came to the gate of the Dauphin's garden,' Cléry continued. 'There I saw some Marseillais, who had just butchered several Swiss and were stripping them. One of them came up to me with a bloody sword in his hand, saying: "What, Citizen! Without arms? Take this sword and help us to kill." However, another Marseillais seized it. I was, as he observed, without arms, and fortunately in a plain frock-coat; for if anything had betrayed my situation in the palace, I should not have escaped.' It was the habit of many royalists to refer to any armed insurgents as Marseillais. The people Cléry came upon were very likely battlefield scavengers looting and finishing off Swiss who had been wounded in the exchange of fire with the National Guards unit stationed at the Pont-Tournant. The fact that another 'Marseillais' seized the weapon offered him showed that the people he had met were short of weapons and were no less civilians than himself.

'Some of the Swiss who were pursued took refuge in adjoining stables,' Cléry wrote. This must be the stables where the previous evening Liancourt mentioned he had a horse ready to escape from Paris.

> I concealed myself in the same place. . . . They were soon cut to pieces close by. On hearing the cries of these wretched victims, Monsieur Le Dreux, the manager of the stables, ran up, and I seized the opportunity, although he did not know me, of going into his home. Monsieur Le Dreux and his wife invited me to stay until the danger was over. In my pocket were letters and papers addressed to the royal prince, and an admission pass for the Tuileries, on which the name and the nature of my employment were written. These papers would have betrayed me, and I just had time to throw them away when a body of armed men came into the house, to see if any Swiss were concealed there. I pretended, on the advice of Monsieur le Dreux, to be working on some drawings that were lying on a large table. After a fruitless search, these fellows, their hands dyed with blood, stopped and coolly discussed among themselves the murders of which they had been guilty. I remained in this refuge from ten [in reality 11 a.m.] in the morning till four in the afternoon, and had before me sight of the horrors committed on the Place Louis XV. Of the men, some were slaughtering the wounded, and others

cutting off the heads of those already slain; while the women, lost to all sense of shame, were committing indecent mutilations on the dead bodies, from which they tore pieces of flesh, and carried them away in triumph.

Not all the insurgents who entered the palace were blood-crazed murderers, unable to reflect on their actions. Le Monnier, the king's physician, kept quietly in his room. When the insurgents entered, his calmness so impressed them that they entered into a dialogue. He was asked what he was doing there. He told them that he was doing his duty, that he was the king's doctor. They asked him if he was afraid. He replied that he saw no reason to be so since he was unarmed. Having made this point, he continued by asking them if they harmed those who could not harm them. They replied: 'Let us go. You are a good old bugger, but it is not well here. Others less reasonable might confuse you with the rest. Where do you want to go?' The doctor replied that he wished to go to the Luxembourg Palace. Perhaps pleased to make some recompense for what they had already done, the insurgents escorted him out of the building and through the crowds outside crying: 'Comrades, let this man pass. He is the King's doctor, but he is not afraid. He is a good bugger!' Showing fear, however justified, was to invite contempt, and was also regarded as a sign of guilt. The doctor did not make the mistake of the unfortunate Abbé.

Le Monnier was not the only one to understand psychology. The sixteen-year-old Pauline Tourzel suggested to the Court ladies in the queen's drawing-room that they close the shutters and light all the lamps and candles. These would be reflected in the many mirrors. The sight would bewilder insurgents when they entered, and give time to communicate with them. The door was left slightly ajar to show they were concealing nothing. When the revolutionaries arrived, they were restrained by a man with a long beard who invoked Pétion in ordering them to spare the women, and not to disgrace the nation. In the confusion of the moment, Madame Campan lost sight of her sister and thought she had fled upstairs to a mezzanine floor between the queen's apartments and the picture gallery above. Madame Campan mounted the stairs to try and find her. She related:

I did not find her, only two maids and one of the Queen's two ceremonial footmen, a very tall man with a military bearing. I saw him deathly pale and sitting on a bed. I said: 'Save yourself, the other footmen have already got away.' He replied that he could not move as he was paralysed with fear. As he said this, I heard a band of men mount the stairs to kill him. I ran back to the other staircase, followed by the two maids. The assassins left the footman to go after me. The narrowness of the stairs hindered the assailants, but I felt a terrible hand grasp my back, seizing me by the clothes. The Marseillais down below cried out: 'What are you doing up there?' The horrible Sans-culotte who was about to kill me replied with a grunt, the sound of which will never leave my memory. The person below said: 'We do not kill women.' I was on my knees when my executioner let go and said: 'Get up, you hussy, the Nation pardons thee.' The grossness of his words did not hinder me from feeling an inexpressible joy which came almost as much from a love of life, as that I was going to be able to see my son and all that was dear to me. An instant before, I had less thought of death than the pain which was going to come from the sword raised over his head. It is rare to experience death so close without suffering it. I can say that all one's senses are at the keenest, and I heard the least words of the assassins as if I was calm and collected. Five or six men took hold of me and my companions and made us climb on the benches under the windows to shout Vive la Nation!

The Swiss and the inmates of the palace were not alone in being victims that day. Innocent doormen were killed purely because their profession was associated with retired Swiss soldiers. Anyone well dressed might attract the unfortunate attention of cut-throats who were able to combine revolutionary zeal for equality with robbery and murder. A young female shop assistant working in the Rue Saint-Honoré, Marie-Victoire Monnard, left some vignettes of this fatal day. She related that a patrol armed with bloody pikes and sabres made a round of the neighbourhood, forcing all the shops to close. 'In less than three minutes, the shops were shut and the streets evacuated. . . . How many horrors I remember having seen through the blinds, among them that of three Sans-culottes holding a tall handsome man by the collar of his frock-coat. This unfortunate person kept saying: "Take me to the Section offices," which they refused to do . . . they gave him a blow on the forehead with the butt of a musket and finished him off. They took his watch, his clothes, and left him dead.' Later she saw at least fifteen women, one after another, standing on top of the corpse with its entrails hanging out, exclaiming that they took pleasure in trampling the aristocracy under their feet. In the afternoon, Marie-Victoire was sent by her employer to find out what was happening at the Tuileries. She witnessed furniture and furnishings, together with corpses, being thrown out of the broken windows.

While the killing in the Tuileries was piecemeal and hidden in countless rooms within a vast and gloomy palace, the so-called massacre of the Swiss Guards at the Hôtel de Ville made a deep impression because it was seen as en masse and in the open. Accounts varied considerably, although all dwelt on the horror. Oddly, the figures given, ranging from 60 to 130, generally refer to those taken to the Maison Commune rather than the specific number killed. The Swiss lawyer François-N.C. Blanc gave a precise figure of 83 sent to the Hôtel de Ville, but typically did not provide a source for this information. This compares with 82 given in a letter written by the Genevese political writer Mallet du Pan at the end of August. For the Swiss in particular, this episode called for ritualistic condemnation, taking on the character of a miniature holocaust where national identity could be affirmed. The anonymous Swiss officer expressed this sentiment in measured terms: 'The appellation Swiss was a death decree, a red coat made it carried out on the spot. But all these atrocities did not approach the cold barbarity with which the pavement of the Hôtel de Ville was covered with blood. This pretended temple of the law, this residence of magistrates, was the theatre for the most revolting scene of this so criminal day. The grenadiers and soldiers who had escorted the King, to the number of 80 to 100, were taken there to be interrogated on events at the palace, under the very improper title of prisoners of the Nation. They seemed to be doubly under the protection of the law. However, hardly had they arrived when they were lined up in a narrow courtyard, and some madmen expressly placed there hurled themselves on them and massacred them without quarter.'

It should be noted that this source stated that the massacre took place in a narrow courtyard within the Hôtel de Ville, contrary to the generally accepted belief that all the killing occurred in the Place de Grève in front of the Town Hall. There seems no doubt that at least some of the killing happened in the confined space of a small interior courtyard dominated by a statue of Louis XIV in Roman costume. This was reported by Nicholas Ruault, who was an eyewitness. He wrote: 'As a result of unforeseen circumstances, I was forced to see the massacre of part of those unfortunate foreigners in the little courtyard of the Hôtel de Ville, at the foot of the statue of Louis XIV. No one could have expected such an execution in that place. They were stripped naked, they were stabbed, and then dragged by their feet to the exterior steps [of the Town Hall] where they were loaded on to carts brought specially into the square up to the entrance. But, to complete the horror, I saw some "cannibals", who, loading the corpses, mutilated them and gave them, while sneering, little slaps on their buttocks.'

There is considerable dispute over how the Swiss came to be at the Hôtel de Ville. Peltier wrote that about sixty soldiers under four officers on the Champs-Elysées were surrounded while retreating to their barracks at Courbevoie, and taken to the Hôtel de Ville. This information is backed by a surviving written report from the second-in-command of the National Guards based in the Section de Roule. This section was situated at the western extremity of Paris which then reached as far as the Etoile. The report explained that Swiss captured in the area had been taken to the section committee offices but there was insufficient space to hold them all. The National Guards officer sought permission to transfer them to the barracks in the Rue Verte. Permission was granted. But the crowd insisted on seizing the prisoners and taking them to the Hôtel de Ville. There is no specific mention of four Swiss officers. However, the report stated that a 'so-called commander of the Swiss' was torn from the hands of the National Guards and massacred. The reporting officer was protesting against these irregularities, which he had tried to prevent. The presence of the armed mob ties in with reports of the despatch of insurgent forces in the early afternoon to seize the Swiss barracks at Courbevoie and Rueil.

The incident about the Swiss officer may tie in with a gruesome and improbable anecdote quoted by Major La Vallière, writing some sixty years ago, concerning the death of Captain d'Erlach. He related that some women in a mob carefully sawed off his head while alive to ensure it would make a good presentation on top of a pike. What really happened to Erlach remains a mystery. F.-N. C. Blanc believed at the end of September that he was en route for Switzerland, although he never arrived there. On the other hand, as related, Deville was told that Erlach was hit by a cannon ball fired from the Place Louis XV.

The nineteenth-century French historian Mortimer-Ternaux, who published the Section de Roule document in his *History of the Terror*, was nevertheless of the opinion that prisoners were also taken from the Convent of the Feuillants. He referred to an incident in the early afternoon when the National Assembly was asked to send deputies to speak to an armed crowd in the Cour des Feuillants. He commented: 'The Section Delegates had ordered the prisoners at the Feuillants to be taken to the Maison Commune [Town Hall]. A first group of sixty or eighty disarmed soldiers were taken away and massacred en route.' Mortimer-Ternaux does not provide any source for this detail, but he had access to and used municipal records which were destroyed during the Commune uprising of 1871. There are no reports elsewhere of a large number of Swiss being massacred on the way to the Hôtel de Ville. It is easy to assume that these were the same Swiss who were actually killed there. The anonymous Swiss officer claimed that the massacred prisoners indeed came from the Feuillants, from members of the king's escort. We know, however, from Deville that this group of prisoners was allowed to escape. Deville mentioned a posse of insurgents entering the Cour des Feuillants at least three times during the afternoon and causing considerable uproar. Unfortunately, he and his fellow soldiers, imprisoned separately in a large room, were unable to look out of the windows for fear of being seen. Deville, who frequently asked his captors what was going on outside, does not refer to any abduction. Such information might have been withheld to avoid panic.

At first sight the known ration count of 112 on 11 August for Swiss prisoners held in the Feuillants might help to solve the mystery. Any solution, however, hinges on the number of troops led to the National Assembly by Durler and Salis. As has been discussed in a previous chapter, there is considerable doubt on the size of this force. A low or medium figure would seem to preclude the possibility that the victims at the Hôtel de Ville came from the Feuillants, and make the Swiss captured in the west of Paris the most likely source. A high figure would make the Feuillants an obvious candidate. Of course, the victims could have come from both, or even several, places. In conclusion, where the Swiss troops killed at the Hôtel de Ville came from cannot be absolutely ascertained.

It has generally been assumed that there were no survivors, but this is very likely not the case. An anonymous letter from Paris dated 13 August suggested the victims were executed one at a time. The confined space must have meant that at the most the Swiss were taken into the small courtyard in batches, where they were stripped, briefly interrogated, and butchered by ruffians who had taken on this task. The remaining Swiss prisoners outside on the Place de Grève would have become rapidly aware of what was going on. Some would have tried to escape. The letter refers to some Swiss defending themselves with their fists. Swiss resistance encouraged the surrounding mob to butcher them, accounting for the stories of massacre on the Place de Grève.

A substantial hint that some succeeded in escaping is to be found in Altishofen's account. At the end of his narration, he acknowledged certain generous French who had shown humanity on 10 August in helping to save some Swiss. Among these was Monsieur Dussaut, Chief Surgeon at the Hôtel-Dieu, who '. . . received wounded Swiss who presented themselves and saved some soldiers who were not wounded. A troop of Marseillais came to the hospital and demanded that the Swiss be handed over. Monsieur Dussaut replied: "I have had a dozen thrown out of the windows, and I will do the same to any more who come." He was not contradicted by any of his assistant surgeons present, and the Marseillais withdrew.' Presumably he was implying throwing them into the Seine, which then passed directly under the back of the hospital. The Hôtel-Dieu, on the Ile de la Cité by Notre Dame, was a considerable distance upstream from the scene of the fighting at the Tuileries and even further from the Place Louis XV or the National Assembly, but is more or less directly opposite the Place de Grève. It seems very likely that Swiss escaped

Some Swiss soldiers may have escaped massacre on the Place de Grève and taken refuge in the Hôtel Dieu on the Ile de la Cité shown in the centre with Notre Dame behind. The hospital was rebuilt last century.

by swimming across the Seine which is divided by the island, or even managed to cross on one of the bridges. Obviously some were wounded in getting away. It is interesting to note that unwounded Swiss also found sanctuary in the hospital, no doubt doing their duty of aiding their wounded comrades.

As for the number murdered, there is a letter which only came to light some thirty years ago, written by a National Guard named René Leprêtre from Rennes, dated 11 August. Its disjointed style bears the signs of considerable emotion. He wrote: 'All the Swiss prisoners were taken together to the Place de Grève. There they blew out their brains. They are traitors that vengeance must sacrifice. What vengeance! All my being trembles. Forty-seven heads at least have been cut. The Place de Grève is covered in dead, and the heads have been displayed on the top of pikes.' He was almost certainly not an eyewitness since there is no evidence elsewhere that the Swiss were shot and at least some of the dead were carted off. However, the precise number of 47 dead is interesting; possibly he obtained this figure from a colleague in the know. Such a relatively low number is in accord with estimates of the overall casualty figures.

Mob psychology was deliberately exploited by Jacobin agitators. Where people were gathered together in sufficient number, mass hysteria could take over. Its influence should not be underestimated. The seven-months pregnant Marquise de Lescure, later the Marquise de la Rochejaquelin, accompanied her husband on a sight-seeing tour on the evening of the 10th, disguised in working-class clothes. From the Champs-Elysées they saw the dark mass of the Tuileries etched by the red glow of burning outbuildings on the other side of the palace. 'After having gone an enormous distance,' she wrote, 'we reached the Louvre. Monsieur de Lescure made me follow the streets which had the most people and which were the best lit. We rubbed shoulders with all those people carrying pikes, most of them were drunk and howling. I had lost my head to such an extent that I started screaming with them with all my might: "Long live the Sans-culottes, burn, break the windows!" Monsieur de Lescure could not calm me down, nor make me stop screaming. We found the Louvre, which was sombre and solitary, and from there the Pont-Neuf, where there were quite a few people and a lot of noise. Finally, we crossed over to the other side of the Seine.' Drink was certainly a primary objective for many who sided with the insurrection. The royal wine cellars yielded some ten thousand bottles, and broken glass was strewn around the Tuileries. There were to be similar scenes after the capture of the Winter Palace in St Petersburg in the Russian 1917 October Revolution. Constant-Rebecque related that the principal concern of many looting the Hôtel de Brionne was the cellars, and he probably owed his life to this single-mindedness.

CHAPTER 17

Fall

Roederer in his *Chronicle of Fifty Days* wrote: 'Who does not know how the opinion of the Assembly gave way, and how in the end it surrendered to so many continuous assaults over a period of forty-eight hours? . . . the interest of conserving an authority which, if it had been lost, would have been seized by the dreadful Commune, together perhaps with the fear inspired by a furious people, and who would not wish to believe it, the hope of returning the people to justice while gaining the time necessary to calm it; all these circumstances decided it [the Assembly] during the day of the 10th, to take measures which at the opening of the session were certainly far from the ideas of the majority.' At the outset, the Assembly had almost certainly been prepared to try to help the king, although at a price. But, as the power of the insurrection made itself felt, and as indignation over the deaths of French citizens at the hands of the foreign Swiss mounted, the Assembly felt it necessary to temporise and then to cave in with woeful and ill-thought concessions. However, as the king rather than the Assembly was the insurgents' target, there is no evidence that the revolutionary Commune was prepared or able to take over the Assembly's functions. If greater resolve had been shown, the Assembly might well have been able to assert its authority.

While the fighting at the Tuileries was raging, the National Assembly wrestled with the problem of dealing with the revolutionary Commune and restoring order. Probably a little after 10.15 a.m., the chair of the Assembly was passed a letter addressed to municipal officers from the mayor saying that he was being confined to his official residence (the Mairie) and was unable to join them in carrying out their functions. The Jacobin Choudieu states in his memoirs that Pétion did not withdraw to the Mairie to act undercover for the insurgents, but rather did everything he could to hinder the Revolution. Pétion's letter to his colleagues ended: 'I am therefore in the impossibility of joining you, and rely upon your zeal and your public spirit to tell the National Assembly what the public interest requires.' Although he was prudent in giving no ideas on this subject himself, he left an opening for the politicians in the Assembly to concert appropriate action with municipal officers present. At the same time, the mayor sent a message to the Department which went even further, telling them that he had intended to go to the National Assembly to inform it of what had happened and to ask them to take the measures the public interest required. He now proposed the Department do all that they believed wise in the circumstances. In other words, he was hinting they might take over the government of Paris. Roederer does not mention this inconvenient communication in his memoirs. In any case, he did nothing. Pétion and Roederer, the two senior officials with executive responsibility for maintaining order in Paris, both failed in different ways to do their duty. If they were not instigators of the revolution to overthrow the Monarchy, fear and complacency made them accomplices.

While Pétion felt he was obliged to pass on the task of restoring order in Paris, the Girondin leaders at the National Assembly had no intention of accepting this responsibility. They urgently and abjectly pleaded for the release of their ally so that he could undertake the task for them. They did not know, however, whether Pétion retained any credibility with the new inmates at the Hôtel de Ville. It was decided to issue a proclamation, of which the somewhat contradictory phrasing reveals the agitation of the drafter, requesting information on the mayor's acceptability as well as asking for his release. 'If the foremost of the legal authorities [the mayor] is still respected; if the representatives of the people, friends of his happiness, are still under the influence of confidence and reason in his regard, they beg the citizens, and in the name of the law they command them, to lift his confinement to the Mairie, and to permit him to appear as first magistrate in the presence of the people.' The conditional phrasing of the request gave the option of refusal to the insurgents in case the Assembly's demand was unwelcome. Timidity could go no further.

The Assembly next turned to consider the command of the National Guards. They did not yet know whether Mandat was dead or alive. Whatever his situation, he needed to be replaced urgently. First thoughts were to appoint Lachesnaye, who had the advantage of being present in the Assembly's corridors, having accompanied the king earlier that morning. Lachesnaye rejected this responsibility, saying it was not his turn but that of Monsieur Pinon, Commander of the 5th Legion. Commanding generals were Legion commanders who served in rotation. This prudence did not save his skin. Nevertheless, Lacroix, the same deputy that Liancourt had reviled as being an out-and-out Jacobin, insisted. Thuriot then intervened, just as earlier in the morning he had helped to derail the attempt to take action on the dismissal of the legally elected Municipal General Council. He claimed that the decision belonged to the Municipality, and the new Paris authorities might have already appointed their own commanding general. Indeed they had done so in the person of Santerre, though this was not yet generally known in the Assembly. Thuriot suggested that for the deputies to make their own choice now might risk civil war. No one pointed out that it was the usurping revolutionary council that would be responsible for such a situation. It was decided to do nothing, and it was reported that the Assembly comforted itself with thoughts that even if no appointment was made, the legal forms would be safeguarded if officers took orders from a higher ranking officer, whoever he might be, and acted in accordance with the law, whatever that might be.

Deputy Jacques Alexis Thuriot de la Rozère was a lawyer who had played a part in the fall of the Bastille at the outset of the Revolution. He had connections with Danton and was believed to be his spokesman in the National Assembly. It seems more than probable that he had been instructed about the takeover of the Commune, and had agreed to do his best to ensure that the National Assembly took no action which might interfere with the success of the insurrection. In this he succeeded only too well, because of the disunity and pusillanimity of those who should have acted to preserve the Constitution. Possibly to revenge Danton, he contributed to the fall of

Robespierre, when presiding over the National Convention on 9 Thermidor 1794, by refusing to allow him to speak. He later became a judge under the Empire.

The National Assembly did not have the courage to take the lead and waited on events. To bolster its waning morale, it feebly decided to back up its earlier resolution, detailed in Chapter 13, to place property and lives under the safeguard of the people of Paris. This time, however, it did not even dare to mention these requirements directly, never mind suggesting support for the Constitution and the legitimate authorities. The now indispensable Thuriot was given the task of drafting the address. He did so in the vaguest terms so as to place minimal restrictions on revolutionary action. 'In the name of the Nation, in the

On 10 August, Deputy Thuriot (1753–1829) ensured the National Assembly took no decisions which might interfere with the success of the insurrection.

name of Liberty, in the name of Equality, all Citizens are invited to respect the rights of man, liberty, and equality.' The Assembly then rose and all swore to defend liberty and equality or die at their post. Orders were given for the two proclamations on freeing the mayor and respecting the rights of man to be printed urgently on the Assembly's presses and to be posted around Paris.

The Girondins do not seem to have anticipated the takeover of the Commune and the neutralisation of their ally Pétion. At a blow, they had been deprived of their indirect control of the Paris National Guards. Instead, they were now commanded by a nominee of the revolutionaries allied to the Jacobin faction. Had they had the fortitude to pass a decree dissolving the insurrectionary Commune, or at least taking over command of the National Guards, history might have taken a different course and the French people spared much suffering. The king looking on from the reporters' box must have known he was being abandoned.

Both the *Journal des Débats et Decrés* (the *Journal*) and the *Logographe* mentioned that the noise of cannon fire died down at this juncture. The former gave the time as around 11 a.m. A deputation now arrived from the moderate Section of the Thermes de Julien [Baths of Julian] in the Latin Quarter of Paris. This section did not belong to the group of twenty-eight present at the Hôtel de Ville around 7 a.m. when a roll call had been made, and they had also denounced the petition sponsored by certain sections for the dethronement of the king on 3 August. While now disavowing their former moderate stance, they challenged the Assembly to declare that it was able to save the State. The Assembly swore that it could. The president took advantage of the opportunity in his reply to tell the petitioners that the people would find the Assembly the true friends of their happiness and liberty. After praising the section delegates for their civic virtue, he admonished them to return and peaceably await the decisions of the National Assembly, while doing their best to carry out the decrees and proclamations already made.

Representatives of the revolutionary Municipal General Council next came to the bar, introduced by the Jacobin Deputy Bazire. They included its new chairman, Huguenin, as well as Bourdon, Tronchon, Deriem, Vigaud, and Bullier. It would be interesting to know when precisely they reached the National Assembly. If it was shortly after 11.00 a.m., as seems possible, then the still armed men of Durler's and Salis' force may have been actually within the Manège at the same time. As previously revealed, there was no specific mention of such a Swiss presence in the Assembly reports, although the official minutes may give a hint by reporting consecutively a number of other items concerning the Swiss immediately following details of the Commune's visit. Reporting the simultaneous presence of the Swiss with the delegation from the new Commune would have tended to negate the revolutionaries' claims that they had risen to defeat a counter-revolution instigated by the king. Yet here was the king having them at his mercy and failing to take advantage of it! Choudieu in his memoirs mentioned that he fully expected the Swiss to be used during the morning to massacre hostile deputies within the Assembly building and was unable to account for this not taking place. While not directly referring to Swiss in the Chamber, he does report noticing surrendering Swiss in the Manège's corridors with white handkerchiefs tied to their muskets.

The *Moniteur* described the delegation from the new Commune as arriving with banners inscribed Patrie, Egalité, and Liberté. The three commercial publications dignified the delegation as the representatives of the new Commune, while the Assembly's minutes referred only to a deputation from the section delegates united at the Town Hall. They had Huguenin explaining that the sections had acted because of the dangers facing the country due to intrigues by the Court. Huguenin went on to mention their association with Pétion, Danton, and Manuel and the nomination of Santerre as commanding general. He referred to the Swiss firing on the people because the king, committing a further crime, had brought them into Paris. In reply, the president thanked the delegates for their zeal with a vague phrase, 'which called them to where the peril was greatest'. He ended with a plea for the mayor's liberty to help in the restoration of order and asked them to assist in the publication of the proclamations recently made by the Assembly. It should be noted that the revolutionaries thought it politically expedient to claim they had Pétion's support.

Guadet, the president, emphasised the deputation's inferiority by having an Assembly official read them the recent proclamations. Nor were they cordially invited to stay on in the Chamber to witness the session which was the normal mark of esteem given to honoured petitioners who spoke at the bar. 'The Assembly asks you to return to your post, for you would perhaps consider it an insult at this moment if you were invited to remain for the session.' Thus, the Assembly wished to pretend that it was still holding its own at this stage and had not yet formally recognised the status of the new revolutionary General Council of the Commune. On the other hand, no remarks were made about standing by the Constitution. It was left to a member of the National Guard, who had accompanied the delegation from the Hôtel de Ville, to come to the bar to protest, saying that he had cast off his uniform and was not returning with his colleagues. He was prepared to die, as he regretted that the Constitution could no longer be maintained.

The *Logographe* and the *Journal*, with similar texts, presented the delegation in a more powerful light. The *Journal* quoted Huguenin as saying:

The Jacobin Deputy Bazire (1764–94), who proposed a motion that the Swiss officers after surrendering on 10 August be placed under the safeguard of the law. He was later a victim of the Terror, accused of peculation and executed at the same time as the Dantonists.

These are the new magistrates of the people who have come to your bar. Circumstances commanded our election, and our patriotism will know how to make us worthy of it. The people, tired at last after four [sic] years of being the eternal plaything of the perfidy of the Court and its intrigues, has felt that it was time to arrest the State on the edge of the abyss. Legislators, it only remains for us to act in support of the People. We are come here, in its name, to ask for measures for the public salvation. Pétion, Manuel, and Danton continue to be our colleagues. Santerre is at the head of the armed force. Let traitors tremble in their turn! This day is the triumph of civic values. Legislators, the blood of the people has been shed. Foreign troops [the Swiss], who have remained within our walls only because of a new crime of the Executive Power, have fired on the citizens. Our unfortunate brothers have left widows and orphans. The People who has sent us, has charged us with declaring to you that it has not ceased to believe that you are worthy of it, but at the same time it has instructed us to tell you that it can only recognise the French people meeting together in the primary assemblies, who are your sovereign and ours, for judging the extraordinary measures to which the necessity of resisting oppression has driven it.

In other words, the new Commune denied the right of the National Assembly to judge its actions, which could only be done by the People meeting together for new elections. There was, however, no disagreement with the official minutes over the substance of Guadet's reply in which he politely ignored the deputation's demand for new elections, while asking it to assist in restoring order. It is pertinent to ask whether the president was influenced in refusing to accept the revolutionaries' rejection of the Assembly's authority because there were armed Swiss in the building, as well as loyalist National Guards at the entrance.

The members of the new Commune left with a parting shot reported by the three commercial publications. Leonard Bourdon addressed the president: 'The people of Paris', he said, 'fear calumnies. We ask you to let us give you a transcription of our [the Commune's] proceedings today for distribution to France's 44,000 municipalities.' In other words, they wished the National Assembly to place its imprimatur on the insurrection. This was also ignored by Guadet who repeated a request that Pétion be set at liberty.

The three newspaper reports on the Assembly's proceedings state that after the deputation from the revolutionary Commune had finished its representations, Deputy Montaut proposed that the National Assembly swear an oath of loyalty to liberty and equality. He went to the speaker's rostrum and addressed the Assembly as follows: 'Messieurs, already twice [this morning] the National Assembly has risen with a common accord and sworn in the name of the Country, Liberty and Equality. If the Tennis Court oath has been famous throughout Europe, these acts must not be less so to the Representatives of the French people, who cherish Liberty and Equality. That is why I ask that the Minutes expressly mention this fact, that one then proceeds to an "appel nominal" [roll-call vote] by all Members, that each on mounting to the rostrum should give their oath in the name of the Country, for Liberty and Equality.' Again Thuriot leapt into the breach and proposed the formula: 'In the name of the Nation, I swear to maintain Liberty and Equality with all my strength, or to die at my post.' To those present, this was not the empty rhetoric it sounds today. The members of the National Assembly were largely atheist or agnostic as regards traditional religion, but they were far from lacking a secular faith in the nostrums of the Revolution. The oath demanded was a reaffirmation of the victory of the Third Estate over the supposed tyranny of the Ancien Régime and the resented social superiority of the nobility. The justice of this achievement was unquestioned.

It is possible that the proposal for the oath represented a real drama rather than a coup de théatre. When Durler left the Logographie with orders to surrender, his account shows that this did not take place without some argument. It may have been in the circumstances of waiting for the Swiss surrender to be confirmed that M. Montaut remembered the Tennis Court oath of 20 June 1789, when the representatives of the Third Estate believed they were threatened by a coup of the royal government, and swore never to separate. If Durler's troops had already entered the Chamber, as he stated, the Swiss might return with glinting bayonets and take control in the name of the king. Ordinary business may have been suspended during the near presence of the Swiss, and Montaut's proposal, as a gesture of steadfastness and solidarity, may have given deputies something to do at this critical juncture. It failed to achieve the historic fame of the Tennis Court oath which it was supposed to emulate.

When normal business resumed, probably after 11.30 a.m., Assembly officials continued to call on each individual deputy present to stand up in turn and take the oath. The first measure now passed was to control the circulation of news outside Paris by suspending the mail until an official statement could be drafted. Petitioners started to arrive with articles taken from pillaging the Tuileries. Instructions were requested for safeguarding the sacerdotal silver in the Royal Chapel. There was a demand to assist a detachment being organised to disarm the Swiss at Courbevoie. Dubouchage advised the Assembly that the latter had been ordered to surrender. A written report was received from a Justice of the Peace about the arrest of Comte d'Affry, Colonel of the Swiss Guards, and about measures taken to safeguard his life by sending him to the Abbaye prison. There was a demand for composing an address for despatch to France's eighty-three Departments. Deputy Duhem made a speech saying that the Ministers no longer had the confidence of the nation and that until they were replaced, the Minister of Justice should stand in for the remainder. The reason for this decision may have harked back to the Ancien Régime, as Dejoly's Ministry had many of the responsibilities formerly belonging to the Chancellor of France. Violent attacks were launched against the Swiss for the deaths they had caused. Finally, some petitioners arrived to complain that the Assembly had not yet declared the king dethroned, nor even suspended him. None of this appeared in the official minutes, which preserved an illusion of unhurried composure.

The peaceable Louis had been unable to defend the Constitution by himself. The equally responsible politicians, with whom he had failed to come to an understanding, now pretended it was not their affair. The Assembly had lacked the political capacity to judge the situation correctly and had failed to ensure the military strength necessary for opposing the insurrection. Nor had they dared to make effective use of their authority to try to restore legality. The Swiss had been allowed to surrender. Now behind the scenes, while a succession of deputies mounted the tribune to take the oath for the maintenance of Liberty and Equality and various petitioners arrived at the bar, Vergniaud and others of the Assembly's Extraordinary Committee had been hard at work drafting the new legislation required to put aside the king – and, even more seriously, to abandon the 1791 Constitution. Guadet ceded the presidency of the Chamber to his fellow Girondin, Gensonné. The decks were cleared for action. Vergniaud came to the rostrum.

He frankly admitted that he came before the Assembly with drastic proposals, composed without due consideration, and that he was fully aware of the distress felt by members caused by recent events. He then launched into a legalistic preamble giving reasons for the proposed legislation, explaining that the king's authority would be suspended and that there would be an appeal to the people.

The National Assembly, considering that the dangers facing the country have reached their limit, that it is the duty of even the weakest Legislative Body to employ all means to save itself, that it is impossible to be effective without going right to the source of the evils, considering that these evils derive principally from the distrust inspired by the conduct of the Head of Executive Power, in a [civil] war undertaken in his name against the Constitution and national independence, that this distrust has provoked, in many parts of the State, the desire for revoking the authority delegated to Louis XVI, considering that nevertheless the Legislative Body must not and does not wish to aggrandise itself by any usurpation, that in the extraordinary circumstances in which it is placed by events unforeseen by all legislation, it is unable to reconcile what it owes to its unshakeable fidelity for the Constitution with its firm resolution to bury itself under the ruins of the temple of liberty, and rather than let it perish, by reverting to the sovereignty of the people, and taking at the same time indispensable precautions so that this recourse is not rendered illusory by treachery, decrees the following.

There were nine articles in all. The first stated that the Extraordinary Committee would put forward proposals the next day for a National Convention to replace the existing Legislature. The second declared that the king was provisionally suspended until the forthcoming National Convention had made a decision on the new form of government. The third and fourth stated that a new ministry would be established later that day, that proposals would be made for its organisation and election, but that in the meantime the existing ministers remained in office. The fifth and sixth proposed the royal family would remain in the National Assembly until order was restored and a new residence was prepared in the Luxembourg Palace. The remainder concerned maintaining order and dissemination of the decree. Each article was adopted by a show of hands.

Guadet (1758–94) like Vergniaud was a Girondin leader and accomplished orator. He presided over the National Assembly during the period when the insurgency triumphed.

Nobody seems to have challenged the measure to suspend the king, although the Constitution of 1791 had no clause permitting provisional suspension, only dethronement. In the preamble, the king was accused of crimes which would have justified the constitutional penalty of dethronement. Vergniaud's statement was disingenuous to say the least. He argued that using the available constitutional remedy to deal with the king would be a usurpation of authority and that liberty could only be preserved by the Assembly surrendering its responsibilities to the People. In other words, the Constitution of 1791 was a scrap of paper which the Girondins now decided to tear up. The previous Assembly (the Constituent) responsible for the Constitution had proposed that it should not require alteration for twenty-five years.

At a stroke the Girondins destroyed the legitimacy and authority of the Legislative Assembly and thus their own power. They abdicated responsibility by agreeing to new elections within a few weeks, which under the existing Constitution were not due for over a year. At the same time, by deciding only on suspension of the king, they ignored the vociferous demands for his dethronement, which had been mounting for the past fortnight. The failure of the National Assembly to decide the matter the previous evening had been the signal for the insurrection. Continuing to delay a decision on the grounds that this should be determined by a new Assembly betrayed only feebleness. The Girondins' weakness lay in their culpable inability to clarify their objectives. While claiming political virtue, they showed themselves shallow and self-seeking. Their faction was easily outmanoeuvred by Robespierre and the Jacobins, until they met their nemesis at the end of May 1793. In his *Coût de la Terreur*, René Sédillot described the Girondins as 'apprentice sorcerers who, unaware, unleashed the abominations of the Terror, and whom the Terror will annihilate'.

The clause in the legislation for taking up residence in the prestigious Luxembourg Palace suggests that the Girondins still looked to preserve the king under their own control, despite undermining their authority by accepting the Assembly's demise. Nor was there any mention of annulling Louis' Civil List. Jacobin deputies led by Choudieu promptly remedied this omission, ensuring that the Girondins would be unable to put their hands on the money. Although Vergniaud and the Extraordinary Committee had left it open for Louis to return to the throne if the situation permitted, the movement of events rapidly showed this to be unrealistic. The Girondins were naturally reluctant to liquidate the political investment they had made over the past few weeks in trying to come to terms with the king. But Louis' presumed association with the resistance of the Swiss Guards, resulting in the death of French citizens, destroyed any prospect of utilising the king. Louis ceased to be a potential Girondin political asset and became the prisoner of a Jacobin-dominated Commune.

Before 10 August, the Jacobins' primary demand had been for the dethronement of the king. The call for a National Convention to establish a new constitution, with the largely undeclared expectation that this would lead to a republic, was less forceful. There were undoubtedly many republicans among leading Jacobins, but in the weeks before the fall of the king it was recognised that republicanism was not yet practical politics. The Girondin Deputy Gensonné wrote in the *Chronique de Paris*, seven months after the fall of the king: 'In the middle of July 1792, the major part of the Nation wished to maintain the Constitution.' The Girondin Buzot, an avowed republican, directly affirmed the widespread support within Paris for the Monarchy at that time. Other contemporaries recorded the same opinion, emphasising that the majority in Paris was constitutionalist, even royalist. In fact, the demand for a National Convention to establish a new constitution was largely a tactical ploy developed by Robespierre, his henchmen and others at the Jacobin Club, partly to undercut the Girondins' power base in the existing Legislative Assembly, and partly to maintain their own political credentials in face of lack of direct involvement in planning the insurrection. Robespierre, as a close disciple of Rousseau, had fallen back on the latter's doctrine of the 'Sovereignty of the People'. But there is little evidence that the demand to hold new elections to replace the Assembly, which had been elected only some ten months previously, was widespread and deeply felt, especially at a time when all energies were needed for repelling the foreign invaders. In effect, only some 10 per cent of electors participated in the two-tier voting process for the new Convention. Only in Paris did the Jacobins make spectacular gains, as the result of the disenfranchisement and massive intimidation of political opponents.

In contrast to the call for new elections, the demand for the dethronement of the king was more deeply felt, based on a wilfully mistaken belief that the king was plotting a bloody counter-revolution. As a result of indoctrination and the judicious use of largesse, this notion found considerable support, particularly in the working-class sectors of Paris, which provided much of the muscle for the coup d'état. If the Girondins had immediately demanded the king's dethronement, which in the circumstances would almost certainly have won the Assembly's support, the 1791 Constitution laid down procedures for appointing a Regent during the dauphin's minority. This would have been the most senior eligible prince of the blood, namely the Duc d'Orléans. For those determined to discomfort the king, Orléans had the advantage that he was hated in royalist circles. As far as the Court was concerned, his intrigues against the Monarchy at the beginning of the Revolution led to the conviction that his hand continued to lie behind many of the Jacobin faction's activities. Although this was untrue, since, at least partly due to lack of funds, he had generally withdrawn from politics after the first year of the Revolution, his relations with the Jacobins were closer than with the Girondins. A Regency under the Duke of Orléans might have been tolerated by the insurrectionists at this juncture. He was placed on the Jacobin slate of candidates in the rigged Paris elections for the National Convention at the end of August, as a potential alternative Head of Executive Power if the Girondins attempted to restore Louis.

Nevertheless, through their influence in the National Assembly, the Girondins could well have ensured a Regency Council packed with their nominees, thus ensuring that the upbringing of the dauphin was under their control. Ferrières stated he believed the Girondins' plan when the king withdrew to the Assembly was to establish a Regency, but failed to comment on why this did not happen. The dethronement of the king and the establishment of a Regency could have been acceptable politics for the Girondins at this juncture, while temporarily defusing the political situation. Naturally, the ability of the Girondins to benefit politically from a Regency would depend on their eventual willingness to confront and control the Paris Commune, now in the hands of their Jacobin rivals. The Municipality, controlling the mob and the National Guards, became the means for intimidating the future National Convention. Power passed increasingly into the hands of extremist revolutionaries who did not hesitate to kill and massacre the French people in the name of 'liberty'. 'O Liberty,' apostrophised Madame Roland on the scaffold as she regarded the nearby statue representing Liberty on the Place de la Revolution [Concorde], 'what crimes are committed in your name!'

The Girondin minority faction dominated the existing Legislature and had no pressing reason for abandoning the 1791 Constitution, which gave them considerable power, and with careful management might have given them more. They had shown no sign of espousing the demand of Robespierre and his followers for an appeal to the People during the previous weeks. Even a few hours previously, they had studiously ignored Huguenin's tactical reference to the sovereignty of the People. It is difficult to explain their sudden volte-face except by sheer funk. Within the verbiage of Vergniaud's introduction to the new legislation, he frankly admitted that the National Assembly could no longer cope in the 'extraordinary circumstances'. Some three hours before, when challenged by a delegation from the Section of the Thermes de Julien, the Assembly had sworn that they were capable of saving the State. Now members were being asked to hand over that task to a new body, thus accepting that they were unable to do so. Nobody apparently objected.

It is doubtful whether the insurrectionists would have been capable of overturning the National Assembly, if the latter had put on a bold front and shown a reasonable amount of finesse. While constitutionally agreeing to dethrone the king and thus defusing the most immediate demand of the insurrectionists, it could have proclaimed any move against the Assembly as Lèse Nation [High Treason]. With strong nerves and the right oratory, control over the Paris National Guards could have been regained. Instead, the lesson that force prevails over legality was to feature in French politics right down to the crisis of the Algerian war in the 1950s or even the student revolt of 1968. Between 1792 and 1871, there were some ten significant insurrections and coups d'état seeking a change of power. If the National Assembly had possessed real backbone, it might have truly preserved both 'liberty' and the 'unshakeable' Constitution of 1791, which they had sworn to uphold. The succeeding two years of Terror and civil war could have been avoided. However, the Girondins might well have defended themselves by stating that they could not foresee the future. They no doubt deplored the situation, the submission to force controlled by others, but were reluctantly prepared to make a virtue out of necessity. The Revolution was moving onwards with the disappearance of the last vestiges of the Ancien Régime. The sheep-like moderates who did not share these radical convictions have less excuse.

Gouverneur Morris, the peg-leg American minister to France, made a political appraisal for Secretary of State Thomas Jefferson in a despatch dated 16 August. He explained that the situation had become polarised between the radicals and the royalists, the latter being divided between those who wanted a monarchic dictatorship, those who wished to return to the Ancien Régime and the traditional society, or a small minority who sought a constitution on British lines. The king belonged to the latter grouping. Morris wrote: 'The King, who has an uncommon firmness in suffering but who has not the talents for action, and who is besides a very religious man, found himself fettered by his oaths to the Constitution which he in his conscience believed to be a bad one, and indeed about which there is now but one opinion in the country, because experience, that great parent of wisdom, has brought it already to trial and condemnation. The King from the causes just mentioned would not step forward, and of course there was no Standard to which the adherents of the two Chambers [a two-chamber legislature] could repair. The republicans had the good sense to march boldly and openly to their object, and as they took care not to mince matters nor embarrass themselves by legal and constitutional niceties, they had the advantage of Union, concert and design, against the disjointed members of a body without a head.'

While Louis had adopted a policy of strict adherence to the new Constitution of September 1791, he sought to change it by legitimate means. No leading moderate politician was prepared to champion this cause openly. Those who might have done so had either withdrawn from politics or were pursuing a military career, hoping that laurels earned might be used for political advantage in due course. Nevertheless, a press campaign was set in motion to influence opinion in the belief that the National Assembly might be persuaded to amend the Constitution. Thus, ironically, the king and the Jacobin faction were following a parallel course but with different objectives. The king had in his possession a new draft constitution, for which, according to his diaries, Gouverneur Morris may have been at least partly responsible. Morris, a lawyer as well as a businessman and personal friend of George Washington, had overseen the final draft of the American Constitution. The draft document in Louis' possession included a two-chamber legislature, liberal laws, and greater authority for the king and Royal Council; in fact similar to the Charter of 1814 at the Bourbon restoration. The document was found among the king's papers at the Tuileries but suppressed. Naturally, the king could not state his position openly. Any proposal to amend the Constitution would be regarded as breaking the oath he had sworn to uphold it. As a result, the French people were kept in the dark about the king's real intentions. Nevertheless, this activity did not pass unnoticed, and the radicals exploited the uncertainty by always imputing the worst designs to the king. Given time, peace, and good management, the campaign for constitutional revision might have borne fruit. But the time was not ripe.

Among the king's advisers, only Bertrand appears to have proposed organising working-class support for the Monarchy within Paris. This was not an altogether impossible project, but attempting it would give rise to the dangerous accusation of counter-revolution. The king and his entourage lacked the political skills to meet such a charge. Louis, who generally avoided taking risks, rejected Bertrand's schemes. The middle-class radicals who dominated the Jacobin Club had no such doubts, and their patriotic egalitarian propaganda and judicious distribution of money ensured the mobilisation of the working classes for their cause. The war was now heightening political tensions and paranoia, particularly as there were no immediate French victories, rather the reverse. This situation benefited the anti-royalists. Patriotism became associated with the political left, which the king and his supporters did little to counter. In effect, even covert measures to bring about an increase in the king's authority were for the moment out of the question. In the circumstances, Louis needed to demonstrate his dedication to the French cause and to the new order established by the Revolution, especially because his brothers' involvement with the counter-revolutionary forces in Coblenz preparing to join the invasion of France made it easy to depict the Court as collaborators. He failed to do so, hampered by a politically crass Court and ministers of inadequate calibre. Even worse, well-meant secret negotiations with the Austrians and Prussians to prevent annexations of French territory and leave the king free to introduce a new constitution in consultation with the French people without interference from the émigrés, led, on the instigation of the Court, to the counter-productive manifesto signed by Brunswick, commander of the Prussian Army. Details of the Brunswick Manifesto became generally known at the beginning of August. It threatened Paris with the sack if harm befell the royal family and undoubtedly alienated potential bourgeois support at this critical juncture.

Against a background of Prussian and Austrian armies about to invade France, there was no effective response to radical propaganda that a counter-revolution was being prepared. Measures which might have improved the king's political standing could have included the despatch of part of his newly formed Constitutional Guard, and the Swiss Guards, to reinforce the armies on the frontiers. Instead, his Constitutional Guard was seen, not without some justification, as a counter-revolutionary weapon and was disbanded by the Girondins. They attempted similarly to deprive the King of his Swiss Guards, but were inhibited by treaties with the Swiss Cantons. Louis and his advisers were unable to see that the Monarchy's true defence lay in wholehearted acceptance of revolutionary France. To this end, Louis could have also dedicated a portion of his sizeable Civil List to the war effort, and have lost no opportunity to denounce the émigrés and to make patriotic speeches. Dejoly frequently advised such gestures during the second half of July, but to no avail. No reconciliation was probable with the extremer radicals, but it was essential to keep their popular support as limited as possible.

The king needed to buy time while awaiting a swing of the political pendulum towards the right. This was to happen in due course, but much too late. He had no valid short-term alternative but to seek an accommodation with the Girondins in the hope of stabilising the situation. It can be argued that the Girondins were unreliable and incompetent, but such a policy offered the only hope of staving off the Jacobin extremists now bent on his immediate dethronement. To maintain their revolutionary credentials, the Girondin leaders' terms for such co-operation would have been harsh. Above all, the king would very likely have had to disown the priests who refused to swear an oath to the Constitution. As a devout Catholic this would have been extremely painful for him. But Louis' scruples might have been overcome by the argument that it was a necessary but temporary accommodation in the long-term interests of the French people. It is possible that a partnership, however unequal, between the king and the Girondins might have caused the latter to moderate their political stance once they appreciated the value of such a relationship.

The king's uncertain politics adversely affected the morale of the National Guards and Gendarmerie defending the Tuileries on 10 August. This was compounded by summoning members of the former aristocracy to help in the defence, giving credence to the belief that the bourgeois militia might find themselves involved in a counter-revolutionary plot. The presence of the Swiss Guards was not altogether unacceptable, since many Parisian National Guards were prepared to see them as a counterweight to the provincial Marseillais. It is a pity the Swiss were well below maximum strength. The detachment sent to Normandy would have been available if the king could have finally decided that he was remaining in Paris. The problem of a shortage of ammunition might have been alleviated by careful planning, though at some political risk. If not available from the Arsenal, it might have been obtained by river from Rouen or elsewhere and taken to the Swiss barracks outside Paris. In view of the known radicalism of the gunners, a serious attempt should have been made to place some guns with ammunition in the hands of the Swiss Guards. They could have made good use of them, as Napoleon was to do some three years later on 13 Vendémiaire. But leadership, prepared to take risks and impose its will on circumstances, was lacking in the higher echelons of the defence.

Moreover, the defence plans failed to allow for the tactics of the insurrectionists. There was a considerable natural reluctance of the Paris National Guards to fire on fellow citizens. The insurrectionists turned such hesitancy into a virtue by making peaceful persuasion their primary weapon. Defence in depth was mistaken, because the insurgents were able to subvert isolated units by walking through them. All forces should have been concentrated in and around the palace. Greater numbers in themselves would have helped to heighten morale. Nevertheless, the risk of defection needed to be countered by a clear political statement defending the Constitution and legality, while not neglecting acceptance of the political gains of the Revolution. This could have been supported by some theatrical expression by the king of his sincere interest in the rights and welfare of the French people, and his determination to defend the Revolution's achievements. Instead, the defence's propaganda was inept, concentrating on the safety of the royal family and loyalty to the king. This was not helped by Louis' silence. In the Review at 6 a.m., the king's entourage devoted their efforts to persuading the National Guards to shout 'Vive le Roi'. A Swiss officer commented that this was a mistake.

The Law of 3 August 1791 ordaining response only in case of attack was inadequate for effective defence. What was required was a declaration of martial law which would have enabled the defence to act positively. The takeover of the Commune which was known by around 7.15 a.m., together with the appearance of insurgent forces on the Carrousel, provided ample justification for the Department to suspend the Municipality's authority and to declare martial law to restore order. No attempt seems to have been made to obtain this declaration at that time. Louis lacked dynamism, while none of his ministers had the character to overawe the self-important and anxious Roederer.

Finally, once the king made the decision to go to the National Assembly, the assumption that the insurgents would leave the Tuileries alone ignored their often stated determination to disarm the Swiss. The latter should have been promptly marched off out of harm's way, possibly to the Place Louis XV where they would have been in a position to intervene if called upon by the National Assembly. Otherwise, they should have been ordered to surrender before firing commenced. Their self-defence at the Tuileries proved disastrous for the king's political position. He could not even claim the virtue of having used them to defend the Constitution. If the king abdicated his responsibility to preserve law and order, albeit with limited resources, could he expect any different action from the National Assembly? The combination of an indecisive king and frivolous politicians was fatal for France.

The overthrow of the 900-year-old Monarchy brutally fractured historical continuity, and ruptured the moral and customary boundaries which define political possibilities and behaviour. The Revolution of 1789 had released a powerful genie. Now the potential of its awesome energy began to be revealed. After the fall of the king, Talleyrand reflected on the event. His written remarks included the now necessary denunciation of the king's treachery, but he ended his commentary by referring to France in general. He wrote: 'The 10 August must necessarily change our position. It has perhaps saved French liberty and independence, it has at least cast aside and punished some traitors, but it has also paralysed us. From this moment, it is no longer possible to answer for events, it is necessary to act on new foundations.'

The foundations progressively established over the next two years were those of ideological totalitarianism. The freedoms established in the 1789 Declaration of the Rights of Man were largely suppressed. Terror imposed by the guillotine, and by mass executions when deemed necessary, became the instruments of political conformity. Some 35,000 to 40,000 French men and women perished directly for lack of zeal for the Revolution and its demands. Another 400,000 in all are believed to have died as a result of the civil war in the Vendée and elsewhere, caused by revolt against revolutionary impositions. Carrier, the revolutionary representative at Nantes, who devised means for mass murder by sealing people in the holds of barges and sinking them in the Loire, talked in terms that Pol Pot would have approved: 'To make the Republic happier, it is necessary to suppress at least half its inhabitants.' One fanatic even went so far as to suggest the guillotine would need to be maintained until the population of France was reduced by four-fifths. The Terror was operating at full stretch when it suddenly crumbled with the overthrow of Robespierre in July 1794. It was followed by twenty years of dictatorship and aggressive war, equally costly in both human and economic terms. The resulting neglect of industrial development and the elimination of France's pre-revolutionary international commerce, which had rivalled that of Britain, left the latter the leading economic power for most of the nineteenth century.

CHAPTER 18

Liancourt's Escape

Liancourt's world was falling apart. He was seething with anger but had to control it. He watched the collapse of the royalist cause with his spirit in turmoil. He saw grenadiers of the National Guards battalions of the Filles Saint-Thomas and Petits-Pères, who had escorted the king and his family to the National Assembly, start to melt away from around the Manège. Some even took possession of a discarded Swiss uniform, cut it up, and spiked the pieces of cloth on their bayonets in order to seem authentic revolutionaries. Liancourt claimed that, by the afternoon, most of the National Guards in the wealthier parts of Paris had taken off their uniforms out of fear and had left the field free to the insurgents – men with trousers and large beards, as he contemptuously described them.

He tells us that although overwhelmed with tiredness and hunger, so great was his disgust at events that he forgot his physical discomfort. Around midday, he decided with some acquaintances to sit in a corner of the Chamber to act out a vigil on the death throes of the Monarchy and the Constitution. They were forced to move by a group of working-class Parisians who insulted them for their fine clothes, and went to sit by the box used by the reporters of the *Moniteur*. Liancourt witnessed the decree suspending the king and heard the roll-call as each member in the intervals of business was called upon to swear to maintain liberty and equality. He listened to the king being insulted, saw pieces of Swiss uniforms being paraded, and remarked on spoils from the pillaged Tuileries being presented to the Assembly – all accompanied by cries and shouts from the spectators.

He sought to remain calm by carefully analysing the situation. Foreseeing the inevitable triumph of republicanism throughout France within a short space of time. Liancourt ruminated over his own relationship with the king. He had decided to devote himself to the Monarchy at the time of the flight to Varennes, the previous summer. He had taken this line despite the senior members of his family who, strongly adhering to the Revolution from its outset, continued to remain constitutionalist. Following the king, he found, was not straightforward, since Louis appeared to be without a clear policy, or at least was unwilling to give his supporters a definite lead. Liancourt could not understand why the king had accepted the constitution in the first place, failing to appreciate the pressures on Louis to agree. Despite his inability to comprehend Louis' politics, he had been content with watching over his safety, ready to sacrifice his life to prevent assassination.

He believed the only viable opposition to the republicans now rested with the émigrés. However, he had to admit that their leaders, the king's brothers, had little credibility in France. Nevertheless, with the king and the dauphin now totally under the control of the radicals, he owed his allegiance to the next in line of succession, the Comte de Provence. He had hesitated to join the émigrés before because of the strongly constitutionalist politics of other members of his family. Since the foundations of such politics were in ruins, he did not think there would be any objection now if he left France. He felt that to remain hiding in Paris would be shameful and unwise since the revolutionaries would seek to exterminate all potential counter-revolutionaries who remained within their reach. Moreover, he had nothing to lose by emigrating as he had no wealth to be confiscated. His sole means was an allowance from his family, which could be transferred to wherever he was situated. The only thing which deterred him was concern that his emigration might draw hostile attention to his relations remaining in France. He tried to justify himself by arguing that they had never consulted him on the actions they had taken and that no families were united in their views.

He wrote that he continued his internal dialogue, his conclusions wavering this way and that. All of a sudden, he was possessed by a blind fury against all the corrupt and dishonest politicians who had started the Revolution and led France to the present disaster. He made up his mind to leave Paris as quickly as possible in order to join the émigrés. But his spasm of anger diminished. He realised that a decision taken in a moment of emotion might affect his entire life. Honest sentiments were not enough. It was necessary to examine the issues more closely and distrust one's passions. He entered into a detailed review of events and politics from the outset of the Revolution, since he wished to make sure that his behaviour had always been reasonable. When he candidly had to admit that it was not always a question of black and white, he resolved that at least republicanism was wrong. Being a young man of twenty-six and in good health, he must be prepared to take risks in serving his country when it was in need, as at present. This meant joining those who were prepared to fight the republicans. The proof he gave himself was that all his friends were of his opinion and they would surely support his choice. Nevertheless, he still hesitated to take a final decision on going abroad. He was not without hope that Rouen, where his father commanded the 16th Military District, might still form a centre of resistance against the anarchy promised by the republicans. Besides, he expected his father would be anxious to learn what had happened to him this day, as the mail might be stopped and the Paris barriers closed. He determined to reassure him by his presence.

Late in the afternoon, he decided to approach the box occupied by the king and his entourage. The guards were drunk and paid no attention. Liancourt was able to open the door and enter the box:

I had the sad spectacle of seeing the King dejected and tired; he was seated at the front of the box, watching coldly with his eyeglass all the villains who spoke one after another, or sometimes all together. Near to him was the Queen whose tears had entirely dampened her handkerchief and neckerchief. She was holding the Dauphin on her knees, who was sleeping and resting his head on Madame de Tourzel's lap. Mesdames Elizabeth and the Princess of Lamballe, together with the Princess Royal, were at the back of the box. I offered my services to the King to soften his woes. The King told me that it would be too dangerous to return and that he would be going that night to the Luxembourg Palace. The Queen asked for a handkerchief. I did not have one, having used mine to staunch the wounds of Monsieur le Vicomte de Maillé whom I had saved from the hands of the pikemen. I went out to find a handkerchief and borrowed one from the head waiter in the Assembly's cafeteria. As I hurried back to the Queen, I found the sentries had been replaced and it was no longer possible to approach the box. They wanted to arrest me and take me to the Commune, assuredly to my death. One of the National Guards said that he recognised me and gave details of my residence without knowing my name. I realised that he was one of those who had arrested me during the week. Fortunately I escaped by running through the dark passageway and withdrew to the cafeteria where a waiter went to find something to disguise me.

Before leaving the Assembly's precincts, Liancourt wished to find his cousin Charles de Chabot. He knew the quick temper of his friend and feared he could have done something stupid and been arrested. He found him doing sentry duty wearing his National Guards uniform. They shared some bread and blackcurrant cordial. He cautioned him to be prudent, since Chabot had angrily stated that he would spit in Condorcet's face if he passed by. The former Marquis de Condorcet, as a leading Girondin politician, had helped to draft the decree suspending the king. Chabot obviously saw him as a traitor to the monarch and his social class. Liancourt replied: 'My dear Charles, you have parents who love you more than you are worth. Think of them, and preserve yourself so as not to cause them sorrow.' Chabot answered that he would. They parted for the last time. Two days later Chabot was imprisoned in the Abbaye, and was one of the first to perish there on 2 September.

Liancourt decided to go about Paris to ascertain what had happened to those of his friends and acquaintances who had been with him at the palace during the early morning, before he left with the king for the Assembly. He first visited the Faubourg Saint-Germain on the Left Bank of the Seine. He found nearly everyone had escaped. So far the fury of the mob seemed to be concentrated on the Swiss. He noted, as did Deville and many others, that all the streets were strongly lit. Going to the Carrousel, he found the adjacent streets full of dead and dying, as well as sleeping drunks. The outbuildings of the Tuileries were on fire, and in the Cour Royale there was a large bonfire of palace furniture on to which the bodies of the Marseillais were being thrown. Other eyewitnesses mentioned that the Swiss were also burned. The people he met in the streets seemed wild and disoriented. Liancourt wrote that he would remember that night in Paris for the rest of his life.

He passed through the Vestibule in the centre of the palace into the Tuileries garden and saw some bloodthirsty people with muskets running through the trees, looking for Swiss and aristocrats. Liancourt was not concerned for himself as his disguise was so convincing. He returned to the Manège and was advised that the king had not after all gone to the Luxembourg but was now a state prisoner held in the Convent of the Feuillants. He left to go and sleep at his brother's flat, fearing that his own rooms might be guarded or watched. Liancourt was still raging with fury because the aggressors, far from being punished, had succeeded. Some hours later, he stated, four Swiss officers including Durler arrived. The latter wrote that after spending a few hours in his own rooms with two other officers, they had left at 4 a.m. to find a safer place. Liancourt explained that a Swiss officer resided in the same house as his brother. This must have been why Durler and his companions went there. They left after an hour.

Liancourt, with his brother who managed a family spinning mill, his brother's wife, and a family friend, were having a late breakfast that morning when they were told that a band of revolutionaries was heading towards their building, looking for the Swiss officer who lived there. They decided to leave and separate. Liancourt mentioned that he intended to go to Rouen. Before doing so, he decided to go to the National Assembly to see if he could be of any further assistance to the royal family. He found the streets much quieter than the day before. Although there were still some groups of malcontents around, he did not feel so threatened. He had a rude awakening when he reached the Place Vendôme which was full of armed revolutionaries demanding the king's head and the queen's entrails and waving about pieces of Swiss uniform, even flesh, at the end of their pikes. They completely obstructed the way to the National Assembly and Liancourt gave up the attempt to go there. He turned into the Rue Saint-Honoré to go down the Rue Royale with the idea of returning to his own apartment across the Seine. On the Place Louis XV, he saw a large crowd gathered around the equestrian statue of Louis XV. It was being pulled off its pedestal with the aid of horses taken from carts and other wheeled transport passing through the square. Some people had climbed up on to the pedestal in order to loosen the fastenings holding the statue to its base. Some distance from the crowd around the statue was a mob armed with batons. They were attacking any passers-by suspected of being aristocrats or looters. Liancourt, who was still wearing his disguise, found himself in the way of an unfortunate wretch at the moment he was caught up by the mob. He wrote: 'Fifty or a hundred of those miserable people fell on an unlucky person and finished him off with blows from their sticks; without any accusation, without speaking to him, or having pity on his cries. They massacred him so close to me that my stockings were covered with blood and brains.' He could not help feeling a sardonic pleasure when part of the statue of Louis XV toppled over on to the crowd, maiming many of those who, he wrote sarcastically, 'had drawn too close hoping to prove useful'. Over the next few days, royal statues were to be tumbled throughout Paris, signifying the end of an era.

He crossed over the Pont Louis XVI where there were still some corpses and returned to his father's residence in the Rue Varenne in the Faubourg Saint-Germain. One of his servants, whom he had told to meet him there, warned him that the house where he had an apartment appeared to be under surveillance. On this information he decided to go to a Madame de Lévis who lived at the end of the Rue Saint-Dominique. When he arrived there, he summoned his own and his father's servants. He gave them instructions to have his groom saddle up two horses and take them to the Military School [Ecole Militaire], covering the saddle of the riderless horse with a blanket to make it look as if it was only being taken out for exercise. He had his servants reconnoitre the area to make sure there were no patrols. He was worried about how to leave Paris safely. His passport was very out of date and he believed he would be sent back if he tried to use it. He decided he would have to exercise considerable care in getting out.

He left Madame de Lévis' on foot, taking with him his English servant to whom he spoke English in a loud voice, hoping to be taken for a foreigner. Near the Military School, they came upon a patrol. Walking fast they overtook it, continuing to make ridiculous conversation all the time in English. He spotted his horses and told his servant to return and give his farewells to his relations and friends. He mounted up and, with a pistol in his hand, took the road for Versailles. For some reason, Liancourt failed to tell how he and his groom passed through the barriers, no doubt manned, in the customs wall surrounding Paris. Being on horseback, however, he would have found it relatively easy to search for an unguarded breach in the wall. One such had been found the previous day by the dauphin's valet, Cléry, who, accompanied by Madame de Rambaut, was also going to Versailles. Whatever happened, he was beyond Paris and continued on his way via Sèvres, avoiding populated areas wherever possible.

Eventually, he reached Versailles. Everything seemed quiet and he hoped it would be possible to stop and rest the horses. He took care to ride his horse close by the sentry as if he had nothing to fear, and ordered his groom to do likewise. The latter was told to hold his tongue, but if asked, to say that his master was an English friend of Madame Sheldon's who was returning to Versailles because he had heard that she was anxious whether anything had happened to him in Paris. It appears that servants, despite ideological propaganda and the fear engendered by the revolutionaries' victory, generally remained loyal to their masters. Weber's servant only gave his master away after being subjected to extreme pressure. A disgruntled servant, however, might be a danger, as in the case of Clermont-Tonnerre's cook who had been dismissed a few days previously. This domestic was reputed to have led the gang which murdered Clermont-Tonnerre on 10 August. Undoubtedly, the loyalty of servants to their masters and mistresses is one reason why they were excluded from the political franchise.

He found the Sheldons very agitated when he arrived at their home. They had heard that the Municipality was going to seek out all aristocrats and others loyal to the king and take them to Paris. Liancourt, disgusted at the atmosphere of fear that was settling over France, decided to reduce the length of his visit to the minimum necessary to refresh his horses. He borrowed some spurs, checked his pistols, dined, and departed. His English friends gave him the address of their bankers in London as Liancourt had left Paris with hardly the proverbial sou. He rode through the forest of Marly, which he knew very well, and reached the château of Madame de Castellane near Equevilly at 10 p.m. He was totally exhausted as he had only slept properly twice during the past week. His voice was hoarse from a sore throat, his eyes were inflamed, and he was hungry. But he wrote that his spirit had more need of rest than his body. He felt morally and mentally overwhelmed by all that he had witnessed – the hatred, the killing, and the destruction of the Monarchy.

He supped at the château and recompensed his hostess poorly with a sad description of all that had happened. He awoke early and departed at 6 a.m., cutting across country and avoiding villages where he might be stopped. Being on horseback gave him the advantage over Weber and Deville whose wheeled conveyances confined them to the roads. He arrived at the family's ancestral seat of La Roche-Guyon on a loop of the Seine near Bonnières. (The château was to be the headquarters of Field Marshal Erwin Rommel at the time of the Normandy invasion in 1944.) He found everyone in a state of general anxiety without knowing the full circumstances. He told them what had happened. He advised his uncle, the titular Duc de La Rochefoucauld and head of the family, that he had heard that Pétion was determined to revenge himself for having been suspended from his functions following the invasion of the Tuileries on 20 June. La Rochefoucauld had been chairman of the Council of the Department of Paris which was responsible for the mayor's suspension. When the Legislature revoked the suspension within a few days, La Rochefoucauld resigned. Liancourt's fears were to be confirmed when the duke was assassinated at Gisors a month later. Liancourt and his uncle had not got on too well in the past, and he was very appreciative when the duke expressed his great pleasure in his survival. He was offered money and given a cabriolet to complete his journey to Rouen since his horses badly needed rest. Liancourt took with him one of the duke's servants who was to return to La Roche-Guyon and advise the duke if Rouen offered a place of safety.

He was reassured during his journey when he heard the latest news of Paris from a stagecoach which had left the city at 11 o'clock the previous evening. There had been no pillaging of houses and the king and his family were still alive. Many in the middle and upper classes expected the insurrection to result in a major attack on property. They were mistaken, having underestimated the authority of the insurgency leadership and the self-discipline engendered by the ideals of the Revolution. Everything appeared quiet on the way to Rouen and he was greeted with questions on the latest news from Paris. The ascendancy of the revolutionaries over the countryside was a gradual process, and it was still possible to move about without being stopped at every turn by busybody militia, as Weber, Deville, and Fonjallaz were to experience a month later.

Liancourt took advantage of his more relaxing mode of transport to consider again his future course of action:

> I reflected much, while going towards Rouen, on what was going to happen to me. I was perhaps going to be obliged to join the people of Rouen, I said to myself, if they had decided to protest against the Republic [a republic had not yet been established and Liancourt was anticipating it in his memoirs] and demand the restoration of the King, if necessary by fighting and resistance. It would be better to stay with them and my father [rather than to emigrate]. But, it was ironic that I would be uniting with those who had sworn an oath to the Constitution! A failed Constitution, that even those who had made it now disparaged their part in doing so. A Constitution which had for one of its foundations a system of equality. Appeal to the populace can only lead to all possible evils. One must prioritise objectives, however. If the constitutionalists wished to put the King back on his throne, even if a tottering one, it was necessary to help them. Perhaps the experience of the outrages that all parties have committed and public misfortunes will decide them to resist. Perhaps, this frivolous nation will return to its natural ardour and find the best way to obtain a better order of things, that is a monarchical government, although one where the King and all individuals who compose the French nation are subject to the

same law. Nevertheless, with rank recognised and property respected, the Throne honoured and the people protected.

It will be observed that Liancourt sought a conservative constitutional monarchy. In castigating his constitutionalist relations, Liancourt failed to criticise those further to the political right who in the summer of 1791 had allowed their dislike of the Revolution to sabotage last-minute attempts to make major changes in the draft constitution, changes which would have strengthened the king's authority. Liancourt's anti-egalitarian views would certainly have been approved by Arthur Young, the celebrated English agricultural economist. Fanny Burney wrote in her diary that she had been invited to stay at the beginning of October at Bradfield Hall, Young's country house, where Liancourt's father was then in exile. 'I have a real obligation towards him,' Young told Fanny, 'and therefore I am anxious to show him every respect and do him service in his present reverse of fortune; but he has brought it all upon himself, and, what is worse, on his Country.' Young meant that it was the duty of the upper classes to provide political leadership. This included keeping the impractical notions of the lower orders in check. In accepting the idealistic tenets of the Revolution uncritically, Liancourt senior had failed to show the responsibility his status required. The British upper classes, long used to governing the state, would not make such a mistake.

The Duc de la Rochefoucauld–Liancourt (1747–1827) as a deputy in the Constituent Assembly. A philanthropist and political liberal, he supported the revolution from the outset. He commanded the 16th Military District centred on Rouen in August 1792. Note the silver buckles on his shoes. These were de rigueur at that period.

Liancourt entered Rouen at 7 p.m. on the 12th, passing through a large crowd. He saw Swiss soldiers of the Regiment Salis–Samade linking arms with National Guards and ordinary people. He hoped that this was a good omen. However, everybody he spoke to was in great anxiety. The previous evening his father, as military commander in the region, had insisted upon the garrison swearing the constitutional oath of loyalty to the nation, the law, and the king. But his son soon became aware that Rouen and the province of Normandy was 'not in a state to overcome the weakness evident throughout France, and fear reigned there as in other Departments. One prepared to bend.' He was told by the chairman of the Department of Seine Maritime (Inférieure), a Monsieur d'Herbouville, that he should restrain his royalism. Liancourt was indignant. To keep silent about his beliefs was dishonourable. The ten-years-older Herbouville counselled prudence. No young idealist like Liancourt, he reflected the attitude of the majority who wished to hold on to their positions or feared for their heads.

That evening, Liancourt's father accepted that Rouen was going to accommodate itself to the revolution of 10 August. Father and son discussed the situation. They decided around midnight that Liancourt senior would go on a tour of inspection towards Neufchâtel in the direction of Dieppe, providing the opportunity to find some little port for sailing to England. It was necessary he should leave Rouen as soon as possible. Liancourt decided he would go first to Havre and look for a boat there; if unsuccessful he would try Dieppe. They would both meet again in London. The young Liancourt was no longer particularly concerned for his own safety. He did not believe he was important enough to merit being pursued by the Paris authorities, while Normandy was not yet exhibiting many signs of republican zeal. Nevertheless, in the morning of the 13th he rode hard and fast with a servant towards Havre, hoping exhaustion would dull the anger in his heart. Everywhere his passport was now demanded. But he did not hesitate to relate what had happened in Paris, including his own sentiments regarding the king and the Swiss who he claimed had done their best to protect the monarch. He found that his views were generally shared. He added, however, that those who followed him might not have such a friendly reception when his account of the happenings in Paris began to sink in. He was right. Events were catching up with him. The same day, the Swiss regiment of Salis-Samade was blockaded in its barracks in Rouen by a hostile crowd. On the 16th, the National Assembly demanded that the Procureur Général Syndic of the Department of Seine-Maritime explain whether Rouen had been involved in counter-revolutionary activities.

Some four leagues from Rouen, at a village called Barentin, they stopped to change horses. He was astonished to see a large number of National Guards and asked what they were doing. He was told that they had just arrested Charles de Lameth travelling on a false passport. Lameth was a leading Feuillant [moderate] politician who had recently served in Lafayette's army. Liancourt enjoyed telling the soldiers that they should guard Lameth well. He had never forgiven him for the time when Lameth was president of the Assembly during the episode of the king's arrest at Varennes. The Duc de Choiseul was one of the officers charged with escorting the king in his planned escape to Montmédy on the frontier. As soon as details of the plot were known, an order was issued for Choiseul's arrest. Lameth had sneered at Liancourt, saying: 'Your friend Choiseul will be hanged.' [Choiseul was pardoned in an amnesty following the king's acceptance of the Constitution.] Liancourt now had the pleasure of seeing Lameth under guard, extremely agitated and in a very bad temper. Liancourt may have been disappointed when Lameth's influential brother was able to arrange his prompt release. He managed to emigrate before an order to arrest him a second time could be acted upon.

Liancourt reasoned that two horsemen arriving in Havre might be noticed, since he was now being continually questioned about the political situation. At the last post-house, he hired a large, dirty, and badly sprung carriage with two nags. When they reached the town, they were asked for passports in five different places. He was told to alight and was escorted to the town hall, where he found at least ten officials gathered together who started to question him. He could not remember precisely what he was asked, but he did recollect that he was extremely tired and in a bad humour. After a few questions, he protested that they had no right to interrogate him, that he would show them his passport, and that was all. They wished to compel him, but Liancourt blustered with anything that came into his head – that he was in the National Guards of Picardy, that he owned extensive property. They became suspicious and called in his servant to corroborate. Not having been briefed beforehand, the servant was in difficulties. They decided to have someone follow Liancourt, who was too worn out to notice at the time, but was warned by the landlord of the inn where they were staying. Liancourt intended to walk to Ingouville where Monsieur de la Borde had a house. This must have been the 59-year-old Benjamin de la Borde, former personal valet to Louis XV. Since the king's death in 1774 he had been made a member of the lucrative Tax Farm. He was also a composer and musicologist. His wife kept a salon in Paris close to the Tuileries which Gouverneur Morris frequented. La Borde was guillotined in 1794.

Instead of walking, he decided to evade the spy by hiring a horse, and setting off at a fast gallop. The agent must have known where Liancourt was going. By taking short cuts he arrived at almost the same time. The exasperated Liancourt rounded on him and threatened to beat him with his riding crop. He wrote: 'I told him that I suspected him and that the profession he followed would well merit several blows with a cane. I would pay homage to the Municipality on his back. All that was not prudent but I was mad with grief and distress.' He told La Borde of his need to quit France. The king was dethroned and his loyal subjects could no longer be of any use to him. He wished to join the French émigré forces. At these words, La Borde hastened to take Liancourt upstairs to a little room where they could not be overheard, going to the door from time to time to make sure no one was listening outside. He gave some inconsequential advice and offered money abruptly without appearing to show any real interest in Liancourt's predicament. At length he asked Liancourt to dine the next day.

Next Liancourt went to see a former friend who might help him to find a ship to take him to England. He was a merchant and an ex-member of the Constituent Assembly. Liancourt hoped his business interests would enable him to recommend a suitable vessel. He was rapidly disillusioned. The businessman, M. Bégouin, had a sound sense of self-preservation which led to a long and successful life. He excused providing assistance by referring to his wife and children, not to mention his property. Liancourt restrained himself from pointing out that all he wanted was the name of a ship's captain or officer to contact. Since he knew English he would not need to compromise anyone else. The next day, 14 August, he was still no nearer finding a boat in which to reach England. Eventually, he remembered an aged acquaintance he had met when in Havre eight years previously. He was Jean–Louis–Roch Mistral, Superintendent of the Navy. He too was unprepared to do anything directly but promised to find means of helping him. Liancourt was touched. When he returned to his inn he received a little piece of paper with the name of an English tavern-keeper on it, a Mr Lake. Liancourt rushed round to see him. He was pleased to find Lake had a robust attitude towards the French authorities and was prepared to consign them all to damnation. Lake agreed to arrange a passage on an English boat and, anxious for further business, pressed Liancourt to recommend his services elsewhere. The price he paid was 6 louis for him and his servant. This was about £5 15s in money of the time, or about 10 per cent of a clerk's annual salary, and probably three times the normal rate. Even so, travel was relatively much more expensive then than nowadays. Lake also charged him 20 livres, a little under a louis which was worth 24 livres, for his own expenses. Liancourt was taken to the captain and it was agreed that they would meet again at 8 o'clock that evening.

In the meantime, Liancourt went off at midday to dine with La Borde whom he again saw privately. The latter was unsettled by his presence and sought to be rid of him as soon as possible. Liancourt touched him for a loan of 20 louis, not wishing to be short of money when he arrived in London. He found a number of guests had been invited to dine, including some leading aristocrats and two municipal officers, one of whom had been particularly inquisitive when Liancourt had first arrived in Havre. He discreetly passed on details about the English tavern-keeper to the aristocrats but decided not to be too circumspect about his opinions. He spoke freely about the horrors in Paris and the bravery of the Swiss. No one dared to contradict him, although everyone was uneasy. After the meal, the municipal officer took him on one side and recommended that he should have his passport countersigned before returning to Rouen, which Liancourt had told the gathering was his destination. He thanked him dryly for the advice but his patience snapped when the official began to question him again. Liancourt ticked him off for his impertinence. He finished by telling him that all these contemptible administrative procedures and insupportable continuous vexations compared unfavourably with officialdom in the Ancien Régime.

He returned to his inn and arranged a rendezvous with his servant at the premises of the English tavern-keeper. While waiting in a little room until dusk, he was surprised to see de Septeuil and his brother, the former being Treasurer of the Civil List. His superior, the Intendant La Porte, was among the first judicial victims of the Jacobin royalist purge, and was guillotined a week later. They left on the boat that night without any searches or delays. Liancourt's first act when on board was to throw his revolutionary cockade into the sea. This gesture proved premature. They had some anxious hours until daylight the next morning due to the lack of wind keeping them almost stationary. Liancourt was concerned that a boat would be sent out to bring them back. Eventually, a wind came and he reached England after a passage of thirty-three hours, very seasick.

Liancourt joined the émigré army and wrote interesting memoirs on its activities. After the defeat of the allied forces, he withdrew to Altona near Hamburg where he met his wife. He then joined his father in the United States, and awaited more settled conditions in France. He returned to France in 1800 and lived on a property in the valley of the Oise. He joined the Corps Législatif in 1809, and served in various legislatures until 1817. At the same time he resumed a military career and served both under Napoleon and later the Bourbons. In 1827, at the death of his father who had succeeded his brother in 1792, he became head of the family as the Duc de La Rochefoucauld. He died in 1848, aged eighty-three.

CHAPTER 19

Fonjallaz's Escape

Grenadier Jacques-Gameliel Fonjallaz left a vivid account of his service in the Swiss Guards at the time of the Revolution. This was not published until 1908. The narration is lively, with much dramatic dialogue. However, the relative unsophistication of the author is evident in places, especially when it comes to indicating lapses of time between different events. Fonjallaz came from a poor Vaudois family living in Vevey on Lac Léman. He seems to have lost his father at a relatively early age and moved with his mother to Cuilly, between Vevey and Lausanne. After working in domestic service for five years, he complained that he did not have enough money to clothe himself. He was twenty-one when he decided to join the Swiss Guards in December 1786.

He walked to Lausanne where he was told he should join Captain de Loys' company based at Courbevoie on the western outskirts of Paris. He was given a louis d'or, equivalent to 24 livres, as travelling expenses, together with a route map. A livre was the daily wage for an unskilled labourer. Walking across the Jura through the snow, he had a near escape from a wolf. He disabled it by striking it in the jaw with his staff. He took a public conveyance for the final stage of his journey to Paris and lost his belongings, including most of his remaining funds. On arrival in the big city, he described a brush with a prostitute who thought he might be an easy victim as the traditional country bumpkin. When he reached Coubevoie, he saw the fourrier [assistant quarter-master] of de Loys' company and was given 4 louis in exchange for signing on for four years. He cheekily asked for an additional 2 large silver écus, equivalent to half a louis. They must have thought him a promising recruit as this was granted on the spot. He was then assigned to a corporal for individual instruction in drill. Since recruiting was haphazard, it seems to have been regarded as more practical to train soldiers on an individual basis rather than in a group. He had drill lessons twice a day and after five weeks he was deemed proficient.

In May 1791, after four relatively uneventful years as far as military activities were concerned, he asked for leave to return to Switzerland. The normal period granted for leave in Switzerland was six months, called a semester. Fonjallaz, however, requested eleven months. This was initially refused. He then pointed out that the period of service for which he had signed up had now expired, and unless his request was granted, he would resign altogether. He does not mention what he did in Switzerland. He returned in due time to Paris in April 1792. On 9 August, he was on guard at the Tuileries by the Porte Royale. He complained about the lack of food. On the 10th, as described earlier, he was on the Great Stairs when Westermann and Granier tried to persuade the Swiss to lay down their arms. He participated in Durler's counter-attack, but his account of the battle is brief and disjointed, a classic example of Joseph de Maistre's famous description of the swamping effect of battle on the soldier's consciousness: '. . . bewildered, carried away by the crash of gunfire and other military weapons, shouted commands which rise and fall, surrounded by the dead, the dying, mutilated corpses, possessed in turn by fear, by hope, by fury, and by five or six other different kinds of madness, what becomes of man? What does he see? What does he know at the end of several hours? What can he know about himself and about others?' Nevertheless, his text does provide some informative details. Although he was a member of Durler's force, he did not participate in the movement to the National Assembly. A possible reason is that Durler and Salis only wished to take properly armed troops with them. Better to use his sabre, Fonjallaz had thrown away his musket when his cartridges ran out. Altishofen was told by a relative present that the Swiss were carefully formed up for their march towards the National Assembly as if on parade.

Fonjallaz said he was obliged to take refuge in the interior of the palace. When the insurgents broke in, he was with four other Swiss in the queen's bedroom. With them was an old lady of 65–70 and a chambermaid aged 25–30.

As we sought to hide ourselves, I could not prevent myself from laughing when the old lady started to say: 'You are fine ones, Mister Grenadiers, to hide yourselves. I would like to see those insolent ruffians come here to misbehave themselves. I would certainly know how to complain to the King.' We heard doors being broken down elsewhere in the palace which made us aware we were not safe. I began to climb up the chimney. The others tried to do the same, but they could only stand up inside it, showing their legs. The women in the room placed a fire-screen in front so the chimney was hidden. A moment later, the door burst open; they were armed with axes and pikes. When they were in the room they took the old lady and threw her out of the window. The chambermaid screaming loudly was treated likewise. The Queen's bed and all the furniture suffered the same fate, while they pocketed small gold clocks decorated with diamonds, and other objects of great price which were on the mantelpiece. One of them knocked the fire-screen and swore that there was something there. They took away the screen and saw the legs of my four comrades in misfortune. They dragged them into the middle of the room, murdered three of them, and threw them out of the window. When they came to the fourth, who was our Drum-Major, a man of 6 feet 5 inches [possibly nearly 7 feet tall after taking into account the difference between the French and English foot], they told him that he was too big. They threw him to the floor, chopped off his legs, and cast him out of the window. Then they took hold of his legs, and one said: 'I bet I can land these on his face.' During this butchery, I climbed ever higher in the chimney. As it made a turn, they could see nothing. They said that the chimney was full of Swiss, and they fired three shots up the chimney. I said nothing, but the powder made me sneeze.

The Swiss had ceased to be valiant fighting soldiers and had become frightened fugitives. The frenzied activity of combat was replaced by the helpless lassitude of defeat. The relatively few remaining rank and file in the palace were isolated in separate rooms, with no officers to tell them what to do. In desperation they had thrown away their weapons to improve their chances of having their surrender accepted, but no quarter was to be granted. It seems very likely that only a small number of insurgents burst into the room where Fonjallaz and his four comrades were hiding, but they had the ascendancy of victors. If the Swiss had been armed and prepared to resist, they might have ambushed their murderers and preserved their lives, at least for a while. Fonjallaz laughed at the old lady whose awe of the king made her believe he might still provide some protection. It is easy to imagine the glee with which the revolutionaries greeted the ridiculous sight of four Swiss soldiers with their heads stuck up the chimney and the lower part of their bodies in plain view. These erstwhile fighting men now allowed themselves to be put to death without even a show of resistance. The grotesque fate of the tall drum-major is hardly believable, but the Parisian working man was partial to gallows humour. Many sources mention victims being jettisoned from windows. This might be explained by a literal desire to cleanse the palace of the king's supporters. The queen's apartments were in fact on the ground floor, and the two ladies may well have survived being thrown out, certainly the younger one. The jettisoning of furniture out of the window may similarly be explained by the revolutionaries' desire to make the palace uninhabitable, so that there was no question of the royal family returning. Regarding the queen's bed, there are stories elsewhere of prostitutes disporting themselves upon it. But these may be due to royalist propaganda.

One might ask how Fonjallaz was able to give so many details since he was up the chimney? It is possible the hearth operated as a sound chamber and he could hear quite distinctly what was going on in the room. But some of the details, such as the weapons the insurgents were carrying and the fate of the drum-major, must have been partly gathered by inference. For instance, if they had uneducated working-class accents, he would know they were likely to have a motley of weapons. The suspicion of some fabrication or embroidery of events cannot be ruled out, especially as Fonjallaz obviously relished making up stories. Nevertheless, his memoirs were not written for publication, and only appeared in 1908. After careful consideration, there seems little reason to doubt the general truth of Fonjallaz's story which contains a number of incidental details which would require detailed historical knowledge to reproduce.

'When the musket shots produced no effect,' Fonjallaz continued, 'they climbed on to the roof to demolish the chimney, but when they were on the roof, they were fired upon from all sides. Seeing this was not a good place to be, they said let us go back into the room where we will demolish it sooner. When they were in the room, they began to demolish the bottom of the chimney. Then I told myself that all was lost. I made a short prayer and asked the Supreme Being to have pity on me. At length, I made an effort to mount to the top hoping to get out by the roof. My aim was to jump from the roof and kill myself rather than be larded with pikes.' It is very improbable that the insurgents went on to the roof to demolish the chimney if Fonjallaz had started in the queen's bedroom which was on the ground floor. It makes better sense that they went to the roof to see if he was escaping. It would be highly likely that they would be shot at by surrounding units of National Guards mistaking them for escaping royalists. Presumably, Fonjallaz must have heard them repeating their experiences when they returned. Being able to hear their conversations may be evidence for only a small number in the room. It is interesting that he considered throwing himself off the roof as did Constant-Rebecque, when he climbed out of the attic in the Hôtel de Malte. As professional soldiers, they would have regarded most of the insurgents as civilian rabble, and being put to death at their hands as highly dishonourable.

Fonjallaz continued: 'I succeeded in breaking through into an adjoining chimney space. The Sans-culottes started to demolish the wall separating the chimney from the room. In doing so they found 1500 louis d'or. They said they would take these to the authorities but probably kept some. By now my knees and elbows were raw with trying to escape higher up the chimney. At length they went away.' Obviously the discovery of the gold distracted his pursuers. Presumably he must have heard them counting the money which would have taken some time. The queen's bedroom would have been a likely place to find a large sum of money, and behind the chimney breast was a good position for concealing it. Revolutionary accounts of the capture of the Tuileries made a great fuss of the insurgents' honesty and the depositing of valuables found there with the authorities. The next day, a number of looters in the palace were summarily executed. However, perhaps many of the insurgents who were initially brave enough to enter the building were not under control. Pillage as well as killing undoubtedly motivated them. Fifteen hundred louis d'or was a substantial sum, roughly equal to a year's pay for forty or fifty skilled workers. No mention of such a sum is made in the National Assembly's proceedings, nor in a summary of the Commune's minutes. It is plausible that such a tidy sum, if handed over at all, would have been brought to the attention of insurgency chiefs who were able and happy to suppress its discovery. Both Westermann and Huguenin were to be accused the next year of having misappropriated money from the Tuileries on 10 August. Danton, who managed to have the charges against Westermann suppressed, was also notorious for his venality. Some of this money may have found its way to the coffers of the Paris Commune's Comité de Surveillance to pay the estimated two hundred or more

Westermann (1751–94) was the principal revolutionary commander when the insurgents occupied the Cour Royale. His demand that the Swiss should surrender their arms proved unacceptable.

executioners recruited for the September Massacres. It is reported they were each given 24 livres for their bloody task, the exact value of a louis d'or.

The evening came and Fonjallaz heard people despoiling corpses in an adjoining room. Around 11 p.m., he descended from the chimney covered from head to toe in soot and his breeches in shreds. He straightened himself up and was surprised by a solitary person in the room he had not heard. 'Are you one of the brigands?' asked Fonjallaz in confusion. 'Have mercy and do not make me suffer,' he cried out. Despite being addressed as a brigand, the person told Fonjallaz to go away quickly before someone else came. Eventually, he found the exit from the State Apartments leading on to the Great Stairs. He saw a sentry keeping guard for a group of twenty-five National Guards sitting around a fire on the landing. He waited until the sentry approached the partially opened door. He beckoned to him, this time being careful not to address him as a brigand. 'Dear friend,' Fonjallaz said, 'with great difficulty I have managed to escape until now. For love of God, let me pass.' Fonjallaz was asked whether he was Swiss, to which he said yes. The sentry replied: 'Comrade, all in my unit are respectable Parisian bourgeois and we have already saved several of your comrades. In fact, we bourgeois do not want anything from you Swiss.' He continued: 'Undo your collar and your hair queue, and pass out boldly without appearing to run away.' The sentry must have seen that the soot largely disguised Fonjallaz's uniform. The principal remaining telltale signs of his profession were his pigtail and high military collar, a circular band of embroidered padded material designed for keeping the head upright. Fonjallaz was lucky in coming across a unit from a moderate part of Paris. It is almost certain that the citizen militia he met belonged to units despatched by the National Assembly late in the evening to restore order and allow the municipal firemen to carry out their functions. The firemen had complained to the Assembly: 'There are 900 toises [1,800 metres] on fire. We are being fired upon. We are threatened with being thrown into the flames.' The firemen then went on to emphasise that the fires might spread into commercial and residential districts. The mob were keen to destroy the Tuileries as a symbol of the Monarchy, despite deputies on the scene pointing out that the palace was a 'national property'.

'I passed by them peacefully,' Fonjallaz wrote. 'None of them paid me any attention. I went down the Great Stairs. I did not know where to go. I decided to jump into the Seine, since I was a good swimmer, and let the current carry me out of Paris. But then I realised that with my wounds and weakened state, this was not a good idea.' Fonjallaz went to speak to one of the firemen in the vicinity, since the Swiss had good relations with the Paris 'pompiers'. He asked one for a jacket but was turned down. The fireman suggested, however, that he should take off his military gaiters.

Fonjallaz suddenly remembered a lemonade seller in the Rue Saint-Antoine who had employed him to whiten harness leather. Lemonade selling from a horse-drawn cart was a major retail trade in Paris at the time. He crossed the Cour Royale into the Cour des Suisses. In several places he was obliged to walk on corpses. 'I saw ten or twelve cannibals', he wrote, 'still drunk and making mockery of the corpses, standing them up, and letting them fall, saying: "Ah! fine soldier, a mere slap will make you fall." They then threw them into the fire they had made in our guardhouse which was fuelled by haversacks, palliasses, and mattresses. I took the small street of Saint Louis, crossed the Rue Saint-Honoré, and made several turns to deceive any pursuers, before arriving at Monsieur Choriac's door. There was a corpse by his doorway which I pulled away by the feet. "Who's there?" he said. "It is the grenadier who whitens your leather", I replied. He got up immediately, let me in and locked the door securely. I then collapsed. An hour later when I came round, I found that I had been placed in a good bed. I began to feel hungry as it was some sixty hours since I had had much to eat. My elbows and knees were in a bad state. I passed the day with Choriac. He went out to find some clothes for me to wear, but they were too small with the exception of a shirt and britches. I threw my regulation britches and shoe buckles down the latrines.'

Fonjallaz left Choriac and went to see a Swiss wigmaker acquaintance who lived in the Rue des Orties which then ran alongside the Galerie du Louvre. Why he had not gone there in the first place, he did not mention. It was only a very short distance from the palace. Presumably when he escaped he was frightened of pursuit and wished to distance himself from the scene of the battle. His friend set about persuading the concierge, a Madame Résillier, to ensure Fonjallaz's safety. She was ready to oblige. He was inscribed in her register under the name of François Vincent. Since it was essential to have suitable papers to avoid suspicion, she took him to the Section Committee Room where she was well known. Someone asked what they could do for her. She replied: 'Citizen, here is a young man who has lodged with me since 1 August and who has no papers.' They asked Fonjallaz what he wanted. He wrote:

'Citizens,' I replied. 'I ask that you have the goodness to hear me a moment.' 'Speak', said the Chairman. As I had been coached what to say, I began my narration in these terms. 'Citizens, I am François Vincent, a native of Saint-Marcellin in the Dauphiné [eastern France]. For thirteen months I was in the service of Monsieur Pluvinal, a Knight of Malta. We were living in Lyons at the Hôtel de Milan, in front of the Place des Terraux. On 20 July, my master said that I must prepare his luggage for departure, because he was going to join the Army of the Princes at Coblenz. I replied that I did not wish to serve against my country and that I had a brother in Paris whom I wished to see. He then settled my wages and I left him to go to Paris the next day. I arrived on the 30th at Montzeron, at three leagues from Paris, and slept there. The next morning, I departed on a public conveyance with my baggage including my papers and wallet. I had 259 Francs d'Assignat [paper money] in my wallet. As the conveyance went very fast, the baton securing my baggage broke and my bag fell off, without me noticing. I noticed my loss in the Faubourg Saint-Antoine where I got off. I thought it useless to return to seek it as there were so many people on the road. Then I arrived at Citizeness Résillier's, Rue des Orties, where my brother Alexis Vincent was staying.' That is what I said word for word. They replied in a friendly tone: 'My friend, it is very inconvenient for you, but be assured you are safe and we will give you an identity card.' I thanked them honestly and felt as pleased as punch. They asked me back to say I would be obliged to mount guard when my turn came.

It is obvious his friend knew Lyons well. Fonjallaz made use of the actual incident of losing his baggage when he had first arrived in Paris five and a half years previously. The 'franc' was formerly a unit of account not used in physical transactions, virtually equivalent in value to the livre. Later on in the Revolution the values of the franc and the livre were equalised, and the description 'franc' then combined the functions of account money and exchange money, replacing the livre. Fonjallaz's reference to francs in his memoir was anachronistic.

Fonjallaz appeared to have had an uneventful time for the rest of August. He made confused allusions to the fate of Swiss Guards who were prisoners. His journal took off again at the beginning of September. At 2 a.m. on the 3rd, his residence was subject to a house search by the authorities. It was usual to make these investigations at night, often in the small hours of the morning. This was probably for the practical reason that all the residents would have returned to their lodgings. But there may also have been an intention to catch people off guard. Fonjallaz wrote: 'My friend the wigmaker and I were fortunately at the top of the house. When they came to the bottom of our staircase, the patrol leader asked who was behind the two doors above. Madame Résillier said: "It is my wood store, and the other is a room where two young men sleep who have been here a long time." The patrol leader replied: "Madame, as we have found nothing suspect in your house, it is not necessary to go up and wake these young men and move the wood about."' It must be supposed that these investigations were tiring for the perpetrators as well as annoying for the recipients. Madame Résillier's reference to her wood store indicated Paris relied upon wood for heating. In London, it would have been a coal store.

After the September massacres, the National Assembly passed a decree that people could leave Paris and travel to within ten leagues of the frontiers without a passport. 'I went and found friends of my acquaintance,' Fonjallaz wrote, 'saying I wanted to go to Switzerland. They gave me clothing and 130 francs [livres] of paper currency and a letter to a Monsieur Bontoux at Lyons.' Certainly, although only a simple grenadier, Fonjallaz was not without resources in Paris. He and his wigmaker companion left Paris on 11 September. They took the stagecoach to Auxerre. Travelling by this relatively expensive mode of transport led locals to assume that they were people of substance, possibly aristocrats seeking to join the émigré army. They were frequently insulted as a result. When they arrived at Arnay-le-Duc, they were arrested for being without passports. It appeared that confirmation of the Assembly's decree had not yet reached this town. They were released three days later when corroboration arrived. Two other men in prison with them were not so lucky. They were political suspects and were sent back under escort to Paris.

They carried on to Chalon-sur-Saône, where they wished to stop and eat, but people cried: 'Wretched aristocrats, you are emigrating. Down with the aristocrats!' They left Chalon without stopping. They continued to Tournus, six leagues down the river. Half way, they were halted by around twenty-five armed men from Provence going towards Verdun, in order to help fight the Prussians. Their information was out of date, since Verdun had fallen to the Prussians on 2 September. One of this group had impaled the head of a man on his bayonet.

Continuing in Fonjallaz's own words: 'They stopped us and asked us where we were going. I replied calmly: "We have left Paris because the Nation is no longer able to arm and kit out everybody any more and they have more volunteers than they can cope with. That is why the Nation has decreed that all can leave who are able to arm and uniform themselves at their own expense. We are going to our homes in Saint-Marcellin in the Dauphiné in order to arm and clothe ourselves, and from there we shall join the Army of Montesquiou which is near the bridge of Beauvoisin." They made us drink several cups of wine, since they had bottles in their pockets which they had purchased in Tournus. The person who was carrying the head said to me: "Kiss this Monsieur." I replied that I would not kiss the head of an aristocrat, but would do so if he was a good Sans-culotte like them. They all said: "Bravo! These are good patriots."' Montesquiou's army was about to launch a successful invasion of Savoy, then part of the Kingdom of Sardinia. Beauvoisin lies some 50 km north of Nimes. Fonjallaz did not explain how he knew the location of Montesquiou's army, assuming he was correct. It is obvious Fonjallaz was seldom at a loss for words and enjoyed the role of spokesman. He gave a cheeky answer concerning the aristocrat's head which might imply that the perpetrators could themselves share the same fate. One wonders what might have happened if he had shown horror at the sight or indicated sympathy for the victim.

'We arrived at Tournus,' he continued, 'with only four Assignats. We asked for soup and a bed. The lady innkeeper enquired whether we would like something else to eat. We replied that we had but little money. She questioned us and we answered her. She seemed to take pity on us and I told her our true situation. She was very touched. "My children," she said, "you must take the river boat [galiote] which passes by at 9 a.m. It will take you all the way to Lyons; you will not be safe on the main road." I then told her we lacked money. She asked us how much we had. I told her only 11 francs in paper currency. She told us that the galiote would only cost us 6 francs. She served us a good supper and gave us a bed for nothing. After thanking her, we bought a four-pound loaf of bread to eat on the boat.'

Assignats were paper currency first created at the end of 1789. Originally they had been printed only in high denominations. By the spring of 1791 they were being printed with a face value as low as 5 livres. The next year denominations of 50, 25, 15, and 10 sous were printed. Twenty sous equalled one livre. For smaller change there existed 'billets de confiance', issued by newly created 'popular' banks and supposedly backed by Assignats held in reserve. The value of Assignats depreciated against metal currency, and when Fonjallaz was en route to Switzerland they were only worth some 70 per cent of coin money. A few years later, reckless over-printing had made them virtually valueless. Fonjallaz shows a poor person's appreciation of money and frequently gives costs and prices. Bearing in mind that they had 4 livres left on reaching Lyons, they must have paid 1 livre for the loaf. The price of bread fluctuated considerably depending upon the overall harvest and local availability of flour. A cost of 1 livre in paper money would not have been regarded as cheap in Paris. The capital was usually favoured in the provision of flour.

In leaving the capital by stagecoach, they obviously wished to put as much distance between themselves and Paris quickly. When Fonjallaz borrowed the money from his friends, he must have carefully calculated the cost to reach Lyons by coach. Unfortunately, the three-day delay caused by detention at Arnay-le-Duc, when they would have had to pay for their meals and possibly tip the gaolers, would have upset their finances. On arriving at Tournus, about 100 km north of Lyons, they must have been concerned about how they could continue their journey. The galiote recommended by their hostess was a long-decked sailing barge for carrying goods and passengers on canals and rivers. This means of transport on the Saône was used seven years previously by an impecunious sixteen-year-old Napoleon Bonaparte when he took up his first military posting at Valence.

'There were three Chevaliers of Saint-Louis on the galiote,' wrote Fonjallaz. 'We sat next to them and started a conversation. This fell on the massacre of the Swiss. When I saw that they were royalist, I told my friend that we had nothing to fear from them. I gave them my story without forgetting to mention that we were without money for the seventy leagues to the Swiss frontier. They made us eat and lodge with them at Macon, paying all our expenses. The next day we arrived at Lyons. With our four remaining francs we went to take refreshments. Afterwards, my friend sought out some wigmakers in order to find work. He found this immediately. I approached Monsieur Bontoux with my letter of recommendation and was well received. He gave me some Assignats and put me up at an inn where he came to see me regularly. He paid for my bed and board but I slept with the servant.'

The Order of Saint-Louis was a decoration freely awarded under the Ancien Régime to nobles for public and other services. In other words, Fonjallaz was saying that the three people concerned were aristocrats. In past times, they may not have cared to strike up a conversation with a lowly member of the Third Estate such as Fonjallaz. Now, people of his station in life wielded power. Nevertheless, he may have been more subservient than he made out. It is almost certain that it was the brash Fonjallaz who initiated the conversation, since he frankly admitted his concern for money and obviously hoped to cadge some. The chevaliers were presumably taking this humble means of transport to Lyons for the same reason mentioned by the lady innkeeper, that revolutionary bands were likely to be met on the road. When this conversation took place, the so-called massacre of the Swiss Guards had occurred around six weeks previously. Even if the chevaliers came from remote parts of the country, it would hardly have been hot news. They may have been discussing the political situation among themselves when Fonjallaz intervened. Unless they were remarkably trusting, he would have had to prove his political credentials before he could take part in a hazardous conversation. The obvious way to do this was to admit that he had been in the Swiss Guards at the Tuileries. In specifically claiming that they arrived in Lyons the next day after spending the night in Macon, Fonjallaz must have either suffered a memory lapse, or did not like to admit that he failed to obtain food and lodging for the next night and had to sleep rough on the boat. The distance between Tournus and Macon is about 30 km and that from Macon to Lyons is at least double. They must have arrived in the latter town two days after leaving Tournus. Obviously Bontoux did not pay too much for Fonjallaz's lodging as he had to sleep with the boots.

Fonjallaz does not indicate how many days he spent in the inn, but it must have been nearly a week. He typically skipped time and wrote that two hours after dinner Monsieur Bontoux came to see him to say that he had spoken to two of his friends who acted as official witnesses for the decisions of a Revolutionary Committee. He was told that he would receive a passport the next day. The notorious Comités Révolutionnaires were not formed until March 1793 and Fonjallaz was probably referring to the municipal Comité de Surveillance (Watch Committee). 'They asked me who I was', he wrote. 'I replied that I was from Geneva but I was living in Lyons and had a wife and three children. I asked them for a passport to go to Geneva to obtain a legacy from the estate of an uncle who had just died. I was asked how much it was. I replied around 2300 francs. Monsieur Bontoux and the two official witnesses then verified the truth of what I had said. I was given a passport for fifteen days. One member of the Committee said that they would have to place my wife under observation. However, the Chairman said that since I was Swiss, this was not necessary. I thanked all those who had helped me and left on 30 September with 68 paper francs. My friend came with me from Lyons one league, where we ate well.'

Fonjallaz seems to have over-elaborated his story by claiming he had a wife and children, a matter very easy to check. The fifteen-day duration of the passport was not particularly generous and would not allow much time to complete his supposed business in Geneva. One member of the committee was suspicious. It seems very likely that the chairman had been at least partly advised of the real situation by the two officials who vouched for Fonjallaz and was acting in collusion, perhaps for a small sum of money. Why otherwise had Bontoux given Fonjallaz an assurance that he would receive a passport? When the chairman intervened to save Fonjallaz by saying it would not be necessary to keep his pretended wife under observation because he was Swiss, and in effect a foreign national rather than French, he was not being strictly accurate. Fonjallaz was claiming to be Genevese, but the city state of Geneva was then not part of the Corps Helvetique and not truly Swiss. Nevertheless, foreigners tended to regard the Genevese as honorary Swiss in view of Geneva's long political association with the Cantons. At that time, the newly declared French Republic was actively concerned to keep the goodwill of the Swiss in view of the Austrian and Prussian military threat in northern France.

Fonjallaz forwarded his luggage from Lyons to Geneva by a regular carrier taking mail and baggage. Since he was walking to Geneva to conserve his money, he needed to travel light. When he stopped at an inn that night to sleep, he was initially refused as he had no baggage with him and might easily slip away in the early morning without paying. He was forced to deposit his wallet in order to obtain a bed. Fonjallaz continued: 'On 1 October, two leagues further on near Fort l'Ecluse, I met one of the gentlemen who had paid our expenses at Macon. After I had greeted him, he did me the honour of asking me to dine [lunch] with him, and told me he greatly feared passing by the fort, since he had no passport. I outlined a plan which succeeded marvellously. I told him to take off his riding boots, put them in his travelling bag, and replace them with shoes. I obtained a dirty overall for ten francs and soiled it even more. I dressed him as a Sans-culotte with a peaked cap. He had the appearance of a field labourer. The next morning, ten minutes before arriving at Fort l'Ecluse, I made him get off his horse and I took his place. At the fort they demanded my passport. I showed it them and they said it was satisfactory. "And the other person?" they asked. I explained that he was a peasant that I had taken to show me the way over the mountains. They accepted this and we continued on our way. We arrived at a village where we ate. We separated after the meal. He took his horse and I never saw him again.'

If Fonjallaz left Lyons by foot on 30 September, as he said, he could not have been at Fort l'Ecluse only some 30 km from Geneva by the next day, as he suggested in his account. The distance between Lyons and Fort l'Ecluse is about 100 km, as the crow flies. Assuming an average distance walked of around 40 km per day, he might have been there by the morning of 3 October. This would agree with his recorded arrival at Vevey on the 7th. Fort l'Écluse is on the Rhône. Because of gorges, the road there leaves the Rhone and ascends into the Jura before going down again towards Meyrin on the northern side of Geneva. The French soldiers may have been rather gullible, since it must have been difficult to explain why he needed to take a short cut across difficult country rather than continuing along the main road from Lyons to Geneva. As for his gentleman acquaintance, he could have ridden into the Jura until he reached Swiss territory at an unguarded place.

When Fonjallaz arrived at Meyrin, he had 12 livres in paper money left. He was leaving France and entering Geneva where his paper currency would not be acceptable. He meticulously noted that he spent 3 francs of this paper money at the inn, and changed the remaining 9 livres for 6 livres in silver coin. Arriving in Geneva, he found a Vaudois battalion in garrison who made him welcome. The events of 10 August had inspired democratic ferment in Geneva. The Canton of Berne had come to the assistance of the Genevese conservative oligarchy by providing a garrison of Swiss troops. Fonjallaz had a Vaudois acquaintance in the garrison to whom he had lent 3½ louis in Paris. He reclaimed them and went to buy some shoes to replace those he had worn out on his fast walk from Lyons. He took a boat a few kilometres to Coppet, thus bypassing the tongue of French territory which then reached the lake at Versoix and cut off direct contact between Switzerland and Geneva by land. When he disembarked, he was taken to the guardhouse and told that his passport was only valid for Geneva but not for Switzerland. Fonjallaz pointed out that he was in fact a Swiss (Bernese) citizen. Vaud was then part of the Canton of Berne. He had to wait for acquaintances to come and vouch for him.

Fonjallaz's journal ended with his return to Switzerland, save for a few brief notes covering the years immediately afterwards. He provided security and other services on the passenger boats plying Lac Léman. In 1795, he was called upon to command an artillery unit during a revolutionary uprising. His final entry refers to a mysterious brief visit to Paris at the end of the century. In 1819 Fonjallaz was one of the listed surviving Vaudois present at the Tuileries on 10 August 1792 who received medals commemorating the Fidelity and Honour of the Regiment of Swiss Guards, which had been decreed by the Swiss Federal Diet in August 1817. His name no longer appeared on a roll of Vaudois survivors on 1 January 1824. The Fonjallaz family in Epesses between Vevey and Lausanne flourished.

CHAPTER 20

Deville's Escape

After being disarmed, young Ensign Deville had gone to the Cour des Feuillants looking for the Swiss staff officers who had formed part of the king's escort to the National Assembly, including the regiment's commanders, Lt Colonel Maillardoz and Major Bachmann. On sighting them, he was greeted by Aide-Major de Vild from Fribourg. At that moment, however, he saw a grievously wounded Swiss soldier being led away. He decided to follow the wounded soldier and offer assistance. Possibly, Deville suddenly realised that he might be reprimanded by his seniors for having abandoned his unit earlier on, taking with him the regimental flag when he followed Captain d'Erlach and his grenadiers. He had since surrendered this standard which he was expected to guard with his life. Whether his act was charitable or due to fear of censure, it was a fortunate one. He was to be the only survivor among the eight Swiss officers who had escorted the king to the Assembly. With the exceptions of Erlach, who was probably killed that day, and Bachmann, who was to be guillotined after trial, the remaining five, together with Louis de Zimmermann, were murdered in cold blood at the Conciergerie on 2 September.

Deville and a National Guard helped the wounded soldier to mount the stairs to a third-floor room in the convent buildings overlooking the alley leading to the Cour des Feuillants. He undressed the soldier and laid him down on a camp bed. There were other Swiss being tended to in the room. Deville sought a surgeon to look after the man he had just brought up. The soldiers present only spoke German and were having difficulty in making themselves understood. He was able to act as interpreter which was much appreciated. Having done all he felt he could, he wished to go downstairs to report to his commanders. He was told that this was most unwise as the mob were demanding the lives of the Swiss. 'I made myself visit,' he continued:

the other rooms of the hospital, where I witnessed a sight as frightful as sorrowful. We Swiss were piled up there, some mortally wounded and others expiring. I found a young soldier of the Lieutenant-Colonel Company, nineteen years old, who had nine wounds, including a musket ball through the neck. He was almost dead. I helped the surgeon staunch the blood and wash his wounds. I visited all the wounded one after the other and had their wounds treated. I fulfilled this duty willingly for one and a half hours, despite the searing memories which scored my mind. [The wounded Swiss helped by Deville were relatively fortunate. Those left behind on the battlefield could expect to be slaughtered without pity.] At length, I returned to the first room and promptly asked to go down. I was given the same reply. In order to pass the time, I started to talk with our Swiss. They told me that when the King had sent them the order to lay down their arms, they had already cleared the courtyards and the Carrousel and had taken possession of six cannons from the Marseillais. Anxious about what was happening outside, I again wished to go out. I went down to the first floor and saw some soldiers' heads through a window. [The window must have been in a wall at right-angles from where Deville was looking.] I approached them and asked why they were there. They replied that they were being confined and that they belonged to the two platoons who, as I have recounted previously, had come from the Assembly to the Feuillants.

Deville's conversation with the wounded soldiers who had fought at the Tuileries confirms that the Swiss cleared the Carrousel as well as the palace courtyards. However, they did not receive an actual order to surrender until they came to the National Assembly. The two platoons seen through the window belonged to the part of the king's escort under Deville's command, which he had abandoned in the Cour des Feuillants. He was naturally reluctant to make this clear in his memoirs. Deville's insistence about wishing to report to his commanders is somewhat belied by what he wrote next:

I considered that since I could not go down without risking being cut to pieces, it would be prudent to remain with our soldiers, because, if there remained any hope of survival, it would be rather for them than for their officers. I then entered the room where they were situated. It was of considerable size, without furniture, supported on each side by six pillars and looked out on to the monks' garden [probably in the cloisters]. I found there around sixty men. They had all taken off their uniforms to be less recognisable and were lying down. They were smoking their pipes and displaying an astonishing tranquillity. I had been chatting with them for half an hour when some sergeants said to me: 'My officer, you ought to take off your uniform. If anyone comes, they will force you to go into the room where the Commanding Officers and the others are confined.' I followed that advice. I took off my uniform and hid it under the clothes of a soldier. A quarter of an hour later, a National Guard came in and told us not to show ourselves at the windows, not to speak, but to remain lying down, because the populace were in the courtyard demanding the heads of our officers. We heard cries and a frightful uproar. The National Guard, however, succeeded in calming the mob by assuring it that the officers would be committed to trial.

Deville's description reveals that the troops who had surrendered earliest belonging to the king's escort were being held separately from Durler's and Salis' men who had been put into the church close by. The crowd referred to was a posse sent by the revolutionary authorities to seize officers and even soldiers, who were needed for interrogation and vengeance. During the afternoon, at least two other posses arrived in the courtyard. Deville continued his story by saying he approached a National Guards officer for some water for his men and this was promptly provided. Cries and other noises continued in the little square outside and he had to prevent the men from going to the windows to look out. In the distance they could hear continued cannon-fire at the Tuileries from which the defenders had long since withdrawn. Such senseless activity was attested by other witnesses. Very likely this cannon-fire was now in symbolic blanks, since a source states that the fabric of the building only received eleven direct hits in all. This seems on the low side, but Swiss sources mentioned that during the battle many shots went over the roof.

A new person entered the room holding a pike. The Swiss were about to jump on him thinking he was the advance guard of revolutionaries coming to massacre them, when they noticed he also held a pitcher of wine. After dividing the wine among themselves, Deville asked the man what was going to happen to them. He replied by placing five fingers on his face representing prison bars. He then stated that all the officers would be killed. They thanked him gratefully for the wine and resumed smoking, resting on their uniforms. Deville says at 2 p.m., but it must have been later, the tumult began again in the courtyard. A gunner captain whom Deville had noticed before came into the room. He warned them to observe complete silence, adding that the crowd had returned to claim the officers' heads, but that the District would do its utmost not to hand them over. He offered to have some straw brought to lie on. A while after he left, there was a further uproar in the courtyard and they heard voices crying out, 'We want his head! . . . He must be handed over! . . . He is at the District offices!' Immediately afterwards, they heard five shots.

Towards 5 p.m., a young man wearing a National Guards uniform arrived with the left sleeve of his coat split and tied up with ribbons. He was accompanied by a serving-man bringing some straw. He distributed a small quantity to each. They asked the young National Guard the reason for the musket shots. They were told that Colonel Carle had been taken to the District Committee's office. The populace had learned that he was there and had rushed to the office to demand that he be handed over. No one dared resist. The Committee were concerned that if the mob forced their way into the building, they would find out where Deville's group of soldiers was hidden. They had preferred to surrender Carle in order to save the lives of the Swiss. Carle was a goldsmith in the Place Dauphine and was commander of the loyalist battalion Henri Quatre. On the night of 9/10 August, however, he had been given command of the detachment of Foot Gendarmerie at the Tuileries which he had been unable to prevent defecting in the morning. Carle's seizure at Les Feuillants is possibly alluded to in an Assembly report when a National Guard arrived at the bar saying: 'I'm on guard here and I've heard some shots. I call on your humanity.' 'It is a question of saving lives!' exclaimed Deputy Chéron. 'Let us appoint a delegation to speak to the people.' This was typical of the Assembly's futile reactions throughout the day when only pikes and muskets counted. It seems that Carle may have managed to avoid being killed in the courtyard and escaped into the Rue Saint-Honoré. There is an anecdote that he sought the protection of Citizen Palloy whom he found there. The latter promptly killed him with his pistol. Palloy was a leading revolutionary and a contractor who had made a fortune out of selling souvenirs of the dismantled Bastille. Such a story would not harm Palloy's prestige and might be apocryphal. Deville later mentioned seeing Carle's corpse, along with eight others, between where he was being held and the Place Vendôme. Unfortunately, he does not specify exactly where Carle was lying.

The young National Guard then took some paper, an inkwell, and pens from his pocket, and placed them on the large table in the centre of their room. He requested those with friends and relations in Paris to write a message asking for civilian clothes. He would arrange that the messages were delivered by a reliable person. At nightfall, those who had received clothes for disguise would be helped to escape. The soldiers immediately took up the pens and wrote to their relations or friends. Deville awaited his turn. He wrote to a family of his acquaintance, not daring to write to his mother direct in case she was threatened. He asked for an old topcoat, a waistcoat, and a hat. He did not sign it in his own name, but pretended to be one of his friends who had also stayed at their house. At 6.30 p.m., the young man returned to take the messages they had written and gave them to a messenger who left immediately. Deville wrote: 'I went up to the young National Guard with my most pleasant expression and gave him my letter, which was addressed to M—, Treasurer of the States of Languedoc. I begged him to take care that it was delivered correctly. He looked at me attentively and replied with an expressive look: "Monsieur, I will take it myself and will bring back the reply." I saw that he recognised me, having seen me in the uniform of an officer at the infirmary. I thanked him in the most moving terms and entreated him not to forget me. I went back to lie down, very anxious about the result of my letter. I saw my life in the hands of this young man, not knowing his intentions towards me. At length, I resigned my fate to the will of God. I confided my fears to one of our sergeants, named Martin, who did his best to give me hope. At last, I went into a deep sleep which lasted two hours and did me a lot of good.'

It must be remembered that Deville had been on duty since the previous evening and was physically and mentally exhausted. When he awoke, Martin told him that the gunner captain had brought some bread and dried sausage. Deville passed into a neighbouring room where he found some soldiers and three sergeants of his company named Kummer, Hauser, and Dozet. There was also some wine and he ate with the appetite of a man who had not eaten for twenty-four hours. After the meal, Sergeant Dozet went up into the room where the regiment's commanders and other officers were confined. When Dozet returned, he told Deville that he had found them very depressed. They had two sentries at their door. The artillery captain returned a moment afterwards to ask if they were pleased with the supper they had just eaten. They asked him further questions on the fate of Swiss soldiers and officers. They were told that the soldiers would surely be pardoned providing they were prepared to join the French armies on the frontiers, but there was much anger against the officers, who would be decimated. The captain was then called away and Deville summoned together the sergeants imprisoned with him.

"'You have just heard," he said, "the captain's words. I believe it is my duty to go and rejoin my comrades. If they are decimated while I am part of their number, I can in dying save one of those fine people." I got ready to leave but the sergeants placed themselves in front of me. "No, my officer," they said, "you will not go out. Your generous manner of thinking will prove pointless. Our brave officers will perish. They will be delivered to the fury of the people and you will be massacred like them, without your death being of any use. All that has happened today is not a matter of war. It is butchery and criminal behaviour. Honour consists of saving your life from the hands of these scoundrels." I asked to go and say goodbye to my fellow officers. The sergeants replied that I would be recognised by the guards and again refused to let me out saying, "Remain with us, we will not let you leave." I went to place myself sadly on my straw and gave myself up to the melancholy thoughts the circumstances warranted. I dwelt upon the natural anxieties which my tender mother must be feeling, who had not been able to receive any news from me.' Deville naturally felt guilty for surviving the grisly fate of his fellow officers at the beginning of September. He was only nineteen and the belief that he had deserted them and not done his duty must have weighed heavily upon him.

Around 8.30 p.m., Deville related that a Horse Gendarme came into his room and rushed up to his son, a private in the Colonelle Company. His father had been in bed with fever when he received the message from his son. Under his uniform he was wearing a topcoat which he gave to his son, who donned it immediately. They followed each other out after cursing all that was happening in the streets. A moment later, two pretty young girls arrived, one of fifteen and the other twelve, from the barracks of the First Battalion of the Swiss Guards in the Rue Grange-Batelière. They were lace-makers working for Madame Hauser, the wife of the sergeant-major with whom Deville had been sitting. They brought a long waistcoat, breeches, stockings, and a hat, hidden under their wide skirts. While Hauser dressed, Deville asked the elder girl to go to his mother's and give her his news. This she carried out about an hour later. Deville embraced Hauser and he departed. Deville was very disappointed that so far his letter had been unanswered. A little later clothes arrived for Sergeant Dozet, two other sergeants, and some privates. Each seemed to escape successfully, which made the remainder believe that the way out was clear. However, when Sergeant Kummer went out a little later after receiving some clothing, he returned immediately saying that the gate leading into the Rue Saint-Honoré was closed and there was considerable noise in the street. Deville promptly asked him to try again. This time he apparently succeeded since he did not come back. Deville waited in vain for the friendly young National Guard to return with his clothing. Soon he was left alone with Sergeant Martin and some soldiers, the others having managed to get away.

Escapes by soldiers in Deville's group are corroborated by a record in the French National Archives. There is mention that two Swiss soldiers arrested on 12 August at the Clichy barrier in north-west Paris belonged to the king's escort to the National Assembly. They were described as having managed to escape from confinement at the Feuillants on evening of the 10th, disguised in clothes provided by unknown people. The lenient treatment of Deville's group was probably due to the fact that they had surrendered without fighting and shedding French blood. Continuing his story, Deville wrote: 'It was then 10.30 p.m., and I saw the District Committee Room well lit up. There was a frightful din coming from it. I went often from my straw to the window to try and see if my National Guard was there. I saw nothing. The time passed painfully till 11 p.m. Then, I saw a door half open which gave on to the balcony in front of our windows. Someone threw a parcel [into our room] in which were wrapped a topcoat and a hat. The soldiers immediately pounced on it and each sought to seize it. I said: "Comrades, the person who threw this parcel is surely going to come up and tell us to whom it belongs." Hardly had I said these words, when my National Guard entered, and decided the issue by saying the clothes were for me. He had thrown this parcel from [across] the courtyard because the sentries were at twelve paces from him. This good young man added that he had taken my letter immediately I had given it him, but fearing he might be discovered, he had returned at 10 p.m. to pick up the garments that he had now brought me. "Hurry up," he said, "I will await you in the courtyard in order to take you out of the Feuillants."'

Deville rapidly put on the clothes. In his pocket he placed his high collar, embroidered with silver filigree and the silver plate he wore suspended from his neck. These were valuable items. He embraced Martin and promised to send him some clothing once he was free. He said goodbye to the remaining soldiers. 'Arriving on the staircase,' he continued, 'I found two sentries who saw me and crossed their muskets saying: "Comrade, no one can pass!" The fear of being questioned stopped me from insisting and I returned sadly up the stairs to the room. I found the soldiers occupied with taking the distinguishing facings off their coats and hats to try and get away. The door remained open and I saw the gunner captain come in. I went up to him and said: "Monsieur, I am an officer and entrust myself to your honesty and goodness." "The devil, my officer friend," he replied, "I am unable to save you, or at least it will be very difficult." However, he added in my ear: "Go up the staircase to the left of the sentry, I will abuse you and even hit you." I slipped towards the staircase and the captain followed, scolding me severely and pushing rudely. "Why have you not come, scoundrel, to measure me for the coat and trousers?"' We arrived thus at the door of Monsieur Dussaut. It was this same red cap [the revolutionary bonnet rouge] in whose room I had tended the wounded at the end of the morning. The captain said to a little servant girl standing by: "Put Monsieur with the others." Then he went out.'

It must be noted that Altishofen gave the name Dussaut to the chief surgeon at the Hôtel Dieu. This was in fact the celebrated P.J. Desault. The similarity in names must have caused Altishofen to confuse witness statements relating to the Hôtel Dieu with those from wounded survivors who were cared for in the Convent des Feuillants.

Deville was frightened he was going to be placed with his fellow officers and asked the girl what the captain meant by his words. She was able to reassure him immediately by saying he meant he was to sleep with wounded Sans-culottes. The 'people' only came to massacre the Swiss and certainly would do no harm to their own kind. This seemed a good idea but he would have much preferred to have got away. As he spoke with Monsieur Dussaut, a surgeon entered to see if the wounded needed his ministrations. He was about to leave, when Deville asked him frankly whether he would help him to escape. The surgeon replied that he would willingly do so. Deville asked him to lend him a lancet case and a bandage. This he did, but insisted that if Deville was held up, he should not appeal to him for help. Deville agreed. They said goodbye to the patients and Deville followed several paces behind the surgeon. On the staircase, the two sentries wished the surgeon good evening, but when Deville came up they refused again to let him pass. He remained a little while saying nothing until the surgeon was out of view and then began to make a scene, that they were not allowing a medical student to follow his master. He demanded to see the commanding officer who, Deville wrote, was fortunately unavailable. Finally, being unable to persuade them, he returned back upstairs to Monsieur Dussaut's room and told him what had happened. One wonders whether the gunner captain was playing a double game and had tipped off the sentries since they had let the others through. Or else, the topcoat and hat he was wearing appeared too fashionable and he was suspected of being someone of a superior class. Just then his National Guard friend arrived and told him that he had been waiting an hour in the courtyard. He informed Deville that a mob was outside the Feuillants in the Rue Saint-Honoré calling for the heads of Swiss officers. He insisted Deville should try and leave immediately as the officers would surely have their throats cut that night.

Deville explained the situation and asked how long it would be before the sentries on the stairway were relieved. He was told it would be in a quarter of an hour. Deville realised that his appearance was now familiar to the sentries and that they might pass on that information to their reliefs. He asked Dussaut to lend him another coat. He brought him a cheap green jacket with white lapels. Deville left him the other coat together with his silver collar and plate in its pockets. He told his friend, the young National Guard, that he had all he needed to pretend he was a surgeon. He was going to make it seem that he had been treating Dussaut who was known to be suffering from a fistula. He carefully rehearsed this role with his friend and asked him to be outside when he reached the bottom of the stairs. Deville told him to greet him warmly, while asking for news about Dussaut in order to convince the sentries in case they had second thoughts. His friend then went down again and came back with the news that the sentries would be relieved in five minutes.

Deville wrote:

It is easy to imagine all that passed in my head during those five minutes. I then started down the stairs led by the little maid with a lamp, while rolling up my dressing and discoursing with her on the state of the invalid. All this was said within range of the sentries, who stood aside to let me pass while saluting me. The maid in leaving me strongly required me not to fail to return the next day. The National Guard was waiting for me at the place we had agreed and embraced me warmly asking for news about Monsieur Dussaut. I replied in monosyllables. During this time we quietly reached the Cour des Feuillants, which was full of National Guards walking up and down. We arrived at the gateway which led [across the Rue Saint-Honoré] to the Place Vendôme. It was opened for us. Outside, we found about one hundred and fifty men armed with pikes and muskets. These were the people who had been demanding our heads. We passed through them boldly, while loudly holding a patriotic conversation, and reached the edge of the Place Vendôme. During this time, we noticed nine corpses including that of Monsieur Carle. I reached the door of Monsieur de M—, Treasurer of the States of Languedoc, and wished to give my faithful guide the sum of 400 livres in Assignats. Despite all my insistence, he refused to accept them. I embraced him. I thanked him with all my heart and all the gratitude possible, promising him never to forget the signal service he had just rendered me. I did not see him go without sadness.

Deville was welcomed by Monsieur M— and his family. After a short while, he went on to his parents' house in the Faubourg Montmartre. On the way, he met several patrols of forty or fifty men and also many drunks. The houses were well lit up. It was 2 a.m. when he arrived home. After looking around to make sure no neighbours had seen him, he knocked quietly on the door, which was opened immediately. His two bulldogs rushed forward to welcome him. He remarked that their eagerness was such that they must have known of the danger from which he had just escaped. He was surrounded by servants who overwhelmed him with questions on how he had managed to get away. With the two bulldogs hanging on to his clothes, he went upstairs to see his mother, who was in bed. He threw himself into her arms and they both burst into tears.

He slept until 6 a.m., when he was awakened by three of his friends. He sent servants out into the town to find out what was happening, while he withdrew to a back room to keep out of sight. Through the window, he spied neighbours speaking in low voices which made him suspicious. He realised, however, that this might be because he had had circulated news of his death. A friend called Houssaye came to dine and mentioned that as there would surely be household searches, he was unsafe. He offered to find a trustworthy family free from suspicion to take him in. Houssaye returned at 7 o'clock that evening with news that he had made the necessary arrangements. Disguised in a servant's costume, Deville took leave of his mother and was accompanied by his friend to the Lycée in the Rue Neuve des Petits-Champs. Passing quickly though the porter's lodge in order not to be seen, he went up to the third floor where Monsieur de la Bouillerie lived. His household consisted of himself, his wife, their son, and a faithful female servant. Deville continued: 'I was received with open arms by this kindly and generous family. I was taken to a very attractive room. After having chatted some time with my hosts, I went to take possession of an excellent bed where I slept a peaceful sleep until the morning. My friend Houssaye came to see us each day and recounted what was happening in Paris. On returning from the Liquidator's Office where he worked, Monsieur de la Bouillerie's son brought us the *Journal du Soir*, edited by Audouin. I always searched for an Assembly decree announcing that one would be able to leave Paris freely through the barriers.'

Deville related that the windows of Bouillerie's salon gave on to the Rue Saint-Honoré on one side and on the other looked upon the Place du Palais Royal. This was a revolutionary meeting place, and Deville had to listen to constant cries of 'Vive la Nation!' or watch the Camagnole being danced. On Sunday 26 August he witnessed a procession in honour of the patriotic dead of 10 August. He estimated sixty thousand National Guards passed under his windows. Recruitment was now open to the poorest. Constant-Rebecque also described this procession which he said lasted three hours. Deville continued to wait for news that one could leave Paris without a passport. He did not wish to spend four hours or so in the District Office applying for one. Moreover, he feared that he might be recognised and obliged to go to the Hôtel de Ville to obtain the signatures of municipal officers. The news of the massacre of his fellow officers in the Paris prisons on 2 September was concealed from him by his hosts.

The next day in the afternoon, when Madame de la Bouillerie had just gone out, he was woken up by strident cries of 'Vive la Nation!' He looked out and saw an immense crowd at the gates of the Palais Royal. In the middle he saw the head of a woman with fine blonde hair on top of a pike. It was the unfortunate Princesse de Lamballe who had been murdered that day at La Force. He recoiled in horror. His hostess returned to say there would be a house search that night. 'We heard,' Deville wrote, 'a knock on the door at midnight. Madame de la Bouillerie came immediately to tell me to go into her son's bed, which was in his father's room, while she made her son another bed with two mattresses on the floor. During this time, the gentlemen of the search force grew impatient and banged with redoubled force on the door with the butts of their muskets. Madame de la Buouillerie opened up and we stayed in our beds. Madame de la Bouillerie was white with fright. I begged her to calm herself. I told her that if she hesitated in her replies, we were all lost. "Have no fear, Madame," said one of the men on entering, "we wish you no harm, we wish only to know what arms you keep in your house and who are the persons lodging here."' The Bouilleries had ensured that Deville would be interrogated in the presence of the family. This exhibited both courage and prudence.

One of the militia having gone through the rooms and found nothing suspect, came up to Monsieur de la Bouillerie to ask the number of weapons that he had in his home. Without leaving his bed, Monsieur de la Bouillerie replied: 'A gun, two pistols, and a good sabre.' 'You must hand them over to us,' said the man. 'But Monsieur', responded M. de la Bouillerie, 'I am obliged to mount guard, and so is my son.' 'You can claim them tomorrow at the District and they will be returned. And what persons have you lodging at your house?' the guard continued addressing himself to Madame de la Bouillerie. Her husband, to conceal his wife's nerves, replied promptly on her behalf, 'my wife, my son, and my nephew'. 'Who is the young man in the bed?' M. de la Bouillerie pretended to be irritated by that question. 'Eh, damn you, I tell you that it is my nephew.' They approached my bed and were amazed. 'He sleeps devilishly well!' 'A drum could beat in the room and he would not wake up', replied M. de la Bouillerie. 'How old is he?' 'Nineteen years.' 'The devil, he is good for the army!' During this time, the porter had come to my bed and stared at me attentively, despite the efforts of the faithful maid to distract him. My simulated sleep was not so profound that I was not seriously alarmed at the direction the conversation was taking. Under my breath I sent the questioner to the nether regions.

Luckily for Deville, the matter was not pressed. He was a reasonable actor, but not a natural storyteller like Fonjallaz, who would have sat up in bed and concocted some long history about where he had come from and how he happened to be in Paris. One of the National Guards went with the maid to visit the cellar. He returned satisfied and asked for a drink of water but was provided with a bottle of Burgundy instead. This was promptly swallowed. At length, they wished them all goodnight and departed. Deville returned to his own bed but could not sleep because of noise made by National Guards in the street.

A few days later, the Assembly passed the decree allowing people to leave Paris without a passport and to travel within ten leagues of the frontier. As there were prospects of further house searches, Deville determined to leave Paris. It was decided that he and the elder Bouillerie should go to Pontgoin, six leagues from Chartres, where Madame de la Bouillerie's mother lived. On 10 September, they dined in Versailles at an inn only a hundred yards away from where 53 prisoners from Orléans had been massacred the previous day. Their heads and severed limbs had been thrown on to a building site opposite. The Assembly had ordered that the prisoners, who were awaiting trial at the High Court based in Orleans, should be taken for safety to Saumur. Fournier, a leading insurgent, had arranged for them to be brought instead towards Paris to be waylaid by an organised posse of killers. Among the victims were de Brissac, former commander of the King's Constitutional Guard, and de Lessart, the former Foreign Secretary. Deville and Bouillerie continued their journey. They were stopped in Maintenon where their passports were demanded, since the news of the decree had not yet reached that place. Fortunately, they had had the foresight to bring with them a copy of the *Journal du Soir* where the decree was published in full. They were allowed to depart and arrived the same evening at Pontgoin.

Deville stayed there until the end of September. He met three sisters, the eldest of whom was a skilled harpsichordist. He accompanied her at times on the violin. He decided to join his father at Coblenz. As the direct route through north-east France meant passing through a war zone, he thought of going first to Switzerland. He contacted a friend in Paris about obtaining a passport, now that Swiss Guards who desired were being officially repatriated. His friend brought the passport to him three days later but advised him that there were rumours that all passports might be rescinded and that it would be perilous to travel through France with documentation revealing that he was a former officer in the Swiss Guards. Deville agreed and decided instead that he would go illicitly to England via Dieppe, and from there travel to Coblenz. After discussing the matter with Bouillerie, it was decided to try and obtain an internal passport from a neighbouring town. At Châteauneuf they found a drug merchant who was also a municipal officer. After making a fuss of him and buying some drugs, they succeeded in obtaining passports for both of them as nephew and uncle. The passports were for Dieppe only, which counted as part of the frontier zone. Obtaining a passport for going abroad was more difficult, as can be seen from Fonjallaz's experience at Lyons. Constant-Rebecque's passport for Switzerland, obtained on false representations in Paris, had received the signature of no less a person than Danton.

Deville, who, having a banker for a father, was obviously not short of funds, purchased what he called an ugly little trap. They used it to go to the home of the municipal officer who had taken a friendly interest in them. He had invited them to sup and sleep at his house, on the way to Dieppe. Two days later they arrived there. They were stopped at a security post and were made to enter a guardhouse where Deville said there were five or six rogues. He pretended to be naïvely fascinated by the spectacle of the sea. Their passports were demanded and scrutinised carefully. Naturally, there were no photographs in those days but a physical description would be given. Deville's mock uncle signed all the necessary documents and told the National Guards that his nephew had wanted to look at the sea which he had never seen before. The militia were satisfied at their replies and they were allowed to go to their inn. They were surrounded by several people when they descended from their trap. Deville made a sign to the landlord who had come to receive them.

'He entered our room half an hour later', wrote Deville. 'I asked him in English whether it was easy to embark for England. He did not hide from me the difficulties, but finished by saying that there was a captain of a mail-boat with whom he was familiar. He left immediately to find out the day of its departure. On returning, he told me that the vessel would sail the next morning and that the captain was willing to take me on board for the sum of forty louis [roughly £38 sterling]. Despite the enormity of this price, it was not too much to be rid of this accursed country. In the afternoon, we went to the port to smoke and to reconnoitre the boat.' Forty louis was approximately the annual wages of a skilled craftsman. There must have been many wealthy boat captains plying the Channel ports that autumn. It is interesting to note that the landlord understood English, no doubt because of the frequency of travellers from across the Channel. Deville's knowledge of English may be due to his having an Irish grandmother. He continued:

The next morning, at 6 a.m., the landlord came to wake me, and Bouillerie accompanied me as far as the vessel. I carried on my arm a basket of provisions and passed near a clerk dressed in National Guards uniform who took me for an Englishman, since I was speaking English to the sailors. I went down smartly into the captain's cabin and he made me enter into a deep hole, in the bilge, and closed the cover on me. I was flat on my stomach, having hardly any air and badly at ease. I heard municipal officials searching every corner of the boat and say, standing on the spot where I was hiding: 'There is no place where a man could hide.' I heard them leave and felt the movement of our boat as the anchor was raised and the sails hoisted. It is one of the greatest pleasures I have felt in my life. At length, a sailor came to fetch us up into the light. I say us, because in going down into the recess, I believed I had crushed a man who had been placed there before me, having paid one hundred louis for his passage. We went up on deck and congratulated each other for having left safe and sound a country where so many execrable crimes have since been committed. We arrived the next morning at 8 a.m. and I took the coach to London, which I reached the same evening.

Deville only stayed a short time in England and went almost immediately to Coblenz to help his father, who was acting as banker for the émigrés, duly bankrupting himself in the process. Deville soon grew tired of banking and sought to take up military service again. He joined the Royal Foreign Regiment in British pay, commanded by Durler and raised by the Baron de Roll, the Comte d'Artois' Swiss agent. Durler had become the acknowledged hero of 10 August. Deville took part in the campaigns of 1794–5 in the Low Countries and was wounded at the battle of the Roer. He left the Royal Foreign Regiment to join the British Army proper, becoming a Cornet in the 7th Dragoons. Apparently he did not progress further in rank. Presumably his father's straitened circumstances blocked the opportunity for promotion by purchase. He visited France at the Peace of Amiens and was arrested as a royalist conspirator. He had an unpleasant two months in prison before he managed to pull sufficient strings to secure his release. He returned to France in 1814, and was awarded the Cross of Saint Louis and promoted Lieutenant Colonel with a grant of Arms. He retired to the country in later life and died in 1847.

CHAPTER 21

Weber's Escape

Grenadier Weber, the 36-year-old foster-brother of Marie Antoinette, spent an unhappy few hours stationed by the entrance to the Manège. It seems that his unit had been ordered to take up this position after being confronted in the Cour des Feuillants. He wrote that they managed to avoid being accused of defending the king or becoming involved in fighting the Swiss, part of whose surrender he witnessed. In effect, the National Assembly entrusted its immediate defence to loyalist National Guards during the critical period before it formally accepted the triumph of the insurrection. This explains why Durler's Swiss were freely able to enter the National Assembly once they overcame opposition on the terrace. Weber claimed his unit was relieved at 3 p.m., presumably no longer needed after the Assembly had caved in to the revolutionary demands. His detachment withdrew through the Cour des Feuillants into the Rue Saint-Honoré where it dispersed. Weber was left with five comrades. Pretending to wipe their faces in the heat to avoid being recognised, they walked in an easterly direction. When they reached the Rue des Petits Champs, Weber separated from his comrades and found himself alone. As he was crossing the Rue Saint-Augustin, his uniform, with its distinctive grenadier's helmet and plume belonging to the battalion of the Filles Saint-Thomas, was recognised by two working-class women. They called him a scoundrel of an aristocrat. One women shouted shaking her fist, 'My husband will know how to kill you. You will escape us as little as those dogs your comrades!' Weber pretended not to hear. A little later, as he was passing two citizens, they addressed him out of the corners of their mouths while looking away from him. 'Monsieur, we know who you are. Do not be concerned but they will search for you, as they will all the Filles Saint-Thomas, and will want to kill you like the Swiss. Do not return to your home in your uniform now as this will indicate where you live.'

Weber realised that his first priority was to rid himself of his uniform. He was acquainted with the Choiseul family whose mansion was close by and managed to obtain a change of clothes. After slipping back to his flat and disguising himself as best he could, he left again to find someone who was prepared to lodge him and his servant for the night. Eventually, he found a Monsieur Arcambal, First Secretary in the War Department. The next day, he learned that the battalion of the Filles Saint-Thomas had been disbanded and its members proscribed. He felt it was necessary to quit France. He hit upon the idea of going to the British embassy in the hope of persuading the ambassador to smuggle him out of France as part of his suite. He rightly expected that the ambassador, Lord Gower, would be recalled because of the king's overthrow. Weber remarked that he did not express any irritation when he was told that Lord Gower was indisposed. Lady Gower, also the wealthy Countess of Sutherland in her own right, was detailed to fob him off. She explained that it was impossible to offer any kind of sanctuary at the embassy because of the presence of Jacobin spies among the servants. She claimed any impolitic action might lead to the embassy being pillaged. Weber was offered money instead. This was not his priority and he effusively declined her offer. Weber was not the only person who failed to obtain assistance from His Britannic Majesty's representative. Gouverneur Morris, who had expressed in his diary designs on the young countess, wrote an entry for the 13th, two days later, that he had gone in the afternoon to ask the British ambassador for a passport on behalf of a supplicant. As he expected, the request was refused. Perhaps in desperation at Weber's continuing importunity, Lady Gower called in her 22-year-old secretary, William Huskisson. He was to enjoy a distinguished political career until, in 1830, he became the first noteworthy victim of the dawning railway age. He was run over by a locomotive at the inauguration of the world's first steam passenger service between Manchester and Liverpool. Knowing Weber to be Austrian, Huskisson proposed that he should seek the help of a German porcelain manufacturer with royalist sympathies in the Rue du Temple.

Weber took leave of Lady Gower and walked towards the Rue du Temple. On the way he decided to call in on another of his contacts, a Monsieur de Mory, the son of the treasurer of the Compagnie des Indes. Mory convinced him that it would be foolish to go to the porcelain factory in the Rue du Temple, since he had heard that the royal family were going to be imprisoned in the Temple and there would be numerous National Guards posted in the area. Instead, he suggested that Weber should come to stay with him. Weber accepted with alacrity as he knew that Mory had a good 'civic' reputation in his neighbourhood. He intended to remain there until it was possible to leave Paris without a passport, when he hoped to travel to London. Thus, he passed six days with his host feeling perfectly secure. Suddenly, as they were sitting down to enjoy the main meal of the day in the early afternoon of the 18th, the door burst open and twelve men armed with pikes rushed in to seize him. He was carried off without even having time to take leave of his host.

Weber had left his servant to look after his apartment. However, he also employed him to bring him news every evening of what was happening in Paris, particularly with regard to his foster-sister, Marie Antoinette. His servant took careful precautions to ensure he was not being followed, walking first to a distant quarter and then jumping into a cab to come back part of the way, and walking the remainder. The revolutionaries were eager to arrest Weber because of his connection with the queen. They soon became tired of being led a wild goose chase by his servant and decided to detain him. According to Weber, they first used blandishments, and when these did not succeed they used brute force. The servant cracked and revealed his master's new address.

While under escort on his way to be interrogated at the section offices in the Rue Vivienne, Weber saw he was passing by a linen shop he had frequented on the Rue de Richelieu. He had over 100 gold louis on him. Having heard that prisoners were often robbed, he wished to deposit a roll of 40 double gold louis (2,000 livres) with the owner of the shop for safekeeping. He obtained permission from his guards to enter the shop. Unfortunately, the owner was away and Weber appealed to his wife, asking her to loan him 100 livres in paper Assignats for living expenses on the security of the roll, which was worth around thirty times as much. She was unable to do so because the safe was locked and her husband had the key. Nevertheless, Weber surreptitiously handed over the roll under the cover of some cloth on the counter and comforted himself that he had saved the larger part of his money. He must have had a trusting nature or his account is an interesting testimony on standards of personal honesty at that time. Weber still had 15 double louis for expenses, equivalent to the annual wages of a skilled worker. It seems evident that he had done well out of his connection with Marie Antoinette.

At the offices of the Bibliothèque Section, covering an area just north of the Palais Royale, he was interrogated by a member of the new revolutionary Commune. This was Collot d'Herbois, actor, theatre manager, and author. He was to become one of the leading exponents of revolutionary Terror. His most noteworthy exploit was the destruction of part of Lyons and mass shootings of its inhabitants. Weber found himself surrounded by a radical crowd who muttered unpleasantly. While he was trying to answer Collot's myriad questions, he was surprised to see the linen shop proprietor's brother arrive with his roll of double louis. 'I am too much of a patriot', the brother said sanctimoniously, 'not to denounce citizen Weber. I declare that he left his escort to enter my brother's shop and deposited a roll of double louis on the counter. He wished my sister-in-law to hold it on deposit. But my family do not want to have anything to do with a person under arrest and I hasten to place this gold on the desk of the citizen chairman.' Weber was asked where the money had come from and what he intended to do with it. This latter question excited some ribald jeers from the onlookers. It was decided that the money should be deposited in the committee's safe.

The main intention of the interrogation was to establish Weber's involvement in the fight on the Champs Elysées between grenadiers of the battalions of Filles Saint-Thomas and Petits-Pères against the Marseillais fédérés on 30 July, together with the royal family's complicity in the event. Weber admitted that he had drawn his sabre but only in self-defence. He was asked: 'Did the Queen take any interest in your situation? Did you withdraw [to the palace] with the other grenadiers?' Weber declared that neither the king nor the queen had been aware of any possibility of a fight. He continued: 'For my part, I do not know what became of my wounded comrades that day. As for myself, I remained with an officer until nightfall.' Collot, aware of Weber's relationship with the queen, then remarked: 'You are very attached to the King and Queen?' 'They are my benefactors,' he replied, 'and I take glory in being devoted to them in life and in death.' Several people noted the animosity with which the chairman wrote down his last remarks, and believing it to be his death sentence, cried out: 'My God, what a mistake! My God, what a blunder to make such a confession! He is lost!' Weber had certainly fallen into hostile hands. In a month's time, Collot as a member of the new Convention made the formal proposal for abolishing the Monarchy.

After signing the transcript of his interrogation, Weber was taken back to the guardhouse for the night where he was subjected to abuse. He claimed he was able to ignore it. At 10 a.m. the next day, they took him in a carriage under escort to the Hôtel de Ville to appear before the General Council. This special treatment reveals Weber's importance in the campaign being undertaken by the revolutionaries to crush any overt royalist support. He was accompanied by a delegate from his section who read out his indictment in a loud voice. He was accused of four crimes of Lèse-Nation. First, of being an enemy national. Second, of being the queen's foster-brother. Third, of being one of the grenadiers of the Filles Saint-Thomas who had drawn sabres against the Marseillais on 30 July. Fourth, of having escorted the royal family to the Assembly at 9 a.m. on 10 August, despite Roederer's injunction to the contrary. This latter charge was technically correct because Weber was not part of the original military escort but had insisted on joining it. The high crime of Lèse-Nation, representing treason against the Sovereign People, had replaced that of Lèse-Majesté. To this indictment, the section delegate added hostile depositions from Weber's landlord and his house porter, concerning the importation of firearms and training aristocrats in their use.

Weber asked that he be allowed to justify himself against these new allegations but was interrupted by jeers from the spectator galleries. Apparently, the revolutionary authorities were concerned his indictment was insufficient. They arranged for a gunner in the audience from the Faubourg of Saint-Antoine to accuse Weber of being in close company with Swiss officers and the General Staff of the National Guards at the Tuileries on the 9th. 'That day, I heard him call for the heads of Pétion and Manuel within half an hour', said the gunner. Weber wrote indignantly: 'This gunner, who had never seen nor heard me, unsatisfied with his own calumnies, called on an old man sitting beside him in a National Guards uniform to witness the truth of his allegations. The old man also had never seen me and now did not even give himself the trouble to look me in the face. From the height of the podium, Pétion and Manuel smiled obligingly at the gunner. After having praised his merited patriotism and having thanked him above all for the means he had given them for immolating another victim, they gave orders for me to be taken away accompanied by gendarmes to the offices of the Comité de Surveillance [Watch Committee], and then to La Force prison.' Weber continued:

The joy of the populace became general when they saw me at their disposal. These menaces and insults of this canaille were cut short by Manuel demanding to speak in a manner a thousand times more distressful for me because the Royal family was the object of his gross pleasantries. The scoundrel amused himself at the expense of the Queen in the most indecent manner, in order to entertain his friend Pétion and the rest of the audience. This is what he said: 'It must be agreed that there is nothing more infuriating in the world than a royal family and its attendants. It is time at last to sweep away this retinue, deprive the Queen of all the women who surround her, and put them in a secure place in order that they do not harm us in the future.' These words excited general applause and cries of 'To the Abbaye! To La Force for those belonging to the Queen!' echoed on all sides. Manuel continued: 'I saw the wife of the King yesterday. She was no longer the unbending haughty woman; I saw her really cry. I spoke to her a lot and to her son also. I can say the little one interested me a great deal. Among the other things I said to the wife of the King, I told her that I would wish to give her ladies of my own acquaintance for her service. She replied that she had no need and that she and her sister-in-law would serve each other. I responded: "Very well Madame, since you will not accept women from my hands for your service, you will not be embarrassed for choice."'

Manuel's reference was to the expulsion from the Temple of the queen's three companions, the Princesse de Lamballe, Madame de Tourzel, and her daughter Pauline. They were imprisoned at La Force were Weber was to be sent. The reference to the dauphin implies that some radical politicians might still be considering the possibility of a Regency. The royal family obviously made some impression on Manuel. He was to vote for reprieving the king after his death sentence. Manuel was guillotined in November 1793, partly for refusing to collaborate in the queen's trial.

It is clear that Manuel made his patronising remarks about the queen to infuriate Weber whose personal loyalty to his foster-sister was well known. Although Weber does not draw attention to the issue, his relationship with the queen was the most dangerous indictment against him. While the Tourzels, mother and daughter, were spirited out of the prison in time, the harmless and philanthropic Princesse de Lamballe was murdered on 3 September at La Force because she was a personal friend of the queen. Her head was displayed on a pike outside the Temple prison in the hope the queen would see it. A similar act of spite was almost certainly in store for Weber. By good fortune, an oversight appears to have saved him.

The gunner who had denounced Weber, accompanied by two officials, came up to hand him over to four gendarmes who were to take him to prison. He was followed to the exit of the Hôtel de Ville by a number of fish-market women and others of violent disposition, despite efforts to restrain them. They called out that they were only leaving the Town Hall for a moment to show the world the queen's foster-brother, someone who had wished to behead Pétion and Manuel. Weber sensed they intended to murder him and urgently sought the protection of a nearby officer in the National Guards. The officer detained Weber until the mob decided to go back into the Chamber to witness the official inauguration of Santerre as commanding general. When the coast seemed clear, the officer released Weber into the hands of the gendarmes. Weber congratulated himself on not having his head displayed on a pike.

After spending some hours close by in the offices of the Comité de Surveillance where the gunner's deposition was formally taken down, he was brought at 7 p.m. under guard by cab to the prison of La Force. He was registered as an inmate and welcomed by the keeper, M. Lebeau, who promised to treat him well. He was put into a cell named after the Prince de Condé. Among his fellow prisoners were de Rhulières who had commanded the unmounted Gendarmerie à Cheval by the Louvre on the 10th and Lachesnaye, who had taken over command of the National Guards at the Tuileries from Mandat. Altogether there were six in the room, including Weber. Three of these were shortly released and replaced by three others. The gaolers accompanied by two large dogs came regularly each day at 7 a.m. to open the cell doors. The inmates were allowed to walk under the shade of two rows of trees in the prison courtyard. Prisoners had to return to their rooms at 8 p.m., when they were locked in. This operation was accompanied by bells and a great deal of noise. Inmates had to provide their own food. Weber and his cell-mates found two cooks among those imprisoned at La Force and hired them to provide meals at 3 francs per head. Some prisoners thought to escape by using wooden beams, stored in the courtyard for building purposes, to batter through a wall into the street beyond. They did not keep their plans secret and the beams were removed.

The evenings were spent writing to friends and loved ones. They learned on 30 August that their mail was not being forwarded by the keeper. Weber and his colleagues also sought legal advice, to which at that time they were entitled by law. He worked on his case to counter the indictments against him. He composed replies for all possible questions he might be asked at his trial. He wrote: 'Reassured a little by this precaution, and more by confidence in the Supreme Being, I waited with resignation the dreadful moment of appearing before the judges of the popular tribunal. We passed several days in a situation it would be difficult to describe.' In retrospect, Weber may have confused the ad hoc 'popular tribunal' which actually judged him with the official Tribunal established by the Decree of 17 August for trying those accused of counter-revolutionary activities on the 10th. This should normally have tried his case if the September Massacres had not intervened.

At 4 p.m. on 2 September, the gaolers made a roll-call of the prisoners and then locked them in their cells. 'The anxious appearance, the serious and confused behaviour of our turnkeys, who came and went continuously, accompanied by gendarmes and National Guards,' Weber wrote, 'gave us so much anxiety as to cause us to remain dressed. At length, tired of hearing noise in the street which we were unable to determine, we threw ourselves on to our beds towards 1 o'clock in the morning to take a little rest. I was hardly on my straw pallet, facing the window, when my eyes were suddenly dazzled by a brilliant light, produced by a great quantity of torches accompanying an armed horde. This troop of people led by the gaolers turned rapidly towards the passage leading to our cell.' Weber continued:

The door opened with a crash and six men armed with pikes rushed in and called for Monsieur de Rhulières, who was among the prisoners in our room. This prisoner who was seated repeated twice, 'It's me, messieurs, it's me.' A Municipal Officer then spoke out, raising his voice in order to be heard by the armed crowd who accompanied him, whose impatient fury the gaolers could hardly contain. 'You are accused, Monsieur de Rhulières,' said the Municipal Officer, 'of being one of the conspirators of 10 August. I come to tell you to recommend your soul to God as the people demand your head! I am sorry to be charged with such a mission but my duty compels me.' The Chevalier de Rhulières replied calmly: 'I have already expected the fate you have announced for some time. I would only have hoped that I might have had a trial.' At this response, the Municipal Officer went towards the door and seeing the people did not wish to wait, he reminded them they had promised to obey the law and had sworn to uphold it. He asked this bloodthirsty mass if he could count on their promise. He continued, 'Would you allow, my comrades, my fellow citizens, Monsieur de Rhulières to be taken to the Clerk of the Court [sic] to be questioned?' They all started to shout: 'Yes, yes, let him come, but he must hurry.'

The Chevalier de Rhulières was thus taken away at 2 o'clock in the morning on 3 September, to be questioned by the popular tribunal established in the Keeper's room. An hour later, they came in the same manner to take the Chevalier de Lachesnaye. Anxious about the fate of de Rhulières, we risked asking a gaoler what had become of him. 'Do not have any anxiety on his behalf,' he told us, 'he is already long since at the Abbaye.' Not knowing then that this phrase meant that the unfortunate person had been massacred outside the entrance of the prison, none of us were concerned. On the contrary, we believed that Heaven had preserved a man as worthy as Monsieur de Rhulières, and we had no more anxiety about the Chevalier de Lachesnaye, seeing that he had in his pocket for his own justification, an order from the Hôtel de Ville by which he was commanded on 10 August to resist force with force. We were far from realising that what ought to have justified him would rather be the signal for his death.

It was only later that Weber understood that the revolutionaries were determined to expunge evidence for legitimate resistance at the Tuileries by the Swiss and loyal National Guards.

The killings, sometimes after summary trials by ad hoc 'popular tribunals', had been spreading throughout Paris prisons since the morning of 2 September. They were nothing less than systematic terror aimed at cowing any royalist sympathisers as the Prussian army moved further into France, and also intended to intimidate Paris voters in the second round of elections for the new National Convention. The massacres, which continued to the 6th, were undertaken by groups of working-class assassins in which butchers featured significantly. A distinction should be made between politically activated killers operating under the unofficial orders of the Municipality's Comité de Surveillance, who probably numbered at least 200 and were paid 24 livres for their services, and subsequent freelance attacks on non-political prisons such as La Salpêtrière and Le Châtelet where rape and pillage were primary objectives. The number slain overall is estimated at 1200–1400. The murdering was done outside in the street as in the case of the Conciergerie and La Force. In other places, such as the Abbaye, it was done in a courtyard. The common factor was expulsion one at a time through a narrow exit, where the victim would be suddenly confronted by a circle of killers armed with sabres, pikes, cleavers, and axes. Death might be far from instantaneous and was almost certainly painful and bloody. Few probably tried to resist. It is said, however, that Aide-Major de Salis, not to be confused with Captain de Salis, succeeded in wounding or even killing one of his murderers before succumbing at the Conciergerie.

At the Abbaye on 2 September, where the massacres included three Swiss officers and a number of other ranks, the killing was described as a corrida and aimed at protracting suffering. 'They piled up the clothing of the victims in the middle of the courtyard like a mattress,' Lenôtre wrote. 'The victim, thrust out of the door into a kind of arena, and passing from sabre to sabre and from pike to pike, came, after several turns, to fall on this mattress soaked and resoaked in blood.' There were onlookers to these spectacles who became experts on how victims might meet their death, whether they would show cowardice or fortitude, whether they would scream loudly or die silently, whether they would try to resist or seek to hasten their end. Benches were set up for the audience in which females featured extensively, though the sexes were kept separate in the interests of propriety!

Weber awaited his turn. He occupied himself by going over the charges against him again and rehearsing his replies. At 4 a.m. Lachesnaye had not returned. The remaining four were eager to know what had happened. They heard prisoners being seized from neighbouring cells with what seemed incredible noise, while cries echoed continuously from the street. At 8 a.m. an armed rabble burst into the courtyard and started looking through the windows of the cells. Seeing Weber and his companions seated inside one, they ordered the turnkey to open the door. 'They entered like madmen,' Weber wrote, 'and took us by the collar and shook us violently, screaming "scoundrels! aristocrats!", and claimed that we had been trying to hide from them. They told us that they would not leave us but were going to make sure who we were.' Weber wrote that he failed to realise then that death awaited him, which enabled him to react indignantly to the mistreatment he was receiving. He seized one of the armed men by the chest and another by the collar, shaking them vigorously. He said: 'The gaolers ought to have told you that we are neither scoundrels nor people who hide themselves. If you have any soul, you ought to respect misfortune and above all remember that the law forbids the mistreatment of prisoners, without knowing whether they are guilty.' They were surprised by his boldness and let go. 'An honest man', he continued, 'does not resist when it is a question of obeying the law but you are only vile oppressors. You are armed and I am not; your behaviour shows that you are cowards. I serve like you in the National Guards. I can like you take up arms, and it is then that I invite you to attack me.'

This caused him and his comrades to be treated with more respect. Guarded each by two men, they were taken into the courtyard to await being called to the keeper's room which contained the popular court. Weber wrote that he lost sight of his companions and was unable to guess the reason for a number of bloody sabres, or why there were shouts of 'to the Abbaye! to Coblenz!' when, from time to time, prisoners were evicted into the street. He waited until 10 a.m. and then was led before the tribunal. On entering the room, he saw a very stout man dressed in a National Guards uniform, decorated with a tricolour sash, seated at a large table with the prison registers placed in front of him. Beside him sat a prison clerk, and around the table were ranged two grenadiers, two fusiliers, two chasseurs, and also two meat porters from Les Halles. The particular composition of this popular tribunal differed from elsewhere. It must have been due to La Force holding loyalist National Guards prisoners. Many Marseillais and other fédérés filled the room as spectators. The person with a sash presiding over the tribunal was Rossignol, a former soldier and jeweller's assistant, now a leading member of the revolutionary Commune who had reputedly shot Mandat on the steps of the Hôtel de Ville. Rossignol survived the Terror despite displaying considerable incompetence as a military commander, saved by his impeccable revolutionary credentials.

Rossignol began his interrogation by asking Weber's name, age, and country of origin. He then looked at the prison register detailing Weber's committal charges. The clerk showed him the place with his finger. Weber saw the entry consisted of some twenty lines. Weber expected searching questions on the four charges of Lèse-Nation, not to mention the gunner's charges of having proposed the death of Pétion and Manuel. He waited as Rossignol glanced at the text. To his great surprise, all he was asked was why he had been at the Tuileries on 9/10 August. Weber replied in great detail as to how and when he had served in the National Guards. He finished by relating he had received orders to form part of a twenty-man detail to reinforce the guard at the Tuileries on 9 August. Rossignol asked for corroboration. All present agreed that the information Weber had given seemed correct.

Rossignol rose from his chair and took off his hat. 'I no longer see', he said, 'the least difficulty in proclaiming the innocence of Monsieur', and started to shout with all the spectators, 'Vive la Nation!' Weber was told to do likewise. The chairman continued: 'You are free, citizen, but since the Country is in danger, you must enlist in the army and leave for the frontiers within three days.' Since Weber now believed himself out of danger, he started to protest, saying that he had an aged mother and a sick sister to look after. He was rudely disabused that he had any option. Two men behind him hissed: 'Citizen, this is not the time for such excuses. The war requires people, the Country needs soldiers. . . .' Rossignol, after glancing at the clerk as if to say it would be Weber's own fault if he perished, looked at him fixedly and said, not without an ironic smile at the absurdity of resistance: 'I warn you, Monsieur, that you must enlist and leave without delay for the frontiers. I see no other course of action for you.' Weber hastened to agree, although he hoped that he would somehow be able to evade serving against his own country, Austria, or the interests of the king and queen. His acceptance called for another round of 'Vive la Nation!' Not to waste any time, Weber was made to enlist there and then.

He received a customary embrace from Rossignol and others of the tribunal, but was shocked when one of the market porters pushed through the crowd to kiss him on both cheeks, after first having asked permission. This form of greeting was then only to be found among the lower orders but has since gone up the social scale. He was told that the porter would look after him and he must follow his instructions. As the killers were Sans-culottes, it was considered essential that his guardian angel should belong to the same social class. Forcibly escorted by two officials from the Military Depot of the Innocents, he followed the porter towards the gate leading to the street. He was told to stop before the gate, while the porter made vigorous shouts of 'Vive la Nation!' to disarm the hostility of the waiting killers. Once outside, he was again held by his arms, while his escorts twirled their hats on the points of their sabres, crying continually 'Vive la Nation!' They went a little way, when the market porter called a second halt. Standing in front of Weber, he shouted: 'Take off your hats!' The large crowd obeyed immediately and waited in silence while Weber was told to swear an oath to the new régime, with his right arm and hand outstretched, the revolutionary salute inherited by twentieth-century fascists. 'I swear to be faithful to the Nation and to die at my post while defending the new order of liberty and equality', Weber intoned. The meat porter then turned towards him and pointed at a heap of bloody corpses; with a strained and ferocious look, he said: 'You see, citizen soldier, that we treat traitors as they deserve.' Once more he was embraced and kissed. He was then passed like a parcel from person to person to receive the same treatment from a large number of National Guards and other persons of the Faubourg Saint-Antoine, almost all drunk, according to Weber. At last his ordeal was over and he was escorted to a church where he found a small number of others that the tribunal had also spared.

Weber had been accused of capital crimes against the Revolution, and there was an obvious intention to kill him, almost certainly to spite Marie Antoinette, as in the case of the Princesse de Lamballe at the same prison. Rossignol had either been insufficiently briefed or his memory was impaired by his sanguinary exertions since around midnight. When he looked at the charge sheet, he would have noted that Weber was a grenadier in the Battalion Filles Saint-Thomas. Despite the arrest of officers of this loyalist battalion from the colonel downwards, no member of this unit was executed at that time for supporting the Swiss on 10 August: this must have been a matter of policy. The need to maintain unity among the National Guards of Paris in face of the growing Prussian threat required a policy of conciliation. Rossignol, aware of this decision, must have failed to read further than an opening statement on Weber's charge sheet that he was a grenadier in the Filles Saint-Thomas.

Weber was told to wait in the church under guard until he was fetched by someone from his section with authority. He gave a note to a young National Guard, together with an Assignat for 5 livres, and told him to take a cab quickly to bring back three or four battalion comrades with the necessary authority. When the emissary reached the offices of Weber's section, formerly La Bibliothèque but since 2 September the Section of 1792, he handed over the note to the new section chairman. He was the well-known playwright Marie-Joseph Blaise de Chénier, younger brother of the famous poet André de Chénier. According to Weber, it had been agreed between Chénier and Collot that he should perish. Chénier immediately sent instructions for Weber to be brought back to his section under strong escort. This note caused some consternation among the authorities of the Arsenal Section where Weber was being held. They wondered whether the tribunal had set free a guilty man. Luckily, the Arsenal Section chairman was an acquaintance of Weber's and was reluctant to move precipitately. Weber's situation deteriorated further when crowds climbed up to the windows of the church, demanding that the inmates be surrendered to them, as being royalists who had escaped justice by trickery. Weber felt that this description was aimed at him. He made his concern known to officials present. Four National Guards then arrived. Weber thought his nemesis had come, but they approached the man sitting beside him, who was told they would take him home and that he need have no fear. Weber later learned that he was the Abbé Bardy, accused of murdering his brother. Bardy refused to leave, protesting his innocence. He was made to go and this seemed to quiet the crowd outside. Weber began to breathe more easily.

A Monsieur Tréfontaine arrived who had resigned from the Filles Saint-Thomas in June and was now a municipal officer in the new Commune. He asked a small boy who was trying to clean some bloody stockings by the altar about M. Chamilly, one of the king's valets. The boy said that Chamilly had been killed at 8 a.m. and he had been given his stockings and hat. Weber waylaid Tréfontaine, who up till then had not recognised him, and explained that orders had been given to take him back to his section. He explained he was frightened of falling into the hands of the mob if he went out in broad daylight, despite being acquitted by the popular court. Tréfontaine promised he would do his utmost to extricate Weber from the dangerous situation. He then departed. Around 4.30 p.m., Weber felt his fears had been justified when he heard that the handsome Abbé Bardy had been seized by the mob from the middle of his escort four streets away and lynched on the grounds that he was an abbé attached to the service of the Court. Time passed and Weber believed Tréfontaine had forgotten him. He dreaded that the guards protecting the church would turn him and his companions out into the street. Suddenly, to his surprise, some of his best comrades from the Filles Saint-Thomas arrived in civilian clothes and his fears dissolved.

The spokesman for this group, a German and the battalion's leading sergeant, named Heck, approached the chairman of the Arsenal Section, and said: 'The Section of 1792 has just learned that Citizen Weber has been declared innocent by the popular court at La Force prison. It has sent us, Citizen Chairman, to thank you and the Committee of the Arsenal for the asylum that you have been willing to grant, in your midst, to a citizen of its Section. The Section of 1792 has charged us with giving you this document, by which you will see they reclaim Citizen Weber whom they desire to see among them again.' Obviously, members of the section committee had bypassed Chénier. The chairman of the Arsenal Section then turned to Weber and said quietly that he was very glad about this turn of events, since he had been impressed by the interest shown by Tréfontaine. Besides, he had met Weber during an evening in 1788 through a mutual acquaintance. He added that he believed he would have ended by helping him himself and offered to escort him to his section. It was arranged that the two recruiting officers from the Innocents' Depot should go independently to deposit copies of Weber's enlistment documents. In due course, Weber was smuggled out of the complex of buildings surrounding the church by a back entrance. He and his friendly escort made detours to avoid crowds, reaching his section offices at 7 p.m. The news of his coming had been brought in advance by the two depot officials. When Weber entered the room, he claimed it resounded with applause for a person who had escaped death by a miracle.

The depot officials had requested a receipt for their documents from the section committee and then withdrew. Examining these documents, a committee member made a statement recognising that Weber had been declared innocent by the popular court but, out of gratitude, had enlisted to join the French army on the frontiers. He continued: 'But he is an Austrian and we cannot demand this sacrifice. We must act as generously as he has. The Committee proposes to refuse the military services of Citizen Weber and to tear up his enlistment papers.' 'Applause came from all parts in response to this motion', wrote Weber. 'All the people of my acquaintance, and an infinity of others who were absolutely unknown to me, joined together in congratulating me on my lucky star. After complimenting me on my good fortune for having escaped death, they advanced with me towards the Chairman to have him sign my acquittal.' Chénier, however, demurred. He had read the serious charges. Weber reported him as saying in a loud voice: 'This case is too grave and one cannot pronounce on a matter of this importance in an instant. Citizen Weber has been accused of crimes of Lèse-Nation. It is inconceivable that he has been acquitted and declared innocent by a judgment of a popular court. This tribunal has certainly been tricked. I will never take it on myself to be involved in his acquittal.' Chénier was referring to the old French judicial principle that the king was incapable of a wrong judgment, unless he was deliberately deceived. The king's attributes had now been taken over by the People.

Chénier's pronouncement was immediately countered by the section meeting. Weber wrote that several members of the committee jumped to his defence, pointing out that the popular courts had been precisely created in order to ensure the People's justice was done. Since the People were sovereign, one could hardly disagree with their verdict. Weber claimed that this revolutionary logic reduced Chénier to a state of fury and he ended by saying that he would rather resign than agree to an acquittal. When this threat momentarily silenced the meeting, Chénier ordered that Weber be confined in a chapel next to the committee room which was situated in a convent. A detail of National Guards was summoned to escort Weber to the Hôtel de Ville for a decision.

The detail arrived half an hour later at 11 p.m., but by that time further protests had had their effect on the young Chénier. He cancelled the order to take Weber to the Maison Commune and instead had him placed in the guardhouse. Hardly had Weber arrived when the post commander notified him that he was free. Weber was surprised and asked the reason for his change in circumstances. Everybody wanted to tell him at once, but the post commander managed to call for silence and was able to explain: 'The Section revolted against the Chairman', he said. 'He employed every Jacobin ruse to have you taken to the Hôtel de Ville. Members of the Committee and your comrades opposed it with much firmness, regarding your death as certain if you were sent before the tribunal on the second night of the massacres. A National Guard, about to join the armies on the frontiers, had challenged the Chairman with greatest eloquence on the basis of revolutionary justice, proclaiming that the will of the people, once manifested, must be held sacred. The Chairman sweated blood and tears, and thrice said he wished to give up his office rather than agree to sign your release. But he was pressed hard, and seeing the National Guards together with his friends becoming furious, he agreed to give me the order to set you free. . . .'

The middle-class district to which Weber belonged was making a demonstration against the Jacobins in general and the horrifying excesses of the massacres in particular. The tide of opinion was now running against the extremists. Weber hastened to thank all his friends and supporters. They were determined to accompany him back to his residence and ensure that he was not further harassed. His landlord, who had testified against him, was told that Weber had been declared innocent by three different authorities and was advised that if he made any further trouble, he would have to deal with all the citizens of the Section of 1792. Weber, however, was unable to enter his apartment as it had been officially sealed. He had to spend the night at a friend's residence. While there, it was suggested that Weber should leave the country as soon as possible because of his Austrian citizenship and his relationship with the queen. This view was reinforced when a few days later some Marseillais, having heard about Weber's release, started to make murderous threats against him and his supporters in the section.

On 11 September Weber managed to have the seals removed from his apartment and was also able to reclaim the 40 double louis left in the section treasury. He left Paris with his friend's nephew who was going to visit his wife on their property over half-way along the road to the seaport of Le Havre. This was not the end of Weber's adventures. After leaving his hosts in the country, he arrived in the evening at a village called Damville and was stopped by the militia for the same reason as Deville and Fonjallaz, because he lacked a passport. Despite his protests that passports were no longer required except within ten leagues of the frontiers, his effects were thoroughly searched. Because of his choice linen and elegant jewellery he was accused of being an escaped aristocrat and threatened with being sent back to Paris. Then the discovery of an expensively bound devotional book convinced the village yokels that they had caught a recalcitrant priest who had refused to swear the oath to the Nation. Weber kept his head and distracted his audience by theatrically declaiming literary excerpts written in a notebook which he had translated from famous English authors. He was now accused of being an actor, a profession happily deemed innocent. Eventually, they were persuaded to allow him to write a letter to his recent hostess, asking her to obtain a letter of recommendation from a relative who was an important local figure. Weber was careful to sweeten his letter, which he read out, with flattering compliments about his captors.

The letter of recommendation eventually arrived. Weber had to cool his heels another hour while an officious young man working in the local tax office meticulously authenticated the handwriting. After being detained for over half a day, he was allowed at last to depart. A few kilometres further on, he was ambushed by two of his recent captors who had taken a fancy to a brace of fine pistols he was carrying in his luggage. Fortunately, the cupidity of these peasants had been well noted and he was rescued by the mayor and municipal officials who had followed them. Arriving at Honfleur, Weber received assistance from important contacts to obtain a passport for England as a German merchant. He sailed on 18 September, reaching London on the 20th. He was soon to be reunited with his mother. He finished the account of his escape by expressing his profound regret that he had been unable to save the queen, to whom he was deeply attached by childhood memories and gratitude.

CHAPTER 22

The Truth about Montmollin?

The historian seeks to answer some questions. More ambitiously, he or she attempts to restore the past to life. Whatever the objective, the historian is dependent upon texts which in general innocently, or sometimes deliberately, conceal as much as they reveal. There is no possibility of cross-examining witnesses except when writing contemporary history. Even then, falsifications of one kind or another must be confronted. The historian has to fall back on reason and imagination. But these instruments are far from foolproof. The reader, who may be carried away temporarily, must retain an enquiring scepticism. Ultimately, although seeking the truth, the historian is only telling a story based on supposed facts.

Pfyffer von Altishofen's work, *Account of the Conduct of the Swiss Guards on the Day of the 10th August 1792*, contains a number of anecdotes gleaned from various sources. One such is the account of the heroic death of a 23-year-old ensign, Georges de Montmollin, who had been inducted into the Swiss Guards the previous day, after serving for several years with the Swiss Regiment Salis-Samade based in Rouen. His letter of 8 August is quoted in Chapter 2. Altishofen related: 'Monsieur de Montmollin had just entered the Regiment and borrowed a uniform from Monsieur de Forestier in order to be able to take part in the fight. He was a battalion standard bearer. He kept his flag until drawing his last breath, which cost him his life. He found himself with some soldiers at the foot of the statue in the Place Louis Quinze, being unable to advance. He fought like a hero. After having killed with his own hand several enemies, he was struck from behind, falling into the arms of a corporal who also died without being able to save him. "Let me perish here", he said to him and thought of nothing but saving the flag. The corporal who was holding him up received at the same moment a mortal wound and Monsieur de Montmollin fell while wrapping himself in his flag. The murderers were only able to take possession of it by tearing it.'

Such an heroic description rightly quickens the pulse; a young man cut down in his prime, fighting against hopeless odds for a tragic cause. Most battlefields generate their quota of valiant acts, but when the action is confused or desperate and leads to disastrous consequences, a comprehensive, responsible account of events may be lacking. The destruction of the Swiss Guards on 10 August 1792 was just such a situation. There were no officer survivors in certain parts of the battlefield. The barracks were sacked, records destroyed, the surviving officers fleeing or in hiding, and within a few days the regiment was officially disbanded. There were no resources available at the time for putting together an official report on the whole action. In due course, Durler and some fellow officers wrote unofficial accounts for that part of the battle in which they were personally involved. Elsewhere, the ground was ripe for invention.

Acknowledgement for details of the following correspondence must be gratefully given to the Neuchatelois historian, Jean-Pierre Jelmini, who partly based his article on research published previously by another local historian, Philippe Godet, in 1904. However, Jelmini does not cite Altishofen or Peltier which would have enabled him to add a new perspective.

Georges de Montmollin was the elder son of a Neuchâtelois owner of a calico printing works who was also mayor of the neighbouring town of Valangin and a state councillor of the Principality of Neuchâtel. The reigning prince was the King of Prussia who had recently ennobled the Montmollins, but this could not add greatly to the lustre of a leading bourgeois family which had been prominent in the principality for centuries. Regarding the young Georges de Montmollin, the Dutch author Isabelle de Charrière, married to a Neuchâtelois, wrote to Benjamin Constant in March 1790: 'Madame de Trémauville has the mind and sense for small change and everyday things. That irritates me a little; there is neither melody in her voice nor elegance in her speech. Her daughter is young, pale, and without ideas, but she is in love which is something and the object of her affections is a handsome indolent person who plays the violin like an angel, and who has all the talents possible. If the springs of this elegant machine were less feeble, most beautiful things would result. Although music is his forte, he hardly needs to read the notes on a score, he also paints prettily. However, I do not believe he has ever drawn an entire face. It cannot be remedied, since seeing how one goes into ecstasies over what he does without effort, he begins to glory in his astonishing laziness. Truly, a violin when he touches it produces sounds as sweet as brilliant. I have never heard anything like it. He has told me that he took a stroll with you in Neuchâtel. He is called Montmollin. He is a tall young man with a fine neat brown head; perhaps you will remember him.'

His great-niece gave another pen portrait of the hero in her memoirs: 'This Georges, of whom we possessed several portraits, was handsome, amiable, and a charmer. He was at the same time the joy and the torment of his parents. At the University of Heidelberg, he only frequented princes, and wherever he went, he was everyone's spoilt child.' In fact, according to Jelmini, Montmollin was never enrolled with the University of Heidelberg but must have been on some study tour in the Palatinate, and no doubt expatiated on all the fine people he was convinced had befriended him. He decided on a military career and aged seventeen obtained a commission in the Swiss Regiment Salis-Samade in 1786. This was subsequently based in Rouen where he came to know the de Trémauvilles in 1789, forming an attachment with their fifteen-year-old daughter, Julie. Monsieur de Trémauville was a marquis and this would have represented a socially advantageous match for Montmollin, while they on their side may have been interested in his parents' money. In due course, he may have tired of provincial life in Rouen. He certainly sought to be accepted into the more glamorous Regiment of Swiss Guards which would give him a chance to participate in the social life of the capital. Montmollin's father obtained a promise from Comte d'Affry in 1791 that he would offer his son a place in the Swiss Guards when one became available. D'Affry failed to act until early in July 1792 when he suddenly wrote that if Georges was prepared to accept the uncertainties over the regiment's future, he could join immediately. The uncertainties to which Affry referred were the possibility of the regiment being disbanded or converted into an ordinary regiment of the line and being sent to the frontiers. D'Affry probably still believed he could keep the regiment safe from any disastrous entanglement such as was to occur on 10 August. However, in the political situation ruling, his policy of non-involvement was becoming increasingly naïve. Montmollin senior had not forgiven the then dead Affry when he wrote a letter in 1796 saying that he suspected Affry knew of the risks the regiment was likely to run in Paris and had heedlessly sacrificed his son.

When the news of the destruction of the Swiss Guards reached Neuchâtel some six days afterwards, Montmollin senior first heard that his son was lightly wounded. Then killed, when he received a letter from his brother-in-law Fréderic Deluze who had participated in the battle. However, Deluze was not an eyewitness of Georges' death since he was with the officers interned with Durler in one of the Assembly's offices and was allowed to escape later that evening. Deluze did not loiter in Paris but made his way immediately to the frontier. On second thoughts, the family continued to hope. Further enquiries were made. Contradictory statements were received. There were rumours that he might be in hiding. A mysterious letter dated 10 September from Paris provided a list of his personal effects, including his violin and a new uniform not paid for, still at the tailors. Montmollin senior charged a cousin with making enquiries, too painful for him to undertake.

On 8 October this cousin, Ostervald, wrote as follows: 'It is only too true that he is no more. . . . He succumbed to numbers on the Place Vendôme. If anything is able to console you for the loss of such a son, it is the manner of his death. He fought with a strong heart and died like a hero. Yes, my dear cousin, he guarded till the end the flag entrusted to him and which cost him his life, because if he had abandoned it, he would have been able to escape like the soldier who has provided details of his end. After having killed several of the assassins, he fell in the arms of a corporal who tried to drag him away and who lost his life in attempting to save him. "Let me die," he said to him, "save yourself and tear up the flag."' No fighting is known to have taken place in the Place Vendôme which was also known as the Place Louis XIV. It is possible Ostervald confused it with the Place Louis XV.

Here we have the source of Altishofen's anecdote which he further embellished. No doubt the family sent him a copy of the letter when he made enquiries prior to writing his history. However, he had Montmollin dying under the equestrian statue, where the obelisk now is, in the Place Louis XV, not in the Place Vendôme which he must have felt was the wrong location. Ostervald's letter at first sight might seem to settle the matter, but does it? Did Ostervald's informant really witness the death of Montmollin and risk staying around to hear his dying words? This seems unlikely. The informant implied that he was able to escape at the moment Montmollin was meeting his fate. It is easy to picture the informant, as he was escaping, seeing Montmollin incommoded by his flag and concluding he must have been killed. Possibly the corporal he included in his story was a personal friend who actually did not survive. He would not be human if he did not wish to honour one of his former comrades. Of course, Ostervald or an intermediary was really only interested in Montmollin. The informant had a chance of receiving a generous tip if he gave an embroidered account of his death. There was less to be gained if he briefly recounted that he did not really know what had happened, since he had left the scene beforehand. The more one considers the account given in Ostervald's letter, the more improbable it becomes.

Why did Altishofen place the death of Montmollin in the Place Louis XV rather than in the Place Vendôme, as in Ostervald's letter? It seems likely he combined Ostervald's account with Peltier's relatively comprehensive record of the battle, published in London in autumn 1792, derived from a large number of witnesses. This described significant action in the Place Louis XV. But Altishofen suppressed some of Peltier's details, preferring Ostervald's heroic version. After all, he was writing to raise funds for a commemorative monument; the more heroes the better. Peltier wrote:

> As for those who escaped up the Champs Elysées, Monsieur Forestier de Saint-Venant retired in good order with thirty Swiss. He saw a similar sized platoon which was fleeing up the Rue Royale with some Gentlemen. He left his force in charge of Monsieur de Mon—, and ran to try and rally the other platoon. He succeeded, but in returning to the Place Louis XV, he no longer found the platoon he had left with Monsieur de Mon—. Shot at on all sides, they had been obliged to fall back into the Rue des Champs Elysées [off the north-west corner of the Place Louis XV]. Monsieur Forestier, seeing himself with so few forces, wished at least to perish gloriously. He charged sword in hand, bayonets at the ready, a body of the enemy posted under the statue of Louis XV. He drove it back three times, but having lost half of his soldiers, he was reduced to retreating with the remaining fifteen up the Champs Elysées. His group dispersed and were killed in detail. . . .
> The little force under Monsieur de Mon— had been confronted by a force of three hundred which had first fled from the Swiss exiting from the Orangerie [Deville's group] but had now returned to the Place Louis XV. Emboldened by their numerical superiority, they cried out for the Swiss to surrender. Some did, and the people surrounded them crying out, 'Vive la Nation!' They led them with their commander, Monsieur de Mon— to the large building, formerly the Mairie and now the Revenue Office, which was being used to hold prisoners. They were escorted thence one by one to the local Guardhouse. From there, they were able to be passed into the District of the Feuillants. The young gentleman who commanded them escaped because of the disorder of his clothes.

This is probably a euphemism for taking off his distinguishing scarlet uniform coat with its embroidered blue facings.

Peltier does not give Monsieur de Mon—'s full name. Either his informant did not know it precisely or Peltier wished to conceal it from the French authorities since an escaped officer was at risk. Whatever the reason, there was only one Swiss officer to whom de Mon— can refer and that was Georges de Montmollin. No other officer had a name beginning with these three letters nor anything like them. Peltier's description of de Mon—, as a young gentleman fits Montmollin. Moreover, if Altishofen's information that he borrowed his uniform from Saint-

Venant is correct, this provides some evidence that Montmollin as a newcomer was under the latter's personal supervision and that they were together on the Place Louis XV. So, perhaps Montmollin did not die after all. If Ostervald's witness was present at all, he was one of the soldiers who did not surrender and managed to escape, as is confirmed in Peltier's account. The description given by Peltier, although at second-hand, is rendered credible by the many plausible circumstantial details, such as where the captives were taken and subsequently sent, and de Mon—'s escape thanks to discarding his uniform.

It appears that Ostervald's letter did not really settle the matter in Neuchâtel once and for all. Madame de Trémauville, mother of Montmollin's fiancée, in particular, remained credulous about rumours which surfaced from time to time regarding his fate. She was told that, after pretending to be dead, he had taken refuge with a widow whose name began with B in the Faubourg Saint-Honoré, adjoining the Place Louis XV and the Champs Elysées. In February 1793, she opened her heart to Madame de Charrière. She told the latter that she hoped it would be possible to approach the woman concerned without frightening her and persuade her to speak with the offer of money. Madame de Charrière reported her as saying: 'If one knew the residence of the woman in question, I will be responsible for ensuring money will not be spared, with that one knows all.' In March, the Neuchatelois financier and public benefactor Pierre-André du Peyrou wrote: 'I reiterate that this poor M. who had only just arrived, necessarily lacked the crowd of acquaintances that those who have lived a long time in Paris must have, and while escaping the first shock, he would have difficulty in avoiding subsequent pursuits . . . . Supposing he survived the massacre of the 10th, it appears impossible that among his comrades, relations even that he had in Paris, none has received any information, while strangers affirm his death and even the circumstances. As for me, without rejecting all possibility of his survival, I reduce it not to one in a hundred, or even a thousand, but to a thousand million and more.'

Let us discount the story of the heroic death or du Peyrou's statistical probabilities, and regard Peltier's account as the truth, that Montmollin did escape. Reverting to the mysterious letter of 10 September from Paris giving details of Montmollin's personal effects, we have additional and intimate information. The letter also said that on the evening of 8 August, he lost 25 gold louis at cards and had remarked: 'It doesn't matter, I will no longer have need of it in a little while.' We learn from his great-niece's memoirs that he had many debts. 'One is told', she wrote, 'that his parents burned all his papers which would show to what extent he had ruined them. Even his brother never knew the figures of his costly follies and one retained of him only a tender memory.' As a fashionable young man who had been in France for six years, it is likely that he had some knowledge of the better quarters of Paris and its pleasure haunts, including the notorious Palais Royal. Knowing his feckless character, it is not hard to imagine that on the evening of his first full day in Paris he decided to go to a gambling club, possibly the celebrated gaming house kept by Andrea Guzman at the Palais Royal. He plays at cards and loses. Let the historian relax a moment and enjoy a little levity. There are a number of attractive ladies present, as one usually finds in such places, and he becomes acquainted with one, the mysterious woman referred to as B, and even spends the night with her. Perhaps she is the author, or at least the instigator, of the letter cited above dated 10 September, giving details of his personal effects and able to quote what he said when he lost a substantial sum at cards. Young widowhood was not at all uncommon in the eighteenth century when adolescent girls were often married to much older men for the sake of an advantageous match. In Paris, such women would find plenty of opportunities for a life of adventure.

When he escapes on 10 August, Montmollin negating du Peyrou's supposition promptly seeks out this lady, who according to Madame de Trémauville conveniently lives in the Faubourg Saint-Honoré. She takes him in, young, charming and handsome as he is, and he lives with her until, as a result of the massacres at the beginning of September, all possibility of counter-revolution is considered crushed, and citizens are allowed to leave Paris without passports. Montmollin decides to take advantage of the situation with the intention of joining the émigré forces on the frontier. We know from a letter written by Montmollin senior, dated 27 July 1792, that before accepting Affry's offer to join the Swiss Guards his son first wrote to the Comte d'Artois to find out whether his services might be of greater interest to émigrés. He was told that the Swiss Guards' duty of protecting the king should have his priority. On leaving Paris for the émigrés, he asks his lady friend to ensure his family has details of his personal effects in case he does not succeed in his venture. It is interesting that the letter is dated 10 September, shortly after the barriers controlling exit from Paris were lifted. The mysterious writer does not mention Montmollin is alive because a letter for abroad might be intercepted and read. However, let us suppose that Montmollin tells the mysterious widow to advise a relative of the Trémauvilles who lives in Paris that he survived 10 August. This news is passed on in due course to Madame de Trémauville in Switzerland where she and her family have emigrated. She then relays it to Madame de Charrière.

As for Montmollin, he does not succeed in joining the émigrés. He is arrested, and as a single young man without papers and unable to account for himself, is press-ganged into the French army which at that time was using every expedient to find extra recruits. It is just possible, allowing free range to the imagination, that he fought at Valmy, helping to save a régime he deplored. He is killed before he can desert. Alternatively, after some vicissitudes he may have used the circumstances to change his identity, ashamed of the substantial debts he has incurred, and to avoid dishonouring his aristocratic fiancée, having fallen in love with the mysterious widow. Despite mentioning his intention to write to others in his letter to his father on 8 August, it seems he failed to write to his fiancée, preferring instead to visit a gaming house. If he decided to make a clean break with his past, there would be an insatiable demand for young men with military experience over the next twenty years and he would have had no difficulty in finding employment. If unable or unwilling to follow a military career, and prepared to accept a decline in social status, his talent with the violin might have enabled him to earn a living. Ensign Montmollin is missing in action, presumed dead. A new life begins!

CHAPTER 23

The End of the Swiss and the King

The Swiss officers who had survived crossing the garden in the force led by Durler and Salis, less three who had become separated, had been taken to safety in the Bureau des Inspecteurs next to the entrance to Terrasse des Feuillants. The eleven present were Captains Durler, Salis-Zizers, and Pfyffer, Aide-Major de Glutz, Under Aide-Majors Alexandre de Zimmermann and de Gibelin, First Lieutenant Emmanuel de Zimmermann, First Under Lieutenants Diesbach de Steinbrugg and D'Ernst, Second Lieutenant Frédéric Deluze, and Under Second Lieutenant Castella d'Orgemont. This is the list given by Peltier which numbers eleven. Gibelin also included Ignace de Maillardoz and Constant-Rebecque. The latter was certainly not present, and there is conflicting evidence about Maillardoz. Deputy Anne-Pierre Coutard from Nantes wrote a letter referring to his being instrumental in saving twelve officers. Another French source reported seeing a dozen labelled uniforms hanging up in the Bureau des Inspecteurs. These could be round numbers, however.

It is easy to imagine the gloom and despondency among this group of defeated officers. It is likely they felt betrayed by the temporising politics of their colonel, while their services had been ignored by the king. Gibelin related that they waited cruelly from midday until 10 o'clock in the evening. After an hour, some members of the National Assembly came to see them, inspecting them, as Durler wrote, like strange animals. Among them were those who were determined to do something positive to save the Swiss officers, whose fate was sealed if they fell into the hands of the insurgents. Gibelin wrote: 'We had the visit of a deputation from the National Assembly, overwhelming us with reproaches, saying that the people were shouting for our heads. But if they could prevent them from doing justice to us and gain time until the evening, they would try to transfer us to the Abbaye in order to protect us from their fury. . . . Among them was a Sieur Bruat who had married the daughter of one named Blum, from the canton of Glaris, surgeon of the Regiment. . . .'

Glutz wrote that after the deputies' visit, they waited several hours in the state of uncertainty, overwhelmed with fatigue and thirst and regretting that they had not been allowed to die with arms in their hands. 'At last', Glutz continued, 'Monsieur Bruat returned, accompanied by a man burdened with a large parcel of clothes and asked us to change as quickly as possible.' Gibelin related that Bruat had sent for 'a second-hand clothes dealer in old topcoats and trousers, to dress us like Sans-culottes. Thus disguised, we were let out two by two through a passageway for a distance lasting several minutes, the exit of which was situated opposite the Place Vendôme.' Durler complained about having to pay dearly for the old clothing. Another officer stated that they exchanged their uniforms for smocks, enabling them to leave the fearsome District of the Feuillants and go to their friends in town. It had been arranged that no guards would be posted to hinder the escape of the Swiss. Of the eleven or twelve officers who were enabled to escape in this manner, three were eventually recaptured and perished in the September Massacres. These were Diesbach, Ernst, and Castella, the first two, at least, betrayed by their Swiss German accents.

The National Assembly definitely attempted to save the Swiss from the bloodlust of the mob. Bruat had almost certainly acted with the connivance, or even orders, of senior members of the Assembly. Among the first business in the Chamber after Durler surrendered seems to have been a decree placing the Swiss officers and men under the protection of the law and the hospitality of the French people. This makes sense, though such timing cannot be certain due to the lack of reference to the Swiss physical presence in the Assembly reports. It is possible that the Jacobin Deputy Bazire, who sponsored the motion, was persuaded to do so as part of a deal between the Assembly and the king in exchange for instructing the Swiss to surrender. The fact that the motion was proposed by a leading Jacobin whose faction now dominated the situation seems significant. While the officers imprisoned in the Bureau des Inspecteurs were allowed to escape, the remainder who had surrendered were next morning sent for their safety to the Abbaye prison of Saint Germain des Prés. This became real imprisonment when the revolutionary Commune insisted that they be brought to trial and they were transferred to the Conciergerie. While eventually the law failed to preserve the lives of imprisoned officers, the Assembly and moderates in the Commune were largely successful in protecting the other ranks.

Throughout the afternoon of the 10th, there were repeated attempts by the insurgents to get their hands on the surrendered Swiss, both officers and soldiers. These were foiled with the help of National Guards based in the District of the Feuillants under the Assembly's control. There were reports of the leading Girondins, such as Brissot and Gensonné, arranging to hide individual Swiss. Genuine humanity played a major part in the Assembly's actions, no doubt partly reinforced by guilt over the failure to defend the Constitution which all deputies had sworn to uphold. Later on, these feelings were augmented by practical concern for the future of Franco–Swiss relations. Whatever the motivation, the Assembly tried to moderate the fury of the insurgents against the Swiss. The young Napoleon noted that there was considerable anger about the Swiss, even among the bourgeoisie, because of the believed wanton killing of French citizens at the Tuileries.

An indication of the Assembly's feelings, in which Jacobin members elated by their triumph took the lead, is demonstrated by the overwrought reporting of an address at the bar by a National Guards wine merchant with the happily symbolic name of Clémence. The wine merchant, after showing his political correctness by attacking the king's supposed treachery, described the Swiss soldiers as slaves who had been compelled to spill blood against their will. The French should respond by treating them with the generosity characteristic of free men. He then introduced a Swiss soldier at his side as one such who had been deceived. But now that he was vanquished, Clémence declared himself his guardian, his defender. The Assembly's minutes went on to describe a scene of pure melodrama. 'At these words, the speaker looked at the Swiss with tenderness, threw himself into his arms, pressed him against his breast, shed tears over him, and, his heart no longer able to sustain the violence of the emotion by which he was moved, he collapsed in a faint. People rushed to help him. Soon, his eyes reopened and fixed themselves again upon the Swiss. "Ah!" he said, "I feel my strength return in seeing the unfortunate victim that I have had the happiness to save. I claim only one payment from him, that he returns to my home, and that he never leaves me. I wish to nourish and care for him; thus do free men revenge themselves on despots."' The minutes went on to state that the Assembly's members had from the first mixed their tears with those of the speaker, and when he had finished, they declared by universal acclamation that this act of touching generosity be placed in the minutes together with the name of the Citizen whose actions so honoured humanity. To have one's name mentioned in the minutes was a distinction. It was further determined that considering the favourable influence that such examples might have on public behaviour, virtuous acts distinguishing this memorable day should be collected by the Assembly's Secretariat and details sent to all the Departments of France. The Jacobin Chabot suggested that Clémence should become the Assembly's personal emissary of peace with the people of Paris.

Actions to save the Swiss imprisoned in the District of the Feuillants continued early the next day, 11 August. The president of the Assembly received a petition from the Section of the Tuileries about preventing the abduction of the Swiss by an armed mob. Santerre was summoned to report on personal security. As a result of a speech by a citizen about the plight of the Swiss rank and file, the National Assembly despatched a deputation to the Feuillants' Church to bring back a number of Swiss soldiers to the bar of the Chamber. The Swiss were made to demonstrate their loyalty to the People by giving the revolutionary salute of an outstretched arm and swearing an oath. They were then asked to denounce their officers. Several soldiers did so. Representatives of the Marseillais stated that they no longer considered the Swiss as enemies, now that they were conquered, and offered to escort all they found in Paris to the relative safety of the Assembly's precincts. The struggle continued, however, between extremists who wanted to submit the Swiss to summary justice and those who wished to preserve or even exonerate them. Pétion and Danton were called on to calm a mob raging at midday around the Convent des Feuillants.

In order to try and control the situation, the National Assembly decreed that a court martial responsible for judging both officers and men be established within twenty-four hours. Officers from the National Guards would be selected to act as judges. It was expected that a court so constituted would incline towards leniency. For this reason it was successfully opposed by the Commune. Nevertheless, the new Municipality joined in the efforts to prevent a massacre. Truchon made a proclamation asking that the People suspend its vengeance. Pétion, now back in office, declared 'that the People, who had enjoyed a first day of justice and vengeance, would dishonour its cause by continuing its hatred against the Swiss who had been misled by their commanders'. It was decided that the security provided at the Feuillants' Church was insufficient and another asylum or prison was sought for the Swiss soldiers. The extremists wanted all to be sent to the Abbaye, where six of the officers who escorted the king to the National Assembly, plus First Lieutenant

Louis de Zimmermann, had already been despatched that morning. There they had been joined by another fifteen Swiss, mainly quartermasters and non-commissioned officers, who had been taken from the barracks outside Paris.

The remainder at the barracks were secured in their guardhouses, though officers were able or allowed to slip away. Eventually, it was decided that the Swiss other ranks in Paris should be imprisoned in the Palais Bourbon, just across the new Pont Louis XVI, in the fashionable quarter of Saint Germain. On behalf of the Assembly's Extraordinary Committee, Condorcet signed a decree late on the 11th ordering the transfer of 112 Swiss Guards from the Feuillants' Church to the Palais Bourbon. Over the next three weeks, the number imprisoned there was to grow to a total of 293. The initial transfer was made not without difficulty. The Swiss were accompanied by a delegation of deputies, including the Jacobins Choudieu, Chabot, and Lacroix. They had to harangue the mob by explaining that in seeking to murder them on the spot, they would hinder enquiries about those who had really been responsible for giving orders to fire on the People.

All along it was anticipated that the fate of the imprisoned officers would differ from that of the rank and file. Apart from actual responsibility by virtue of command, there was also a class bias: the officers were seen as belonging to the aristocracy, while the lower ranks were viewed as belonging to the common people. In a letter dated 16 August addressed to his brother in Geneva, a Swiss bank employee in Paris wrote that it was hoped that the soldiers of the Swiss Guards at the Palais Bourbon would not be condemned to death but he believed the officers would have difficulty in escaping it. This was not necessarily so. Despite a special tribunal under Jacobin control being established by the National Assembly on 17 August to try those who were regarded as having committed counter-revolutionary crimes, the authorities were slow to bring the Swiss officers to judgment. This was at least partly due to concern over the judicial clauses in the treaties regulating the Swiss regiments in French service. If these were ignored, the Swiss might have cause to join France's enemies at this critical juncture. Nevertheless, it was accepted as almost inevitable that some example needed to be made and the desire for vengeance propitiated. It is possible to argue, from the texts of the court judgments following the trials of Colonel d'Affry and Major Bachmann that the latter alone had been selected for the role of scapegoat.

On 25 August, d'Affry was the first to be tried. He was acquitted but was promptly re-arrested. However, the Jacobin authorities ensured that he was set at liberty in the nick of time from the Conciergerie at 8.30 a.m. on 2 September. Only Major Bachmann, among the other officers, had definitely been scheduled for trial by the beginning of September. If the intention was to limit executions of the Swiss to the single instance of Bachmann, it was overtaken by events when those who instigated the September Massacres temporarily controlled the situation in the prisons. The Swiss unfortunate enough to be held at the Abbaye, La Force, or awaiting possible trial at the Conciergerie, to the total of ten officers and some forty other ranks, were murdered. Perhaps less than half these other ranks had actually been at the Tuileries on the 10th. Bachmann alone survived for a day because he was being formally tried at the time. Even so, a mob broke into the courtroom in an attempt to seize him.

Count d'Affry (1713–93), Colonel of the Swiss Guards, in full regalia. He was the only Swiss to be given the highest royal order of the Holy Spirit, which can be seen on his breast. His long service to the French crown included a period as ambassador to Holland. He was also a lieutenant-general in the French Army and had commanded all the regular troops in and surrounding Paris in 1791.

Bachmann was guillotined in the Place du Carrousel about 8 a.m. on 3 September, facing the Tuileries where he had been second-in-command of the Swiss. On the scaffold, he was reputed to have said: 'I shall be avenged.' No doubt he was referring to the approaching Prussians. His expectations were to prove false. The Swiss NCOs and soldiers being held in the Palais-Bourbon were moved to the refectory of the Abbaye of Saint Germain-des-Prés and safeguarded with difficulty. It had been intended for some time that these soldiers should be enrolled in the French armies. This aim was now achieved by bringing them to the Hôtel de Ville for enlistment en masse under threat of massacre and forming them into a unit called the Franc Battalion.

On 21 August the National Assembly had passed a decree disbanding the Swiss regiments in French service, on the reasonable grounds that it was difficult to employ troops in wartime which, as a result of treaties, could only be utilised in restricted circumstances. The decree, which could not be implemented immediately, was generous in intent and designed to conserve the traditional friendly neutrality between France and Switzerland. The Corps Helvétique, the official designation for the Swiss polity at that time, was thanked for the services it had provided. France guaranteed to meet all its financial obligations to the former Swiss regiments, including pensions payable to former officers, in specie rather than depreciating paper Assignats. Generous terms were offered to Swiss who wished to enrol in the French Army. It was not until 5 September that an extraordinary session of the Swiss Diet at Arrau confirmed the recall of all Swiss regiments to their homeland.

The same day, the French government officially accepted Colonel d'Affry's offer to remain in Paris to help administer the termination of the service of Swiss regiments in France. From the middle of September d'Affry, seconded by Bournonville, Chief Clerk of the Swiss Bureau, became actively engaged in overseeing the repatriation of Swiss soldiers, including members of the former Regiment of Swiss Guards. He was given full access to the regiment's surviving records. In October, he negotiated terms, including pecuniary assistance, for individual soldiers wishing to return to Switzerland. They could apply for passports and two months' pay. By mid-November, he was able to produce figures giving a breakdown of what had happened to the personnel of the Swiss Guards. These details, first published by von Mülinen in 1892, have been ignored over the past hundred years by most historians, who have adhered to earlier more sensational figures. D'Affry wrote on 12 November to the Swiss authorities that according to his approximate calculations, the number of Swiss dead from 10 August, including those massacred on 2 September, amounted to 300. However, there were 175 men whose fate he was unable to determine, which must have included escapees like the self-reliant Fonjallaz. He then itemised the remainder. A total of 300 had been sent to Normandy and were separately disbanded at Dieppe, 375 others had been provided with documents to return to Switzerland, and 300 had enlisted in the French Army. On 22 November, he corrected this latter figure to 350. In other words, the maximum number of Swiss dead was 425 out of a total 1450, of whom 750–800 had fought at the Tuileries.

At first sight it is difficult to reconcile this relatively low figure with eyewitness accounts by Napoleon, Dr John Moore, and others. The Emperor stated on St Helena: 'I chanced to penetrate into the garden [of the Tuileries]. Never since have any of my battlefields given me the idea of so many corpses as presented to me by the masses of Swiss; be it because of the smallness of the locality made the number stand out, be it because it was the first time I experienced this kind of thing.' Peltier, who heavily influenced later writers, estimated some 700 Swiss killed. However, Mallet Du Pan, writing at the end of August, indicated a lower figure. Informed by a Swiss officer, he stated that 'out of 800 Swiss more than 400 were massacred [killed].' Peltier even more grossly inflated the figures for casualties among the insurgents, which were officially stated at a little less than 400 dead and wounded. The actual dead appear to have been around one quarter of this figure. The French figures, based on claims for pensions awarded for those who supported the insurrection on 10 August, may be a slight underestimate. Immigrant workers from the provinces, of which Paris was full, might have had no relatives available to make claims.

In 1817, the Swiss Confederation decided to issue a medal inscribed 'Treue und Ehre' [Loyalty and Honour] to all those who could prove that they had been at the Tuileries on 10 August 1792. This provided material for later research. The Swiss historian Von Gonzenbach, writing in 1866, unaware of d'Affry's correspondence, examined a number of cantonal records and calculated the death roll might be as low as 350 on the basis of 800 combatants at the Tuileries. Recent research involving an in-depth investigation of the archives of the cantons of Vaud and Fribourg, which were leading contributors to the force at the Tuileries, indicate a death rate well under 50 per cent. While precise figures for other rank losses cannot be ascertained due to imperfect records, the case is different for the officers whose individual fate was carefully explored. Out of 38 combatant officers, 26 or 27, if Montmollin is included, survived the fighting on 10 August. This represents a loss of about one-third.

Pity was not absent from Paris on 10 August, even in the case of the Marseillais. Napoleon claimed to have persuaded them to save one Swiss. Those who escaped from the fighting were soon able to find shelter with friends and relatives until they could leave Paris, as is evidenced by the accounts of Deville, Fonjallaz and Constant-Rebecque. The latter also personally provided for three soldiers, giving them clothing and money. As related, Deville described how soldiers confined with him in the afternoon of the 10th were enabled to write to contacts in Paris to obtain clothes for disguise and escape. Altishofen mentions a Monsieur Coquet who lodged a dozen Swiss for three weeks. In 1820, the insurrectionist commander of the troops from the Faubourg Saint-Marceau, C.A. Alexandre, recounted how he and Santerre had saved many Swiss in the afternoon of the 10th, soldiers who had continued to be taken to the Hôtel de Ville after the massacre earlier. It had not been possible then to protect the Swiss but now there were sufficient reliable National Guards at hand. The Swiss were hidden in the attics and given food and clothes to replace their uniforms. When the danger from extremists was past, they were sent on their way. Many of these agreed to join the French Army.

Since soldiers in the Swiss Guards were allowed to take on temporary civilian jobs, many would have built up a range of potentially useful contacts. Some, of course, were married to Frenchwomen. A number were actually French themselves. Recruiting standards had been relaxed because of the shortage of new recruits from Switzerland as the Revolution progressed. The Swiss Guards based over the long term within and just outside Paris were foreigners by nationality but expatriates by experience. Apart from friendly French, there was also a considerable Swiss colony in Paris. For instance, Captains Durler and Pfyffer were safeguarded many months by such a Swiss resident. The idea that a few hundred Swiss soldiers could successfully conceal themselves in and around Paris during the crucial days after 10 August, remaining for the most part undetected, may at first sight seem difficult to accept. Nevertheless, it must have been the case. In conclusion, the number of fatal casualties suffered by the

Swiss Guards stationed at the Tuileries on the 10th, together with those later massacred in prison, was at the most around 400 and possibly nearer 350. This compares with figures of 600 for the 10th alone quoted by Simon Schama in *Citizens* published in 1989, or in McLynn's *Napoleon* in 1997. Of course, even some 350 dead out of a force of 800 engaged would represent an exceptional fatality rate for a military engagement of this period. At the famous battle of Lodi in 1796, the Austrians only lost 153 killed out of 9,600 present at the battle.

After the suspension of the king from his powers in the early afternoon of 10 August, the National Assembly set about regularising the situation. The Jacobin Bazire proposed the recognition of the revolutionary Commune. This was carried. A special summary of the decree suspending the king's executive power was devised for use on posters. Deputies were sent out into the streets to advise the populace on the Assembly's activities. Arrangements were made to circularise details of events to the 83 Departments. Legislation was passed on the procedure for electing new ministers. Orders were given to secure the papers of the former ministers, especially those concerning foreign affairs. A decision was taken to send delegates to France's four frontier armies and another to compensate French victims of the fighting in Paris.

It was only late in the day that the Assembly found time to use the new legislation for replacing the king's ministers. The Girondins now rewarded themselves for their complacent accommodation with the revolutionaries, and proposed the reinstatement of their three ministers who had been dismissed or resigned in June, namely Clavière, Roland, and Servan. This was agreed by the Assembly. Votes were then taken for the three remaining ministerial posts, by which Danton obtained the Ministry of Justice with the largest number cast. After serving relatively briefly as minister, he resigned to take up a place in the new National Convention, illustrating that the Executive was the shadow, and the Legislature the substance of authority.

The king and his family were kept cooped up in the Logographie until 2 a.m. on the morning of the 11th. They were then taken with some of their entourage to sleep in cramped quarters in the convent buildings adjacent to the National Assembly, without change of linen or other comforts. The legislation to make the Luxembourg Palace their new residence, now that the Tuileries had been rendered temporarily uninhabitable, was never carried out. It was declared that underground passages would make escape too easy from the Luxembourg. During the daytime of the 11th, the royal family were back in the Logographie watching the debates and again returned to the Convent of the Feuillants in the evening. Madame Campan visited them with her sister and described their distress.

She wrote that they were lodged in three small cells below the cloisters. The king's hair was being cut and he offered a lock to each of them. Madame Campan wished to kiss his hand. He forbade it and formally embraced the two sisters. The queen, in the third of the cells, was less philosophical than her husband and did not bother to conceal her distress and bitterness in a series of outbursts: 'Come, unfortunate ladies,' she said, 'and see one even more unfortunate than yourselves, since it is she who has made your misfortune in everything! We are lost! Here we are after three years of all the outrages possible and now we succumb to this terrible revolution! Many others will perish afterwards! Undone by men who wanted change at any price, ambitious for their fortune, for the most violent Jacobins wish for gold and position, while the crowd expects pillage! There is not a patriot in all that infamous horde! The émigrés had their intrigues and projects, foreigners wish to profit from the dissension within France, everyone takes part in our misfortunes!' She went on to complain that the foreign embassies in Paris had provided no personal assistance with the exception of Lady Gower, who had sent fresh linen for the dauphin.

The royal family were told to dismiss most of their attendants, who, knowing the king had no money, begged him to take what they had on their persons. He refused their offer, saying he believed they had longer to live than he had. On the evening of the 12th, they were taken to sleep in somewhat better conditions in the Hôtel de Sceau, housing the Ministry of Justice, now under Danton's control. In the

Madame Campan (1752–1822) was in charge of the queen's domestic staff and a confidante of the royal family. Her lively memoirs are an important source for 10 August.

meantime, the Commune had insisted that it should be responsible for the safekeeping of the king and his family. On the evening of the 13th, they were moved to the walled complex of the former priory of the Knights Templars, the Temple. Its principal building was the late palace of the Comte d'Artois, built by Mansart in the seventeenth century. The Commune had scant sympathy for royalty, and the king and his family were instead first lodged in spartan conditions in the smaller of two medieval keeps. There they were submitted to a régime of close round-the-clock surveillance. Later they were moved to the larger tower.

Their remaining Court attendants, Madame Tourzel and the Princesse de Lamballe, were taken away to prison towards the end of August. Madame Campan appealed personally to Pétion to be allowed to join the queen but was threatened with arrest if she persisted. By the beginning of September, with the imprisonment of Huë, only Cléry remained of all the servants the Monarchy had once possessed. He attended the whole family, helping to dress the hair of the ladies as well as waiting on the king and dauphin. With dignity they suffered constant insults and humiliations. Their consolation, a considerable one, was the bonds of family duty and affection. Fortunately, they were allowed ample reading matter which was used to educate the children and provide the hapless king with necessary distraction. He himself read some 250 volumes during the few months remaining to him.

The royal family dining in the Temple. The king was made to lodge separately from his family and one of the bourgeois-clothed municipal officers on the right is looking at his watch to announce that time is up and the family must separate. This action is out of synchronisation with the king's valet Cléry who is just serving the meal. The gaoler on the left is a typical sans-culotte. Two municipal officers were on constant duty to supervise the imprisonment.

On 20 September, the Prussian advance was checked at Valmy. The next day, the National Convention decreed the abolition of the Monarchy. On the 22nd, France was declared a Republic. French armies began to conquer and by the end of the year France had absorbed the Savoie and Nice, and had conquered much of Belgium and the west bank of the Rhine. In November discussions started on the trial of the king. On 11 December, Louis was summoned to the bar of the Convention to answer to his indictment. Henceforth, the king was cruelly separated from his family. On 25 December he wrote his will, in which he offered his much-quoted advice to his son, encapsulating his own political views. In his convoluted style he wrote: '. . . if he has the misfortune to become King, to think entirely of only what is owed to the happiness of his fellow citizens, that he must forget all hatred and resentment, specifically concerning the misfortunes and suffering I have experienced; that he can only make the people content by ruling according to the laws, but at the same time

Louis XVI on trial at the bar of the Chamber on 26 December 1792. His counsel Desèze looks towards him. As it is winter, a stove is situated in the centre. The description on the print wrongly refers to the preliminary hearing of the charges against him (Interrogatoire).

he can only make them respected and do the good in his heart, in so much as he has the necessary authority, as otherwise being circumscribed in his activities, and inspiring no respect, he is more harmful than useful.'

His trial in the Convention began the next day. On 15 January 1793 he was declared guilty without dissent, although there were a few abstentions. On the 17th it was voted that his punishment should be death. After last-minute efforts to find some way of bringing about a reprieve, it was decreed early on the 20th that he should be guillotined the next morning. He had long prepared himself to follow in the footsteps of Charles I of England. He was allowed to see his family again in the evening, when they made their final emotional farewells. He was also granted a priest of his choice. With typical consideration he nominated a foreign national less likely to be victimised, the Irish Abbé Edgeworth, but only after first approaching Edgeworth for his agreement.

Early next morning, the 21st, after hearing Mass Louis received Communion from Edgeworth. He had been told the latter could accompany him to the scaffold. For a man with strong Catholic faith, this would have been a great consolation. A heavy snowfall must have muffled noises during the slow one-and-a-half-hour journey to the Place Louis XV, renamed the Place de la Révolution. Security measures were massive. The route was heavily guarded and spectators were discouraged. On mounting the platform with the uprights of the guillotine framed against the wintry sky, he addressed the crowd in a clear voice. It was related that after a short instant his speech was drowned out by a drum-roll ordered by Santerre. His reported words, before he was seized, thrown on to the plank and moved under the blade, proclaimed his innocence and forgave those responsible for his death, while hoping that the shedding of his blood would cause no suffering for the French people. These sentiments appear very much in tune with his character and beliefs.

It seems fitting for this book to be ended by Cléry, who faithfully served Louis during his captivity and perhaps even more so after his death by his moving journal. Its closing words were: 'I was behind the King, near the chimney place. He turned towards me and I offered him his overcoat. "I have no need", he replied. "Give me only my hat." I handed it to him. His hand encountered mine and gripped it for the last time.' Cléry recounted as the king left the room he apologised to the Warden of the Tower for some sharpness two days previously. 'I remained alone in the room,' Cléry finished, 'distraught and almost numb. Drums and trumpets announced the King had left the tower. An hour later artillery salvos, and cries of "Vive la Nation!" and "Vive la République" were heard — the best of kings was no more.'

Bibliography

General Sources (Books)

Aftalion, F., *The French Revolution, an Economic Interpretation*, trans. Martin Tome, CUP, Cambridge, 1990
Bradby, E.D, *The French Revolution*, Clarendon Press, Oxford, 1926
Cambridge Modern History, *The French Revolution* (Vol. VIII), CUP, Cambridge, 1907
Carlyle, Thomas, *The French Revolution*, James Fraser, London, 1837
Cronin, Vincent, *Louis and Antoinette*, Collins, London, 1974
Hardman, John, *Louis XVI*, Yale University Press, London, 1993
Hibbert, Christopher, *The French Revolution*, Penguin Books, London, 1982
Horay, Pierre, *Guide de la Révolution Française*, Editions Horay, Paris, 1989
Hunt, Lynn, *Politics, Culture and Class in the French Revolution*, Berkeley, UCLA, London, 1984
Kelly, Linda, *Women of the French Revolution*, Hamish Hamilton, London, 1987
Loomis, Stanley, *Marie Antoinette and Count Fersen*, Fontana, London, 1973
Maillard, Robert (ed.), *Chronicle of the French Revolution (1788–99)*, Chronicle Communications, London, 1989
McLynn, Frank, *Napoleon*, Jonathan Cape, London, 1997
Rose, R.B., *The Enragés, Socialists of the French Revolution*, Melbourne University Press, Melbourne, 1965
Schama, Simon, *Citizens*, Penguin Books, London, 1989
Sedillot, *Le coût de la Révolution Française*, Perrin, Paris, 1987
—— Réné, *Le coût de la Terreur*, Perrin, Paris, 1990
Thompson, J.M., *The French Revolution*, Basil Blackwood, London, 1955
Williams, G.A., *Artisans and Sans-culottes*, Edward Arnold, 1968
Yalom, Marilyn, *Blood Sisters, The French Revolution in Women's Memory*, Pandora, London, 1995

Specific Sources (Books)

Braesch, Fritz, *La Commune du dix août 1792*, Hachette, Paris, 1911
Buchez, P.J.M. and Roux-Lavergne, P.C., *Histoires Parlémentaires de la Révolution-Française*, Vols. 15–18, Paulin, Paris, 1834–8
Campan, J.L.H., *Mémoires sur la Vie Privée de Marie-Antoinette*, Baudouin Frères, Paris, 1826
Choudieu, P.R., *Mémoires et Notes*, E. Plon, Nourrit et Cie, Paris, 1897
Cléry, Jean-Baptiste Cant Hanet, *Journal etc.*, de Baylis, London, 1798
Dejoly, E.L.H., *Mémoires inédites etc.*, edn Jacques Godechot, Paris, 1947
de Molleville, Bertrand (trans.), *Private Memoirs Relative to the Last Year of the Reign of Louis XVI*, J.B. Millet & Co., Boston, 1909
de Sainte-Croix, L.L., Bigot, *Histoire de la Conspiration du 10 Août 1792*, R. Edwards, London, 1793
Dominique, Pierre, *10 août 1792, La monarchie est mortel*, Perrin, Paris, 1974
Ferrières, C.E., *Mémoires etc.*, Baudouin Fils, Paris, 1820
von Gonzenbach, A., *Der 10. August 1792 mit besonderer Rüchsicht auf die Haltung des Schweizer-Garderegiments*, Haller, Berne, 1866
Huë, François, *Dernières Années du Règne et de la Vie de Louis XVI*, Cadell and Davies, London, 1806
Johnston, R.M., *The Corsican, a Diary of Napoleon's Life in his own Words*, Houghton Mifflin, Boston & New York, 1910.
Mathiez, A., *Le 10 août 1792*, Hachette, Paris, 1931
Morris, Gouverneur, *A Diary of the French Revolution 1789–93*, Harrap, London, 1939
Mortimer-Ternaux, L., *Histoire de la Terreur 1792–4*, Vols II and III, M. Lévy, Paris, 1862–6
—— *La Chute de la Royauté 1792*, Lévy Frères, Paris, 1864
von Mülinen, W.F., *1792 Das Französische Schweizer Garde-Regiment am 10. August*, Räber Brothers, Lucerne, 1892

Peltier, Jean Gabriel, *Dernier Tableau de Paris, ou récit historique de la Révolution du 10 Août 1792*, the author, London, 1792.
Pfyffer, d'Altishofen, *Récit de la Conduite du Régiment des Gardes Suisses à la Journée du 10 Août 1792*, Abraham Chervuliez, Geneva, 1824
Reinhard, Marcel, *La chute de la royauté 10 août 1792*, Gallimard, Paris, 1969
Roederer, Pierre L., *Chronique de Cinquante Jours 1792*, Impr. Lacevardière, Paris, 1832
Roland, Madame, *Mémoires*, Baudouin Fils, Paris, 1820
Sagnac, Philippe, *La Révolution du 10 août*, Hachette, Paris, 1909
Sayous, A., *Mallet Dupan, Mémoires et Correspondance etc.*, Amyot/J. Cherbuliez, Paris, 1852
Scott, Sidney (ed.), *A Journal of the Terror etc.*, Folio Press, J.M Dent, London, 1974
Thompson, E.M., *English Eyewitness Accounts of the French Revolution*, Basil Blackwell, Oxford, 1938
de Tourzel, Duchesse, *Mémoires etc.*, Duc des Cars (E. Plon), Paris, 1883
de Vallière, P.F., *Honneur et Fidelité, Histoires des Suisses au Service Étranger*, La Presse Française et Étrangère, Paris, 1940
—— *Le dix août*, Payot, Lausanne, 1930
Weber, Joseph, *Mémoires concernant Marie-Antoinette etc.*, Firmin Didot Frères, Paris, 1847

Archives, Newspapers, Periodicals, Monographs, Articles and Theses

D'Affry, *Déposition*, Archives Nationales, Paris
D'Affry, *Jugement*, Archives Nationales, Paris
Bachmann, *Jugement*, Archives Nationales, Paris
Chronique d'une Mort Héroique, J.-P. Jelmini, Château de Penthes
'Chronologie des Événements du 10 août 1792', Jérome Bodin (*Le Messager Suisse*)
The Compromising of Louis XVI, the Armoire du Fer and the French Revolution, Andrew Freeman, Exeter University, 1989
'Le Dernier Combat du Régiment des Gardes Suisse', A.-J. Crouz-Tornare (*Revue Militaire Suisse*)
'L'Enseign Gabriel Deville', *La Revue des Deux Mondes*, Paris 1928
'Le 10 août 1792 et son Mythe', A.J. Crouz-Tornare (*Le Messager Suisse*, October 1992)
'Lettre de Constant-Rebecque', *Revue Historique Vaudoise*, 1964
Lettre de Mallet Dupan à M. de B. du 31 Août 1792, Geneva University Library
'Relation de Mr Dürler', *Helvetia Peregrina* (1986)
Extrait d'une Lettre de Paris du 13 Août 1792, Archives of the Château de Penthes
Les Fribourgeois aux Tuileries le 10 août, A.-J. Crouz-Tornare (Institut Fribourgeois d'Heraldique et de Généalogie, June 1992)
Unterleutnant G. B. Good from Canton of Uri, 'Letter dated 10 August 1792 from Paris', *Neue Zürcher Zeitung*, 1 August 1916
'L'Histographie Suisse de la Journée du 10 août 1792', A.J. Crouz-Tornare, *Revue Suisse d'Histoire*, 1993
'Histoire d'un Grenadier Suisse', *La Revue de Paris*, 1908
'La Journée du 10 Août 1792', *Revue de la Suisse Catholique*, 1893
'François de La Rochefoucauld, Souvenirs du 10 Août 1792', *Revue, Amis de Versailles*, 1964 (3)
Le Procés Verbal de l'Assemblée National 10 Août 1792
'National Assembly Proceedings', *Le Logographe*, 10 August 1792
'National Assembly Proceedings', *Le Journal des Débats et Decréts*, 9/10 August 1792
'Un Récit Inédit du Massacre des Gardes-Suisses', F.N.-C. Blanc, *Cahiers du Musée Gruérien*, 1992
'La Récuperation du 10 août', A.J. Crouz-Tornare, *Le Messager Suisse*, October 1992
'Repond et Castella, des Officiers disparu aux Tuileries', *La Gruyère*, 8 August 1992
'La Révolution Française et ses représentations mythiques à Fribourg: le cas du dix-août', Alain Jacques Tornare, *Annales Fribourgeois*, LXI 1994/5
Les Révolutions de Paris, Issues for July and August 1792
Nicholas Ruault, 'Mémoires', *La Revue d'Histoire Moderne et Contemporaine*, Vol. XII
'Les Suisses et le dix août', *Société Suisse des Amis de Versailles*, 1960
Les Troupes Suisses Capitulées et les Relations Franco-Helvetique à la Fin du XVIII Siècle, A.-J. Crouz-Tornare, PhD thesis, Paris, 1996
'Les Vaudois au combat des Tuileries à Paris le 10 août 1792', *Revue Historique Vaudoise*, 1958

Index